ECONOMIC CHANGE IN PRECOLONIAL AFRICA

Senegambia in the Era
the Slave Trade

Philip D. Curtin

ECONOMIC CHANGE IN PRECOLONIAL AFRICA

Senegambia in the Era of the Slave Trade

The University of Wisconsin Press

Published 1975
The University of Wisconsin Press
Box 1379, Madison, Wisconsin 53701

The University of Wisconsin Press, Ltd.
70 Great Russell St., London

Copyright © 1975
The Regents of the University of Wisconsin System
All rights reserved

First printing

Printed in the United States of America
For LC CIP information see the colophon

ISBN 0-299-06640-1

TO

Steven, Charles, and Christopher

CONTENTS

vii

ILLUSTRATIONS

xi

MAPS

Maps and figures drawn by the Cartographic Laboratory of the University of Wisconsin, Madison

TABLES AND FIGURES

TABLES

FIGURES

PREFACE

This book is an experiment in a kind of history sometimes called interdisciplinary, sometimes analytical history, or even historical sociology. More specifically, it might be called historical economic anthropology, to identify the disciplinary bounds to be crossed. Or a purist might insist that any study of change in human societies is a study of history, implying that this particular kind of history is still history, neither more nor less. Fundamentally, the label should make no difference, though it does create expectations. This book has to do with historical change, and it brings in some of the theory and concepts of anthropology, economics, and geography; but it is not written to any particular disciplinary model.

Analytical history calls first of all for the study of regularities, uniformities, and similarities in the way human societies operate. This means that the specific and unique aspects of the past, while recognized to exist, are not the center of attention. Nor is it possible at present to discover historical laws equivalent to the regularities in the physical universe. It is possible, however, to look for more limited uniformities of pattern in the way societies work, in the ways they change through time. Perhaps these could be called styles of history or styles of change, to avoid the suspicion of ironclad determinism.

The kind of history aimed at here will depart from two fundamental attitudes of most previous history. It will try to avoid both ethnocentricity and elitism. It seeks the perspective of world history, relating events to their meaning as part of the process of change in human society generally, not to the particular national or cultural setting of the author and his probable audience. It seeks to avoid the elitist bias that has made so much of history an account of men in power, great ideas, important inventions, top nations, or the winners on the field of battle. Economic history, for example, has been concerned almost entirely with the economic growth of the industrial world.

xix

This book is concerned with the process of economic change in a society that still lay outside the industrial world, had not yet become a European colony, yet was linked to the Western economy through trade. My underlying assumption is that generalizations based on the Western economy or on other industrialized economies cannot be an accurate picture of economic change in human society, but only in a particular segment of human society. One object, in short, is to help extend our understanding of economic change beyond the Western and industrial societies that have so far been too narrow a basis for generalization about human behavior.

The subject is an African economic region, not a nation state but a sufficiently homogeneous set of societies for convenient study. Senegambia was a comparatively small and unimportant economic region between the late seventeenth century and the middle of the nineteenth. This book is not principally concerned to explain how Senegambia became as it was at the end of this period. It is concerned with Senegambia as an example of the way an economic system operated on the fringes of the world economy during the centuries before it fell under the economic domination of the West. Its contribution should be first of all an examination of uniformities and styles of historical change within Senegambia itself, though it may then aid comparison between this economic region and others.

Needless to say, the book did not begin with those objectives; few books ever end as they were first planned. It grew instead out of a long-standing concern about race relations in the United States, which had already been translated into historical writing about Africa and the West Indies. It was apparent to Africanists generally during the past quarter-century that the treatment of the slave trade in American historical literature was peculiarly biased. If the trade is conceived as having, broadly speaking, four stages—enslavement, shipment within Africa from the point of enslavement to the coast, shipment across the Atlantic, and sale to the ultimate owner—only the last two appeared in detail. The African aspect was left hidden behind the myth of a "savage" Africa, with the unstated assumption that "primitive" people were probably easy to enslave—or behind the nineteenth-century abolitionists' active mission to show that the trade was evil and should be ended. It *was* evil, and they succeeded. But historians for a century thereafter turned away from the slave trade, especially from the slave trade within Africa.

In the process, they left unanswered a flock of questions that are now crucial. What, for example, was the impact of the slave trade on Africa? If Africa was supposed to be savage and primitive, how is it that the African commercial system of the 1760's was able to deliver more than 100,000 men, women, and children to the coast for sale to the European slavers in a peak year? Both sellers and buyers might be called savage, but the commercial system within Africa was far too complex to be called primitive. Other unanswered questions remain. Why were slave prices on the African coast so low that slaves from Africa replaced European workers throughout the American tropics? Were Africans captured *for* sale to the Americas, or were those already enslaved sold off because their labor in Africa was less profitable to the owners than the price paid by the European slavers?

My direct concern with some of these questions began in the early 1960's, when I began to put together a collection of historical sources about the slave trade within Africa, drawing on accounts mainly by those who were themselves victims of the slave trade. That research made it obvious that source material existed for the slave trade within Africa and that a study in depth would have to have a regional focus. Since I had edited and commented (in *Africa Remembered*) on the account of a certain Yuuba Jaalo (Ayuba Diallo or Job ben Solomon) from the Senegambian kindgom of Bundu, a man who had been a slave in Maryland and then returned to Africa, Senegambia seemed a convenient point of departure. Because Senegambia was a complex region with many linguistic and cultural variants, it seemed wise to begin with Yuuba Jaalo's home country of Bundu as a place for orientation to Senegambian culture, for the collection of oral traditions, and for what field work was possible in the retrospective ethnography of commercial culture. Yuuba Jaalo had, in fact, been a merchant, and Bundu lay across the main trade route from the east to the navigable Senegal or Gambia. It was also close to Gajaaga, where the French had maintained a fortified trading post most of the time from the late seventeenth century onward. This meant that European records would be available for early periods and from a spot well in the interior.

The project advanced in 1966 to field research in Senegal and the Gambia. At that stage, however, the objective was still quite different from the present outcome. I hoped to write two short books. One would deal with the trade route running from the Niger valley through Bundu to the coast, its working concept "the biography of a trade route," while the other was to be a study of Bundu's policies toward the slave trade that crossed its territory. In the optimism of those days, I hoped to finish one of these books by 1967 or so and the other by 1968 or 1969. In fact, neither book appeared; and it may be that neither will ever appear, though work continues with the Bundu material.

In the summer of 1967, I took time off the Senegambian research to write an essay I had promised J. F. Ade Ajayi and Michael Crowder for their *History of West Africa* (1971), an essay that was to be a synthetic treatment of the slave trade in general from a West African perspective. When I came to the paragraph that had to tell how many slaves were shipped from West

Africa at what times, I began following the numbers from footnote to authority, through his footnotes to his authorities, till it was finally clear that historians had only been copying from one another back to the middle of the nineteenth century. Only Noel Deerr's *History of Sugar* had even tried to make new estimates, and no one at all had systematically gone through the monographic literature to add subtotals and pull together a total number for the slave trade and its parts. The task seemed worth doing immediately, so I put off the Senegambian material once more to write an article. The projected article then took on a life of its own and grew into an unplanned book called *The Atlantic Slave Trade: A Census* (1969).

Long before the book appeared, the Senegambia material began to dictate its own priorities. In the beginning, the slave trade had been the main focus. The core of the investigation was the way slaves were acquired, shipped to the coast, and transferred to the Europeans. It seemed at that time to be sufficiently Africa-centered, since it carried the slave trade from origin to point of sale to the Europeans. In fact, it also carried its own weight of ethnocentric distortion. By focusing on the slave trade alone, it abstracted from Senegambian reality the one economic feature that tied it closely to the West at the height of the slave trade.

Abstraction from the total reality is legitimate and necessary for any social science, as it is for most writing. The decision is not whether to abstract a part from the whole reality, but which abstraction will add most to our understanding at the present state of knowledge. As the research continued through still another academic year of leave in Paris and London in 1968–69, it seemed increasingly clear that highest priority did not belong to a mere pursuit of the slave trade into the heart of Africa. Just as the slave trade was a sub-system of the Atlantic economy (even within Africa), it was also a sub-system of a broader pattern of West African society, attitudes, religion, professional standards, self-identity, and much else. First priority was to recapture as much as possible of the broader patterns of Senegambian life in precolonial times, then the economic life in particular, and finally commerce, of which the slave trade formed a part. Only then could the slave trade emerge in a perspective that was not dictated from America. It was only then that the project crossed the imaginary line from economic history to historical economic anthropology.

In the writing, it changed again, but not so crucially. One decision was to write from the inside out, beginning in chapter 1 with a synthetic view of what might be called Senegambian history, with no special emphasis on external factors. In the chapters that follow, the influence of the broader Atlantic world is uncovered layer by layer down to a final quantitative summary of external trade. Each new chapter pulls out some particular aspect for examination. Each should be readable in itself, but the book was written to be read straight through from the beginning, and it should still read best that way. The companion to this volume, subtitled *Supplementary Evidence,* contains added information for those who would like to pursue the subject further.

It would be pleasant to believe that the result is like peeling an onion layer by layer, until finally nothing remains to be explored. Such, unfortunately, is not the case—not merely because history never produces the whole truth, but even more because the quality and quantity of evidence available for more recent history within Western culture is not and will never be available for distant times in less literate societies. At best, it must be a more partial truth than produced by social scientists studying the recent past, but its contribution could be equal or greater because the starting point is so far behind.

The crux of the problem is exactly the same for any social scientific investigation of long-run phenomena. In the short run of the present and recent past, it is possible to define the problem and then generate data for solving it. You can ask questions. Further back in time, you can still ask questions, but the answers have to be discovered in the evidence the past left, either by chance or with intent. This explains why historical economic anthropology cannot make the most desirable kind of contribution to existing theory in either anthropology or economics. The trade-off is that *only* historical studies can say anything at all about change over the long run.

Precolonial history of sub-Saharan Africa also has some special handicaps of its own. Even though Senegambia was a literate society using Arabic as the language of religion, comparatively little of the surviving documentation in Arabic is useful for a study like this one, and the rest of the written record was left by foreigners. They were mainly temporary residents of the trade enclaves Europeans maintained along the coast and rivers. Everything they wrote has kept the biases of their time, place, and social status in Western society. Few indeed even tried to understand the African societies around them. For any historian, even present-day Senegalese or Gambian historians, these sources pose a constant threat of "brainwashing" or unconsciously imposing their point of view. The "Senegambian point of view" of two or three centuries ago is probably unrecoverable beyond its vague outlines. The best that can be done is to avoid the culture-bound attitudes of the Western present, to try for a perspective on Senegambia in the broader framework of human society in general.

Other special problems of Senegambian historiography are more annoying than serious. Colonial education left its impact on the customary orthography for Senegambian languages, in spite of the recent Senegalese effort to reform and phoneticize, and the orthographic heritage was double—one in French and one in English. As a result, members of the same family, pronouncing their surnames identically, are likely to spell them Diop in Senegal and Jobe in the Gambia, Diallo in Senegal and Jallow in the Gambia, Cissé in Senegal and Seesay in the Gambia. European map makers dotted their maps with even more various approximations of the proper names they actually heard. In many cases the erroneous name stuck so firmly that no possible extent of intellectual decolonization is likely to unstick it.

One solution I followed in the past was to accept the map name as it is, no matter how far from actual pronunciation, and to accept modern spellings for the names of historical figures. Now, however, the government of Senegal has provided a way out in its new phonetic alphabet, which has already been widely used by Senegalese historians and promises to be standard in the near future, however unfamiliar it may look at first. The Senegalese orthography published in 1971 has the advantage of allowing the same letter to stand for the same sound in the major Senegalese languages—Wolof, Sereer, Pulaar, Joola, Malinke, and Soninke—using a total of forty symbols that can be written with a standard international typewriter. These are described phonetically in tables P1 and P2.

The obvious answer of simply adopting the Senegalese alphabet for all Senegalese names is not as simple, however, as it might appear at first. Official transliterations of place names have not yet been made, and all place names are not pronounced quite the same way by all people—even by those who live

Table P1

Consonants in the Official Phonetic Alphabet for Senegalese Languages

	Labial	Dental	Palatal	Velar	Uvular	Glottal
Closed	b	d	j	g		
	p	t	c	k	q	
Implosive or glottalized	ɓ	d˄	y˅	g˅		
	p	t	c˅			
Constricted	f	s		x		h
Lateral		l				
Trilled		r				
Nasal	m	n	ñ	ṅ		
Semi-vowels	w		y			

Letters not found on an ordinary international typewriter may by typed as follows:

ɓ	ƀ	í	i̧	p˅	p̂
c˄	ĉ	ñ	n̂	f˅	t̂
d˄	ḑ	ŋ	n̈	ū	u̲
g˄	ĝ	ó	ọ	y˅	ŷ

Source: *Journal officiel de la république du Sénégal*, 116:623–28 (no. 4171, 28 June 1971), p. 624.

Table P2
Vowels in the Official Phonetic Alphabet
for Senegalese Languages

	Forward	Central	Rear
Extremely closed	í		ú
Closed	i		u
Half-closed	é	ë	ó
Medium or half-open	e		o
Open		a	
Extremely open		à	

The long form of these same vowel sounds is produced by doubling the letter.

Source: *Journal officiel de la république du Sénégal*, 116:623–28 (no. 4171, 28 June 1971), p. 624.

close by. (Think of the problem of a "correct" phonetic spelling for New Orleans.) In time, usage will straighten out most of the existing problems, but foreigners who hear some Senegalese say Bambuhu, while others say Bambugu, must wait until an accepted phonological spelling emerges.

We are, in short, in a transitional stage of some uncertainty, and complete consistency is difficult. The Senegalese orthography is therefore used for all historical personal names, but not for the names of living people, which are spelled as they are by the people themselves. It is used for most place names, but not for those of French or English origin. This is true not only of Bathurst and Saint Louis (still widely called Banjuul and Ndar respectively, and Banjuul has reemerged on the official maps) but also of place names like Kayes, in Mali. Phonetically, it should be Xai, as pronounced locally, but most people in Senegal and Mali know it is Kayes and pronounce it *kai*. For that matter, Kayes was a colonial town of no great consequence before the railroad was built. It would only be confusing and pedantic to change to Xai at this point.

And a further shift from strict adhesion to the Senegalese alphabet is made here in regard to the symbols, ɓ and ɗ respectively, which stand for the implosive that sometimes occurs in Pulaar. For typographical convenience, these symbols will appear only the first time a Pulaar term is used, and they will be indicated in the index reference to proper names. It seems unnecessarily pedantic to preserve the full distinction in a book written for an English-speaking audience, few of whom could either make the distinction in pronouncing the words or readily distinguish the difference in hearing spoken Pulaar.

Weights, measures, and currencies present another problem of translation. Weights and measures reported in old French or English measures are easily enough translated into metric equivalents, accepting the authority of H. Doursther, *Dictionnaire universel des poids et mesures anciens et modernes,* unless otherwise noted.

The problem is more severe with currencies. Money is supposed to be a standard of value, but it has never been a very reliable, stable, or convertible standard. The sources for Senegambia refer either to French livres tournois (later francs) or to English pounds sterling. But the structure of prices in Europe was not identical with that in the Senegambian trade enclaves, so that a pound sterling in England was not really equal to a pound in the Gambia, and the same with metropolitan and Senegalese livres tournois. In Europe, even when the silver value of the two currencies was constant, the market price fluctuated within a reasonably wide range. In addition, the silver content of the livre tournois fluctuated considerably, which meant that the par value shifted as well, especially in the early eighteenth century. The pound sterling, however, remained constant at 111.60 grams of pure silver from 1611 onward until after 1850, though it was officially bimetallic through most of the eighteenth century and subsequently shifted to a gold standard. The changing ratio of gold to silver values, however, made no practical difference until the 1840's, so that the value of the pound sterling was nearly the value of a constant quantity of silver throughout the period.

Recognizing that any monetary translation is bound to involve incommensurates, it nevertheless seemed preferable to translate all Senegambian values into a single standard. Because of its constant quantity of silver, the pound sterling was chosen as the standard of reference, and livre or franc values are translated at the uniform annual rate shown in appendix 9 of *Supplementary Evidence.*

Any historical study of this size has a large accumulated load of obligation to those who helped along the way. Financial support has come from the Carnegie Corporation of New York through its grant to the Program in Comparative World History at the University of Wisconsin, from the Guggenheim Foundation for a fellowship in 1966, from the National Endowment for the Humanities for a Senior Fellowship in 1968–69, from the Graduate Research Committee of the University of Wisconsin for a variety of financial aid from funds voted by the State Legislature, and in recent years especially from the Ford Foundation through its grant to the Wisconsin Research Program in African Economic History. I can only hope that the results will be seen in retrospect to justify the confidence they showed, though nothing written here should be taken to represent the views of any of the sponsoring bodies.

The obligation to research institutions is equally great, and especially to the courteous and efficient service offered by the Memorial Library at the University of Wisconsin, by the Archives nationales du Sénégal and the library of the Institut fondamental de l'Afrique noire (IFAN) in Dakar, by the National Archives of Gambia in Banjul, by the Bibliothèque nationale, the Archives nationales, the Archives de la Marine, the Centre d'études et de documentation sur l'Afrique et l'Outre-Mer, the Centre universitaire international, and especially by the Section Outre-Mer of the Archives nationales in Paris, by the Public Record Office, the British Museum, and the Institute of Commonwealth Studies in London.

The greatest obligation of all is to my Senegalese friends and fellow workers in the field, who guided my steps from the beginning of my research. In this respect, I am especially grateful to Amadou Maktar M'Bow for his early interest in this project. In Bundu, Koli Sy performed the invaluable role of introducing me to those who could best help, while in Dakar, Abdoulaye Bathily, Makhan Bathily, and Mamba Guirassy helped with the translation of oral traditions in Soninke, Jahaanke, and Malinke. Most important of all was the unfailing courtesy, friendship, and good advice of Hammady Amadou Sy, who not only translated the Pulaar traditions for me but also acted as my principal informant and guide into the intricacies of Senegalese society, culture, and history.

At a later stage in the work, I received most valuable assistance from my colleagues and friends George Brooks, Lucie Colvin, Anne Curtin, Stanley Engerman, Steven Feierman, Allen Howard, Martin Klein, David Robinson, and Jan Vansina, who were kind enough to read the manuscript and to give me the benefit of their advice.

ABBREVIATIONS

AM	Archive de la Marine, Paris
ANF	Archives nationales de France, Paris
ANF-OM	Archives nationales de France, section Outre-Mer
ANS	Archives nationales du Sénégal
BIFAN	*Bulletin de l'Institut fondamental de l'Afrique noire;* formerly *Institut français de l'Afrique noire*
BN	Bibliothèque nationale, Paris
C6	In reference to ANF, carries the unstated implication that the indication is the colonial series of documents
CC	Curtin Collection of oral traditions of ʾBundu and Gajaaga, on deposit at IFAN, Dakar, and at the African Studies Association, Center for African Oral Data, Archive of Traditional Music, Maxwell Hall, Indiana University, Bloomington
CEA	*Cahiers d'études africaines*
CEHSAOF	*Bulletin du Comité des études historiques et scientifiques de l'Afrique occidentale française*
CI	Compagnie des Indes
CO	Colonial Office series, Public Record Office, London
FF, NA	Fonds français, nouvelles acquisitions, Bibliothèque nationale
IFAN	Institut fondamental de l'Afrique noire, Dakar
JAH	*Journal of African History*
JHSN	*Journal of the Historical Society of Nigeria*
JRGS	*Journal of the Royal Geographical Society*
MC	French Ministry of Colonies or Ministry of the Navy
PP	British Parliamentary Sessional Papers
PRO	Public Record Office, London
RAC	Royal African Company
RHCF	*Revue d'histoire des colonies françaises, Revue francaise d'histoire d'outre-mer*
RMM	*Revue du monde musulman*
Supplement	*Economic Change in Precolonial Africa: Supplementary Evidence*
T	Treasury series, Public Record Office, London

ECONOMIC CHANGE IN PRECOLONIAL AFRICA

Senegambia in the Era of the Slave Trade

1 | SENEGAMBIA: THE REGIONAL PERSPECTIVE

The lower valleys of the Senegal and Gambia rivers mark off a region of special significance for African history. Senegambia shares two distinct styles of history—one in common with other maritime regions along the western coast, and a second in common with other regions along the *sahal*, the southern shore of the Sahara. During the stretch of more than four centuries from about 1450 to the European invasions in the 1880's, European traders appeared along these coasts of the Atlantic and the Gulf of Guinea, once the part of Africa furthest removed from contact with the outside world to the north and east. Maritime contact with the Europeans posed common problems for the west-coast states and peoples, and their solutions to these problems helped to produce a common style of history. This is not to say that contact with Europeans was the dominant force in shaping African history of this period; it was certainly not so in the earlier centuries, though it left a detectable pattern even then in such matters as the response to the Atlantic slave trade, or political controls over trade and trade routes. It became more important from the last two decades of the seventeenth century as the slave trade became the dominant trade for many African regions. Finally, the European presence and pressure became crucial all along the coast during the century from about 1780 to 1880, the "pre-colonial century"; as the slave trade began to end, other trade became more important, and western Africa began to be pulled into closer interaction with the outside world, a process that has been continuous ever since.

Senegambia was a key region in this maritime pattern. It was the closest sub-Saharan region to Europe. In the early centuries of the slave trade, it was the largest single contributor to the repopulation of the New World. The twin water route to the interior gave Senegambia a deep commercial hinterland, reaching to the upper valley of the Niger, which was one reason why Sene-

3

gambia was never quite so dependent as other regions on the slave trade alone—gum, gold, hides, ivory, and beeswax were also important. In the early nineteenth century, when the Europeans stopped buying slaves for export, Senegambia was the first West African region to shift successfully to other products. Finally, it was a key region for cultural interchange between Africa and the West through a series of Afro-European communities in the coastal towns. These towns in turn were to be among the first in Africa to have modern, representative government. Senegambia, in short, was not so much typical of the maritime style of history over these centuries as it was a paradigm of what was to happen elsewhere, often to a lesser degree.

But Senegambia was simultaneously a desert-edge region, practicing rainfall agriculture, but with steppe and desert to the north. Here too was a region of culture contact, since the desert functioned in many respects like the sea. With camels, people could easily cross it, but a sedentary life was not possible outside the oases which functioned as islands. Senegambia was thus a point of desert-caravan contact with the Islamic civilization of North Africa—and beyond to the whole Middle East. This sahal contact with Islam was older than the maritime contact with the West, and it was more intense. Taking simply the index of religious change, being offered both Islam and Christianity from the outside, most Senegambians today have chosen one or the other in preference to the older local religions, and the great majority have chosen Islam.

From 1450 onward Senegambia was thus in contact with two civilizations of the intercommunicating zone—the civilizations stretching from Morocco through India to China, which had been in nearly continuous contact since before the birth of Christ. The rest of Guinea knew very little of Islamic civilization before the nineteenth century, and the rest of the sahal knew even less of the West.

The Senegambians were conscious of their position at this point of three-way contact, and their ordinary view of the world often saw the contrast in ecological terms. Senegambian social traditions place a low value on occupational specialization and a high value on cultivating the land. They therefore tended to think of themselves as people with the correct values, who grew crops and maintained a proper relationship with the earth and its Creator. People related to the land in other ways were inferior and possibly dangerous. This was true of the Moors who pastured their animals on the steppe and desert, and were forced to trade animal products for the very clothes they wore and the grain they ate. Just as the Moors were desert people, the Europeans were water people whose realm was the sea and the rivers. Some of the more unsophisticated Senegambians believed that Europeans lived constantly on their ships. And the traders and mariners were also a specialized, unbalanced community, forced to trade in order to exist, skillful enough at what they did well but lacking a proper relationship to the forces of creation.

These underlying attitudes of Senegambian folk culture were so pervasive and durable, it would be hard to overrate their importance for the course of history and equally hard to trace that importance in detail with solid evidence at every point. The Senegambian perceptions, for example, help to underline the fact that this meeting point of three civilizations was not a meeting point of three complete civilizations. Senegambian culture was representative enough of the African civilizations stretching away to the east and southeast, but the desert nomads of the Sahara were fringe people in their relationship to Muslim civilization as a whole. Nor did the motley and invalid crowd of merchants and sailors at the European trading posts fairly represent the West. In this sense, the Senegambians were right in seeing both sets of alien culture-bearers as representative of specialized, incomplete subcultures. That fact in itself has an important bearing on culture contact and the course of historical change.

Another aspect of sahal history drew still more directly from differences between the sedentary and nomadic ecologies. Anywhere along the world-wide frontier between the steppe and the farmland, relations between farmers and herdsmen tended to be both competitive and cooperative. The basis for cooperation lay in specialized production. The herdsmen had milk and meat, and animals to sell for the farmers' cloth and grain. But the two groups were in competition for the use of land that was marginal to both, and the terms of exchange could often depend on the threat of force. In their power relations, nomadic and sedentary peoples had quite different advantages and disadvantages. The fact that nomads had to keep moving to feed their flocks gave them an enforced mobility that could be turned to military ends. Though they were comparatively few, they could concentrate for raids into the sedentary territory. The sedentary peoples were comparatively rich, numerous, and immobile—attached to their farms, stores of grain, and sources of irrigation water. They could use these advantages in different ways. One possibility was to buy off the nomads with tribute. Another was to build elaborate frontier defenses, a heavily capitalized military effort. Still another was to organize full-time troops, and hence attain the countervening mobility of frontier guards or even extend sedentary control over the steppe itself.

The result of these factors was a style of history along the desert fringe marked by alternation of strength between farmers and nomads. Some nomadic attacks were not merely raid-and-withdraw, but went from an initial victory to the foundation of nomadic dynasties ruling over sedentary empires. When sedentary empires were strong and well organized, however, they were able to control the marginal lands and police the steppe itself, so that nomadic raids were hard to mount. This style of frontier relations is traceable as far back as written records extend for the western Sudan, nor is it limited to West Africa. It is found along both fringes of the great Afro-Asian dry belt stretching from Mauritania to the Sea of Okotsk. While the first detailed theoretical attention paid to these phenomena had to do with relations between the Sahara and North Africa, the most recent detailed studies have had to do with the great-wall frontier of China.[1]

For Senegambia, therefore, the desert was partly a route of contact with Islamic civilization—and this part was shared with the rest of the Sudan as far as the Red Sea—but it was also associated with a style of sedentary-nomadic relations that was shared far more broadly. During the four centuries preceding 1880, however, the pattern of Senegambian relations to the nomads of the north was most closely parallel to that of the other sub-Saharan peoples between the Atlantic coast and Lake Chad. Broadly speaking, the sixteenth century was one of sedentary successes, while the seventeenth and especially the eighteenth witnessed nomadic incursions all along the line. Senegambia's special place in West African history came from the fact that there and there alone the pattern of desert-edge history was overlaid on the maritime style of commercial contacts by sea.

The Region and Its Political Framework: Sixteenth-Century Realignments

The historical region of Senegambia was so called long before the European colonies of Senegal or the Gambia came into existence. The name came from the rivers, but Senegambia was not simply a physical region demarcated by the rivers, and nothing more. It was also a region of homogeneous culture and a common style of history. Three of the principal languages, Sereer, Wolof, and Pulaar, are closely related members of the West Atlantic language family. The fourth, Malinke, is part of the Mande language group centered further east, and the Malinke came into the Gambia valley only six to eight hundred years ago. Malinke culture, on the other hand, is not far different from that of the Wolof-, Sereer-, or Pulaar-speakers. Living as neighbors over several centuries also led to interchange among the peoples, so that Sereer and Wolof today have more in common with the Malinke on the Gambia than they do with the West-Atlantic-speaking region of stateless societies and micro-states that lay to the south of the Casamance River.

The discontinuity of culture patterns to the north of the Senegal is far more

1. The historical analysis of ecological frontiers as a factor in historical change goes back at least to Ibn Khaldun (1332–1406). It was especially developed in this century by Owen Lattimore, *Inner Asian Frontiers of China,* 2nd ed. (New York, 1951).

obvious. The people there speak Arabic or sometimes Berber, Afro-Asiatic languages far different from the West Atlantic and Mande language groups, which are usually classified as part of the even broader Niger-Congo language family spoken in most of the rest of West Africa. The ecological difference between cultivating the land and practicing nomadic pastoralism is still more striking, and a difference in physical appearance is usually reocgnizable. Both the desert people and those to the south are a mixed race, but the mixture is more Negroid south of the desert and more Caucasoid in the steppe. These obvious differences are so obvious, indeed, that they threaten to obscure many similarities—in social structure, for example, in pre-Islamic religious belief and kinship forms, or in music—similarities built up over millenia of contact between the different peoples in the western Sahara and its fringes.[1]

Toward the interior, the regional boundary is harder to draw. With culture and interstate relations alike, the break is not sharp. Fuuta Tooro, in the middle valley of the Senegal River, has interacted over centuries with the Wolof states on the coast, as it has with its upstream neighbor, Gajaaga (Gadiaga), which speaks Soninke or Sarakoole. Gajaaga, in turn, had close historic relations with its neighbors to the east, who share the Soninke language and other aspects of culture. It is therefore hard to draw a sharp line, and unnecessary as well. In rough terms, Senegambia probably ends as a historical entity at about the present eastern frontier of the Republic of Senegal. Of the precolonial African states, that line would include Bundu (Bondu), which had occasional influence on the state system as far west as the Atlantic, but it would exclude Xaaso (Khasso) and Kaarta, both of which were historically and culturally more nearly within the orbit of the Manding region.

Cultural homogeneity had ancient roots, but the tug of political consolidation sometimes came from outside the region. Ancient Ghana incorporated part of Senegambia. So did Mali, moving in from the southeast, and even Sõñrai (Songhai) may have had a distant and indirect form of control over part of the region, at least for a time. But still another focus of early state formation was in Senegambia itself, on the middle and lower course of the Senegal. This northwest focus was a natural center of dense population in the lands watered by the Senegal; it was a point of cultural interchange with desert people, and through them with North Africa. Takrur, predecessor of the later Fuuta Tooro, was an early center of Islam south of the desert. Its first Muslim ruler, War Jaabi, died as early as 1040. Later, in the second half of the twelfth century, a Wolof leader, Njajan Njai, founded a new state

1. For an impressive hypothesis explaining some of the possible trans-Saharan culture contact see Daniel F. McCall, "The Cultural Map and Time Profile of the Mande-Speaking Peoples," in C. T. Hodge, ed., *Papers on the Manding* (Bloomington, Ind., 1971).

centered just south of the river. In time, this empire of greater Jolof came to exercise some form of hegemony over virtually all of the western Senegambia, including Dimar, the westernmost province of Takrur.[2]

The power of Mali began to be felt on the opposite corner of the region in the thirteenth century, as Mali pulled in the eastern part of Senegambia, leaving Jolof in control of the west. Oral traditions date the Malinke push down the Gambia valley to the reign of Sunjaata, in about the middle of that century, but the establishment of a Malinke-speaking population on the lower Gambia was more likely a long process extending over several centuries. The Gambia was a natural objective for Malians. Salt was rare and valuable throughout the Manding region, and the Gambia was a highway leading to the salt flats on the tidal reaches of the Gambia and the Saalum rivers. When Mali was strong, its political control reached down the trade route to the Atlantic, and its hegemony extended briefly over all of Jolof as well.[3]

In the second half of the fifteenth century, when Portuguese accounts first become available, the power of Mali no longer stretched unbroken to the sea. Many of the north-bank states were already independent under Malinke rulers, and many that were to play a continuing role in Gambian history over the coming centuries were already present—Ñomi (Niumi or Barra) at the mouth of the river, Rip or Badibu next upstream, Ñaani (Niani) and Wuuli (Wuli or Oul) dominating the north bank to the head of navigation at Barokunda Falls.

The political situation in the south was more complex. Portuguese accounts mention several of the later Gambian states, like Kantora, opposite Wuli: these states were still under Malian hegemony in the late fifteenth century, but Malian rule was exercised indirectly through Kaabu, the province that occupied the pre-forest region from the Gambia southward to the Corubal— roughly the present-day upper Casamance and the eastern end of Guinea-Bissau. This province appears to have kept a degree of centralized power under the descendents of Tiramakan Traore, who had been commander of the original Malian conquest of the region. At various times, its authority was recognized along the whole south bank of the Gambia, except Kombo, the

2. See Al-Bakri in V. Monteil, trans., "Al-Bakrî (Cordoue 1068), Routier de l'Afrique blanche et noire du Nord-Ouest," *BIFAN*, 30:39–116 (1968). This account of early Senegambian history is based principally on J. Boulègue, "La Sénégambie du milieu du xve siècle au début du xviie siècle" (Ph.D. diss. [3rd cycle], University of Paris, 1969); B. Barry, "Le royaume du Walo, 1659–1859" (Ph.D. diss. [3rd cycle], University of Paris, 1970), recently published as *Le royaume du Waalo, 1659–1859: Le Sénégal avant la conquête* (Paris, 1972); P. Diagne, *Pouvoir politique traditionnel en Afrique occidentale* (Paris, 1967).

3. S. M. Cissoko, "La royauté (mansaya) chez les Mandingues occidentaux d'après leurs traditions orales," *BIFAN*, 31:325–39 (1969), pp. 325–26.

Joola region at the far west. Even after the central power of Mali itself weakened, that of Kaabu was to continue.[4]

To the north, Jolof was still a united empire in the late fifteenth century, but much of the real power had slipped to the level of the provinces—the metropolitan province of Jolof proper, Kajor (Cayor), Waalo, Bawol, and Siin—each of which had once been an independent state and would be so again. Of the prominent Wolof and Sereer states, only Saalum was missing; it was founded about 1500. On the middle Senegal, a Takruri state still existed, independent of Jolof but possibly under the overlordship of Jara (Diara) in the sahal further east.

During the century and a half after 1450, the political map of Senegambia was redrawn, and the main changes were the disintegration of Jolof and Mali. That left a series of medium-sized successor states, normally independent, though closely linked to the others through family ties between ruling houses and diplomatic relations between courts, and occasionally falling briefly under the broad hegemony of one of the strongest. This new situation then stabilized through the seventeenth and eighteenth centuries. It was only after 1850 that religious revolutions swept Senegambia, changing political geography once more on the very eve of the European conquest.

Direct European influence during the sixteenth century was small. After an initial piratical phase, the Europeans learned that trade was more profitable than raiding. One exceptional episode broke the pattern of European non-intervention, though lessons learned on that occasion may well have helped to freeze the pattern for the future. In 1489, a certain Jelen, the *Bumi* of Jolof (the second in command to the *Burba* or king), was ruling over the empire in the name of his half-brother, Burba Biraam, but he fell from power in a palace coup. Biraam was assassinated by his other brothers, and Jelen took refuge first with Portuguese traders on the coast and then in Portugal itself. It was part of the regular pattern of Senegambian politics to take refuge at a friendly court after a fall from power and to ask the host for military help to regain power. Jelen did this, and the Portuguese acceded, on condition that he become a Christian and a vassal of the Portuguese crown. João II came through handsomely with a major expedition of some twenty caravels—a fleet as large as the one that established Portuguese dominance of the Indian Ocean off East Africa a dozen years later. But this fleet was less successful; it sailed into the mouth of the Senegal; the commander quarreled with Jelen and

---

4. S. M. Cissoko, "Introduction à l'histoire des Mandingues de l'ouest: L'empire de Kabou (xvie–xixe siècle)," B. K. Sidibe, "The Story of Kaabu" (papers presented at the Conference on Manding Studies, School of Oriental and African Studies, University of London, 1972).

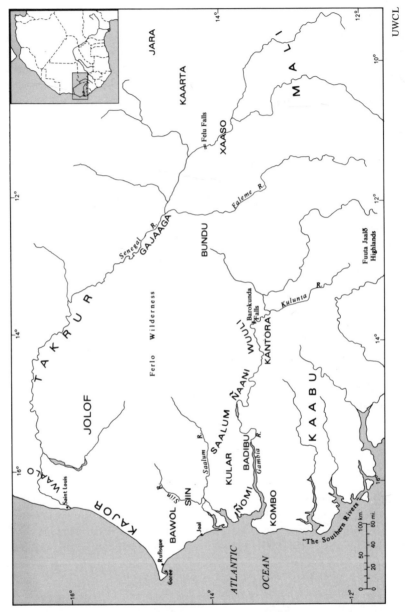

1.1 Senegambian States about 1700

killed him, and the fleet withdrew. The Portuguese never again tried to place a major trading fort on the Senegambian coast.[5]

The more serious threat to Jolof domination came from the interior. In about the 1490's, a Puulo (pl. Fuulɓe) adventurer named Kooli Teengela Baa had recruited a force of pastoral Fuulbe and others and begun a career of conquest in the western Malian region of weakening central control. He made one entry into Senegambia following down the Gambia river through Wuuli, then crossing to the south bank and on through the south-bank kingdoms until he was finally stopped by the Biafada. Defeat forced him to retreat as he had come, to a fortified camp in Fuuta Jaalõ (though it was not yet called that). After rebuilding his force he set out once more for Senegambia in about 1510, moving first to the north and then down the Senegal valley. This time he was successful in establishing his hegemony over the ancient state of Takrur, which he refounded under a new dynasty, the Deñankooɓe (sing. Deñaanke), who were to rule until the 1770's. Details of Deñaanke relations with Jolof are not known, but it is clear that Kooli Teengela recaptured Dimar and pushed the metropolitan province of Jolof back from the river.

The coming of the Deñankoobe not only meant that Jolof now had a strong and troublesome neighbor; it also affected the strategic situation within the kingdom. Cavalry was the dominant military arm, but horses were hard to breed in Senegambia proper. Remounts were mainly imported from the Moors, or even from North Africa. The Moors apparently tried to keep their position in this trade by refusing to sell mares under any circumstances. The interposition of the new Deñaanke state between the heart of Jolof and the Moors weakened Jolof access to remounts at the very time when the coastal provinces of Waalo, Kajor, and Bawol had a new source of remounts from their trade with the Europeans. The result was further decay of Jolof's central authority over the provinces.[6]

At an uncertain date, probably in the late 1540's, Kajor led a move toward full independence for the provinces. Not only was it successful, but metropolitan Jolof even fell for a time under the suzerainty of the Deñankoobe. Kajor moved ahead in the late sixteenth century to be the strongest state in the region in a period remembered still as one of prosperity. But Kajor did not try to refound the Jolof empire under her own control. It was enough to keep Waalo within reduced frontiers and to join Kajor and Bawol in a dual monarchy, where the same man held the titles *Teeñ* of Bawol and *Damel* of Kajor.

Meanwhile, the southwestern part of Senegambia suffered its own conquest

---

5. João de Barros, in G. R. Crone, ed., *Voyages of Cadamosto* (London, 1937), pp. 128–41. A. Texiera da Mota, "D. João Bemoim e a Expediçao portuguesa ao Senegal em 1489," *Boletim cultural da Guiné portuguesa*, 26:63–111 (1971).

6. J. Boulègue, "La Sénégambie," pp. 177–203.

from the interior and its own shift of power toward the Atlantic coast; and this movement was also associated with the weakening of Mali. Somewhere near the middle of the sixteenth century, Kaabu made itself independent of Mali and began a course of expansion on its own, pushing westward and southward into the earlier kingdom of Kasa and against the stateless peoples in the hinterland of the southern rivers.[7] An offshoot of Kaabu expansion even skipped over the Malinke states on the north bank of the Gambia and attacked the stateless Sereer along the Atlantic coast north of the Saalum River. Malinke adventurers from Kaabu first attacked near the coast under leaders associated with the ruling lineages in Kaabu itself, gradually winning Siin for the Gelwar dynasty. With Siin as their base, they then conquered still more territory, this time returning toward the east to create a second Gelwar-dominated state—Saalum, with its capital at Kawon near the present-day city of Kaolak on the Saalum River, ruling over territory stretching still further east and south to reach the northward bend of the Gambia near Kaur.[8]

This whole process remains obscure, and it certainly took several decades. By the end of the sixteenth century, however, Saalum had emerged as one of the most powerful states in Senegambia, with its authority extending over Ñomi, at the mouth of the Gambia, and over Badibu and Kular. By this time, the Gelwar dynasty had become Sereerized, but the two Sereer states were separate. Siin remained relatively small and homogeneously Sereer, while Saalum had a Sereer majority, a Malinke dynasty, and important ethnic minorities.

Both the expansion of Kaabu and the Gelwar kingdoms in Sereer country can be associated with the new opening for trade on the coast and up the rivers. Kaabu was beautifully placed to catch the trade moving from the interior to the south bank of the Gambia, and on to the southern rivers. The movement may also be associated with the demand for slaves. Sample data about the ethnic origins of African slaves in both Mexico and Peru in the middle years of the sixteenth century indicate the importance of these Senegambian military and political changes for the source of slaves bound toward the New World. A combination of the Mexican and Peruvian samples can give a reasonably accurate picture of the probable makeup of slave exports from Africa toward the Caribbean and beyond. (See table 1.1.) These data are important, because they confirm the probable course of political events in Senegambia. The Wolof 20 per cent for that particular quarter-century suggests that the wars associated with the breakup of Jolof had already begun. The low proportion of Fuulbe would be expected from the

7. S. M. Cissoko, "Kabou," p. 10.
8. A. S. Diop, "La genèse de la royauté Gueleware au Siin et au Saalum" (paper presented at the Conference on Manding Studies, School of Oriental and African Studies, University of London, 1972).

Table 1.1
Projected Contributions of African Regions to the
Northern and Transatlantic Slave Trade, 1526–50

Region and ethnic group	Regional percentage of total exports	Ethnic percentage
Senegambia	37.6	
Wolof		20.4
Fuulbe		0.6
Sereer		8.3
Malinke		8.3
Guinea-Bissau	40.8	
Kasanke		1.7
Bañuun		4.5
Biafada		18.7
Bram		15.9
Sierra Leone	4.2	
Cape Mount to Cameroon	8.6	
Congo-Angola	6.2	
Southeastern Africa	2.4	
Total	100.0	

Source: P. D. Curtin, *The Atlantic Slave Trade*, p. 100. The total here
is not the whole of Atlantic exports from Africa, since São Thomé was
a major importer, but only of the slave exports into the transatlantic
trade.

stability of a newly founded dynasty that was no longer expansionist. The
Sereer figures are relatively higher, as would be expected at a time when the
conquest of Saalum was still in progress. Finally, the very high percentages
from the south suggest that the expansion of Kaabu was an important
military operation. If the Sereer and Malinke figures are taken along with the
others from present-day Guinea-Bissau and both are taken as a symptom of
this last major phase of Malinke expansion to the west, that expansion
accounted directly and indirectly for more than half the slaves exported from
Africa in this quarter-century. But that expansion ran its course before the
end of the sixteenth century, and Senegambia settled down to two and a half
centuries of relative stability.

Senegambian Agriculture: The Economic Base

Like other pre-industrial societies, most people in Senegambia
were concerned most of the time about crops, not states, and the period
between the mid-seventeenth century and the mid-nineteenth was one of
comparative stability in agricultural technology. The American crops like

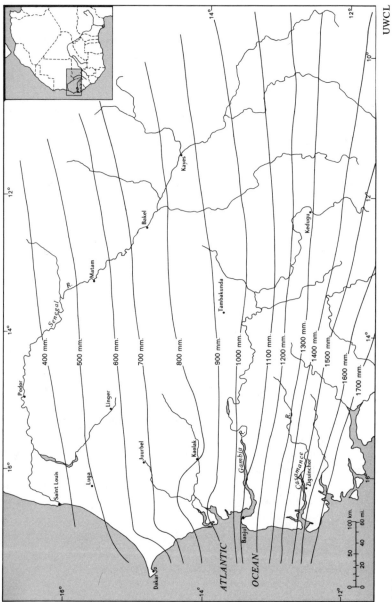

1.2 Senegambian Annual Rainfall

14

maize, peanuts, and tobacco had been assimilated and fitted into the set of available cultigens in the previous two centuries. The next major change was to be the enormous expansion of cash-crop peanut growing in the second half of the nineteenth century, followed by the spread of agricultural colonization in the twentieth. The period between these dates was stable, but not changeless. Senegambian villages were not isolated from the larger world. They were rarely self-sufficient, producing all they consumed; hence they were connected to markets and trade. Although no mass migrations took place, people were constantly moving back and forth, lured by opportunity or pushed by the usual pressures of war, pestilence, and draught.

Senegambians had long since adjusted to the particular problems and advantages of their environment, though some adjustments could not be completely successful. One of the worst problems was erratic rainfall. Located at the extreme northern limits of possible rainfall agriculture, Senegambia might be expected to be dry; but the climate was (and is) dry in its own peculiar ways. The basic seasonal pattern of rainfall is produced by the northward sweep of the intertropical convergence zone, which follows the apparent northward movement of the sun during the northern summer. The zone is a convergence of two different air masses. Monsoon-like winds in these months blow tropical maritime air over the land areas of West Africa. At the same time, a tropical continental air mass moves south from the Sahara, overriding the moister air from the sea. When the wedge of moist air under the dry reaches a depth of 1,500 meters or more, a band of rainfall occurs.[1] This band of rain is comparatively narrow and comparatively intense, and a dry belt follows it, giving a double rainy season to some parts of West Africa further south than Senegambia—one as the intertropical convergence zone moves north and a second one later in the summer when it returns.

The result for Senegambia is a brief seasonal peak of rainfall just at the edge of the desert, the most northerly reach of the convergence zone. A place in the north, like Podor on the Senegal River, has had an annual average of 316 mm of rain in recent decades, but 45 per cent of it fell in the single month of August, and the growing season for rainfall agriculture is barely two months long. More important still, the intertropical convergence front may not arrive at all, or it may not stay as long as expected. In the period 1887–1927, Podor's mean rainfall was 300 mm, but the annual variation ran from 513 mm in the highest year to 128 mm in the lowest. Meanwhile, at the other extreme of the Senegambian region, at Ziguinchor south of the Gambia, the recent annual average rainfall has been about 1,500 mm, distributed over a

1. W. B. Morgan and J. C. Pugh, *West Africa* (London, 1969), pp. 176–210; P. Pélissier, *Les paysans du Sénégal: Les civilisations agraires du Cayor à la Casamance* (St. Yrieix, 1966), pp. 3–18.

growing season from mid-June to early November—five times the rainfall at Podor, twice the growing season, yet the distance from Podor is less than 500 kms or less than Boston to Baltimore, London to Edinburgh, or Calais to Lyons. And Ziguinchor also lacks the insecurity of northern Senegambia. Between 1887 and 1927, the variation from the mean of 1,500 mm was from 2,146 mm in the highest year and 705 in the lowest. Ziguinchor's worst year, in short, was better than Podor's best. The Ziguinchor's variance is not much less than Podor's, but the maximum and minimum are within an acceptable range for agriculture.[2]

Historical climatology has not yet succeeded in explaining the variations in weather along the northern fringe of the African savanna. The sequence of wet and dry years appears to be cyclic to some degree, since four or five relatively wet years have been followed in recent decades by a slightly longer sequence of dry years. Some scientists once associated this sequence with sun spot activity, but the connection has never been proven; nor has the "cycle" been conclusively proven not to be simply random change.

Another, longer-term variation can be documented back to the sixteenth century. Some dry and wet periods affected the western Sudan as a whole and are attested by simultaneous observations at the Niger's northern bend and at the mouth of the Senegal. (See *Supplement,* appendix 1.) Around 1500, the intertropical convergence zone apparently moved further north each summer than it does today, carrying the whole pattern of rainfall further north as well. At that time, rainfall agriculture appears to have been generally possible in southern Mauritania, and the Senegal valley was within the belt of safe dependence on the rains.[3] These relatively favorable conditions seem to have lasted until the end of the sixteenth century. Then dry years became progressively more frequent until a maximum aridity was reached about the middle of the eighteenth century. This long-term arid phase corresponds to a European cold phase with similar timing; the steepness of the arctic-to-tropics temperature gradient is one factor that determines the northward reach of the intertropical convergence front. A cooling of the northern latitudes tends to push the deserts of the arid belt further south, causing what has been called the "Sahelian effect" (responsible for the period of comparative aridity that began to be felt along the southern fringe of the Sahara in the late 1960's). It goes without saying that these shifts from inadequate to adequate rainfall and back again had enormous importance for human history in the sahal.[4]

2. Pélissier, *Paysans du Sénégal,* pp. 3–18, 97–100; F. Brigaud, in J. G. Adams, F. Brigaud, and others, *Connaissance du Sénégal,* fasc. 3, Climat-Sols-Végétation (St. Louis du Sénégal, 1965), p. 48.

3. S. Daveau, "La découverte du climat d'Afrique tropicale au cours des navigations portugaises (xve et début xvie siècle)," *BIFAN,* 31:953–88 (1969), p. 986.

4. Reid A. Bryson, "The Sahelian Effect" (mimeographed prepublication paper, Institute for Environmental Studies, University of Wisconsin, 1973).

Northern Senegambia has one natural protection against irregular rainfall. The Senegal River flows from further south and from higher elevations. The combination of high altitude and low latitude guarantees a good supply of water each year, and the Fuuta Jaalō highlands where the river begins have an annual average rainfall of more than 2,500 mm. Each year, as the rains begin in June or July on the middle and lower Senegal, the river begins to rise, and it stays high even after the local rains have finished, sustained by the longer rains to the south. Finally, about early November, the waters begin to recede, and people sow crops on the wet fields. The residual moisture in the soil is enough to carry the crops until they can be harvested between March and May. In addition to guaranteeing against total starvation if the rains fail altogether locally, the use of the Senegal water has a second virtue. It makes agricultural work possible at a time of year when work on rainfall agriculture is finished, enormously increasing the productivity per capita. The Futaanke have a saying, "Fuuta is a double-barrelled gun."[5]

The flood waters, however, had their own form of inconstancy; flood levels varied from year to year, and a few meters difference in the vertical height of the water could mean thousands of hectares difference in the amount of land covered. In the decade 1941–50, for example, the highest flood covered some 280,000 hectares, while the lowest covered only 80,000.[6] But even with this variation, the flood waters improved the statistical chance for a reasonable harvest, since the rainfall crops depended on local rain, while the flood depended mainly on rain that fell far up the watershed. A low-rainfall year in one place could be a high-rainfall year in the other.

Long before the seventeenth century, the people of the middle Senegal valley had developed an intricate response to the peculiarities of their environment. They classified all land as either *jeeri*, land for pasture or shifting cultivation using rainfall alone, or *waalo*, floodland usable in the following dry season. Waalo land was further subclassified according to the likelihood of its being flooded, over a range from the low-lying land certain to be flooded every year, up to the highest land that was flooded only by an exceptionally high crest. Jeeri land was also subclassified according to the type of soil and the possibility of getting a crop in a low-rainfall year.

In effect, the Senegal valley downstream from Bakel to the mouth had many characteristics of an oasis river flowing through desert. In this case, though, it was not real desert but an erratic semi-desert, and farmers responded, when they could, by planting different kinds of crops for the

5. *Fuuta ko fetel jabaaji.* See H. Gaden, *Proverbes et maximes peules et toucouleurs, traduits, expliquées, et annotés* (Paris, 1931), p. 310.

6. J. L. Boutillier, P. Cantrelle, J. Causse, C. Laurent, and Th. N'Doye, *La moyenne valée du Sénégal (étude socio-économique)* (Paris, 1962), pp. 98–99; Y. Wane, *Les Toucouleur du Fouta Tooro (Sénégal): Stratification sociale et structure familiale* (Dakar, 1969), pp. 22–23.

different conditions. A plot planted was partly an act of faith and partly a wager in a complicated game played against the environment. For the waalo lands, the Futankooɓe had a choice of four or five different species of sorghum (called *gros mil* in Senegalese French), selected according to the particular conditions of a specific plot, though the most common was *Sorghum cernum*. For the jeeri the staple was millet (*petit mil* in Senegalese French, botanically *Pennisetum*). Again, two varieties were available in Senegambia, but the choice in the semi-arid north was almost always the one known in Wolof and Pulaar as *suna,* which had the shortest growing season. In recent years, the jeeri has produced about 42 per cent of all cereals grown along the middle Senegal, while the waalo produced 58 per cent. The annual floods are therefore enough to mitigate famine, but not enough to prevent it altogether if the rains fail.

The Senegal valley was also the center of an important pastoral industry. Even though the jeeri well away from the river received as much rainfall as any other land in the region, it was not dotted with permanent villages. The dry-season water table was often too low to be reached by wells before modern drilling equipment came into use, though some dug wells went as deep as 30 meters. Land beyond the reach of permanent villages was therefore left to transhumant pastoralists, who stayed near the river and the sources of water in the dry season and then went out to the north or south of the river when good pasture and surface water returned with the rains. The fact that cattle-keepers had to be away from settled lands exactly when the jeeri cultivation was at its peak meant that pastoralists and cultivators were sharply divided (though pastoral people could and did often raise a millet crop near their temporary cattle camps), and this occupational division has left a deep imprint on the culture and history of the Senegal valley.

It has also left a heritage of enormous confusion in the ethnographic and historical literature. The people of the middle valley call themselves Halpulaar (meaning speakers of Pulaar), regardless of occupation as cattleman or farmer. The fact that they live apart during a good part of the year, however, tends to accentuate the marks of a pastoral subculture. French ethnographers in the nineteenth century began to make a new distinction, dividing the Halpulaar into two different "tribes." The agricultural they called Toucouleur or Tukulor, and the pastoral they called Peuhl or Peul, borrowing a Wolof term. This distinction persisted down to the present, but only in Francophone scholarship. When English visitors to Africa ran into Halpulaar in northern Nigeria they called them Fulani, regardless of occupation, borrowing the Hausa word. When other English met Halpulaar in the Gambia and Sierra Leone they called them Fula, borrowing from Malinke. The confusion only increased when Anglophone scholars read the work of their French colleagues and added "Peul" and "Tukulor" to their ethnographic data. As a result, people with an essentially similar language and culture are found in the literature under at least four different names—many more, in fact, since many communities of Halpulaar origin scattered through West Africa have achieved a separate identity by partly assimilating the culture of their neighbors.

This confusion in terminology was influenced by the most serious error of nineteenth-century science. In the seventeenth and eighteenth centuries, Senegambians and Europeans alike seem to have thought in terms of three broad categories of people—sub-Saharan Africans, Moors, and Europeans—categories that were essentially cultural, but were also marked by recognizable racial differences that made the individual recognizable on sight. In the nineteenth century, however, pseudoscientific racism was virtually unchallenged in Europe. Early anthropologists assumed that race determines culture, and they became sensitive to smaller racial differences, as between so-called Nordic and Mediterranean in Europe itself. They noticed that the pastoral Halpulaar tended to be more "Caucasian" in appearance than their sedentary neighbors in Fuuta, though everyone on both sides of the line between savanna and desert is actually racially mixed in varying degrees. The slight racial difference among the Fuulbe, however, was enough to make nineteenth-century ethnographers distinguish the Peuls from the Tukulor, thus elevating occupational subcultures to ethnic entities.

The two terms come from different linguistic roots. *Tukulor* goes back to a root that means sedentary.[7] The other root, *pul* or *ful,* is associated with the people's name for themselves regardless of occupation, as in the names of the language they all speak (Pulaar in Senegambia, often Fulfuulde elsewhere) and of their country (Fuuta), or as a general collective for all Halpulaar (Fuulbe). In the Senegalese Fuuta, however, the term Fuulbe can also have a narrower meaning of pastoral Fuulbe, which some informants say originated as a short way of indicating the Fuulbe *Wooɗaɓe,* or red Fuulbe, so called for their Europeanoid skin color. This usage has tended to make many people say Halpulaar in the Senegalese Fuuta when they refer to all the people, without regard to occupation. Elsewhere in West Africa, however, the most common single term for all people who speak the common language is Fuulbe, and this wider meaning is the one I will use here, though much of the time it is necessary to distinguish between Fuulbe political units and talk of the Futankoobe as the people of Fuuta Tooro on the middle Senegal, the ɓundunkooɓe (sing. ɓunduunke) for those of Bundu to the southeast, and so on.

Many different hypotheses have sought to explain why people who have the same language, very similar culture, but different occupations should also tend to have somewhat different racial mixture according to occupation. The

7. C. Monteil, "Le Tékrour et la Guinée," *Outre-mer,* 1:388–99 (1929).

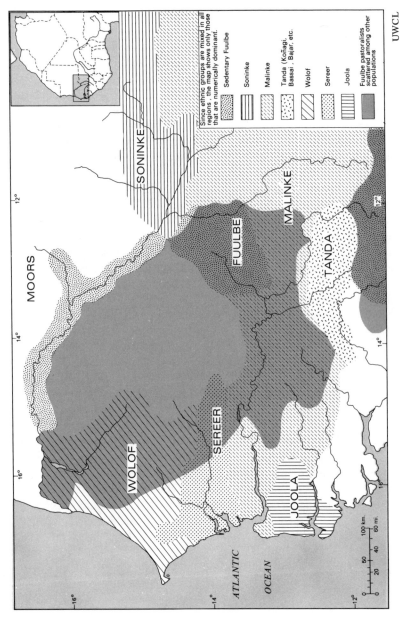

1.3 Ethnographic Map of Senegambia

Since ethnic groups are mixed in all regions, the map shows only those that are numerically dominant.

Sedentary Fuulbe
Soninke
Malinke
Tanda (Koñagi, Bassai, Bajar, etc.)
Wolof
Sereer
Joola
Fuulbe pastoralists scattered among other populations

MOORS

SONINKE

FUULBE

MALINKE

TANDA

WOLOF

SEREER

JOOLA

ATLANTIC OCEAN

12°

14°

16°

100 km.
60 mi.
0   20   40   60
0   50

most reasonable explanation begins with Fuulbe oral traditions saying that they came from the north, supported by the fact that they once controlled a great deal more territory to the north of the Senegal than they now do. These early Fuulbe were sedentary, and they were negroid in appearance. They settled along the middle Senegal, while the Sereer who speak a closely similar language moved on to settle in the region between Cape Verde and the mouth of the Saalum River. Meanwhile, the Wolof had been neighbors of the Fuulbe and Sereer in their original home to the north. Wolof, for example, is a related language, but not as closely related to either Sereer or Pulaar as Sereer and Pulaar are related to each other. The Wolof moved south in their turn and settled near the mouth of the Senegal, southward to Cape Verde, and eastward into the later core area of Jolof. In this way, they put a wedge of Wolof speakers between the Sereer and Fuulbe.[8]

As a next step, probably after the Wolof occupation of the lower Senegal, Zenata or Sanhaja Berber pastoralists followed the sedentary migrations. The evidence now at hand suggests that the pastoral Fuulbe were an offshoot of these Berber migrations. Not only do the caucasoid Fuulbe pastoralists look a little like Berbers; serological evidence also suggests a Berber connection. The probable course of events is that some Berber pastoralists attached themselves to the denser communities of sedentary Fuulbe. In time, they assimilated Fuulbe culture and intermarried with the negroid Fuulbe to produce the present racial mixture,[9] and the geographical conditions of the Senegal valley suggest why this process of cultural and racial change may well have been relatively rapid. Pastoral peoples who crossed to the south of the Senegal valley could practice wet-season movement into the Ferlo wilderness to the south, but they would return each dry season to the dense Fuulbe populations along the waalo lands of the Senegal. Interchange and intermarriage with the sedentary people could produce major changes in culture within a few generations. Meanwhile, Berbers who practiced the same kind of transhumance north of the Senegal, as many Moors still do, would retain continuous contact with people of their own culture. This hypothesis certainly oversimplifies; but it helps to explain changes that had already taken place by about 1000 A.D., when the pastoral Fuulbe of recent history were already on the scene with a physical appearance and culture not unlike that of the present day.[10]

8. This hypothesis has been adopted by a number of different authorities. See Pélissier, *Paysans du Sénégal,* passim.

9. Racial mixture has been continuous for centuries along the southern Sahara fringe where negroid and caucasoid peoples meet, producing a variety of different mixtures. Serological studies among the pastoral Fuulbe in northern Nigeria indicate that the mixture there tends to be stabilized with a larger number of negroid than of caucasoid genes. (R. G. Armstrong, *The Study of West African Languages* [Ibadan, 1964], p. 28.)

10. This passage follows the main lines of the hypothesis, based partly on linguistic evidence, published by Armstrong in *Study of African Languages,* pp. 25–28.

But the Fuulbe puzzle is not ended there. Fuulbe are not found merely in Senegambia, near others who speak related languages. They are scattered across the West African savanna belt as far east as Cameroon and Chad. By the 1950's, Fuulbe were estimated to be 6,000,000 in all, but barely 200,000 (or around 3 per cent) still occupied the original homeland in the middle valley of the Senegal.[11] Part of the explanation seems to be that Fuulbe filled an unoccupied ecological niche in the western Sudan. Some farmers there kept cattle, but they were not able to take full advantage of transhumance as long as they were tied down to their fixed villages and crops. Pastoral Fuulbe on the move found they could prosper through a division of labor with sedentary farmers. Their numbers could therefore increase, while those who stayed at home were limited by the carrying capacity of the middle Senegal.

Transhumant pastoralism was itself an encouragement to migration. As long as the group moved north each summer with the rains, it was easy to seek a new dry season base if the need arose; and the need could arise from conflict with other pastoralists, from conflict with their sedentary hosts, from weather conditions, and from much else.[12] Nor was the pattern of transhumant drift followed by the Fuulbe alone. The Shuwa Arabs began a similar drift on the Sudanese shore of the Red Sea and gradually moved westward as the Fuulbe were moving east. By the late nineteenth century they had actually overlapped, with some Shuwa west of Lake Chad and some Fuulbe to the east. The timing of the Fuulbe drift outward from Fuuta is uncertain, but it had apparently begun before the year 1000.

One other encouragement for the Fuulbe diaspora lay in the physical environment of Fuuta itself. A cycle of good years with high rainfall, good crops, and good grazing on the jeeri would encourage the herds and even the human population to increase. When the dry years came, it was a natural reaction of the mobile pastoral Fuulbe to move out. Unlike their sedentary neighbors, they rarely had waalo land to fall back on. The Senegal valley conditions were therefore like a demographic pump; a few decades of mostly good years filled the cylinder with people and their cattle, while a series of bad years like the early 1970's pushed them out to begin a process of transhumant drift.

The basic economic and work unit among the sedentary farmers in Fuuta Tooro was the narrow family made up of a man, his wives, and his children, with the possible addition of a few close relatives or slaves. With the agricultural technology that prevailed into the recent past, this unit could work only a small plot of land, perhaps 1.5 hectares of jeeri and 2.25 hectares of waalo.

Control over the use and produce of these plots was set in a complex and

11. D. J. Stenning, *Savannah Nomads* (London, 1959); Boutillier and others, *Vallée du Sénégal*, pp. 19–20.

12. For transhumant drift in recent decades as a pattern for such movement see Stenning, *Savannah Nomads*, esp. pp. 206–33.

historically determined system of land tenure. The basic right over land belonged to the man who first cleared it (and his descendents), or in the jeeri to the one who dug the first well. The holder of this kind of claim was called *jom jengol* (master by right of fire) or *jom levre* (master by right of the ax). He could farm the land himself or rent it out on a variety of tenures. A second kind of claim was created by the state, superimposed on that of the jom jengol. This second title was *jom leeidi* (master of the land), and it was usually held by court favorites, important officials, or others who had earned the gratitude of the ruler. Their estates were often substantial, usually managed by a slave official called a *jagraf.* The jom leeidi simply collected annual dues and special inheritance payments from the peasant who worked them in the status of jom jengol, or from the jom jengol's tenants.

As of the late 1950's, about a fifth of the cultivated land in Fuuta was under a jom leeidi. Another 37 per cent was worked by tenants who paid the jom jengol for the right to cultivate, usually a substantial payment of 10 to 50 per cent of the harvest. Another third of the land was worked by the jom jengol, without a separate jom leeidi over him. The remainder, about a tenth of the whole, was joint-family property whose co-proprietors formed a segment of a lineage. Nearly 60 per cent of the land, in short, was worked by men who owed part of the income to other private claimants. When the rights of the jom leeidi are traced back in time, however, many of them are found to have originated in the period of religious warfare at the end of the eighteenth century. In the seventeenth or early eighteenth century, a far higher proportion of the land was owned by the peasants who worked it.[13]

As one moves up the Senegal valley through upper Fuuta and into Gajaaga the environment changes in important ways. The floodplain of the river is narrower, which means less waalo land; but the rainfall is greater, which means that the jeeri is progressively more valuable. At present, the average rainfall doubles between Podor and the frontier between Fuuta and Gajaaga. It reaches 800 mm a year in central Gajaaga and northern Bundu, 900 in central Bundu, and 1,000 mm in southern Bundu. Over the same distance the natural vegetation also changes from open grass with only a few trees, to dry savanna and sparse woodland, and then into a dry forest so thick it is rarely possible to see more than a few hundred meters, even in the dry season.[14]

13. The chief authorities for more detailed studies of Futaanke land tenure are H. Gaden, "Du régime des terres de la vallée du Sénégal au Fouta antérieurement à l'occupation française," *CEHSAOF,* 18:403–14 (1935), and M. Vidal, "Etude sur la tenure des terres indigènes au Fouta," *CEHSAOF,* 18:415–18 (1935). The simplified version given here is largely that of Boutillier and others, *Vallée du Sénégal,* pp. 112–15. See also D. Robinson, "Abdul Bokar Kan and the History of Futa Toro, 1853 to 1891," (Ph.D. diss., Columbia University, 1971), for nineteenth-century relationships of political change to changing land tenures.

14. For Senegambian zones of natural vegetation see J. Trochain, *Contribution à l'étude de la végétation du Sénégal* (Paris, 1940).

Millet and sorghum give way to a greater variety of crops in these latitudes with their longer growing season—rice along the streams, maize, cotton, indigo, and peanuts on the higher land, along with millet. In Bundu, the land used for rainfall agriculture is called *niaruwaal* or *seeno*, rather than jeeri as in Fuuta, and it is far more important to the economy. The lowest of the waalo land along the Faleme, the part certain to be flooded every year, is nowadays planted with eggplant, tobacco, onions, and an African bean called *ñeebe* (*Vigna sinensis*), while sorghum is moved to higher land that might or might not flood in a particular year. The waalo, in short, is hardly more than a kitchen garden, while the major crops are grown with rainfall alone.[15] The other major change from the Futaanke pattern is the presence of American crops like maize, peanuts, and tobacco. Their first appearance is not documented, though they were present and important by the 1720's.[16] This suggests an indefinite date of introduction sometime before the end of the seventeenth century. Millet, however, remained the principal export crop from Bundu until the middle of the nineteenth century, while peanuts were kept for home consumption and soap-making. Today, of course, the situation is reversed; peanuts are sold overseas, while millet is kept or sold locally.

Bundu and Gajaaga kept the general principles of Senegambian land tenure—that ownership belonged to the lineage that first cleared and made the land productive, though the state reserved some rights to itself (like that held by a jom leeidi in Fuuta). Most land, however, was distributed at the village level, where it was owned and worked by an extended family. Some fields were assigned to the family as a whole, and the produce of those fields was redistributed by the lineage head. Other fields were assigned to the nuclear family, and the produce of those fields was redistributed to the smaller group. Even slave families were assigned a small parcel of land. The state-held land in Gajaaga was mainly rented to those who worked it. The *Tunka* or ruler appointed a slave official called the *jagarafu* to manage these lands, in much the way the jagraf did in Fuuta, but no land-holding nobility stood between the Tunka and the peasant.[17]

Bundu was again different. The usual work unit was the small or nuclear family, as in Fuuta; but virtually all land was held by the village, even more

---

15. A. M. M'Bow, "Enquête préliminaire sur le village de Sénoudébou, canton du Boundou Septentrional, subdivision de Goudiry, cercle de Tambacounda" (mimeographed study dated May 1954 in the series "Térritoire du Sénégal, education de Base," ANS), pp. 20–34.

16. P. Charpentier, memoir of 1 April 1725, ANF, C6 9; P. D. Curtin, ed., *Africa Remembered* (Madison, 1967), p. 47.

17. I. D. Bathily, "Notices socio-historiques sur l'ancien royaume soninké du Gadiaga," *BIFAN*, 31:31–105 (1969), p. 73. (Edited and introduced by Abdoulaye Bathily.)

than in Gajaaga. In fact, land in Bundu has no scarcity value except along the Faleme and other streams;[18] and no evidence suggests that it did in the past, though population densities before the middle of the nineteenth century are thought to have been higher than they are today. A recent study showed the region of Bundu as a total of 1,795,000 hectares, of which 88.9 per cent were unsuitable for cultivation (largely because laterization had turned the surface to rock); 5.6 per cent were judged suitable, but only 1.6 per cent had ever been cultivated in the past and only 0.9 per cent were being cultivated at the time of the survey.[19] In these circumstances, uncleared land acquired value only through the labor of those who cleared it. They kept their control over it until its fertility was gone and it returned to fallow. After a few years in fallow, it was again ready for use, but it had to be cleared all over again by the new occupier assigned to it.

Wolof agriculture on the Atlantic coast faced different problems and met them in different ways. Aside from the waalo land along the Senegal in the country called Waalo, the Wolof had to depend on rainfall agriculture—but with only about half the rainfall normal to Bundu or Gajaaga. On the other hand, the soils were comparatively light and easy to work, which meant that low yields per hectare could be balanced by cultivating more hectares per man. If the rains came in the right quantity and with the right timing, yields per worker could be as high as anywhere in Senegambia. The Wolof therefore grew a combination of crops that balanced many possible kinds of diversity against one another. They grew the suna variety of millet near the village, the *sonio* variety further out, and sorghum on scattered patches of clay soil. Near the house, cotton, peanuts, and manioc were common, supplemented by goats and sheep. The Wolof also kept cattle; but they often consigned them to the care of the Sereer or to Fuulbe herdsmen for the cycle of trans-humance. This meant that manure was not available as fertilizer to permit continuous cropping without a period of bush fallow.[20]

Wolof land tenures bore a family resemblance to others in Senegambia, but with their individual peculiarities. The primary claim came through descent from the man who had first settled and cleared it. This claim, however, was held by the lineage, not the individual, and it usually included much more land than a single family could work. The head of that lineage held a claim called *borom dai* (the right of fire), and his office of *laman* (often translated as "master of the land") also included obligations to the earth deities—

18. Land in and near towns and villages obviously had a site value, but this was apparently slight.

19. The remaining 3 per cent were forest reserves. See M. Baro, B. Fall, D. Diarra, D. N'Diaye, and B. Dieye, *Le Sénégal oriental, étude régionale* (mimeographed study for CINAM and SERESA, c. 1957), ANS, B. I. 4° 174), p. 104.

20. Pélissier, *Paysans du Sénégal*, pp. 149 ff.

obligations that have often disappeared in recent centuries with the progressive introduction of Islam. The laman who held borom dai collected customary payments from each of the families that actually worked the land, though these payments were usually more nearly a ritual token of recognition than an economic rent. Those who worked the land held another kind of right, *borom ngajo* (right by ax), more sharply distinguished here than in Fuuta from the "right by fire." This claim normally covered the amount of land a family actually worked; it was equally heritable with borom dai, and it was a secure tenure as long as the symbolic payments to the borom dai were made regularly.

It is usually assumed that the lamanate preceded the establishment of states. When higher authorities like the Burba of Jolof, the Damel of Kajor, and the Teeñ of Bawol came on the scene, they simply superimposed their power, leaving the laman in office with their old functions. But the state needed to reward loyalty, and it began granting tracts to those it favored. This movement paralleled the similar grant to a jom leeidi in Fuuta, but it differed in its consequences. The level of dues collectable under these government grants of lamanate remained at the low, symbolic levels of the past. If the territories controlled were large enough, they might produce a significant income; but they were not the source of inequality that similar grants were to be in Fuuta. Many of the grants covered areas that had no pre-existing laman; in this case the government appointee simply began to collect the dues a laman might have collected. Later grants were in the core areas of the various kingdoms, but they tended more often to extinguish the rights of the existing laman than to impose a second layer over him.

Here, as in Bundu, land had little scarcity value. Where the only real value of land was the capital cost of clearing it, command over land was not an important source of social differentiation; but command over people was. By the nineteenth century, a military aristocracy of slave origin, the *ceddo* (*thiedo*), became more and more important in all the Wolof states, but their power came from their influence over the court and from their ability to harass and plunder the peasantry, not from enforced collection of regular dues or rents.[21]

Sereer agriculture and Sereer life in general were different from the Wolof in ways that transcend the southward step toward more dependable rainfall. Where the Wolof peasants tended to be mobile and impermanently fixed, Sereer villages and people had a quality of closedness, stability, and cohesiveness—all of which are aspects of their tendency to fend off foreign

---

21. See Pélissier, *Paysans du Sénégal*, pp. 124–32; C. T. Sy, "Amadou Bamba et l'islamisation des Wolof," *BIFAN*, 32:412–33 (1970), pp. 420–21; L. A. G. Colvin, "Kajor and Its Diplomatic Relations with Saint-Louis de Sénégal, 1763–1861," (Ph.D. diss., Columbia University, 1971), passim; Martin A. Klein, *Islam and Imperialism in Senegal: Sine-Saloum, 1847–1914* (Stanford, 1968).

influence. Where Islam had long been a crucial force, if not the only religious force, in the Wolof states, the Sereer kept to their religion based on the worship of ancestors and of the tree and the earth spirits, through many centuries of contact with Islam, though many have only converted to Christianity or Islam in the past century. This meant that the Sereer laman had quite a different position from the Wolof equivalent. He held the land by right of fire (*yal o niai*), but his position was mainly religious, a link between the land and those who worked it. The payments he received therefore kept the significance of religious contributions longer than they did among the Wolof.

The continued ritual functions of the Sereer lamanate may be one reason it and the peasantry together were more successful than the Wolof were in defending their position against royal encroachment. The very foreignness of the Gelwar rulers may also have made them sensitive to the danger of seeming to interfere with the local religion. In addition, the individual economic units among the Sereer peasantry tended to be larger and more stable than they were among the Wolof, possibly providing a stronger organization for resistance. Here, the basic economic unit was the extended family, living in a single compound (*mbind*). The lineage held the land by right of the ax (*yal bakh* in Sereer). Its total work force might vary between ten and forty people associated with a single matrilineage and represented by a lineage head who was normally the eldest male.[22]

Sereer agricultural technology was also strikingly different from other Senegambian systems, though the crops were the same. Millet was the basic cereal, especially the suna variety, though in recent years Sereer have grown more ñeebe and cotton than the Wolof, and less manioc. The real difference was the Sereer use of penned cattle, held in the fields soon to be cultivated, rather than sent out for transhumance with the Fuulbe shepherds. The manure made it possible to use some fields year after year, and the cattle pens were integrated with the use of the *Acacia albida*. The peculiar feature of this tree is a deep tap root which enables it to act as though the seasons were reversed. It sheds its leaves just before the rains begin—thus providing humus for the soil about to be worked and opening the fields to sunlight. At the beginning of the dry season it grows new green leaves, and the leaves on the lower branches serve as fodder for the cattle toward the end of the dry season when other food is scarce. Although this tree is grown intensively in Sereer country and elsewhere in West Africa, it is not native to the region, and it requires horticultural care from farmers who want to benefit from it.[23]

22. This discussion of Sereer agriculture is based on Pélissier, *Paysans du Sénégal*, pp. 183–299.

23. The *Acacia albida* is not used in quite the same way elsewhere in Africa, but it has become a common tree in scattered regions from Senegal to Lake Chad. How or when it came to West Africa is not known, nor is its place of origin, though North Africa is suspected.

As a result of this combination of cattle, millet, and Acacia albida, the Sereer were able to use the land more intensively than their neighbors and therefore to have denser patterns of settlement. Present-day population densities cannot be read back into the past, but they help to measure the relative productivity of agricultural systems that have not changed drastically. Where Wolof densities in recent decades have been on the order of ten to thirty people per square kilometer, the heart of the Sereer region carried at least sixty and sometimes seventy-five people in an equivalent area.

This density of population dropped off sharply between the mouth of the Saalum River and the mouth of the Gambia. For reasons that are still not clear, the Malinke occupation of the Gambia valley stretched only a short distance north of the river, leaving the region further north sparsely settled, with only scattered fortified villages of varying ethnic identity. This underpopulated region was one of those available for planned agricultural colonization in the twentieth century.

Ethnic heterogeneity marked the middle valley of the Gambia as well, where the Gelwar monarchy of Saalum ruled a population that was not merely Sereer but Wolof, Malinke, and pastoral Fuulbe as well. The wedge of Malinke population stretching west from the greater Manding culture area in present-day Mali was not merely a wedge in the sense of splitting apart the West Atlantic languages; it also had the shape of a wedge, with a point in Ñomi on the north bank at the mouth of the Gambia. Moving inland, it became appreciably wider, with Ñaani and Wuuli on the north bank matched by Malinke dominance over Kaabu on the south.

The Gambia River had little of the agricultural importance of the Senegal in Fuuta, partly because its water was not easily used for irrigation and partly because better rainfall made irrigation less necessary. The floodplain is much narrower than the floodplain of the Senegal. Though the Gambia's annual rise is nearly 10 meters, it floods a much smaller area. More serious still, the Gambia is tidal during low water as far as the head of navigation at Barokunda Falls. Even in the time of the annual flood, the tides still reach as far as MacCarthy's Island, 195 kms in direct line from the mouth of the river or 283 kms following the river. With the end of the rains, the tides begin to push inland again, bringing salt water as far as 350 kms up river at the end of the dry season. The salt destroys the possibility of easy dry-season cultivation on the floodplain of the lower river. Techniques that have been used recently to remedy some of these problems were available only in this century.

It is hardly worthwhile trying to determine at this distance in time why or whether the Malinke system of agriculture was less efficient than it might have been. It was certainly not as efficient as the Joola rice cultivation of lower Casamance, which today supports a population as dense as sixty people per square kilometer, through careful control of fresh and salt water by a system of dykes. The Malinke on the Gambia on the other hand put the main emphasis on upland millet and other grains, leaving rice to women, as a secondary crop, when women were already largely occupied with other chores. Either as a result, or because they had small alternative, Malinke rice cultivation was comparatively inefficient, with seeds sown broadcast in swampy areas and with small attention to transplanting or hydraulic controls until recent decades.[24] And one result was to leave the Gambia valley so sparsely populated that immigrants from other regions had to be attracted as "strange farmers" when peanuts began to be grown for export in the middle of the nineteenth century.

This is not to say that the Joola system of rice cultivation would have worked along the Gambia. What appears today as inefficient may actually reflect an optimum use for that environment, given the technology available. The valley of the Kuluntu, a southern tributary to the Gambia, is completely unpopulated, even today, though it has a broad floodplain and annual flooding that could easily be adjusted to intensive rice cultivation. Yet the people of the region stay in the surrounding uplands and grow millet under conditions clearly inferior to those in the valley floor, because the price of using those resources is simply too high; the gallery forest along the river provides protection for tsetse fly and hence the danger of sleeping sickness, while the river itself is home to the variety of snail that acts as intermediate host for "river blindness" (*Onchocerca volvulus*).[25]

Senegambian Society

Just as the new state structure of the late sixteenth century was comparatively stable, the social patterns were also comparatively stable. As a result, recent field studies are in broad agreement with historical records, and this congruence makes it possible to use both sources in reconstructing the patterns of past society. Some of the detail is inevitably lost in this process, and much of the change through time that might be apparent from better historical evidence is simply not visible, but the main outlines are clear enough.

Almost everywhere, the fundamental social division was tripartite. First, the free men, *jambuur* in Wolof, *riimɓe* (sing. *diimo*) in Pulaar, *horō* in Malinke.

24. For Malinke agriculture see M. R. Haswell, *Economics of Agriculture in a Savanna Village* (London, 1953) and *The Changing Pattern of Economic Activity in a Gambia Village* (London, 1963). For Joola rice cultivation see Pélissier, *Paysans du Sénégal*, pp. 623–891, and J. J. Lauer, "Rice in the History of the Lower Gambia-Geba Area" (Master's thesis, University of Wisconsin, 1969).
25. Pélissier, *Paysans du Sénégal*, pp. 507–9.

Then came the so-called caste people belonging to endogamous occupational groups such as blacksmiths, leather workers, or minstrels, called collectively *ñeño* in Wolof, *ñeeñbe* in Pulaar, or *ñamahala* in Malinke. Finally came the class of servile bondsmen, sometimes called slaves (*jam* in Wolof, *maacube* in Pulaar, *jōo* in Malinke). In a broad sense, the three major divisions were a hierarchy of rank, but wealth, status, and power did not line up neatly in the ranked order. Many finer lines and divisions could exist within any of the three divisions, so that in fact they overlapped. Those who were best off in either of the lower groups, in terms of wealth, status, and power, were better off than the lowest ranks of free men.

Several distinctions were drawn among the free men. The mere fact of being free might mean no more than belonging to the mass of the Wolof peasantry, the *baadolo*. It was thus a neutral status, a zero point, to be added to or subtracted from. Some men had less, by virtue of membership in the occupational "castes" or being bondsmen. Others had more, by virtue of office or personal reputation, and above all by membership in a privileged lineage. The root of the free man's self-identity and the framework for his day-to-day relations with others was kinship. In pre-Islamic times this meant a matrilineage for the Wolof, Sereer, and Fuulbe—inheritance passed from male to male, but following the female line. For the Malinke, the normal form of reckoning descent was in the male line, though either system could change to the other. The Fuulbe who converted to Islam changed to the Muslim patrilineage, though traces of matrilineage remain in Fuuta and among the pastoral Fuulbe down to the present. Patrilineal descent also gained a great deal of ground in Wolof territory, though it never replaced the important matrilineages. At the same time, the patrilineal Malinke who became the rulers of the Sereer states and of Kaabu changed over to a system that emphasized matrilineage, though keeping some patrilineal elements.[1]

Whether patrilineal or matrilineal, the largest kind of lineage group in Senegambia, sometimes called a clan, was one made up of all people who traced their descent back to a common ancestor (usually a male ancestor, even when traced through the female line). The members of this clan had (and still have) a common surname, called *jaamu* in Malinke, *yetoode* in Pulaar, *sant* in Wolof, but there are more lineages than surnames, so that quite separate lineages may have the same surname. In any event, the whole clan

---

1. For the upper class or free people generally see C. A. Quinn, "Traditionalism, Islam, and European Expansion: The Gambia 1850–90" (Ph.D. diss., University of California, Los Angeles, 1967), pp. 71–73, recently published as *Mandingo Kingdoms of the Senegambia: Traditionalism, Islam, and European Expansion* (London, 1972); Wane, *Les toucouleur*, pp. 29–34; Diagne, *Pouvoir politique*, pp. 56 ff.; Barry, "Royaume du Walo," pp. 45 ff.; Cissoko, "Kabou," pp. 12–13; Y. Person, *Samori: Une révolution Dyoula*, 3 vols. (Dakar, 1968–).

was not an effective social unit. It was usually scattered in villages hundreds of miles apart, and its distribution cut across linguistic, ethnic, and state boundaries, though most prominent surnames have a known original ethnic identity. All the people of a clan were linked by the belief that they were kin, and by common totemic animals. One, called *tana* in Malinke, was the totemic animal proper, associated with the ancestors and never to be harmed in any way. The other animal symbol was called *bemba* in Malinke, *ele* in Pulaar, and it was repugnant rather than attractive or protective. This system of dual animal symbols extended far beyond the Senegambia. In spite of the coming of Islam, it was found in recent years from Wolof country on the Atlantic coast, through Fuuta, and on east into the whole of the greater Manding region.

But the clan was too broad to be an effective political or social unit. The effective lineage was the segment living together in a single town or village, often having contiguous compounds of a ward belonging to that clan alone. This local unit (*lu* or *kabilo* in Malinke, *gale* in Pulaar) had an active head, normally the oldest member, who represented its interests to higher officials, settled internal quarrels, and sometimes acted as a central agent for receiving and redistributing income from the group's economic efforts. This local unit usually included the bondsmen subordinate to members of the lineage of free men, and might include some clients and especially some of the associated "caste" people. In this way, the position of the free lineage often determined the status of subordinate ranks as well.

But the "caste" people were not set in a social hierarchy so much as set aside from the rest of society. This is one reason why the Portuguese-Indian term *caste* tends to be confusing in the West African setting. Like Indian castes, the West African ñeeñbe were endogamous and they were associated with particular occupations, but there the similarity ends. The West African caste groups were not separated by religious prohibitions, either Muslim or pre-Muslim. They were defiling to others through sexual contact but not necessarily through social contact, such as common dining. Caste rules in this respect differed from place to place. While the free people everywhere thought of them as separate, they were not necessarily inferior. Whether they were or not depended on the particular caste. Blacksmiths, for example, were feared, but also respected for their technical expertise—not for skill or virtuosity alone, but because they had to deal with the tree spirits to make charcoal and with the earth itself to extract ore for making iron. These dealings required special ritual and spiritual contacts that ordinary people were well advised to stay clear of.

Minstrels were a group with variable status. People looked down on some of them as mere entertainers, just as Europeans of the seventeenth and eighteenth centuries placed "players" at the bottom of the social hierarchy along with domestic servants. But the Senegambian minstrels were not merely at the bottom of a social hierarchy; they were outside it, and their potential for defilement was so strong that they were formerly buried in trees to avoid polluting the soil. At the same time, many were close to the nobility and the centers of power. Not only could they have informal influence through their advice, they often had a formal political role as well, especially in diplomacy and above all in diplomacy between factions within the same lineage. Leatherworkers and woodworkers, on the other hand, were craftsmen whose work itself was defiling. Woodworkers dealt with trees, which were the home of the spirits in the pre-Islamic religion. It was therefore necessary for them to deal with the supernatural in ways that could be dangerous in the same way that it was for blacksmiths, while leatherworkers were defiled by the necessity of breaking certain blood taboos.[2]

The institution of the ñeño or ñamahala is at its most complex, strongest, and probably oldest along the Senegal valley, especially with the Wolof and the Fuulbe. The Wolof in the seventeenth century distinguished five separate occupations as the basis for endogamous social groups—fishermen (*cubaalo*), weavers (*rabb-ser*), woodworkers (*lawbe*), smiths (*tegg*), and minstrels (*gewel*). This would be a maximal list of occupations, even though some societies counted two or even three different kinds of minstrels. Approximately the same complexity of caste division still survives in the middle and lower Senegal valley.[3]

The number of divisions and the strength of the institution then tends to diminish with distance from the mouth of the Senegal, but the diminution is not directly proportional to distance. It weakens rapidly to the north and the south, for example, but it stretches far to the east. In Fuuta, the fishermen shift into the group of free men, but a small group of potters is added to the Wolof list. In Bundu and in some parts of Fuuta the weavers tended to be grouped with minstrels, and weavers drop from the list altogether among the Malinke both in the Gambia valley and the Manding heartland. Otherwise, the core of the institution, distinguishing smiths, leatherworkers, woodworkers, and minstrels of two kinds, persists into the whole of the Manding culture area.[4] It begins to weaken sharply only with movement still further east—for example in Mossi country of the present-day Upper Volta, where only blacksmiths persist as a separate "caste."

2. For the origins of the ñeeñbe generally see H. Zemp, "La légende des griots malinké," *CEA*, 6:611–42 (1966); L. Makarius, "Observations sur la légende des griots malinké, *CEA*, 9:622–640 (1969); P. Smith, "Notes sur l'organization sociale des Diakhanké: Aspects particuliers à la région de Kédougou," *Bulletin et mémoires de la Société d'anthropologie de Paris*, 8 (11th ser.): 263–302 (1965), pp. 290 ff.

3. Barry, "Royaume du Walo," pp. 34–42; Wane, *Les Toucouleur*, passim.

4. Person, *Samori*, 1:54–58.

With movement north or south of the Senegal, on the other hand, the number and importance of the ñeeñbe also decreases sharply. To the north, the Moors of the Mauritania distinguish only two endogamous groups, minstrels and praisers on one hand (*'iggawan,* sing. *'iggīw*), and a group of all the craftsmen on the other, including smiths, soapmakers, leatherworkers, and so on (called *m'allmīn,* sing. *m'allam*).[5] To the south, even the Sereer borrowed the institution from their Wolof and Fuulbe neighbors within recent centuries, and in many instances the "casted" people themselves were immigrants from the north. The institution is strong with the Gambia Malinke, but here it is intrusive and reflects its strength in the Manding region to the east. South of the Gambia, caste distinctions drop off altogether. The Bajaraanke, Koñagi, and Basari of southeast Senegal, who once lived much further north, believe that blacksmiths have a special relationship with the supernatural, but the smiths are not endogamous.[6]

Whatever its origin and cause of diffusion, the institution of "casted" occupations is not coterminous with other aspects of culture. It exists among sedentary people speaking West Atlantic languages, as it does among nomads speaking Afro-Asiatic languages like Arabic and Berber. It appears strongest among West Atlantic speakers like the Wolof and Halpulaar, but it stops short of other West Atlantic speakers like the Bajaraanke, and it has only recently reached the Sereer, who are close linguistic relatives of the Fuulbe. It corresponds somewhat better to the region that has a long historical experience of elaborate political institutions of the state type, but even there the correspondence is far from perfect.

The presence of the ñeeñbe as an institution affected society at large. Where ñeeñbe were important, a strong sense of occupational solidarity was often found among free men, and members of particular lineages tended to follow the same occupation generation after generation. Interest groups or professional groups that came into existence in particular historical circumstances could be frozen by inheritance and then separated somewhat from the rest of society by the tendency toward endogamy. A recent example is the Tooroɗɓe of Fuuta, who began as a religious party which strongly supported Islamic purity in the eighteenth century; many were Muslim clerics by profession. They then won power in the religious revolution during the last quarter of that century, tended to become a hereditary aristocracy, not truly endogamous, but enough so to make some authorities identify them as a "caste." In

5. Miské, Ahmed Baba, "Al-Wasît: Tableau de la Mauritanie à la fin du xixe siècle," *BIFAN,* 30:117–64 (1968).

6. D. P. Gamble, *The Wolof of Senegambia* (London, 1957), p. 101; Diagne, *Pouvoir politique,* pp. 71 ff.; W. S. Simmons, *Eyes of the Night: Witchcraft among a Senegalese People* (Boston, 1971); M. de Lestrange, *Les Coniagui et les Bassari* (Paris, 1955); M. Gessain-de Lestrange, *Les migrations des Coniagui et Bassari* (Paris, 1967).

a somewhat different way, some Moorish tribes tended to be identified as clerical or zwāya, while others were military. In fact, both kinds had some Muslim clerics, both had to fight, and both contained "casted" occupational groups of minstrels and smiths.[7]

The boundaries between ñeeñbe and riimbe were not always absolute. Smiths and minstrels were clearly and permanently ñeeñbe, but others have changed status within historical memory. The jawaanɓe (sing. jawaanɗo), for example, were something like minstrels in Fuuta; they too were courtiers and advisors to the rulers, though they were sometimes merchants. In Bundu and Fuuta alike, they were usually considered to be ñeeñbe in the nineteenth century, but in recent decades they have begun to take wives from the class of free men. In much the same way, the subaalɓe (pl. of cubaalo) were fishermen in Fuuta and among the Wolof, but in Fuuta they were considered riimbe, though the seventeenth century Wolof called them ñeeñbe.[8] Subtle shifts with time and place make the historical role of Senegambian castes especially liable to misunderstanding.

The third major group, slaves or captifs, is also liable to misunderstanding for other reasons, especially so because the West itself recently had a social category called slave, marked by the legal right of one person to sell another person at will, like any other chattel. The key was the property right, the salability that distinguished the owned from the owner. Purchase was the mechanism for transferring African slaves to the Americas, but it was really a shift of institutions more than a simple change of geography. Senegambian slaves were not property in the Western sense, and most of them could not be sold at all without judicial condemnation. The distinguishing mark of slaves as a social group was the fact that they were foreigners or descendents of foreigners who had entered the society in which they found themselves by capture in war or by purchase.

But these African "slaves" fell into three quite distinct categories. First, there were trade slaves who had themselves been captured or purchased. They were called jam sayor in Wolof, pad okob in Sereer, jiaado in Pulaar, and a variety of different names in different regional dialects of Malinke. Trade slaves had no legal rights at all. Second came the category of slaves born in captivity or accepted as members of the household of the master, called jam juundu in Wolof, pad bin in Sereer, maccuuɗo (sing. of maacube) in Pulaar.

7. H. T. Norris, "Znāga Islam during the Seventeenth and Eighteenth Centuries," Bulletin of the School of Oriental and African Studies, 32:496–526 (1969); Wane, Les Toucouleur, pp. 34–38; Robinson, "Abdul Bokar Kan."

8. A. Raffenel, Voyage dans l'Afrique occidentale exécuté en 1843 et 1844 (Paris, 1846), p. 204; F. Brigaud, Histoire traditionelle du Sénégal (Saint Louis, 1962); P. Cantarelle, "L'endogamie des populations du Fouta sénégalais," Population, 4:665–76 (1960), p. 671; Wane, Les Toucouleur, pp. 42–50.

From the moment of purchase, a trade slave began gradually to change status as he was assimilated to the new society. For those born in the new society, the status was that of a subordinate membership, including a fictitious quasi-kinship relationship to the master's lineage which carried with it a complex web of rights and obligations. The slave's general well-being depended a great deal on the kind of work he did. Some were settled in slave villages, where they did the work of ordinary peasants and had much the same kind of life, except that they owed a portion of the harvest to the owner. Others served the master more directly in his own fields. Still others were allowed to follow crafts like weaving. Some females were taken as concubines by their masters, or even as wives, since the slaves were not set apart from the rest of society by sexual prohibitions like those against the ñeeñbe. In several Senegambian societies, marriage to a free man that ended after a child was born automatically shifted the mother into the ranks of the free, since it would not be proper for the mother of a free child to marry a slave.

In a separate category came royal slaves used for military or administrative purposes. These were called *ceɗɗo* in Wolof, Sereer, and the Pulaar singular (*seɓe* in the plural and often spelled *thiedo* in French).[9] The potential power and wealth of a royal slave was enormous, and the chief among them sometimes were second only to the king himself. In most Senegambian kingdoms they were the only people available to serve as bureaucrats, because all others had obligations to their own lineages standing in the way of efficiency and loyalty to the king. In the same way, the royal slaves were usually the only standing army, in much the same tradition as the Janissary corps in Turkey, the Mamluks in Egypt, or the corps of black slave-soldiers in eighteenth-century Morocco. This position gave them access to power that could be used to influence the choice of the ruler, or to lord it over the peasantry or even over civilian officials. By the early nineteenth century, the slave-soldiers in the Wolof states and some Malinke Gambian kingdoms had become a branch of the ruling class who happened to be military specialists, and they fell more and more outside of royal control. Their habit of pillaging the countryside, with or without the king's agreement, made them increas-

9. The importance of this group differed greatly from place to place in Senegambia, and the terminology also differed. In the Malinke kingdoms, a term cognate with *ceddo* included slave administrators as well as slave soldiers. (Quinn, "The Gambia," p. 88.) The Pulaar *ceɗɗo* had a variety of different meanings. In Fuuta, even today, it refers to free men descended from the Deñanke dynasty and its followers. In Bundu, however, the original meaning slipped still further, and the word became the generic term for foreigners, especially for Wolof or the Soninke of Gajaaga. (Wane, *Les Toucouleur*, pp. 29–34.) In much the same way, the current meaning in Wolof and Sereer is also extensible in certain usages to mean non-Muslims generally, or simply a member of the precolonial ruling class. (Klein, *Islam and Imperialism*, p. 9.)

ingly unpopular with the peasantry. In the second half of the nineteenth century, this unpopularity combined with reformist Islam in a series of insurrections that overturned the political order from the lower Gambia northward to Kajor and Jolof.[10]

The numerical balance of class and caste differed greatly from one place to another, and from one time to another, influenced by the rise and fall of states, the incidence of warfare, or the political success of particular lineages. In recent Fuuta Tooro, a sample of sedentary Fuulbe showed 20 per cent descended from "slaves" (maccube), 6 per cent in the occupational "castes" (ñeeñbe), and 74 per cent riimbe.[11] This may be close to the general pattern in the Wolof and Sereer states as well, but the upper Senegal had a different pattern. Administrative estimates in 1904 put two-thirds of the population of Bundu and lower Gajaaga in slave status at that time. Travelers on the Gambia toward the end of the eighteenth century also guessed that three-quarters of the population of the Malinke states were slaves. Other Malinke in Bambuhu, on the other hand, kept no slaves at all in some regions, and very few in others. On balance, the administrative estimate for all of French West Africa in 1906 was about 25 per cent slave.[12]

One final institution cut across the lines of status, descent, and kinship. This was an age-grade organization, grouping all men or women who were initiated to adulthood at about the same time. In many African societies, the age grades were a crucial cement joining those who were otherwise split into jealous and competing kinship groups. In Senegambia, their importance was uneven. It was greatest in the Manding culture area to the east of Senegambia proper. There, the age grades helped to work across the grain of separate lineages that competed within the framework of the small Malinke state or *kafu*. A new age grade was created each seven years, and the previous grade promoted for a total of six promotions, yielding a cycle of forty-nine years in all. The Gambia Malinke, however, did not preserve the full force of this system; rather than having a cycle of seven named grades repeated over and over they kept only four. Even so, this was a more important age-grade system than was found in most of Senegambia. Age grades had some importance among the Sereer, but they dropped to insignificance with the Wolof.

10. Colvin, "Kajor," pp. 41–45; Klein, *Islam and Imperialism,* and Quinn, "The Gambia," passim.

11. In this case the jawaanbe, often counted as riimbe, were counted as ñeeñbe, but they were only 1.8 per cent of the total, so that the change is not significant. (Cantarelle, "Endogamie," p. 671.)

12. "Questionnaire sur le sujet de la captivité," 1904, ANS, K 18; J. B. L. Durand, *Voyage au Sénégal,* 2nd ed. in 2 vols. (Paris, 1807), 1:129 (first published An X [Sept. 1802–Sept. 1803]); M. Park, *Travels in the Interior Districts of Africa,* 2 vols. (London, 1816–17), 1:32–33; Boucard, "Relation de Bambouc," June 1729, AM, mss. 50/2, f. 61; Deherme, "L'esclage en AOF," ANS, K 25, p. 218.

The Wolof, however, had a related institution, the *mbar* or circumcision group; and it could have importance later in life, as it did when those men who had passed through circumcision with a potential Damel would later become the core of his military support. The sedentary Fuulbe kept only an unimportant age association, while the Soninke of Gajaaga had age associations for adolescents but not for adults.[13]

Government

As elsewhere in West Africa, the essential element of political life in Senegambia was kinship; lineages were the building blocks out of which a constitutional order had to be made. Lineage determined eligibility for office, and some states had a single royal lineage from which the ruler was chosen—the Deñankoobe in Fuuta, the Baacili (Bathily) in Gajaaga, the Sisiɓe (Sy) in Bundu, the Gelwar in the Sereer states, and the Naanco (Nantio or Nyancho) in Kaabu. Others had a number of different lineages that were eligible for office in a multidynastic system of rotation, as in Kajor, Waalo, and most of the Gambia Malinke states. Whether one dynasty or several, all Senegambian political constitutions were in the nature of a compromise between the most powerful lineages. The terms of the compromise were privileges or favors promised to other powerful lineages in return for their acquiescence in a one-lineage monopoly of the monarchy.

Below the level of the ruling lineage or lineages (called *garmi* in Wolof and *sumakunda* in Malinke), still other lineages had an inherited right to provide candidates for lesser offices at the provincial level or in the central government. This class of nobility was known as *kangam* in Wolof, sometimes as *riimɓe ardiiɓe* in Pulaar. It was sometimes made up of the descendents of local rulers, like the laman, who had been subordinated in the aggregation of small states to make a larger one. In other places, subordinate offices were reserved for junior members of the dominant lineage. The Naanco of Kaabu had a regular hierarchy for non-royal Naanco, formed by an interesting imposition of patrilineal descent on the dominant matrilineal pattern borrowed from the Sereer. The form of succession was such that only a female Naanco, in effect a royal princess, could give birth to a true Naanco, eligible for the kingship. A male Naanco's sons and daughters were therefore non-Naanco unless their mother was also a Naanco. But these non-Naanco grandchildren of a Naanco princess were nevertheless eligible for certain subordinate offices and their children in turn were eligible for lower offices, and so

13. Gamble, *Wolof,* p. 53; Pélissier, *Paysans du Sénégal,* pp. 211–13; Bathily, "Notice sur Gadiaga," pp. 76–79; Wane, *Les Toucouleur,* pp. 27–29.

on until the fourth generation down the male line from the Naanco princess were nothing but ordinary free men.[1]

The constitution of Waalo is one illustration of the way the powers of royal lineages were balanced against those of the non-royals. To be a candidate for the office of Brak, a man had to be qualified by descent through both the male and the female line. He had to belong to the patrilineage (or sant) of Mboj, and he had to belong to one of three royal matrilineages (or *men*)— Logar, Joos, or Teejek. The choice between potential candidates, however, was in the hands of a three-man council (called *Seb ak Baor*). The councillors were themselves men of *kangam* status, eligible for high office in the central government, for provincial command, but not for the kingship. Their origins in most cases would have gone back to the lamanate, and their rights to choose and remove the Brak was thus a form of compromise between the old rulers and a central government. Even in the central government, the rules of eligibility divided power among three powerful matrilineages. The council was not bound to appoint a Brak from each in turn; but some kind of informal order must have been maintained, since all three continued to be appointed with reasonable frequency down to the French conquest.[2]

Such neat balance of authority by constitutional compromise may not, however, work out well in practice. During the last centuries of Waalo's independence, the Brak's powers came to be too limited in practice as well as in theory. His control over the provinces was very weak indeed, and even in the central government, the *Bökkneeg Jurbel* or chief of the royal slaves succeeded in making his office into a form of prime ministership equal in power to the ruler himself. Several Bökkneeg Jurbel made the office heredi-tary for a time. The constitutional balance in this case was an adequate guard against autocracy, but not against anarchy.

None of the Senegambian constitutional arrangements was fixed perma-nently. Kajor, Waalo's neighbor to the south, began with a similar constitu-tion, which developed in a different direction. At the emergence of Kajor from the greater Jolof empire, the Damel had to bear the sant of Fal and belong to a particular branch of that patrilineage. He also had to belong to one of a prominent group of matrilineages, though in fact the approved list kept getting longer and longer through the late sixteenth and seventeenth centuries, as each Damel who had not been legitimate on his mother's side

---

1. Quinn, "The Gambia," pp. 71–73; B. Barry, "Royaume du Walo," passim; B. Barry, "Le royaume du Walo du traité du Ngio en 1819 à la conquête en 1855," *BIFAN*, 31:339–442 (1969), pp. 278–87; Boulègue, "La Sénégambie," passim; Brigaud, *Histoire traditionnelle*," pp. 63–69; Colvin, "Kajor," passim; Cissoko, "Kabou," pp. 12–13; Sidibe, "The Story of Kaabu."

2. Barry, "Royaume du Walo" (thesis), esp. pp. 71 ff.

added his own matrilineages to the approved list. As in Waalo, the choice of Damel lay with a council of non-royals.

Then a powerful figure came to office and the situation changed. Lat Sukaabe (ruled c. 1697–1720) not only added his matrilineage to the list, the seventh matrilineage to be so added, but also changed the constitutional practice. From then on to the French conquest, all seven matrilineages were counted as eligible, but each Damel was in fact chosen from the Geej matrilineage to which Lat Sukaabe had belonged. In theory anyone from the sant of Fal could be ruler, but in fact the senior branch, which had ruled up to this time, never supplied another Damel. Instead, all later rulers came by turn from two junior branches. Just as the constitutional balance was effectively a compromise between lineages, the terms of the compromise could be changed as the power and influence of the lineages themselves changed.[3]

While the lineages at play in the political game were usually only free lineages, this was not necessarily the case. In Jolof, the Burba was chosen from a single patrilineage (with no privileged matrilineage at all), but the electoral council was made up of the lineage heads of five important, named patrilineages, plus the village heads of two particular slave villages belonging to the royal family.[4]

The Sereer states exemplify a constitutional order that sought to balance the rights of a conquering dynasty, the Gelwar, against those of the local people. The Gelwar first of all transformed themselves into a matrilineage, out of deference to their subjects' way of doing things. They also allowed the conciliar principle to enter on a continuous basis, not simply when a ruler had to be chosen. This was done through an assembly of village heads (*jaraf*) and village-level administrators (*sak-sak*), which was entitled to elect the Great Jaraf, a cross between an elected prime minister and a tribune of the people representing the Sereer peasantry at the court of the Malinke rulers. The Great *Farba,* chief of the crown slaves and head of the military forces, was a third important figure balancing the power of the *Bur* and that of the Great Jaraf. Perhaps because so many lineages were represented on a continuing basis, the Sereer monarchies were able to keep order in the late eighteenth and early nineteenth centuries, when the Malinke to the south and the Wolof to the north were seriously disturbed by their anarchic military aristocracies of slave soldiers.[5]

3. Colvin, "Kajor," pp. 46–60.
4. Brigaud, *Histoire traditionelle,* passim; V. Monteil, "Le Dyolof et Al-Bouri Ndiaye," *BIFAN,* 28:595–636 (1966).
5. Diagne, *Pouvoir politique,* pp. 56–94; Pélissier, *Paysans du Sénégal,* p. 199; Brigaud, *Histoire traditionelle,* pp. 143–71. Oral traditions in both Sereer country and Kaabu associate the Naanco and the Gelwar lineages.

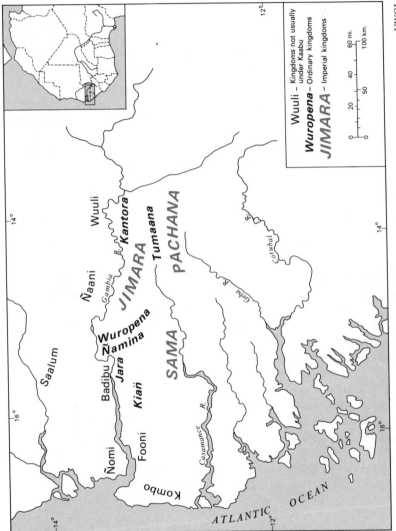

Wuuli – Kingdoms not usually under Kaabu
Wuropena – Ordinary kingdoms
JIMARA – Imperial kingdoms

1.4 The Lower Gambia Valley, Showing the Riverside Provinces of Kaabu

While the Malinke states of the Gambia bear a family resemblance to other political forms in Senegambia, they also belong to the Manding political tradition stretching out to the east.[6] The fundamental political unit was the local segment of a patrilineage—called *lu* in the east, but often *kabilo* on the Gambia. The word *kabilo* means a ward or section of a village, but with overtones suggesting that only people with the same jaamu would live together. Hence the head of the kabilo (*kabilo-tigi* or *kabilo-tio*) was simultaneously the head of the ward and the head of the extended family, and the office passed in succession through a line of brothers before dropping one generation to pick up again with the eldest son of the eldest brother. In practice this meant that the kabilo-tigi was usually also the eldest male in that kabilo.

In the greater Manding world, several different political forms have linked the local lineage to the state. Common forms along the Gambia were like the Sereer and Wolof systems, having a council to represent important lineages and multidynastic succession. Unlike the Wolof system, however, which tended to let the electoral council choose a ruler from any eligible lineage, the Malinke system passed the office from one to another in a fixed order. Ñomi or Barra, for example, had three royal lineages (Jame, Mane, and Sonko), but the office of *Mansa* actually circulated in a set order to the kabilo-tigi of each of seven different towns dominated by one or another of the royal lineages. The council (*beng*) therefore had nothing to say about the choice of a Mansa, though it had to be consulted on all major decisions and it (or the Mansa's own lineage) could depose him if either strongly disliked his rule. This was true even in states like Wuuli where a single dynasty ruled.[7]

The political system in the south-bank Malinke states was somewhat different because they were theoretically part of the much larger state of Kaabu, formerly a province of Mali. Each of the smaller kingdoms that made up the empire of Kaabu had its own Mansa and its own particular dynasty or dynasties eligible for rotation to the kingship. In all, some twenty to thirty mini-states of this kind made up Kaabu at its height, including a row of states along the south bank of the Gambia. From west to east these were Kiañ, Jaara, Wuropena, Jimara, Tumaana, and Kantora—all of the south-bank states ex-

6. Person, *Samori,* 1:43–88, is a good introductory discussion to problems of unity and diversity in Manding history in recent centuries. For recent studies of Malinke social and political organization, in the Gambia and in the Manding heartland, see P. M. Weil, "Political Structure and Process among the Gambia Mandinka: The Village Parapolitical System," and N. S. Hopkins, "Mandinka Social Organization," in C. T. Hodge, ed., *Papers on the Manding* (Bloomington, 1971), pp. 249–72, 99–128.

7. Quinn, "The Gambia," pp. 72 ff.; A. Rançon, *Dans la haute Gambie: Voyage d'exploration scientifique 1891–92* (Paris, 1894), pp. 53, 69; Cissoko, "Royauté mandingue," p. 331 and passim.

cept Ñamina, tucked into the northern bend of the river opposite Saalum, and the two dominantly Joola states in the far west, Fooni and Kombo. The imperial office could only be held by a member of the patrilineage Sane or Mane who was also a Naanco in the maternal line, and these same qualifications applied to the office of Mansa of the imperial kingdoms of Jimara, Sama, or Pachana. In practice, the emperor was chosen because he was the eldest ruler of any of these three kingdoms,[8] though his authority seems to have been merely nominal in the seventeenth and eighteenth centuries.

Fuuta Tooro resembled Kaabu and the Gelwar states in being ruled by a foreign dynasty, established by right of conquest near the beginning of the sixteenth century. But the seventeenth- and eighteenth-century constitutional pattern in Fuuta is obscure. The political narrative preserved by oral tradition reflects the play of conflicting interests within the state, but without explaining their formal relations. As rulers, the Deñankoobe could not simply override local interests. They had to balance diverse ethnic differences. They had to balance those of their own followers, some of whom acquired large territories as jom leeidi at the time of their conquest, against those who held land as jom jengol. They had to balance the interests of the transhumant pastoralists against those of sedentary farmers—and during a period when the Moorish nomads from the north were especially aggressive. They had to balance a demand for religious reform against the ideas and practices of others who were not completely Muslim. Some of the Deñankoobe were themselves pious Muslims; others were less so, but they were all swept from power by the religious revolution at the end of the eighteenth century. It was this revolution that obscured the formal constitution of the earlier period by superimposing its own forms.

Meanwhile Bundu, a second sedentary Fuulbe state, was founded at the end of the seventeenth century by Futaanke emigrants who followed a Muslim cleric named Maalik Sii (Sy) into a sparsely settled region populated by a mixture of Malinke, Soninke, Tanda, and emigrant Futaanke. Since his leadership was based on religious prestige, Maalik Sii took the religious title of *Eliman* (later changed to the more Pulaarized version *Almaami*), derived from the Arabic *al-Imām*, leader of prayer. This was the first of a series of almamates founded by religious insurrection or conquest. When Maalik Sii died about 1700, other lineages claimed their turn to rule. For a time in the 1720's, one of them, the Giiroɓe, became dominant, but the Sisibe returned in the 1730's under Maalik's grandson and made the almamate hereditary in their lineage alone. An electoral council had a voice in choosing which Sii was to rule, but the succession was supposed to pass through a line of brothers before returning to the eldest son of the eldest brother—and the council included only other Sisibe, though other lineages would be consulted if there

8. Sidibe, "The Story of Kaabu."

were sharp disagreement within the family. Bundu was thus a model for a potentially more autocratic state than most, as though the prestige of religious leadership strengthened the hand of the Sisibe in their dealings with other lineages.[9]

The Bundu model was thus available when the Toorodbe emerged as successful leaders of a similar religious revolution in Fuuta. The first Almaami of Fuuta was Abdul Kaader Kaan, a serious Islamic scholar, a sincere Muslim, and a man who wanted to enforce Islamic law in a purified Muslim state. As the revolution moved toward its final victory, however, many joined who were not quite so religiously motivated. In 1806, a group of these men conspired with the Almaami of Bundu to divide the forces of the religious party and kill Abdul Kaader. With that coup, five of the conspirators (and their descendents after them) emerged as the real power in the country. They inherited membership in an electoral council, but the electoral lineages were barred from the office of Almaami. Instead, the office tended to rotate among another group of lineages, more famous for their religious prestige than for their political acumen.[10] The Bunduunke model was thus partly followed by Abdul Kaader Kaan but abandoned by his successors—not by choice but by force of circumstance.

Gajaaga, the Soninke state next upstream from Fuuta, passed through a similar and more complex series of constitutional changes. The oral traditions suggest that the kingship originally belonged to the segment of the ruling Baacili (Bathily) family that came from the town of Tiyaabu (Tuabo), even though Tiyaabu was only one of several towns in which the Baacili were important. This primacy for Tiyaabu disappeared at an unknown date, to be replaced up to the 1830's by a multidynastic succession involving different branches of the Baacili. The office of Tunka for Gajaaga as a whole went in order to the eldest male Baacili from each of six towns, in a fixed order—Tiyaabu, Kotere, Lani, Maxaana, Musaala, and Tambukaane.[11] In the period from the 1830's through the 1850's, the system broke down in intertown rivalries and efforts to monopolize the possible profits from the newly intensive trade on the Senegal, with the result that the original Gajaaga was

9. A. Rançon, "Le Bondou," *Bulletin de la Société de géographie de Bordeaux,* 17 (n.s.):433–63, 497–558, 561–91, 593–647 (1894), remains the best general study on Bunduunke history. See also Raffenel, *Voyage dans l'Afrique,* pp. 268–75; Demba Sembalou Sok, CC, XX T3 (1); P. D. Curtin, "Jihad in West Africa: Early Phases and Inter-Relations in Mauritania and Senegal," *JAH,* 12:11–24 (1971).

10. Robinson, "Abdul Bokar Kan," pp. 24–50.

11. Bathily, "Notice sur Gadiaga," pp. 66–67; Levens, Report of 10 July 1725, BN, FF,NA, 9339, f. 145; Simon to Governor, 25 October 1827, ANF-OM, Sénégal IV 15. Some of the early authorities suggest matrilineal elements in the succession to office in the more distant past. See P. Labarthe, *Voyage en Sénégal pendant les années 1784 et 1785, d'après les mémoires de Lajaille* (Paris, 1802), p. 45.

split (under French pressure) into two kingdoms—upper Gajaaga or Kamera, along the south bank of the Senegal from the Faleme nearly to Kayes, and lower Gajaaga or Goi, from the Faleme downstream to the frontier with Fuuta. The capital of upper Gajaaga was usually Maxaana, while Tiyaabu became the usual capital of the smaller Goi.

All of these Senegambian states were territorially defined, but autonomous enclaves might also exist within the territory—a tendency that may have been more widespread than records indicate. It apparently originated from the fact that some conflicts could be resolved by giving contestants a share of power or a turn in office, but others were better avoided by creating independent or autonomous jurisdictions, where possible dissidents could peacefully go their own way. Throughout the western Sudan, Muslim clerics were often found with their own ward in a town, sometimes with a separate town alongside the secular town, or simply with the right to apply Muslim law to Muslims while the non-Muslims followed their own customs. In Gajaaga, a dozen or so of the towns along the Senegal River were dominated by clerical lineages, especially by the Draame. They enjoyed autonomy from the secular government of Gajaaga by long tradition, and they kept that autonomy through all the constitutional changes of the Baacili regime. A similar autonomy was granted to at least one other group of alien immigrants. Sometime during the eighteenth century, a segment of the Njaiɓe, the ruling lineage of Jolof, came to Gajaaga as refugees who had lost a struggle for office. They were granted permission to settle at Bakel, which then became an autonomous center of Njai power. It was partly this autonomy that made the French establish their fortified post there in 1818 and led to the later rise of Bakel to commercial predominance in northeast Senegal.[12]

The broad similarity of Senegambian political constitutions helped to give it a relatively homogeneous political style. Even the Gambian regimes of Manding origin were influenced by their centuries of political interaction with non-Manding neighbors. This influence is most apparent in changes from patrilineal to matrilineal reckoning of descent, but it also appears in the way the Gambia Malinke developed kingdoms of approximately the size and stability of others in Senegambia. In the Manding area to the east, the removal of Malian imperial rule tended to leave the somewhat smaller unit generically called a kafu. Thus the greatest discontinuity in political constitution lay between Wuuli, the easternmost of the medium-sized Malinke kingdoms on the Gambia, and the congeries of Malinke and Tanda mini-states to the east and southeast. A little to the north, a similar discontinuity fell

---

12. J. B. Labat, *Nouvelle relation de l'Afrique occidentale,* 4 vols. (Paris, 1728), 3:338–39; C. Monteil, "Le site de Goundiourou," *CEHSAOF,* 11:647–53 (1928); P. Charpentier, Memoir of 1 April 1725, ANF, C6 10; Samani Sy, CC, T4 (1).

between Bundu and the neighboring Malinke region of Bambuhu, to the east of the Faleme. There, the political units were smaller than those of the Gambian states, and the rulers made no claim to the title of Mansa, used by the emperors of Mali. The fundamental unit for many purposes was the village, ruled by a *Farin*, who was usually the lineage head of the principal lineage. Larger states grouping several villages were also present, but they might have no more than two to five villages, and the ruler carried the title of *Saatigi*. In fact, he was usually the Farin of one village in the group, and his authority was greater there than it was in the others.[13]

But the similarity of constitutions should not obscure the variety of actual regimes that could masquerade behind the forms. These constitutions included a web of checks and balances, which meant that some regimes *could* function reasonably well as governments with the consent of the governed. But the checks and balances could easily become mere rules for dividing power among members of an oppressive oligarchy.

One source of this contrast between outward forms and their actual content was the fact that Senegambian bureaucracies were too rudimentary to deal directly with individuals. They dealt instead with corporate groups, normally lineages; these corporations were then responsible for their internal self-government. This meant that the monarch's writ might run very unevenly through the territory of his state. A strong provincial governor could carry his province into a temporary de facto independence, or a strong king could upset the theoretical balance of the constitution and become genuinely autocratic. The main outlines of political geography could therefore remain stable one century after another, while the political realities of power and its application changed rapidly.

The tendency to deal with corporate groups also helped the European trading concerns when they appeared off the coast. If the Europeans asked permission to build a factory or set up a town of their own, Senegambian practice had plenty of precedents with dealing with aliens through their own chiefs. From the African point of view, a European trading post was not ceded territory, merely another religious minority, more easily dealt with by letting it live under its own laws. In other respects, the Senegambian monarchies were acutely interested in trade, and especially in the tolls that could be collected from traders. Each state had an official in each port in charge of

13. Boucard, "Relation de Bambouc," June 1729, AM, Mss. 50/2, ff. 23–28; Person, *Samori*, 1:64–88. The title Saatigi was also used by the Deñankoobe of Fuuta Tooro, and it has a broader sense of meaning a leader of a caravan, or of a moving body like a body of migrants. The distinction between *Saatigi* and *Mansa* in Malinke is therefore not simply one distinguishing the size of the state; it has overtones, rather, of the distinction between *Laamiɗo* and *Aarɗo* in Pulaar—that between the ruler of a sedentary state and the leader of a band of transhumant pastoralists.

European relations, normally under the title *Alkaati,* and a Grand Alkaati might also exist at the central level. In Waalo, for example, this post, held by a royal slave first appointed to deal with Atlantic commerce, gradually rose in importance over the course of the seventeenth century to make its occupant a kind of minister of foreign affairs.[14] Fuuta, Kajor, Siin, and the Gambian kingdoms all had a similar official, often known along the Gambia as the *Tubabmansa,* literally "king of the Europeans."

Religion and Political Change

Over two centuries and a half, from the early seventeenth to the middle of the nineteenth, the maritime trade on the Senegambian coast was a new element of some importance, but it was rarely of first importance. The Europeans were no physical threat; external dangers from the Moroccans in the first half of the eighteenth century, and from the Bambara in the second, were far greater. The European cultural impact was minimal before the end of the eighteenth century, and it was insignificant compared to the influence of Islamic civilization until well into the colonial period. The most important general theme in the political history of Senegambia was, indeed, Islamic. It was the problem of adjusting the political forms of pre-Islamic society to the religious and legal claims of Islam.

Islam was hardly a new religion at this period, though Senegambia lay on the far outskirts of the Muslim world, a borderland inhabited by converts, incomplete converts, and non-converts; but this had been so for centuries. Islam was first taught as early as the tenth century. By 1700, it was already more than six centuries since the Almoravids rode north from the Sahara (Senegambians among them) to conquer Morocco and Spain. In all that time, the advance of the religious frontier was not very obvious—either in the percentage of converts south of the Sahara, or in the smaller percentage who fully followed the teaching of Islam. The question was not whether the Islam of Senegambian believers was "pure" by Middle Eastern standards, which is beside the point. The question, rather, was whether Senegambian Muslims took the local version of Islam seriously as a standard of conduct in personal and public life. This was the point of intersection between religious belief and political change.

This question was important all along the religious frontier, but the religious frontier was a zone, not a line, and the frontier zone in the seventeenth century stretched to the south of the Gambia and northward far into the desert. In the western Sahara, the Sanhaja or Znãga Berbers had been the core of the Almoravid movement, but they were no longer the dominant desert

14. Barry, "Royaume du Walo," p. 71.

nomads. Beginning about the fourteenth century, they were joined by an Arab migration, branching southward and extending the major movement of Arabs from Arabia toward the Māghrib, which had begun in the eleventh century. As these Arabs moved into the western Sahara, the tribal units divided, forming new tribes, which subdivided in their turn. This process is one cause of the genealogical complexity and shifting terminology that besets Mauritanian history. The Arab nomads who finally came to live north of the Senegal by the end of the sixteenth century and established their dominance over the Berbers already there are sometimes called the Banū Ma'qīl, after the oldest remembered male ancestor—or else Hassānī after the leader of a later fission, or Maghfar after a leader later still.

Whatever name is used, the coming of the Arabs introduced a division in Mauritanian society that has lasted to the present. They were Muslim, but they did not pay very great attention to Islamic learning or to commerce. Their specialty, other than pastoralism, was fighting, and they were able to supplement their pastoral income by levying tribute and "protection money" from others in the region, both nomadic and sedentary. In time they came to be known by their occupation, so that Ma'qil, Hassānī, or Maghfar was synonymous with the grouping of "warrior tribes." The Berbers meanwhile passed through a long-term process of cultural assimilation, adopting Arabic rather than Berber for everyday use—as they had done long since for learned discourse—but they kept their special tradition of Muslim learning, linked to a commercial tradition as well. In time, they came to be known as the *zwāya*, clerical, or "marabout" tribes.

The same pattern of serious and less serious Muslims extended south of the Sahara as well. European visitors of the sixteenth century reported that Senegambians were Muslim, which indicates that the surface forms of Islam were practiced at the courts and in commercial circles. Later evidence suggests that courtiers and merchants were more likely than the rest of the population to be Muslim, and that otherwise, Islam was often a superficial layer on a non-Muslim base. Muslims were a probable majority of the peasantry only in Fuuta Tooro. Elsewhere the religion appears from scattered evidence to have been similar to that of the present-day survivals among the Sereer or the non-Muslim Malinke. They recognized a high god who created the world and may in some variants have withdrawn into neutrality, though Rog Sèn, the high god of the Sereer, is an immanent deity, still active in the world's affairs, though he acts in the world through supernatural beings, some purely spiritual and others that can take human form.[1] Some spirits in these pre-Muslim religions were associated with particular trees, termite hills, or water courses. Others were the spirits of ancestors, or in some cases non-ancestral spirits that could nevertheless act as intermediaries between the

1. For Sereer religion see H. Gravrand, *Visage africain de l'Eglise* (Paris, 1961).

living and the dead. Lineage heads and rulers, with their powers derived from kinship, therefore had a crucial role as representatives of the living to the dead of the same lineage, just as they represented their people to other lineages among the living. Hence political leadership at all levels was partly a religious office, sanctioned by religion and requiring ritual acts by the office holder.[2] The conversion of a ruler to another religion was therefore an act with potentially profound political implications, not simply a personal choice of belief.

Islam itself raised political issues. Alongside the emphasis on the hereafter and ultimate justice in heaven, Islam was more insistent than Christianity has been on the proper organization of the here and now. Rather than distinguishing a realm for Caesar and one for God, Islam obliged a ruler who was a true Muslim to see that Muslim law was enforced within his territory. And Islam came equipped with attitudes and techniques that carried further political implications. It was a religion of the book, which meant that good Muslims were also literate at a time and place where literacy was a rare and valuable skill. This skill was most useful, or most remunerative, at the courts of Senegambian rulers. Through Muslim scribes, the rulers were introduced, at least in a small way, to the norms, values, and practices of Muslim civilization in North Africa and the Middle East. Finally, Islam south of the Sahara was an occupational religion. Merchants from North Africa carried it across the desert. Their most common converts on the sahal were their merchant counterparts from black Africa, who in turn became the carriers of Islam further south through the savanna and into the forest; and this fact too had political implications.

Taken together, these factors conditioned the form and speed of Islamic penetration. Merchants on the move tended to form little clusters of foreigners, travelers, or Muslims—in fact, these three categories were one and the same in the eyes of a mainly peasant population. Some of these clusters appeared in capital towns as well, with the result that Islam first appeared not as a moving frontier of mass conversion but as a series of urban enclaves at the centers of trade and political power, while the mass of the peasantry remained little affected for centuries. For the Gambia, a Portuguese visitor writing in about 1570 mentioned three specifically clerical towns, Sutuko in Wuuli, Malor in Ñaani, and a third unnamed town near the mouth of the river. There were to be many more a century and a half later. In this respect, at least, the progress of Islam was continuous.

This pattern of propagation heightened the political problem. After the

2. These religious functions should not be taken to indicate that Senegambian rulers were in some sense "divine kings"; they were not. For a review of divine kingship see M. W. Young, "Divine Kingship of the Jukun: A Re-evaluation of Some Theories," *Africa,* 36:135–54 (1966).

merchants themselves, rulers and courtiers tended to be among the first converts. This fact would have posed no problem if the whole country had also been Muslim, or if the ruler had had an autocratic bureaucracy capable of imposing Islam; but none of the Senegambian rulers had the political power or the bureaucratic machine to enforce Muslim law. Rulers who converted therefore did what they could; they became nominal Muslims and enforced the law insofar as they could without compromising the loyalty of the non-Muslim majority. In most cases, however, they also continued to carry out their pre-Muslim duties of office.

The result was a crucial tension within the Muslim community—always implicit, sometimes rising to a crisis. All Muslims were not themselves so well instructed in the full Islamic doctrine as to be troubled, but those who were found themselves caught between the obligation to insist on full enforcement of law and belief, and the recognition that politics was the art of the possible. The result, over time, was a chronic demand for religious purity and religious dominance within the state. The reform movement was capable of turning to revolution on occasion, especially when the religious issue could join other issues in a common cause. At first, from the second half of the seventeenth century through the first half of the nineteenth, the religious revolutions were sporadic, rarely affecting more than two or three adjacent states at the same time, rarely recurring more frequently than once a generation. From the middle of the nineteenth century to the European conquest, the series of separate crises spread into a pandemic and continuous crisis marked by warfare, mass migration, anarchy, and a steadily greater weight of European power to intervene.

The first recorded of the early crises occurred on both sides of the ecological frontier between steppe and savanna. It began with Nasīr al-Dīn, a zwāya cleric of southern Mauritania, who preached the need for reform, first among his own people but then throughout the Muslim world. He claimed to be caliph, with a right to rule as successor of the Prophet, and he sent out missionaries to preach in his name and proclaim the new order. He was successful at first among his own people, even among some of the militaristic Hasanīya, and he gained support among the common people of the sedentary zone as well. The movement was peaceful until 1673, when Nasīr al-Dīn called for jihad, in this case not against pagans but against Muslim rulers who were incompletely Muslim. This too was successful at first; he conquered and set up viceroys over Fuuta, Waalo, and Kajor, but he failed to keep the full support of the desert nomads. When he asked them for the *zakāt* traditionally paid to a Muslim sovereign, most of the Hasanīya revolted under the leadership of a certain Hāddi b. Ahmad b. Dāmān. The war that followed is known in Mauritanian history as the war of Shur-bubba. The Hasanīya won in the desert by 1677; the former rulers won and returned to power in the three sedentary states.[3] For the time being, the reformers had lost quickly and completely.

A generation later, in the 1690's, Maalik Sii emerged as a new Fuutanke religious leader with a military following, and he succeeded in founding Bundu as a new Muslim state. This was not a religious revolution within a Muslim state so much as a Muslim war of conquest setting up a new state in non-Muslim or weakly Muslim territory. Maalik Sii's use of the title of Eliman (later Almaami), however, recalled Nasīr al-Dīn's use of an Arabic equivalent *Imāmūna*, and Almaami was adopted by most of the later religious revolutionaries down to Samori Ture in the late nineteenth century.

The third revolt followed a generation later, in 1725, in Fuuta Jaalō. Here, as in Bundu, Fuulbe had been moving gradually into previously Manding territory, and their insurrection had aspects of a Fuulbe ethnic revolt as well as of a jihad against rulers who were incompletely Muslim. The result was a new almamate that was to last, like Bundu, until the French conquest at the end of the nineteenth century.

Another kind of outcome from Nasīr al-Dīn's jihad appeared on the desert edge. Hāddi b. Ahmad b. Dāmān capitalized on his leadership of the anti-clerical forces among the Hasanīya to form the first of a group of Mauritanian emirates with a territorial jurisdiction, replacing looser tribal groupings.[4] Hāddi's foundation was called the Trarza emirate, after an eponymous ancestor who led a subdivision of the Banū Maghfar, and it dominated the region north of the lower Senegal until the French conquest. By the end of the seventeenth century, a second Maghfar division was reorganized as the Brakna emirate dominating the region north of Fuuta Tooro.

About the same time, still another subdivision of the original Banū Maʿqīl, the Mbārek or Mubarek, established a similar state in the steppe much further east, in the region known as Hodh, north of Ñoro (Nioro) in the present-day Malian sahal. This was the state the eighteenth-century Europeans called the kingdom of Ludamar. Finally, about 1775–1800, the last of the Moorish states that were to be important for Senegambian commerce took form midway between the Brakna to the west and the Mbārek to the east. This time, the dominant tribe was not of the Banū Maʿqīl but was one of the

---

3. P. D. Curtin, "Jihad in West Africa," but see also Barry, "Royaume du Walo," for a different interpretation of these events as they affected Waalo. Chambonneau, "L'histoire du Toubenan," in C. I. A. Ricthie, ed., "Deux textes sur le Sénégal (1673–1677)," *BIFAN,* 30:289–353 (1968), is the crucial written source for these events.

4. This discussion of Mauritanian history is based on G. M. Désiré-Vuillemin, *Histoire de la Mauritanie* (Nouakchott, 1964), esp. pp. 138–40; Paul Marty, *L'émirat des Trarzas* (Paris, 1919), *Etudes sur l'Islam et les tribus maures, les Brakna* (Paris, 1921), and "Les Ida ou Ali, chorfa Tidjanïa de Mauritanie," *RMM,* 31:223–73 (1915–16); and A. Leriche, "Notes sur les classes sociales et sur quelques tribus de Mauritanie," *BIFAN,* 17:173–203 (1955).

zwāya. These people, called the Idaw 'Aish (or Dowich by the Europeans), had first been submerged in the common zwāya defeat in the 1670's, but they gradually recovered and rebuilt a substantial power.

This new cast of characters beyond the northern boundaries of Senegambia was important enough in itself, but its emergence was simultaneous with the intervention of Morocco in Mauritanian and Senegambian affairs. Morocco had been interested in the trans-Sahara since the late sixteenth century. The successful Moroccan expedition against Sōñrai in 1591 led to the collapse of the Sōñrai empire, but the Moroccan expeditional force was small, only about 4,000 men. Even with later reinforcements, the Moroccans were unable to conquer what Sōñrai had once held. Instead, they settled down in an uneasy occupation of the Niger bend. In time the garrison and their descendents, called the *arma*, made themselves an independent power and slipped from Moroccan control.

In the 1670's, simultaneous with the war of Shur-bubba, Mulai Isma'il (ruled 1672–1727) became Sultan and began extending his authority over parts of the Sahara. He soon took over a slave army recruited in the Sudan and began to build an even larger slave army of his own. This effort called for a series of expeditions into the Sahara and then to the Sudan itself. In 1689, Mulai Isma'il led an especially important expedition in person. It moved south through Chingetti, the principal Moroccan base in the Sahara, with a force said to have been nearly 40,000 troops mounted on horses or camels, and fell on a stone-built town called Tarra in the European reports, probably a little north of present-day Ñoro in Mali.[5] Neither this nor the later expeditions to the south tried to establish permanent Moroccan control over any part of Sudan, but Mulai Isma'il was able to secure recognition of his hegemony from most of the Ma'qīl leadership in the western Sahara. One of his wives came from the Banū Maghfar and became mother of the later Sultan, Mulai 'Abdullah b. Isma'il, and Mulai Isma'il drew important military resources from the Sudan throughout his reign.[6]

5. Some of the soldiers who went inland with Cornelius Hodges participated in the attack, but Hodges himself was in Bambuhu at the time. He reported it at 457 kms distance ENE from the gold working at Neteko (Netico). By dead reckoning from modern maps, that would put it between Nioro and Jaara (Diara) in Mali. It is possible that Hodges' "Tarra" was actually the present-day Jaara, or else Nara, somewhat further east. (C. Hodges to RAC, 16 September 1690, printed in T. G. Stone, "The Journey of Cornelius Hodges in Senegambia," *English Historical Review,* 39:89–95 [1924].) But Mungo Park's *Travels* (1:156–57) opens still another possibility. When he was in Jara in 1796, he inquired after Major Houghton, an earlier British traveler who had disappeared in that region. He was told that Houghton left Jaara in the direction of Tichit (which is due north). After two days' travel, he had to turn back, and he backtracked to a watering point called Tarra, where he died.

6. The principal authorities on Mulai Isma'il's activities in the Sahara and Sudan are Muhammad al-Wufrānī, *Histoire de la dynastie Saadienne au Maroc* (Paris, 1888–89), p.

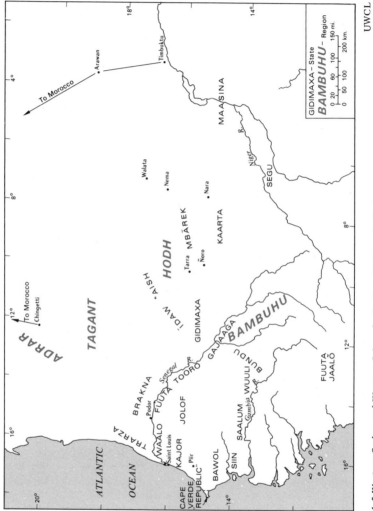

1.5 Western Sudan and Western Sahara in the Late Eighteenth Century

52

UWCL

At first, the primary Moroccan targets were further east, but Senegambia began to attract expeditions almost annually after the 1690's, and especially in the 1720's and 1730's. The expeditionary forces varied in size, but they were considerably larger than the small force that caused the collapse of Sõñrai. Reports mention 12,000 Moroccan troops operating on the upper Senegal in the closing years of the seventeenth century, and another force of 30,000 men and 60,000 camels in the 1730's. The full intentions and extent of these expeditions can only be known when they have been studied from the Moroccan sources. Reports from the Senegambian side, however, make it clear that the Moroccans devastated much of the northern savanna from Kaarta west as far as the Atlantic coast and south at least into Bundu, Jolof, and the Sereer country. The commanders of the Ormankoobe[7] (as these troops were called in Fuuta) also played a major role in the Senegambian politics of the period. They operated in alliance with a variety of Sene-gambian and neighboring states—among others, with Trarza, Brakna, Fuuta Tooro, Gajaaga, and Bundu—and they were able to act at times as the arbiters of local political quarrels, making and unmaking the Saatigi of Fuuta Tooro at their whim. But the Ormankoobe were no easier to control from Morocco than their predecessors the Arma had been. On at least one occasion, in 1737, two separate Moroccan expeditions in the Senegal valley were fighting each other.[8] In spite of many puzzles that still surround these Ormaanke expedi-tions, it is clear that European intervention in Senegambia never approached this scale before General Faidherbe's expeditions on the Senegal in the 1850's.

505; Ismāʿil Hāmid, ed. and trans., *Chroniques de la Mauritanie sénégalaise* (Paris, 1911), p. 9; Ahmed Ennasiri Esslaoui [Es Slawi], "Kitab Elistiqsa [Kitab al-Istiqsal]," trans. E. Fumey, *Archives marocaines,* vols. 9 and 10 (Paris, 1906), 9:74–77; G. Mouette, *Histoire des conquests de Mouley Archy* . . . (Paris, 1683), reprinted under a different title in H. comte de Castries, *Sources inédits de l'histoire du Maroc de 1530 à 1845,* 2nd ser. (Paris, 1924), 1–199, p. 135; F. de La Chapelle, "Esquisse d'une histoire du Sahara occidental," *Hésperis,* 11:35–95 (1930).

7. The Pulaar version, which is a plural form, may disguise the fact that the name *orma* or *arma* is the same by which similar Moroccan forces were called in the region of the Niger bend.

8. Labat, *Nouvelle relation,* 3:339; T. Pellow, *The Adventure of Thomas Pellow, of Penryn, Mariner,* ed. Robert Brown (London, 1890), p. 195 (first published in 1740, the only known account by a participant in the Moroccan expeditions); Violaine to Director, Fort Saint Joseph, 2 August 1720, ANF, C6 6; A. Delcourt, *La France et les étab-lissements français au Sénégal entre 1713 et 1763* (Dakar, 1952); Barry, "Royaume du Walo," (thesis), pp. 155 ff.; Saint Adon to CI, 20 April and 22 July 1737, ANF, C6 11.

It is not yet possible, and it may never be possible, to trace in detail the activities of the Ormankoobe. The records of the Compagnie des Indes preserved in the French archives are full of detail because they regularly contain the despatches from Fort Saint Joseph in Gajaaga—but only up to the middle of 1738, when this series breaks off abruptly.

One remaining puzzle is the relationship of the Moroccan expedition to the climatic patterns of the seventeenth and eighteenth centuries, and of both to a general weakness of sedentary society in the face of nomadic advance from the Senegal eastward past the Niger bend to Aïr. The climatic record is sufficiently clear. (See *Supplement,* appendix 1.) The number of dry years was greater in the seventeenth century than it was in the sixteenth, and the first half of the eighteenth was worse still, down to the great famines of the 1750's. It is possible that the Moors in the west and the Tuareg in the east were forced from their usual grazing areas into the country of the sedentary farmers, while the farmers in turn were driven south by their inability to cultivate. What is not known is why the Moroccans came at the time of worst climatic crisis, and why they withdrew when the worst of the crisis had passed—though it could have been no more than coincidence.

Whether coincidence or not, the Moroccans played a role in the pattern of sedentary decay during the first half of the eighteenth century, but a reform movement began to be more and more vocal from the middle of the century, just as the Moroccan danger receded. This movement drew on diverse sentiment—opposition to the Ormankoobe, to the raids by the Moors into sedentary kingdoms, to enslavement of Muslims and their sale into the Atlantic slave trade. The issues involved were not logically tied to the demand for Islamic reform, but they were pulled into the reform movement, just as that movement drew new strength from the currents of reform in the Islamic world at large. The intellectual center of the movement was at Piir in Kajor, which had been a center of Muslim intellectual activity, partly Moorish and partly Senegambian, and it was probably through Piir that the zwāya resentment of the Hasanīya worked its way into the movement.

The currents from Piir were found in most Senegambian states, but the movement turned to active revolution first in Fuuta Tooro. The Toorodbe became a military force in the early 1770's under Suuleiman Baal. About 1776, leadership passed to Abdul Kaader Kaan, who gradually established his authority over Fuuta and took the title of Almaami. Since Abdul Kaader Kaan had been a student at Piir, they were close to similar reformers in Kajor and Bundu. At first the reform influence was comparatively peaceful. Abdul Kaader asked the Damel, Birama Faatim Penda (ruled c. 1777–90) to accept the Kaadiri order (Qādirīyya in Arabic),[9] which he did, but his successor Amari Ngoone Ndella Kumba (1790–1809) was less pious. Early in the reign, he became involved in a quarrel with Malamin Sar, an important cleric, and

9. The Qādirīyya was one of the largest and most widespread of the *sūfī* orders in Islam. It was not necessarily a reformist order in all times and places, but it functioned as such in the western Sudan of the late eighteenth and early nineteenth centuries, where it was associated with the whole group of religious revolutions before the 1850's, from Cameroon to Fuuta Tooro.

the quarrel grew into a general clerical revolt against the secular state. The Damel of Kajor defeated the rebels decisively near Piir, but some of them managed to escape and take refuge on the Cape Verde peninsula in the far southwest of the kingdom. There they built fortified lines across the base of the peninsula and defended themselves as an independent state under clerical rule, attracting a steady trickle of like-minded refugees from Kajor and Bawol.[10]

Meanwhile, Abdul Kaader Kaan had established himself in full power in Fuuta, the decisive step being his defeat of the Trarza in 1786, which assured Fuuta's security from the desert and brought in large numbers of new followers who were not necessarily as religious in their motivation as the original nucleus had been. With this, Abdul Kaader was able to follow a more adventurous foreign policy. He forced Waalo and Bundu to accept his hegemony, which they did peacefully. Then, in 1796, he invaded Kajor, but the Damel defeated his army and captured the Almaami himself, though allowing him to return to Fuuta after humiliation and a few months in captivity. The next year, Abdul Kaader moved against Bundu, where he seized the Sisibe Almaami, Seega Gai, and put him to death for acts unfriendly to Muslim clerics. This move led on into a civil war in Bundu, partly a war between two candidates for the almamate, partly a contest between a clerical and an anticlerical faction, and partly a war of independence from Futaanke control. The winner was Amadi Aisaata Sii, of the anticlerical side. By the first years of the nineteenth century, Abdul Kaader was successful in Fuuta, but he had failed to spread the reform movement into other states.

In the end, this effort to export the revolution backfired and ended its forward movement in Fuuta itself. After his victory in the Bundunke civil war, Amadi Aisaata made an alliance with the aggressive Bambara state of Kaarta for a war of revenge against Abdul Kaader. He also made secret arrangements with a number of powerful figures in Fuuta, nominal followers of Abdul Kaader but in fact not serious Muslims or serious reformers. The invasion of Fuuta came in 1806-7. Abdul Kaader's support melted away, and Almaami Amadi Aisaata had no trouble finding and killing him. The Sisibe of Bundu thus had their revenge, and the conspirators came to power in Fuuta as the electors who were to dominate the almamate and reduce the office of Almaami to a nearly meaningless honor. Fuuta Tooro after 1807 represented an effective victory for the counter-revolution.

Senegambia drifted into the first half of the nineteenth century under a

10. This account of the religious revolution of that late eighteenth century is based principally on Colvin, "Kajor," pp. 164-85; Robinson, "Abdul Bokar Kan," pp. 17-61; Barry, "Royaume du Walo," pp. 190 ff.; Maxwell, Responses to H. M. Commissioners, 1 January 1811, CO 267/29; and A. Sylla, "Une république africaine au xixe siècle (1795-1857)," *Présence africaine*, nos. 1-2 (n.s.): 47-65 (1955).

double shadow. On one hand, the unfulfilled movement for Islamic reform was pushed underground; but it had active followers, and the suppression of reform again built up revolutionary tensions. By the 1850's these tensions were present throughout Senegambia, with the possible exception of Siin. The second threat came from the industrial revolution in Europe. Before the 1820's, the European presence was confined to a few rented islands in the rivers or off the coast. These were fortified, but mainly only for defense against other Europeans. They had diplomatic and military exchanges with African neighbors, but they were usually militarily weak, though they were sometimes useful as auxiliaries supporting African allies.[11] When they returned in force after the Napoleonic wars, the new European presence was different from the communities of merchants who had run the slave trade in the past. They no longer bought slaves in quantity, and European economic growth meant that Europe was a growing market for other African products. By the 1830's, the value of Senegambian maritime exports was already more than three times the level reached at the height of the slave trade (see below, table 8.7), and the Europeans came back with a new kind of military advantage based on their new industrial technology.

The Europeans still followed a policy of entrepôt, with no intention of ruling over African territory; but their attitude toward Africans was different, and their sphere of informal influence beyond their trading towns was greater. Both changes can be traced in part to the industrial revolution. The Europeans had a new self-confidence in their own abilities, in their own standing among world civilizations. They became more arrogant in their dealings with non-Europeans, and this attitude fitted their biological thought about race difference. As a result they adopted a cluster of ideas and attitudes, with pseudoscientific racism at the core, surrounded by multi-variant layers of cultural arrogance and ethnocentricity.[12] It was partly this attitude, and partly the new technology of power, that made France in the Senegal and Britain on the Gambia shift from a policy of merely trading on the river to one of trying to dominate the trade. They rebuilt or built a new series of fortified posts along the rivers, and they forced the African states along the banks to grant them a variety of political and commercial privileges. They sometimes tried to create an economic monopoly over one or more branches of trade, but this policy never succeeded for long. The intention, however, was to control the rivers' trade, not their banks. In spite of incidents

11. As, for example, when the French in Saint Louis took the antireligious side in their efforts to suppress the jihad of Nasīr al-Dīn. See Chambonneau, "L'histoire du Toubenan."

12. See P. D. Curtin, *The Image of Africa* (Madison, 1964), esp. pp. 27–57, 227–58, 363–87, and *Imperialism* (New York, 1971), esp. ix–xxiii.

like the French annexation of Waalo in 1855, the actual conquest of major Senegambian territory came only in the 1880's and afterwards.

Before the shadow of colonial rule began to be a reality, the shadow of religious revolution completely destroyed the old political and social order. Insurrectionary episodes occurred in Jolof and Waalo in 1820 and in Fuuta in 1828–29, but they were suppressed. The almamate in Fuuta was strong enough to keep order. Elsewhere in the Wolof states and those of the Gambia Malinke, the ceddo were a source of anarchy, but they were also able to suppress opposition to governments too weak to keep them under control. One solution sometimes available to clerical reformers was enclavement. Muslims who wanted reform, or simply security from ceddo raids on their villages, joined together in separate Muslim villages under a clerical leader. They could protect themselves, and they could enjoy autonomy from the secular state, and in time they came to constitute scores of nuclei for a more aggressive role against the state.[13]

The active phase of the new Senegambian religious revolutions began when Umar Taal, a cleric from Fuuta, returned from pilgrimage in Mecca with long stops at the centers of religious reform elsewhere in the western Sudan— the Caliphate of Sokoto and the Caliphate of Hamdullahi in Maasina.[14] He finally settled at Dingirai on the outskirts of the Almamate of Fuuta Jaalō. Rather than follow the Kaadiri order of the earlier reformers, Shaykh Umar accepted the Tijaani way, and his call for reform was not so much aimed at the purification of Islam in his own homeland as it was at jihad against pagans to build a new Muslim empire. He criticized the three previous almamates in the two Fuuta and Bundu, but he apparently had no original intention of attacking them—rather of using them as a recruiting ground for the military strength he needed for the jihad. He and his agents therefore began organizing a following in all of the almamates during the second half of the 1840's, and the call for jihad came in 1852. The result for Senegambia was a series of military campaigns on the upper Senegal in the mid-1850's, an enormous emigration of Fuulbe to join Shaykh Umar in the conquered territories to the east, but not yet a renewal of the older revolutionary tradition in Senegambia itself.

A new and more inward-looking phase of revolution opened about 1860 in Badibu (Rip), a north-bank kingdom on the lower Gambia. There, the enclaved Muslim communities joined together under a religious and military

13. Barry, "Royaume du Walo," *BIFAN*, 31:387 ff. For the background to revolution in Siin and Saalum see Klein, *Islam and Imperialism*.

14. He signed himself in Arabic 'Umar al-Fūtī, more formally he was called al-Hājj Shaykh 'Umar al-Fūtī, but he is remembered in the oral traditions as Laaji Umar Taal, or sometimes simply as Shaykh Umar. The Pulaar forms will be used here and below.

leader known as Maa Baa.[15] He was first successful in overturning the local secular state. By 1862, he began to spread the revolt to the neighboring countries. It then broke out almost everywhere, not so much by transmission from Badibu as from local causes. To the south of the lower Gambia, Foode Kaba, a cleric originally from Bundu, established a new Muslim state. Upstream on the south bank, the succession of Alfa Molo and Muusa Molo led a revolt that overturned Kaabu, though in this case the rising was not so much reformers against unreformed as Fuulbe from Fuuta Jaalō against the Kaabunke. In the Wolof north, the new religious thrust had dampened political consequences because of the French presence, but the 1860's and 1870's saw a new beginning toward the complete conversion of Senegambia to Islam.

The final act in Senegambia was the rising of Mamadu Lamiin Draame in Gajaaga in the mid-1880's, after the colonial conquests had already begun further east. This movement, which combined Muslim reform with anti-French and anti-Fuulbe elements, followed a checkered course from Bakel through Bundu to the middle Gambia, where the leader was finally tracked down and killed by a French column in December 1887.

The most general phase of the religious revolutions, like the colonial conquest itself, lies beyond the chronological limits of this book, in a very different era on Senegambian history. The three decades before 1850 were in fact a period of transition, when time was running out for the political and social and economic forms that had prevailed since the seventeenth century. It might have been wise to stop the account short at the end of the eighteenth century, before. the transition began, but I will nevertheless carry on to the middle of the nineteenth, though conscious that many of the social, political, or economic forces that were to become important in the future will be slighted in favor of those rooted in the more distant past.

15. Quinn, *Mandingo Kingdoms,* is the best recent treatment of these wars on the Gambia, where they were called the Marabout-Soninki Wars in the nineteenth century. But the name is confusing, since the clerical party were not all marabouts, or clerics, and the anticlerical party were not Soninke in the ethnic sense but non-Muslim Malinke, the word Soninke in this sense being derived from a Malinke term meaning to make a sacrifice. (Person, "Les ancêtres de Samori," *CEA,* 4:125–56 (1963), pp. 130–31, *n.*)

2 | TRADE DIASPORAS AND THE SENEGAMBIAN JUULA

Trade between people of differing culture has been an important source of culture contact and culture change through the whole of human history, and it always poses special problems. Exchange between people with a common way of life can take place in an atmosphere of confidence, while aliens are always a little mysterious and probably dangerous. The ubiquitous, if mythical, stories of silent trade represent one form of solution.[1] They imagine trade on a frontier between two cultures, where nothing changes hands except the trade commodities themselves. Alien traders appear, leave some goods, and then go away. If they return and find an equivalent that satisfies them, they take the equivalent and go away. If they are unsatisfied, they retire again and wait for an increase in the return. This model of trade without communication is ingenious, but it actually involves a high level of tacit understanding between the parties, and most trade we know about has taken place away from the cultural frontiers.

An analytical model closer to historical reality would depict an individual who crossed the cultural frontier, settled in the alien territory, learned about its culture so as to be able to act as a cross-cultural broker. That single individual would function as an embryonic trade diaspora, one of those networks of trade communities scattered along the routes of commerce, living as a series of alien enclaves in the host societies to facilitate the passage of trade. The term *trade diaspora* originated with Abner Cohen, who called it "a nation of socially interdependent, but spatially dispersed, communities."[2] His own studies were first made in West Africa; but the phenomenon itself runs through human history on a worldwide basis.

1. L. Sundström, *The Trade of Guinea* (Upsala, 1965), pp. 22–31.
2. A. Cohen, "Cultural Strategies in the Organization of Trading Diasporas," in C. Meillassoux, ed., *The Development of Indigenous Trade and Markets in West Africa* (London, 1971), p. 267.

59

The utility of a trade diaspora clearly grew from the fact that trust and communication are far easier between people who share values, language, legal system, kinship ties, and other sources of social solidarity than they are across cultural barriers. The functions of the trade diaspora, stripped to the essentials, were two—agency and mediation. The trader of the diaspora mediated by gaining a specialized knowledge of other cultures along the trade route. He had to deal with political authorities so as to make way for trade to pass through several different jurisdictions, and he had to deal with the aliens at the point of exchange. The obvious archetype of the cross-cultural middle-man in West Africa is the landlord-broker. The second function necessary to long-distance trade was an organized form of agency. The model of the peddler carrying his wares from place to place as a one-man operation is possible, but not common. Efficient long-distance trade needed sources of market information, and it needed people who could be trusted to act for the principal at a distant point.

Trade diasporas dominated trade in all parts of the world until at least the end of the eighteenth century, and cross-cultural trade today is possible without them only because the commercial culture everywhere has become that of the West. However different existing cultures are in other respects, long-distance trade is no longer cross-cultural.

At earlier stages in history, chains of trading posts, commercial networks, and diasporas are found in great diversity. The chains of Phoenician trading posts and some aspects of Greek colonization are familiar examples from the classical Mediterranean. Within the broadly homogeneous world of medieval Europe, trade diasporas were linked with the local and semiseparate economic regions. International banking spread out of Italy with Italian bankers until *Lombard* became an alternate term for banker. The Hanseatic League in the Baltic was based on an earlier trade diaspora outward from Cologne during the twelfth and thirteenth centuries. The prior existence of merchant communities with commercial and family relations scattered among the Baltic and north European trading towns made it possible to organize a formal league of towns.[3] Even short-distance trade between different countries was easier if traders of the same nationality were resident at either end of the route. The Hanseatic League, for example, kept a privileged enclave in London (called the Steelyard) into the early sixteenth century. Meanwhile, English wool trade to the Continent went through an English enclave at Calais, under English sovereign control, while the Company of Merchant Adventurers which regulated the export of English cloth kept its headquarters in Antwerp—not in England.

Nor was the phenomenon mainly Western. The East African trading towns of the thirteenth to sixteenth centuries became cosmopolitan centers because

3. R. L. Reynolds, *Europe Emerges* (Madison, 1961), p. 199.

they received trade diasporas from Persia and Arabia. By the fifteenth century, a set of coastal enclaves stretching from southern Somalia to southern Tanzania had evolved a common culture and adopted a common religion.[4] Further east, Gujerati traders formed a network of commercial settlements from northwest India to Malacca, where it intersected with similar Chinese networks coming from the north, and both existed alongside settlements of Indians from the Malabar coast and Indonesians from Java.[5]

Some of these trade networks were established by force, with political authority exercised over the trading posts from a central point—a variation on the trade diaspora sometimes called a "trading post empire." It was a short step, in any case, from a series of homogeneous communities stretched out along a trade route to making each community dominant over a trade enclave, thus opening the possibility of controlling trade. Attempted trade control came into the Atlantic and Indian Ocean trade networks simultaneously with the outburst of the Portuguese in the second half of the fifteenth century and the first half of the sixteenth, armed with better ships and cannon than their Asian or African rivals. The Portuguese operation in the Indian Ocean and South China Sea became the classic overseas-European model of a trading post empire, with controlled enclaves at Macao in China, Malacca in Malaya, Goa in southwest India, and Mozambique in southeast Africa. In retrospect, the attempted monopoly of the spice trade in the Indian Ocean was not as successful as many thought at the time, but it was nevertheless copied by others.

Europeans in West Africa quickly shifted from "ship trade," where the ships' personnel did their best to mediate between differing cultures, to shore-based trade. But the Portuguese, as the leading alien power on the African coast, were not interested in controlling local competition so much as they were in keeping other Europeans out of their private commercial preserve. They therefore seized and fortified offshore islands, not coastal enclaves. Their three strongpoints of the late fifteenth century were Arguin Island, some 500 kms north of the Senegal, the Cape Verde Islands, 800 kms due west, and Elmina far away on the Gold Coast. Portuguese went ashore to trade, but they did so under the peaceful conditions of a nonmilitarized trade diaspora. With the exception of the brief attempt to seize a post at the mouth of the Senegal about 1490, the Europeans remained a set of enclaved merchant communities on the African mainland. The first attempts to switch to trading post empire came only with the mid-seventeenth century.

By that time, Europeans had some experience with overland trading post

4. For a recent authoritative survey see N. Chittick, "The Coast before the Arrival of the Portuguese," in B. A. Ogot and J. A. Kieran, eds., *Zamani: A Survey of East African History* (Nairobi, 1968), pp. 100–118.

5. See M. A. P. Meilink-Roelofsz, *Asian Trade and European Influence in the Indonesian Archipelago between 1500 and about 1630* (The Hague, 1962), esp. pp. 60–88.

empires, as well as the overseas variety. One of the best known, and certainly the best known to the Portuguese, grew with the spread of the *bandeirantes* into the Brazilian backlands during the course of the seventeenth century.[6] Similar trade networks pushed westward with similar timing in North America, from the Saint Lawrence valley into the Great Lakes country and beyond—and a little later from Hudson Bay to the south and southwest, while the Russians extended their fur trade along the Siberian watercourses until they reached the Pacific by the end of the seventeenth century. In the North American and Siberian cases, the operation was an overland trading post empire, with central control over the trading posts and attempted control over the trade that passed between them.[7] The bandeirantes served an economic demand for gold and slaves that ultimately reached back to Europe, but they were seldom under close control from São Paulo, much less from Lisbon. They were more nearly a self-governing community of traders, a trade diaspora less militarized and less controlled than a real trading post empire; and they were less European in culture. Their ordinary language was Tupí, not Portuguese, and their culture was further from European norms than that of the coureurs de bois in North America or the forest cossacks of the Russian forests and Siberia.

In West Africa, on the other hand, the Europeans had no need to send out overland trade diasporas, much less develop trading post empires. The African merchants had already established trade networks in long distance trade, some of them extending back in time to the thirteenth century if not before. These trade networks had long since been linked to the Mediterranean networks through the trans-Sahara diaspora of North African merchants who had established themselves in the desert-edge towns south of the Sahara. Eleventh-century reports from Gao on the Niger bend and others from the capital of ancient Ghana tell of double cities, one for the ruler and his court and the other for the foreign merchants. These and similar towns on the sahal were the points of exchange between the North African diaspora and the West African merchants who operated the trade routes further south into the savanna and ultimately into the forest. Since the Soninke were the dominant people of the northern savanna between the Niger bend and the Senegal, it was only natural that their diaspora to the south carried the first known long-distance trade into West Africa.

The trade diasporas of recent African history are thus part of a much larger and more various family of similar socioeconomic institutions, and they need

6. The best English introduction to the bandeirante literature is R. M. Morse, *The Bandeirantes* (New York, 1965).

7. The most useful introduction to the Russian-fur-trade literature is found in G. V. Lantzeff, *Siberia in the Seventeenth Century* (Berkeley, 1943), and R. Fisher, *The Russian Fur Trade, 1550–1700* (Berkeley, 1943).

to be understood in this broader perspective. One form of analysis is to distinguish the types of trade diaspora by a variety of political, cultural, economic, and social variables. The obvious and key political variables were in the relations, first, between a minority merchant community and its host population, and second, among the individual merchant enclaves in the same network, though these two do not exhaust the possible variables.

The relations of the traders to the host community can be seen as a broad spectrum of possibilities. One would be for the host state to dominate the people of the diaspora completely, keeping them in a dependent position in order to milk their commercial income. This was close to the actual situation of West European Jewry during the Middle Ages, and of East European Jewry into the early twentieth century (though the Jewish diaspora was more diverse and complex than a mere trade diaspora). Through the middle ranges of the spectrum would be various relations of autonomy or dependence, but at the far end the merchant enclave would be found not merely independent of the host society but dominant over part of it. This was the actual situation of the Portuguese trade enclaves in Malacca and Macao, or Dutch rule over Cape Town in the eighteenth century.

The second political variable concerns relations among trade enclaves. Some enclaves had no formal political ties with any other enclave, or at most only such weak ties as might be carried by a sense of solidarity based on common religion, nationality, or profession. This was, in fact, close to the African pattern in Senegambia and much of West Africa; and it contrasts sharply with the overseas-European extreme of a centralized trading post empire where autocratic control extended from a central point to each individual trading post, and the whole trade of the network was centrally directed as a single economic enterprise. At certain periods of its history the Dutch East India Company approached this ideal, and it was pursued by the Compagnie des Indes and the Royal African Company in their Senegambian operations of the late seventeenth and early eighteenth centuries.

Some implications of the geographers' "central place" theory are relevant to the West African tendency toward acephalous trade diasporas and the overseas European tendency toward strong political ties.[8] With a relatively simple commercial technology, individual West African traders or small firms could carry out all necessary commercial functions on their own, independent of specialized facilities for banking, marketing, communication, and the like.

8. For some implications of central place theory for urban history see E. Lampard, "Historical Aspects of Urbanization," in P. M. Hauser and L. F. Schnore, eds., *The Study of Urbanization* (New York, 1965), pp. 519–54. For a systematic application to African economic history see A. M. Howard, "Big Men, Traders, and Chiefs: Power, Commerce, and Spacial Change in the Sierra Leone–Guinea Plain" (Ph.D. diss., University of Wisconsin, 1972).

Each commercial enclave could then stand alone, without having to depend for essential functions on a multifunctional urban center. In theory, greater specialization of function would lead to greater efficiency in commerce. But historical experience and central place theory alike suggest that specialized functions will not be distributed in space at random but will concentrate in a central place where other specialized functions are also located. The result has usually been an urban hierarchy, the apex occupied by the central place with the largest concentration of different functions, descending through levels of decreasing functions to the most specialized settlement on the periphery of the system. The multifunctional central place gains an automatic advantage over the less-diverse places in the region. It performs functions which all require but it alone can perform. It is essential to the rest, but no *single* center lower in the hierarchy is functionally essential to the central place. In this rudimentary form, the model is extremely simple, but it has useful implications as a tool for the analysis of historical relations between cities, and it will be used in discussing the changing Senegambian trade networks. For the present, it merely points out the theoretical expectation that functional dependency within a commercial system is likely to be the basis for political dependency; the more specialized and divisible the commercial functions, the stronger and more centralized the possible political control.

The political variables are also influenced by cultural variables. One important distinction is the degree of cultural difference between the trading community and the host society. A Hanseatic German resident at the London Steelyard was not far removed from the cultural pattern of the English. An employee of the Dutch East India Company on their island off Nagasaki would be far less at home. In the Senegambian setting, the traveling merchants of Manding culture who passed along the Gambia toward the coast were culturally on home ground, while those in the European trade enclaves were not. These differences were modified in turn by another variable—the degree of contact between the enclave and the host society. Some enclaves tried to seal themselves off by their own choice, like the overseas Europeans in the Chinese treaty ports before 1939; others were sealed off on the initiative of the host, like the Dutch post at Nagasaki during the seventeenth and eighteenth centuries. Others, however, had easier relations that led to intermarriage and finally to so much assimilation of the host's culture that a new blend came into existence, containing elements from both parent cultures. Sometimes the blend became a separate people with its own identity. The bandeirantes of Brazil or the mixed bois brûlés of Manitoba come to mind as examples.[9] Similar cultural blending was to have an important role in the shifting fortunes of Senegambian trade enclaves—not merely the blending of African and European cultures at coastal points but also the interaction of

9. On the bois brûlés as a new nation see J. K. Howard, *Strange Empire* (New York, 1952).

the African traders' culture (and especially their Muslim religion) with the cultures of less-mobile farming peoples.[10]

A trade diaspora served economic ends; it is therefore only natural that the range of discriminating economic variables should be very wide. They are too many, in fact, to be listed here, though several will recur in connection with specific trade networks of Senegambia. Some idea of the range of variation can be had by comparing the possible size and makeup of the individual firm or basic, self-directing economic unit. For some of the European trade diasporas, the whole trading post empire was a single firm, controlling the fleets and forts and goods in transit, while at the other end of the scale was the single small-time African trader or *juula* with his entire capital tied up in a single load of kola nuts carried on his own back.

The size of the firm was largely independent of the size of the system, and it was again independent of functional specialization. The commercial system of a trade diaspora can be broken down for analysis into a number of discrete functions—whether performed by one man or several. Some men, acting as a small independent firm, might do nothing but serve as broker between buyers and sellers, never or rarely trading on their own account and never moving from a fixed point. Others would buy goods in one place and sell them in another. Others acted as transporters, taking charge of other peoples' goods in transit. Still other firms performed all or many of these functions. The whole trade process, in short, can be subdivided for analysis into many different functions, various combinations of which could fall to a particular individual or firm. As the Senegambian trade diasporas changed through time, one of the crucial aspects of that change was to be the shift of particular functions from one type of firm to another.

The range of social variation in trade diasporas was still wider than the range of economic difference, though many social types available in the worldwide spectrum of trade diasporas were not present in Senegambia. The Senegambian examples, however, were sharply divided between one social type for the African commercial enclaves and another for the overseas Europeans. African enclaves normally reproduced the full range of class, caste, and occupation found elsewhere in the vicinity, though with more people in commercial occupations than was normal. The European communities, however, were almost entirely made up of adult males, resident for short periods only. Most of these men died after a short period in Senegambia, because they lacked immunity to the endemic diseases of the region.[11] Those who lived tended to return to Europe after a residence of three

10. Person, *Samori,* 1:143–48, discusses the degree and form of culture change among merchants in the preforest zone of Guinea-Konakry and northern Ivory Coast.

11. Curtin, *Image of Africa,* esp. pp. 438–87; K. G. Davies, "The Living and the Dead: White Mortality in West Africa 1684–1732," in Engerman and Genovese, *Race and Slavery,* passim.

to ten years, rarely longer. Without their own women, overseas Europeans could not recreate a model of the home society. Most took local concubines or mistresses, which meant that the second generation was racially and culturally mixed. This mixed community was constantly renewed with new immigrants from Europe, and it was just as constantly dissipated as third- and fourth-generation part-Europeans lost touch with the overseas-European culture of the posts and merged with the general African population.

The death rates of new arrivals to West Africa were higher than equivalent rates for overseas Europeans anywhere else, which suggests that the West African pattern may well mark one extreme in a range of overseas-European social patterns; but the comparative study of these communities, and of trade diasporas in general, is only now beginning.

Islam and Commerce

The vast majority of merchants in long-distance trade were Muslim, often clerics, while the vast majority of people in other occupations were incompletely Muslim, or at least not clerics. This fact helped to build a feeling of solidarity among merchants and give them an identity separate from the rest of the population. A separate identity for a professional group fitted the Senegambian social setting, where craft specialists were set aside in endogamous "castes." In practice, merchants also tended to marry their daughters to Muslim clerics or to other merchants, though their usual social ranking was that of free men, generally one step lower in prestige than the military and political élite.

Islam and commerce were first associated in West Africa because Islam came across the Sahara carried by merchants, and contacts on the sahal were between merchants. It was natural enough for the savanna merchants to adopt the new religion and carry it further south. But mere contact may not be explanation enough; the Wolof were in contact with Islam for nearly a thousand years before they finally converted in the full sense of the term. Merchants, on the other hand, found particular advantages in the new faith. Islam was friendly to commerce from the beginning in Arabia, and it was also a universal religion where belief carried a valuable sense of solidarity with other believers. The local pre-Islamic religions were often particular to specific places and specific ancestor spirits. A local community that propitiated the spirits of the fields and streams and trees had a spiritual investment reinforcing other ties to the land it worked. Islam lacked this intimate tie to nature, but its universality meant that the believer's spiritual investment was good anywhere. A Muslim trader could look down on pagans, whose nature spirits were simply genies in the Muslim context, and he had the temporal advantage of dealing with fellow traders who were also fellow Muslims.

Islam also carried the prestige of literacy and association with court life, a prestige that held good even with non-Muslims. Their own religions were not exclusive, and they were happy to seek Muslim clerical aid to help them manipulate the world of the supernatural. Islamic clerics and merchants therefore had a lucrative sideline in the manufacture and sale of charms. These were the "gri-gris" of the European travelers, the most common being verses from the koran or other symbolic words written on a piece of paper, then sewed into a flat leather container 3 to 5 cm square (called *talki*, sing. *talkuru*, in Pulaar). Others were made from various powders, kept in hollowed cow's horns (*galuuje*, sing. *alaadu*). All these forms of charm had close parallels in pre-Muslim practice. One common charm, for example, was the *aye*, made by writing verses from the koran on a wooden plaque, then washing the plaque with water, which absorbed the spiritual power of the written words. The pre-Islamic counterpart in Bundu was a similar liquid made by mixing water with the ritually prepared bark or roots of certain trees. The aye thus drew its power from wood of the plaque as well as the words of the koran.[1]

Non-Muslim respect for Muslim spiritual powers also helped to protect Muslims moving through a variety of different political jurisdictions. It was worth a trader's while to encourage a reputation for magical powers, and some clerics were less than zealous about spreading Islam to the unconverted, preferring to claim esoteric powers for their own group.[2] This use of religion as a passport was noted by Richard Jobson, writing about clerics on the Gambia in 1620: " . . . they have free recourse through all places, so that howsoever the King and Countries are at warres and up in armes, the one against the other, yet still the Marybucke [marabout or cleric] is a privileged person, and many follow his trade or course of travelling, without any let or interruption of either side."[3]

Some of the merchant-clerics claimed a special protective power for their religious knowledge, even beyond the powers of other clerics. The Jahaanke (French Diakhanké, English Jahanka) were one such clerical community whose villagers were scattered widely in the hinterland of the Senegambia, and their claims rested on non-Muslim as well as Muslim sources of religious prestige. They trace their origins back to Ja (Dia) on Niger above Timbuktu, a town famous for its outstanding place in the supernatural order of things on Muslim and pagan grounds alike.[4] Today, the Jahaanke lay greatest emphasis

1. Annotation by Hammadi Amadu Si to narrations by Demba Sembalu Sok, CC, T 5 (1) and Idi Ja, Ts (2).

2. Person, *Samori*, 1:133.

3. R. Jobson, *The Golden Trade, or a Discovery of the River Gambia* . . . (London, 1932), p. 106. First published 1623.

4. G. Dieterlen, "Mythe et organisation sociale au Soudan français," *Journal de la Société des africanistes*, 25:39–76 (1955) and 29:119–38 (1959), esp. pp. 124 ff.

on their special techniques for reciting the *alfatiya,* the first verse of the Koran, so as to produce good or evil consequences for particular individuals, and some claim that all Jahaanke are endowed from birth with the powers of a *waliu* or Muslim saint.[5] This use of religious prestige to protect long-distance traders was not peculiar to Islam in West Africa. In southern Nigeria, for example, both the Awka and Aro, commercial specialists and subgroups of the Ibo, used the powers of their associated local dieties to assure their safety throughout Iboland.[6]

The merchant as Muslim also fitted the ancient West African division between the religious, commercial, and clerical calling on one hand and the military and political on the other. The distinction appears at many points in the thought and practice of the western Sudan and western Sahara. The division between so-called warrior and marabout tribes in the desert extends from the distinction between Hasanīya and the zwāya in Mauritania eastward to the Tuareg northwest of Lake Chad. One aspect of dichotomy was the belief that the political-military group had a right to rule, but the clerical-mercantile group had a right to autonomous jurisdiction over their own affairs. This distinction appears early in West African history with the double cities at Gao and ancient Ghana, where the segregation of foreign merchants was in effect a segregation of Muslims as well.

The practice of segregation and autonomy for Muslims continued, and certain clerical towns—most famous of which was Jahaba (Diakaba) on the Bafing—had the right to autonomous government and to give sanctuary to fugitives, even in the great days of Malian power.[7] Elsewhere Muslims were grouped together in a quasi-independent village under clerical leadership, in a special ward of a mixed village, or sometimes in a double town. This separation was important to the isolation of the communities of a trade diaspora, as it was later on for the enclavement of Muslims on the eve of the great religious revolutions.

Juula Communities in Senegambia: The Soninke of Gajaaga

The clerical-commercial communities scattered through Senegambia and its hinterland were an offshoot of a much wider net of associated trade diasporas spread across the whole of West Africa. In the sector west of the Niger bend, these diasporas had begun with a southward movement of

5. Baku Kaba, Tambura, CC, T 13 (1); Mamba Girasi, translator's notes, CC, T 13 (2).
6. B. W. Hodder and U. I. Ukwu, *Markets in West Africa: Studies in Markets and Trade among the Yoruba and Ibo* (Ibadan, 1969), pp. 127–36.
7. M. Kâti, *Tarikh El-Fettach,* trans. O. Houdas and M. Delafosse (Paris, 1964), pp. 714–15.

people from the desert edge, setting up trade communities to serve the trans-Sahara trade. Some were Soninke from ancient Ghana, who traded overland to the Bambuhu gold fields. Others used the upper Niger river transportation which extended from the edge of the desert nearly to the edge of the forest. The boatmen on the river itself were mainly Sõñrai (Songhai), but merchants, often of Soninke origin, moved south to carry the overland trade that branched off from the river itself. One important branch, in operation well before 1500, dropped due south from the Niger at Jene through Bobo-Julaaso (Bobo-Dioulasso), Kong, and Bunduku to the Asante goldfields. In the process of developing this route, the merchants dropped the Soninke language and picked up a dialect of Malinke, modifying their culture in the process. In time, they adopted a self-identity as Juula (Dioula or Dyoula in French), *juula* being the Malinke word for merchant—now adopted to mean a particular people and their way of life.

Other Soninke followed trade in other directions and went through a similar transformation. Those who moved from Ja on the Niger to a new center at Jahaba on the Bafing came to be known as Jahaanke, and they too Malinkized. Other Soninke moved inside the Niger bend and were called Marka, while those who became associated with the Voltaic states became Yarse. Still other Soninke merchant colonies are found out in the desert oasis towns like Tichit and Walata, while others branched south from the Niger to work the north-south kola trade through Kankan in upper Guinea, and the trade colonies spread further until they reached the sea through Sierra Leone, Guinea, and Senegambia.[1]

Just as many of the originally Soninke trade diasporas changed to Malinke patterns of language and culture, some Malinke joined them by choice or through intermarriage. Other Malinke became Muslim and took to long-distance commerce on their own, founding new trade networks of Malinke Mori or Muslim Malinke. These were especially important in the westward salt route from Mali to the Gambia and in the southern kola routes from the Manding culture area to the forest edge. By the seventeenth century, the Senegambian hinterland had at least three distinct but interrelated trade diasporas—Soninke who remained Soninke in speech and culture, principally based in Gajaaga; Jahaanke, or Malinkized Soninke, principally based at Jahaba on the Bafing but gradually pushing their sphere to the west and south; and the Malinke Mori, mainly important along an east-west axis stretching from the Gambia mouth to Bamako on the Niger. In spite of the danger of confusion with the Juula of the Jene-to-Asante axis, the most

---

1. See Monteil, "Le Tékrour et la Guinée," p. 397. Some of the twentieth-century survivals of these networks are described in Meillassoux, *Indigenous Trade and Markets*, esp. pp. 199–284.

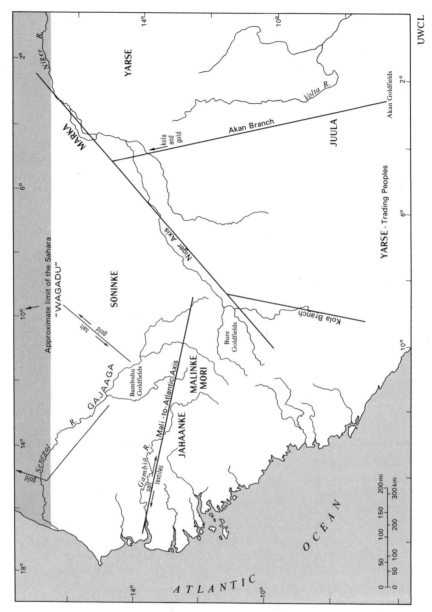

2.1 Schematic Outlines of Early West African Trade •

70

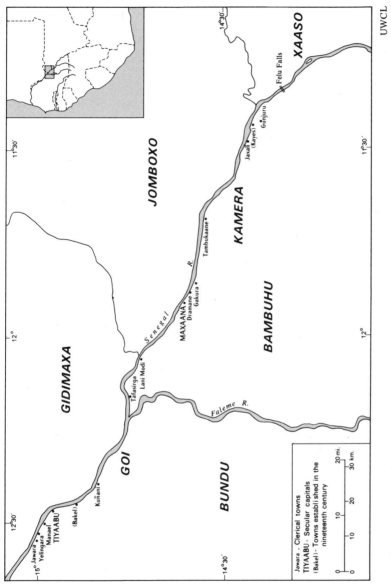

2.2 The Clerical Towns of Gajaaga   (Sources: Bathily, "Notices sur Gadiaga," *BIFAN*, 31:31–105 (1969);
Monteil, *Khassonké*, p. 360)

71

accurate collective name for all three groups is still *juula,* the ordinary Malinke word for a trader.[2]

The Soninke juula of Gajaaga were centralized more than the others, as a clerical enclave in a Soninke state otherwise dominated by the secular-minded Baacili lineage. They had a base, therefore, in a culturally homogeneous region, and their role as mediators of cross-cultural trade began only as they traveled away from that base. Oral traditions trace these people back to the dispersal of all Soninke from Wagadu, and they hold that the Baacili arrived in Gajaaga together with the clerical lineage of the Tanjigora, who were in fact collatoral descendents from a common ancestor. Other clerical lineages of Soninke later joined from other directions. The Draame were most important, coming either from Tichit in the desert (according to one tradition) or from Mali (according to another). Other clerical lineages, Saaxo (Sakho), Dukure, Ba, and Jombera (Diombera) were also present by the early twentieth century, each dominant over part of a town or an autonomous town scattered among other Gajaaga towns governed by Baacili.[3]

Clerical autonomy for some at least of these towns was already old by the seventeenth century. The *Tarikh al-Fattāsh* bracketed Gunjuru, the principal clerical town in Gajaaga, with Timbuktu and Jahaba as towns with a special judicial status stretching back to the period of Malian dominance. " . . . it was the town of the cadi of that region and of the ulama. No soldier may enter it nor any official reside there so as to oppress his charges. Nevertheless, the king of Gajaaga would visit the ulama and the cadi of that town each year in the month of Ramadan according to the custom of the country, bearing presents which he would divide among them. When the 'night of destiny' came round, the king would order food cooked, and then he would have it placed on a large plate or rather in a large calabash which he would place on his head. He would then call those who studied the Koran and the young people who were learning to read, who came to eat the food from the calabash on the king's head, he being seated while the others stood in order to eat. The king acted thus in order to honor them, and the custom lasted down to our own time according to what I have been told by al-Hājj Mamadu Sire, a native of Gajaaga."[4]

2. Although the word passed into Ghanian English as a proper name for a particular ethnic group, it passed into Gambian English in the broader sense, often as "julaman," a trader or peddler.

3. Bathily, "Notices sur Gadiaga," pp. 57–58; C. Monteil, *Les Khassonké* (Paris, 1915), p. 360.

4. Translated from the French translation by O. Oudas and M. Delafosse published as M. Kâti, *Tariih El-Fettach.* The "night of destiny" is one of the last nights of Ramadan, in which it is believed that God sets the events that are to occur during the coming year. The translation places Gunjuru in Kaniaga rather than Gajaaga, though the error is corrected in identifying Mamadu Sire's birth place as Gajaaga.

The number and fortunes of the various clerical towns varied somewhat over time, but they were all under at least the moral authority of the Draame—first the Draame of Gunjuru, but later those of Dramane (after Gunjuru itself was annexed to Xaaso in the early eighteenth century). Even then, the Draame of Gunjuru became the principal religious advisors of the rulers of Xaaso, as their relatives in Dramane were in Gajaaga.[5] It seems doubtful, however, that the Gajaaga clerics ever had a "marabout republic" or league of clerical towns, as described by some of the European visitors of the late seventeenth and early eighteenth centuries.[6] They had the mutual solidarity that bound merchants to act together in favor of commercial privilege, and they had the usual solidarity of serious Muslims, but their relationships stretching beyond Gajaaga were sometimes as close as those within the country.

Each major lineage was merely the local segment of a broader lineage distributed far beyond that region. A Draame, for example, was a kinsman of other Draame scattered very widely by the Soninke dispersal, and the connection had obvious value for traveling merchants. Another kind of tie could result from a tight and permanent alliance between lineages. Such alliances (jõñu in Soninke) were traced back to an inviolable oath, sworn after a memorable event had demonstrated the friendship of the two families or earned the gratitude of one to the other.[7] The Saaxo and Ba in the lower-Gajaaga towns of Jawara and Yelingara have a tradition of a first dispersal from Wagadu to Fuuta Tooro. There they became jõñu, and they remained so after their final move to Gajaaga; the tie still continues, and it is binding on others of these two lineages wherever they may be.[8]

Though the clerical towns might sometimes act together in war, they were often on their own in defense against the nomads from the desert, or their neighbors, the Baacili. Like other Gajaaga towns each was defended by a

5. Gunjuru kept its religious prestige and political autonomy under Xaaso as well. After Mamadu Lamiin Draame of Gunjuru led a religious revolution against the French and the Sisibe rulers of Bundu in 1885–87, the French destroyed the town in the course of suppressing the revolt. The site is now the village of Dugubo, 6 kms south of Kayes in Mali. See C. Monteil, *Les Khassonké*, p. 124, and "Le site de Goundiourou," *CEHSAOF,* 11:647–53 (1928), and Robert Arnaud, "Vestiges de la vénération du feu au Soudan," *Revue d'ethnographie et des traditions populaires,* 4:193–200 (1923).

6. The principal accounts are in Labat, *Nouvelle rélation,* 3:339–39; La Courbe, *Premier voyage du Sieur de la Courbe fait à la coste d'Afrique en 1685,* ed. Pierre Cultru (Paris, 1913); P. Charpentier, Memoir of 1 April 1725, C6 10, or printed version in J. Machat, *Documents sur les etablissements français et l'Afrique occidentale au xviiie siècle* (Paris, 1906); Levens, Report of 10 July 1728, ANF, Col. C6 9, or BN, FF, NA, 3999, f. 144.

7. This kind of relationship is found very generally in western West Africa, not merely in Gajaaga. See Bathily, "Notices sur Gadiaga," p. 68.

8. Al-Hājj Bukari Saaxo (Sakho) of Jawara (Diawara), CC, T 4 (2).

substantial adobe wall (called a *tata* in most Senegambian languages), and the interior was subdivided into smaller defensible areas, each with its own tata. Some clerical towns were single, while others were paired with a secular community to make a double town, religious and mercantile in one half, military and secular in the other. Lani, for example, was traditionally a double town of this kind, Lani-Modi and Lani-Tunka. In 1849, when they were both sacked by a French force, the two towns were about 1.2 km apart, each within its separate wall. The clerical town was the larger of the two, with a main tata measuring about 400 meters by 90 and subdivided into four separately walled interior tatas.[9] The usual population of Gajaaga clerical towns was from four or five thousand for a large one down to perhaps two thousand for the general run. This was unusually large for a purely agricultural village of the time, and roughly half the population of Gajaaga was associated with the clerical towns. But most of their people were slaves and members of the occupational castes of minstrels, leatherworkers, woodworkers, blacksmiths, and the like. Only a minority were able to follow the call of religious learning as a full-time occupation, though many more participated in commerce.

The trade network of the Gajaaga merchants led mainly eastward from their home base on the upper Senegal, one branch running through the sahal to Jaara (Diara) just south of the Sahara, and occasionally on to the Niger bend. A second branch veered off to the south to catch the trade further up the Niger, usually at Segu, and an intersecting north-south route exchanged the products of the steppe for those of the savanna.[10] The Gajaaga-based trade network was thus an extension outward in three directions from a junction point between networks. It was the normal terminus for the pack oxen from the east, donkeys from the south, and camels from the north, and it was the transfer point to Senegal River trade.

But the normal was not invariable. If the Senegal route was blocked by political disturbances in Fuuta Tooro, as it often was in the eighteenth century, Gajaaga merchants were willing and able to go overland to the upper Gambia, or even through to the coast itself if necessary. The fact that they could do this without having their own Soninke network stretching in that direction on a permanent basis is one indication that facilities for brokerage and the like were available to any Muslim juula, regardless of nationality. In this sense, the Soninke trade rested on the whole network of trade enclaves

9. Map enclosed with Reverdit to Governor, 7 October 1849, ANF-OM, Sénégal IV 19.

10. For the nature and range of Gajaaga trade see Charpentier, Memoir of 1 April 1725; Park, *Travels*, 1:95; Paul Marty, *Etudes sénégalaises* (Paris, n.d. [c. 1926]), p. 179; Governor Senegal to Minister of Colonies, no. 60, 20 February 1832, ANS, Dakar, 2 B 14; Al-Hājj Bukari Saaxo, Jawara, CC, T 4 (2).

and trade communities that stretched across the Manding cultural region and west to the ocean.

Some additional Soninke settlements, however, were founded by dispersal from Gajaaga, some by political refugees, others for commercial reasons. One small cluster emerged along the western frontier of Bundu in the direction of Wuuli. Since Bundu was a Fuulbe state and Wuuli was Malinke, this was a cultural frontier and one marked by chronic warfare—so much so that the frontier between the two states was not a line but a zone of man-made wilderness. The Soninke villages of Julingel and Juumi were convenient take-off points for crossing the wilderness bound for the Gambia, or for entering Bundu on the way back. Sabi in the valley of the Ñeriko (Nieriko) was another Soninke center between the Gambia and the interior. Isaaco, Mungo Park's former guide, stopped there in 1810 to enjoy the hospitality of the family of one of his wives, though he himself was from the neighboring kingdom of Wuuli. A decade later Major William Grey employed Isaaco's cousin Yusufu to carry a message from Gajaaga to Segu—one of the occasional glimpses of family patterns strung out along the trade routes which sometimes come through the otherwise impersonal reporting by European travelers. Other Gajaaga settlements were still more distant, on the northern fringes of Fuuta Jaalō, where in the early nineteenth century they helped to forward Soninke traders with gold from Bure or slaves from the upper Niger on their way to the Portuguese posts on the Geba-Corubal river system.[11]

Jahaanke and Others

The Jahaanke resemble the Soninke of Gajaaga so much that the two trade diasporas have often been confused.[1] Both were originally Soninke in speech and culture, Muslim in religion, commercial and clerical by occupation. Both lived in commercial enclaves, with as much freedom as possible from the interference of the secular state. The Jahaanke, however, trace their origins back to Ja, in Maasina on the Niger, just as the Juula of the Asante hinterland do. They, like the Juula, passed through a process of Malinkization, and they regard the eastern Juula as a related people. The

11. William Gray, *Travels in Western Africa in the Years 1818, 19, 20 and 21* (London, 1825), pp. 102–3; "Isaaco's Journal" in Park, *Travels*, 2:239–40; William Fox, *A Brief History of the Wesleyan Missions on the Western Coast of Africa* (London, 1851), p. 462; Gaspard Theodore Mollien, *Travels in the Interior of Africa*, trans. from the French by T. E. Bowdich (London, 1820), p. 288; A. Rançon, "Le Boundou," *Bulletin de la Société de géographie de Bordeaux*, 17 (n.s.):433–63, 465–84, 497–548, 593–647 (1894), pp. 629–32.

1. Initially by Charles Monteil, *Les Khassonké*, pp. 357–61, whose authority was accepted more recently by Pierre Smith "Les Diakhanké: Histoire d'une dispersion," *Bulletin et mémoires de la Société d'anthropologie de Paris*, 8 (11th ser.):231–62.

clerics of Gajaaga, on the other hand, trace a different course from Wagadu to their present location, they belong to a different set of lineages, and their home base remained in Soninke-speaking territory.

In effect, both the Juula of the Asante hinterland and the Jahaanke were peoples formed by a trade diaspora—formed, indeed, by the same trade diaspora—but the two went in different directions and both lost regular contact with their common source (which is no longer Soninke, in any case). While insisting on their ultimate origin in Ja, the present-day Jahaanke make much more of a formative period of residence at Jahaba on the Bafing in the border area between Bambuhu and Gāgarā. They trace their identity as a people to the experience of living there together, and to the religious teaching of al-Hājj Salimu Sware (Arabic Salīm Suwari, also called Mbemba Lai [Laye]). The chronology is uncertain, but data assembled by Ivor Wilks suggest that Salimu Sware must have flourished after 1485 and before 1650.[2] At either of these dates, the Jahaanke were comparative latecomers to the western trade, but they became so important in the last decades of the seventeenth century and the early decades of the eighteenth that their name became virtually synonymous with merchants among the Europeans on the Gambia or the upper Senegal, though with many variant spellings such as *Guiaca* in French, *Junko* or *Jagga* in English.

The date of the outward movement from Jahaba is uncertain, though Jahaanke traders no doubt moved up and down the trade routes for some time before they actually began to establish new towns at a distance. One of their principal moves was into Bundu, where Maalik Sii's new clerical state, founded in the 1690's, provided a welcome for Muslims, along with easy access to the Bambuhu gold fields from the coastward side. The first two Jahaanke towns in Bundu, Diide (Didé) and Gunjuru (Goundiourou, not to be confused with the Gajaaga town of the same name), were founded in the reign of Maalik Sii himself. The thirteen or so that followed all trace their origin to one or the other of the pioneer settlements.[3]

2. The earlier date is suggested by the fact that Salimu Sware's teaching laid great emphasis on a religious work that was not available until 1485. Other evidence from *silsila* or intellectual genealogies suggests a date in the sixteenth rather than the seventeenth century, but the first mention to my knowledge of the Jahaanke in European sources is that of Francisco de Lemos Coelho in 1669, in *Duas descriçoes seisentistas da Guiné de Francisco de Lemos Coelho,* ed. Damioo Peres (Lisbon, 1953), p. 23, saying that the "Jagancazes" were the most important merchants on the routes eastward from the upper Gambia. I have revised my earlier belief that the Jahaanke founded Sutuko (P. D. Curtin, "Pre-Colonial Trading Networks and Traders: The Diakhanké," in Meillassoux, *Indigenous Trade and Markets,* pp. 229–30); they may have done so, but the only evidence is that they lived there in the late eighteenth century, much too late to be conclusive.

3. Hammadi Madi Si, Madina Kojalani, CC T 7 (1 and 2); Arfā Alkasana Gasama, T 13 (2); Kadiali Diakite, C1P(1); Anon., "The History of the Gassama," Fonds Curtin, IFAN, Dakar, unpublished collation and translation by Lucy Quimby from mss. nos. 1, 27, and 29.

A second Jahaanke town was founded about the same time to the south of Jahaba, in Dentilia. This time the commercial significance was not the gold trade but the general east-west route between the upper Niger and the upper Gambia. Other new towns followed further west on the same route. Silakunda, Lamiinia, and Samekuta (Sillacounda, Laminia, and Samécouta) are on or near the Gambia where it changes its general course from north to west, near the present Senegalese town of Kedugu (Kédougou). Though the date of foundation is uncertain, these towns were already flourishing by the early eighteenth century, maintaining close relations with their kinsmen in Bundu, Dentilia, and Jahaba. By the late eighteenth century some Jahaanke were found at Sutuko (Sutuco) on the navigable Gambia to the west, though Sutuko may not have been purely Jahaanke. By that time, the Jahaanke trade diaspora had spread along the main east-west route from the Niger to the Gambia.

Nineteenth-century expansion took a north-south direction as well. Jahaanke had been moving into Fuuta Jaalo for the kola trade over many decades, but their first town in that region was founded in 1804 by al-Hajj Salimu Gassama, called Karamoho Ba (literally, "the great teacher"). He was not so much a man of commerce as a man of letters who was born in Diide in Bundu, studied in Ñaani on the Gambia, in Gunjuru in Xaaso, and had taught in Kākā and Timbo before he asked the Almaami of Fuuta Jaalo for permission to found his own town on the northern frontier of that country. The town had to be moved in 1815, but both settlements were called Tuba, and the second (often called Tubaba) became a major center of Islamic learning through the remainder of the century. Tuba was also a center for the Jahaanke dispersion further south, into the kola-producing regions and on to the coast. This further dispersion, however, was mainly one of small groups settling in their own sections of existing towns, rather than founding new, all-Jahaanke settlements. Though diffuse, it may have been more influential on surrounding peoples than the older pattern of settlement had been, and the Jahaanke were among the most important of a number of northern elements moving through Fuuta and onto the coastal plain during the course of the nineteenth century.[4]

At this same time, the network further north also began to change. The rise of Kaarta in the final decades of the eighteenth century was a menace to all of northeastern Senegambia, and disaster to Jahaba. As the trade routes were cut again and again for long periods, inhabitants drifted away to the Jahaanke towns in Bundu or downstream to the Gajaaga clerical settlements. Finally, Tiginkoro of Kaarta (ruled c. 1808–11) destroyed Jahaba and drove the

4. P. Marty, *Islam en Guinée* (Paris, 1921), pp. 106–7, 133 ff.; P. Smith, "Les Diakhanké," esp. pp. 246, 251; Anon., "History of the Gassama"; A. Wurie, "The Bundukas of Sierra Leone," *Sierra Leone Studies*, 1 (n.s.): 14–25 (1953); A. Howard, "Big Men, Traders, and Chiefs," passim.

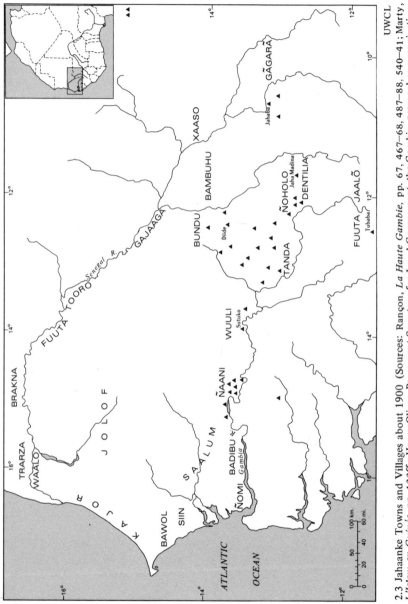

2.3 Jahaanke Towns and Villages about 1900 (Sources: Rançon, *La Haute Gambie*, pp. 67, 467–68, 487–88, 540–41; Marty, *L'Islam en Guinée*, pp. 133ff.; Henry Oliver, Permanent Secretary for Local Government, the Gambia, personal communication, May 1966; Kadiali Diakité, CC, CIP (1)

survivors off to the west. According to tradition, 500 years passed from the founding of Jahaba to its destruction.[5]

The final shifts in the spacial disposition of Jahaanke towns came with the religious revolutions. As serious Muslims, the Jahaanke could hardly ignore the call of Shaykh Umar Taal for a *fergo* or emigration into Kaarta to found a new Muslim empire. Some from Bundu followed him, and their descendents still live near Ñoro (Nioro) in Mali. Most Jahaanke, however, were in the Kaadiri brotherhood, while Shaykh Umar was a leader of the rival Tijaani order. Jahaanke traditions also centered on a self-protecting isolation from the quasi-pagan world, not military action to transform it. They were to be more ripe for action, though, some three decades later, when Mamadu Lamiin Draame appealed for their support at a time when the kind of society they had known seemed to be in full collapse. Many Jahaanke from Bundu followed Mamadu Lamiin on his final flight toward the Gambia in 1886, and they settled there when the leader was killed and the revolt collapsed.[6]

Although they have had no common political ties since their departure from Jahaba, the present-day Jahaanke think of themselves as a separate nation or people, unified by the special religious tradition incorporated in the teaching of Salimu Sware. But the Jahaanke people in the broad sense are defined linguistically as those who speak their special dialect of Malinke. In a slightly narrower sense, they are counted as Jahaanke if they live in a dominantly Jahaanke village, whether free people, members of the endogamous craft groups, or former slaves (jōo).[7] In fact, the "slave" group were more important to the Jahaanke than to most Senegambian peoples; it was their work in the fields that freed the upper class for koranic learning and commerce abroad. Tuba in Fuuta Jaalō was reported as 60 per cent slave at

5. Anon., "The Ulama of Jaha," Fonds Curtin, IFAN.

6. Kadiali Diakite, CC, C1P(1); Rançon, "Le Boundou," pp. 632–39; Humphrey Fisher, "Field notes," 7:1650, 1663 (unpublished mss. seen through the kindness of the author). Eight Gambian villages were officially classified as Jahaanke in 1966.

7. In a still narrower sense, a true Jahaanke would be a person descended from those who lived in Jahaba in the time of Salimu Sware, though in fact many leading Jahaanke today are descended from lineages of Halpulaar or Malinke origin which have since become assimilated to the Jahaanke way of life. Some traditions claim that the key Jahaanke patrilineages from Jahaba were originally a single matrilineage, since each of the founding ancestors of the patrilineages was born to one of a set of full sisters with the jaamu Suduro. On the other hand, Jahaanke villages differ as to which patrilineages belong in the inner circle. Sware (alternate forms, Sanbaheesi or Sise), Draame, Giraasi (alt, Fofana) are most commonly listed. Kaba (alt. Jaakite), Dibasi, and Jabi (alt. Gasama) occur on some lists but not on all. See Hammadi Madi Si, Madina Kojalaani, CC, T 7 (2); Monteil, *Les Khassonké*, p. 357; Smith, "Les Diakhanké," passim; Arfa Ibrahima Gasama, Tombura, CC, T 13 (2); Mamba Guirassy, "Etude sommaire sur la race Diakha" (unpublished mss. seen through the kindness of the author, Ministère d'Education Nationale, Dakar).

the beginning of the colonial period, and this is close to the figure given for other Jahaanke towns as well.[8]

Like other juula, the Jahaanke valued automony from the secular authorities, Islam as a religion, and commerce as their chosen occupation, but they went further still and held that the use of force and the exercise of political authority were incompatible with the religious calling. These ideas are attributed to Salimu Sware and are found among the Juula of the Asante hinterland as well,[9] but the Jahaanke gave them a special twist. The theological formulation of Swarian pacifism was to reject physical jihad and to assert that the only correct form of jihad was the spiritual struggle for righteousness. Later Jahaanke thought drew out the fullest possible implications, holding that all warfare is morally wrong and the use of violence even in self defense may not be legitimate. They explain many of their shifts from one place to another as a decision to move rather than fight. The Jahaanke of Bundu have a tradition that, when they first arrived, their ancestors made an agreement with Maalik Sii, who promised they would never be asked to fight in Bunduunke wars but could do alternate service building fortifications and giving prayer for victory. Many traditionalists still claim that Jahaanke caravans moved through the country armed only with the power of prayer, though others concede that prayer was most effective when supplemented by firearms.

The avoidance of political power emerges most forcefully as a theme running through Jahaanke historical traditions, which tell again and again of a noble cleric, so respected by the people that they offered him the kingship. Yet he declined, proving by his renunciation that he was indeed a great waliu. The Jahaanke reaction to the Umarian jihad of the 1850's is neatly illustrated by the Jahaanke account of Shaykh Umar's visit to Tuba. There he met the famous Jahaanke scholar and waliu Karā Tasilimu, and the tradition tells how each performed a series of miracles to demonstrate his supernatural powers. After they had reached a mutual recognition of spiritual equality at a high level, Umar asked Karā Tasilimu to join his jihad, but the Jahaanke saint proved his ultimate superiority by answering that he was a Jahaanke, and Jahaanke fight only against the temptation to dominate others.[10]

The general range of Jahaanke trade ran from the navigable Gambia on the west to the Niger on the east, rarely extending further than Segu or Sikasso, where it linked up with other trade networks in the Niger valley. On occasion in the eighteenth century, they might go through to the sea at the *petite côte* north of the Gambia mouth, but the southern route to the sea in what was to become Guinea-Conakry appears to have developed only in the nineteenth

8. Marty, *L'Islam en Guinée,* pp. 126–32; Smith, "Les Diakhanké, pp. 249–51.

9. I. Wilks, "The Transmission of Islamic Learning in the Western Sudan," in J. Goody, ed., *Literacy in Traditional Societies* (Cambridge, 1968), p. 178.

10. (Arfan Diame Diakhabi, CC, T9 (2). See also Kadiale Diakhite, T2 (1); Ibrahima Diasigui, Sututa, T 10 (2); Baku Kaba, Tambura, T 13 (2).

century. Even then, most Jahaanke originating as far north as Bundu would trade only as far as Tuba or Kankan, leaving the trade from there to the coast to a few traders with large capitals or to those whose base was further south. Jahaanke merchants took their caravans to Gajaaga, just as the Soninke did, but they seem to have left the east-west route along the sahal to the Soninke, rarely going further to the northeast than Xaaso.[11]

In spite of the web of relationships giving separate identity to the Jahaanke or the Soninke of Gajaaga, those networks were only subdivisions of a broader net that encompassed all the juula of Senegambia, with linkage to other juula networks beyond. Several different groups of *Malinke mori* or Muslim Malinke were involved in long-distance trade. Virtually any Muslim Malinke town could contribute some merchants, though most Malinke juula appear to have come from the core area of Manding culture, especially from its southern fringes, less often from the Muslim villages on the Gambia itself. The Gambian Afro-Portuguese, for example, translated *juula* as *mercador,* and the English called them *mercadores* at first before settling on *merchant* as a term for a specific group of people, not just those with commercial occupations; and the usual designation for the Malinke region east of the Gambia was simply "the merchants' country."

Juula involvement in Gambia trade, however, led early to the development of juula settlements on the Gambia which were not specifically identifiable as Jahaanke, or Soninke, or Malinke Mori. In 1507, for example, Sutuko on the Gambia was a commercial enclave on the fringes of the Jolof empire but independent of it. It then had about 4,000 people and was a site of major exchange between Malinke juula from the interior and Portuguese river traffic. Even at this early date, gold exports through Sutuko were 23 to 28 kgs in a good year. A century later, in 1620, Sutuko was still the most important up-river town, with a walled area more than 1.5 kms in diameter, though the enclosed area was greater than the built-up area, to allow grazing for the large number of transport donkeys. After another century, in about 1730, however, the main trade center had moved downstream to Kaur, which took the form of a triple town having one Wolof section and two separate sections for Muslim traders.[12]

Nor was Kaur alone. Francis Moore's map of the Gambia in about 1735 showed eighteen different villages identified as "morecunda" or "juncocunda" (Muslim town or Jahaanke town). (See below, map 3.2.) By the 1790's, even more of the principal merchants in long-distance trade had

11. Kajaali Jahite, CC, T 2 (1).

12. The old Sutuko is the village shown on present-day Gambian maps as Sutukoba (literally "great Sutuko"), not the one marked Sutuko a little to the north of Basse. See D. Pacheco Pereira, *Esmeraldo de Situ Orbis,* ed. and trans. Raymond Mauny (Bissau, 1956), pp. 63, 65; Jobson, *Golden Trade,* p. 89; Francis Moore, *Travels into the Inland Parts of Africa* ... (London, 1738), pp. 101–2.

moved to the Gambia. Mungo Park visited a certain Jemafu Mamadu, the "richest trader on the Gambia," who lived in one of the clerical villages, but other prominent juula in the Gambia trade still kept their main residence hundreds of kilometers to the east, usually in enclaved Muslim towns, but scattered very widely in places as diverse as Xaaso or the Muslim part of a double town he called Kamalia in the heart of Manding a little west of Bamako—in either case near the eastern terminus of the normal caravan route to the Gambia. Still others lived halfway along the route. One juula Park visited in 1797 had his headquarters at Madina (Médine), a village which was his sole property, near Satadugu on the Faleme. But the Gambian influence was apparent in the Gambian English architectural style of his house and in the fact that his meals were served on imported pewter dishes.[13]

Other ethnic groups also contributed a few traders to the general juula community. The Sereer and coastal Wolof were notable for their relative scarcity, but many of the Futankoobe of the middle Senegal were juula. North of the Senegal, many zwāya Moors were active in the gum trade and in the more general exchange between desert and savanna. The usual point of exchange for gum was the north bank of the river, but zwāya caravans came as far south as Cape Verde and occasionally to the Gambia as well, so often that all of Kajor and Waalo fell within a Moorish trading zone. The Moors also operated east-west camel caravans that sometimes covered the whole distance between the coast of Mauritania and the Niger bend. One group especially active in this trade was known to the Europeans of the 1730's simply as the Arabs of Haire, Haire being the desert region due north of Gajaaga.

In one sense, all of these different long-distance traders were in competition with one another, but their competition was moderated by other aspects of Senegambian social organization. A useful distinction can be made between two different kinds of solidarity, a corporate solidarity and a feeling of solidarity based on common status. In the first case, an individual may feel that his interests are bound up with those who bring differing contributions to a common effort. The present-day example would be the solidarity of all who belong to the same university or work for the same firm; in Senegambia, it would be the solidarity of a village regardless of rank or caste. But the individual may have an equal or stronger feeling of status solidarity with those whose position is equivalent to his own, but in other firms, other universities, or other villages.[14]

The normal pattern in Senegambia was very strong corporate solidarity exemplified by strong persisting ties between former masters and their former slaves, or between the "caste" people and the ruling class. Juula on the other

13. Park, *Travels,* 1:126, 380, 525.
14. The distinction recalls Durkheim's discussion of "corporate" and "mechanical" solidarity; but it is not identical, nor are Durkheim's full set of theoretical overtones implied.

hand lived in peculiar circumstances, where their religion normally bound them to fellow Muslims and separated them from the rest of society. Their special function as cross-cultural mediators in commerce also separated them somewhat from others of their own language or ethnic group. The juula tradition laid a very strong emphasis on status solidarity with other merchants. Jahaanke today still insist that they have a bond not merely to other Jahaanke but to other juula, and especially to other juula in the same line of trade. A multinational caravan representing several ethnic groups—Jahaanke, Soninke, or Futaanke—would tend to subdivide according to the branch of trade, not the ethnic identity.[15] The road through status solidarity to nationhood based on that solidarity—the road followed by the Juula of the Asante hinterland—had already been followed some way by the Senegambian juula as well.

When Richard Jobson visited the Gambia in 1620, he met a juula named Bokar Sano who appealed to Jobson's own sense of juula solidarity. In Jobson's words, "In our time of trading together, if it were his owne goods he bartered for, he would tell us, this is for my selfe, and you must deale better with me, than either with the Kings of the Country or any others, because I am as you are, a Julietto, which signifies a Merchant, that goes from place to place, neither do I, as the Kings of our Country do which is to eate, and drinke, and lye still at home amongst their women, but I seeke abroad as you doe; . . ."[16]

Over the long run, however, juula solidarity in Senegambia reached neither the nationhood it achieved in the Asante hinterland nor yet the revolutionary role that allowed Yves Person to identify the rise of Samori Ture as a "juula revolution."[17] A detailed explanation will have to await further research in specific Senegambian societies; but in general the juula solidarity of earlier centuries disappeared into the broader movement for religious reform and Muslim supremacy. This was possible in nineteenth-century Senegambia because Islam and the status of juula were no longer coterminous in Fuuta Tooro, the Wolof states, or even the lower Gambia; Muslims outnumbered merchants many times over, while in Samori's country or the Asante hinterland they continued to be nearly one and the same.

The Politics of Trade: Juula Communities and the Competition between the Rivers

It is difficult in most periods to disentangle the role of the juula in the maze of political maneuver, negotiation, violence, and threats of violence that marked the shifting relations between coastal or riverain polit-

15. Hammadi Madi Si, Madina Kojalaani, CC, T 7 (1).
16. Jobson, *Golden Trade*, p. 125.
17. Person, *Samori*, passim.

ical authorities, the European juula from overseas in their trading forts or factories, the African juula from the hinterland, and occasional extraneous forces, such as the Moroccan raiders who were present along the Senegal so much of the early eighteenth century. The somewhat abstract model of juula society, religion, attitudes, and spatial distribution is nevertheless only a part of reality. Another part of that same reality is the day by day, year by year play of power and profit surrounding the movement of commerce. The data needed for a continuous account are not available. Even if they were, a full chronicle of these political relations would be redundant, where the essential is the style of history, the recurrent pattern that emerges from the more detailed narrative. Some of this style can be seen in a sequence of crises in the 1720's and 1730's, centering on the strategic rivalry of the Senegal and Gambia rivers as carriers of east-west trade.

The two rivers were nearly equal as potential routes to the interior, but their advantages and disadvantages were different. The Senegal was navigable as far as Felu Falls, just above Kayes in present-day Mali, 560 kms in a direct line from the mouth, 925 kms by river. The Gambia on the other hand was only navigable to Barokunda Falls, 265 kms in direct line from the mouth, 470 kms by river—roughly half the distance. But the Senegal had contravening disadvantages. Oceangoing ships found it difficult to cross the bar at the mouth of the river, and even harder to navigate further inland than Podor (180 kms direct, 269 by river from Saint Louis). In practice, goods were transshipped at Saint Louis for a river voyage in specialized vessels. The Gambia had none of these transshipment problems. Oceangoing sailing vessels could go all the way to Barokunda Falls, though they found the upper reaches so difficult they often stopped further down. Even today, oceangoing steamers sail regularly as far as Kuntaur, 153 kms in direct line from Bathurst, 240 kms by river.[1]

The hydrography of the two rivers was also different. Where the Senegal was tidal only to Podor, the Gambia was tidal all the way to Barokunda. This meant that, even with unfavorable winds, a sailing vessel could go upstream by drifting with the favorable tides and riding at anchor during the unfavorable. But on the Senegal, navigation above Podor was only possible during the "high season" when the river was in flood, rarely before July or after December, and usually only in August through November. During the rest of the year, any sailors from the coast who happened to be in Gajaaga were cut off till the next high season. Though the Gambia was not seasonal in this definitive sense, the best trade season there was the dry season, when the tides were comparatively strong and the current comparatively weak, say late January through April. It was also the best season for European sailors to avoid malaria and for juula to avoid muddy tracks and streams in flood. This

---

1. F. Brigaud, *Connaissance du Sénégal*, pt. 2, *Hydrographie* (Saint Louis, 1961).

meant that the two rivers offered complementary seasonal advantages, and the average transit time from the coast to upper Gajaaga and back was not very different. (See map 2.4.) The combination of Gambia River plus caravan came to about thirty days each way, while the Senegal route took about fifty days upstream and fifteen days down.

The game of competition between the two rivers included as players the French traders from overseas on the Senegal and the English on the Gambia. Each had a route to the interior which it sought to monopolize against other Europeans. The two positions were roughly competitive but not symmetrically so. The Senegal, being harder but longer, had two strategic advantages balancing its navigational problems. The need to transship for the upriver voyage meant that control of Saint Louis carried full control of the river trade, whereas easier entry into the broad estuary of the Gambia meant that interlopers or well-armed enemy ships could sometimes sail past the forts at the river mouth. The longer reach into the interior also put the French in a position to use force or diplomacy to set up a prohibitive screen from their base in Gajaaga to block trade from passing through to the Gambia. The French strategists suggested again and again that the Company either sign treaties with Bundu, paying Bundu to prevent the passage of caravans, or else that the French themselves set up a series of armed posts along the line of the Faleme in Bundu or Bambuhu. Both lines of suggestion (and combinations of the two) led to recurrent if unsuccessful action from the 1710's until after the 1850's.[2] The countering English strategy was to use the navigational superiority of the Gambia to pay higher prices for African produce, prices high enough to compensate for the extra days of travel by caravan from Gajaaga. This policy also called for forward diplomacy to keep the roads open and the tolls low.

The various groups of juula were also in the game, not only as the carriers on the overland extension into the interior from either river route, but also as potential competitors between the head of navigation and the coast. In this respect, the European trade diasporas had the advantage of relatively cheap and efficient water transportation, but this advantage carried concomitant disadvantages. The rivers were fixed in place, and the river mouth was easily blockaded from the sea. Nor was it possible to detour around an unfriendly state that might try to stop shipping along the river. The contrasting juula advantage was mobility. They could switch their trade from one route to the other, bypassing both rivers if necessary and selling directly on the coast.

The degree of functional differentiation between nodes in the trade net-

2. See anonymous memorandum of 1723 quoted in Machat, *Documents,* pp. 22–23; Estouphan de la Brüe to David, 10 February 1753, ANF, C6 14; Guillet, "Mémoire de remise de service," Saint Louis, 24 September 1837, ANS, 13 G 22; Raffenel, Reports of 14 and 17 March 1844, *Revue coloniale,* 4:154 and 197 (1844); Paul Holle to Governor, Bakel, 5 June 1846, ANS, 13 G 165.

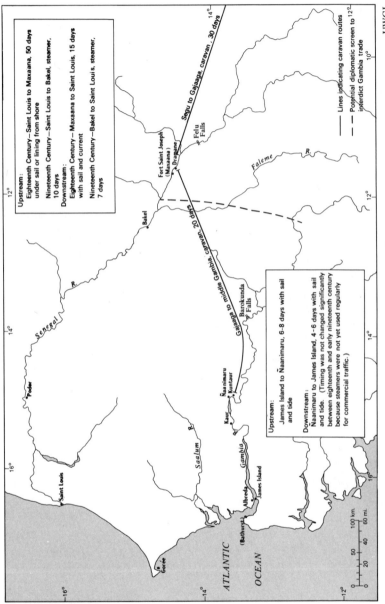

Upstream:

Eighteenth Century—Saint Louis to Maxaana, 50 days
under sail or lining from shore

Nineteenth Century—Saint Louis to Bakel, steamer,
10 days

Downstream:

Eighteenth Century—Maxaana to Saint Louis, 15 days
with sail and current

Nineteenth Century—Bakel to Saint Louis, steamer,
7 days

Segu to Gajaaga, caravan, 30 days

Felu
Falls

Faleme R.

Fort Saint Joseph
(Maxaana)

Drajane

Bakel

Senegal R.

Gajaaga to middle Gambia, caravan, 20 days

Barokunda
Falls

Podor

Saint Louis

Saalum R.

Gambia R.

Ñaanimaru
Kuntaur

Kaur

Albreda
(Bathurst)
James Island

ATLANTIC
OCEAN

Gorée

Upstream:

James Island to Ñaanimaru, 6–8 days with sail
and tide

Downstream:

Ñaanimaru to James Island, 4–6 days with sail
and tide. (Timing was not changed significantly
between eighteenth and early nineteenth century
because steamers were not yet used regularly
for commercial traffic.)

Lines indicating caravan routes

Potential diplomatic screen to
interdict Gambia trade

0   50   100 km.
0 20 40 60 mi.

2.4 The Strategy of Competition between the Two Rivers

86

work played a role here. The waterborne trade network was more complex, with greater division of labor and greater spatial distribution of functions. Central direction was in London or Paris, with either James Fort or Saint Louis dependent socially and economically and politically on its respective central place, just as sloop captains, heads of out-factories, and other personnel in Africa were dependent on James Fort or Saint Louis. When either fell to enemy forces in wartime, the whole trade operation came to an end or was diverted to the service of a new master. But this was not so of the juula, where each node in the network performed much the same functional roles as any other. The Soninke of Gajaaga had central places on the upper Senegal, and they performed some basic functions for the diaspora as a whole—like clerical education, or basic socialization of each new generation of traders. But the Gajaaga clerics could shift their trade in an emergency to keep it clear of Gajaaga. In much the same way, the Jahaanke network was able to continue alive and healthy even after the fall of Jahaba, the center of its seventeenth- and eighteenth-century dispersion. Specialization and functional differentiation were potentially more efficient, but the trade off of efficiency for mobility may well have been the appropriate strategy for the juula to follow.

The secular African states were also in the game, with still another hand of cards. They had power—more power locally available than the Europeans could usually muster, and far more than the African juula. But the African states were comparatively small; none had enough extension in space to stop the flow of trade by individual action. They were therefore at the mercy of juula mobility. If they tried to raise tolls, at some point the juula would find it easier to take another route than to pay. Even the European juula had a long-term kind of mobility that could be played against the greater power of the African states. If it appeared that high tolls would make their operations unprofitable for the foreseeable future, the European headquarters would simply withdraw its Senegambian outposts, removing the source of revenue altogether. In this sense, the secular rulers, the European juula, and the African juula were set in a hierarchy of increasing mobility, running counter to another hierarchy of decreasing power.

The sequence of crises chosen to illustrate this pattern began in 1719, when the Ormankoobe were operating in the region of Gajaaga. Ñame, the Tunka or ruler of Gajaaga, became friendly with the Moroccan commander and decided that the Moroccan presence strengthened his position. He therefore asked the French representative of the Compagnie des Indes to increase the tribute or "customs" he paid each year. At first, the French agreed; they could do little else, but they waited for a chance to reassert their position. That chance came in 1722, when Charpentier, the French commandant, escalated the latent conflict into open war by attacking the Tunka's capital at

Maxaana, adjoining the French fort, driving away the Tunka and killing many of his people.[3] Both Ñame and Charpentier were probably guilty of overplaying their hands, but the incident illustrates a pattern of force and threat of force by which the Europeans of the entrepôt and the African rulers established the share of revenue that each would have from the passing trade.

Late in 1722 or early in 1723, the juula came into the picture with their own demands on the French post. Masatā Draame and Jagu Draame, the most influential of the merchant-clerics of Dramane, demanded that the French raise the price paid for slaves to equal that paid by the English on the Gambia. This time the French refused, thinking that they could pay a lower price in compensation for their longer route to the coast, but the Draame sent word through to the Gambia, offering to divert the entire gold and slave trade to that river, and to bring an Englishman through to Gajaaga so that he could see for himself the potential value of the trade;[4] and they carried out the first part of the threat. From the end of the high season in December 1723, Gajaaga people stopped delivering gold or slaves to the French post; even caravans that came through as far as Dramane were diverted to the Gambia. At this stage, then, the play was a commercial boycott to win a commercial advantage.

At the next stage, beginning early in 1724, the separate pressures expressed through commercial boycott and military force joined in a more complex pattern. The Ormankoobe returned, along with a separate force of Futankoobe under Samba Gelaajo Jegi, formerly Saatigi of Fuuta Tooro, now in retreat or military exile (*fergo* in Pulaar) waiting for a chance to make another try for the kingship.[5] Meanwhile, the Moroccans and the Fuulbe

3. Saint-Robert to CI, 28 December 1722, ANF, C6 7.

4. Extract of Orfeur to RAC, 6 June 1723, T 70/7.

5. The custom of retreat to a nearby kingdom after a political defeat was very common throughout Senegambia, and it was governed by diplomatic conventions that ordered hospitality for the refugees. Gajaaga was the traditional place of fergo for defeated Futaanke politicians, so much so that one of the Pulaar names for Gajaaga was *leeidi fergooji*, or country of refuge. (Gaden, *Proverbes et maximes peules*, pp. 284–85.) *Fergo* is also the usual Pulaar translation of the Arabic *hijra*; it therefore recalls Mohammad's retreat from Mecca to Medina. The great fergo in recent Futaanke history was the movement organized by Laaji Umar in the 1850's.

The individual in this narrative is the famous Samba Gelaajo Jegi, probably the best known of all traditional heroes in Senegambian oral literature. Many different stories about Samba's life are still told, and the whole corpus of Samba stories is much like the European epics of Roland or King Arthur. In this case, the immense scholarly task of disentangling the historical Samba from the maze has not yet begun. The principal recorded traditions are Oumar Kane, ed., "Samba Gelajo-Jegi," *BIFAN*, 32:911–26 (1970); C. Steff, "Histoire du Fouta Toto" (unpublished mss., 1913, Fonds Gaden, IFAN, Dakar); Lanrezac, "Légendes soudanaises," *Revue economique française*, 5: 607–19 (1907); L. J. B. Bérenger-Féraud, *Recueil des contes populaires da la Sénégambie* (Paris, 1885), pp. 39–49; A. Raffenel, *Nouveau voyage au pays des nègres*, 2 vols.

raided and stole cattle up and down the Gajaaga countryside, keeping terms of vague friendship with the French. This was as damaging to the Draame as it was to the Baacili and their followers, and the Draame raised their demands on the French by asking that they not only increase prices but also make the Ormankoobe take their raiding north of the Senegal. In fact, the French post in Gajaaga lacked the force to end the raids, but they did settle the commercial question on juula terms, raising the price of slaves to 30 iron bars or equivalent and adding valuable presents for Masatā and Jagu Draame. In time, the Ormankoobe and Samba Gelaajo both drifted away.

Tunka Ñame tried once more in 1725 to raise his own payoff, but the clerical towns tacitly supported the French, and a brief Franco-Baacili war ended in May 1725, nearly simultaneously with Tunka Ñame's death. Muusa Baacili of Tiyaabu was elected Tunka in July; Levens became the new French commandant, and both men were willing to compromise the extreme stands of their predecessors for the sake of their common interest in moving trade once more.[6] If any general lesson is to be drawn from these events of 1719 through 1725, it is that the French and the Baacili both tended to overplay their bargaining position based on force, while the juula position based on a choice of routes was much stronger. The juula, however, held no cards valid against raiders like the Ormankoobe.

The two European-based networks meanwhile tried to exploit their own particular advantages, especially when the competing network was in difficulties. In 1728, for example, the Royal African Company in London learned that the French shipping had failed to reach Gajaaga during the high season because of trouble in Fuuta. It automatically increased the trade goods bound for the Gambia in order to take care of the predictable increase in demand.[7] As disorders associated with the Ormankoobe persisted into the 1730's, the Royal African Company pushed forward its effort to attract a larger share of trade. In 1726, it had operated only two factories upriver on the Gambia— "Joar" near Kaur in Saalum, and "Cuttejar" near present-day Karantaba in upper Ñaani—but increasing trade encouraged a move toward new posts further up, at Buruku and Fatatenda.[8] In 1733, it discovered Yuuba Jaalo, a

---

(Paris, 1856), 2:320–44; Frantz de Zeltner, *Contes du Sénégal et du Niger* (Paris, 1913), pp. 151–57; F. V. Equilbecq, *Contes indigènes de l'ouest africain français*, 2 vols. (Paris, 1913), 2:3–42. Several different versions are found in CC, of which the longest and most detailed is by Saki Njai, translated into French on T 13 and 14.

6. Procès verbaux of 19 May 1724, 1 July 1725, ANF, C6 7; P. Charpentier, Memorandum of 20 June 1724, ANF, C6 8; Levens, reports of 10 July and 19 July 1725, ANF, C6 9 (also in BN, FF, NA, 9339). A narrative of the events in Gajaaga in this period is also given by Delcourt, *La France au Sénégal*, pp. 157–65.

7. African Committee of RAC to Robert Nasmyth and others, 18 October 1728, T 70/55. Boucard, Memorandum enclosed with dispatch of 1 April 1732, ANF, C6 10.

8. RAC to Anthony Rogers and others, 29 February 1727/28, and 17 December 1730, T 70/55.

juula from Bundu who had been kidnapped and sold into slavery in Maryland. It purchased his freedom and sent him back home with the idea that he might be a useful agent to further the Company's interest—as in fact he was. In 1735, he took Thomas Hull to Bundu, though they were unable to pass on into Bambuhu to visit the gold field. In 1736, he again guided Hull to Bundu, though Hull apparently never returned. Yuuba Jaalo, however, went on to the French Fort Saint Joseph in Gajaaga in June 1736, looking for a shipment of goods the Royal African Company had sent him by way of the Senegal.[9] The French immediately arrested him and put him in prison for guiding an Englishman toward Bambuhu.

The move was in line with the French blockade strategy, but it was a mistake. The juula response was a telling example of juula solidarity. Even though zwāya from Mauritania, Jahaanke, and Soninke were all important in the trade of upper Gajaaga—and Yuuba Jaalo was none of these, but a Puulo from Bundu—trade stopped abruptly, and from all sources. Where the Compagnie des Indes had been shipping at least 200 slaves a year, even in the slack period of the recent past, the boats came back to Saint Louis after the high season of 1736 without a single slave. When the French released Yuuba Jaalo, trade began again.[10] The whole affair was an interesting play of cross-cultural misunderstanding. The French arrested Yuuba for a crime that was essentially ethnic—giving aid and comfort to the national enemy, though this was peacetime between France and England in Europe. The response they met was completely professional, crossing ethnic lines but uniting a great variety of different and competing juula groups.

At that point, the relative simplicity of game-like trade competition was complicated by other factors. In fact, the politics of commerce could not be closed off from other events. It was only one of a number of overlapping political games that were simultaneously in play. A second one was a very complex system of dynastic competition for the office of Saatigi of Fuuta Tooro. Fuuta drew little of its revenue from trade; the prize here was command over land and people in Fuuta itself. The Ormankoobe were a third factor, related to still another political system in the Sharifian Empire beyond the Sahara.

The man who claimed credit for bringing these three systems together was Saint-Adon, French commander at Fort Saint Joseph, acting to improve the Company's trade position in Gajaaga. Samba Gelaajo Jegi was still on fergo,

---

9. See T. Hull, "Voyage to Bundo" (unpublished mss. from the library of the Duke of Buccleuch, 1735); Curtin, *Africa Remembered*, pp. 27–59; D. Grant, *The Fortunate Slave: An Illustration of African Slavery in the Early Eighteenth Century* (London, 1968), passim.

10. Saint-Adon to IC, Gajaaga, 2 December 1736; Conseil du Sénégal to CI, Saint Louis, 6 November 1736; and Devaulx to CI, 20 March 1737, ANF, C6 11.

living mainly in Bundu. In 1737 and 1738, Saint-Adon formed a tripartite alliance between the Compagnie des Indes, Samba Gelaajo, and the local commander of the Ormankoobe, for a joint attack on Saatigi Konko Bubu Muusa of Fuuta. If it succeeded, the Moroccans would get booty (and perhaps some control over Samba Gelaajo once he was in power), Samba would again become Saatigi, and the French would have the right to build a fort in Fuuta for the greater security of their trade. They also hoped, of course, for the friendship and cooperation of a grateful Saatigi put in power by their efforts. The campaign began early in 1738 with the sack of Dramane, the leading clerical town in Gajaaga—perhaps a way of punishing the juula for their earlier actions—and in March it moved on to an attack on Fuuta itself.[11]

The historical record is anything but clear on points of detail, but the coalition apparently won. Samba returned to power, though only for a short time. Trade revived on the Senegal route, as the Gajaaga juula came back to their natural outlet on the upper river. The Royal African Company lost its initiative in the Gambia trade. Though trade on that river continued to be important, it moved from the hands of the Company into those of separate English traders. But these developments were part of the changing way the Europeans sought to organize their trade sphere on the two rivers. Before going forward, it is best to go back to the earlier history and background of these juula from overseas.

11. Saint-Adon to CI, 20 April 1737, Devaulx to CI, 20 March 1737 and 15 February 1738, and Conseil du Sénégal to CI, 14 May 1738, ANF, C6 11.

3 | TRADE DIASPORAS FROM OVERSEAS

Although the European trade diasporas in Senegambia belonged to the same family of socioeconomic institutions as their juula
counterparts, their political, social and economic norms were alien to the
Senegambian way of doing things. Most obvious was their dependence on the
European metropolis, and European control over the trade enclaves on the
coast. The pattern of dependence and control affected even the most inde-
pendent-looking separate trader who sailed the coast trading from shipboard,
free of all relationship to his fellow Europeans in the trade enclaves; even this
apparently free agent was tied to outfitters, port facilities, shipbuilders,
armorers, pools of skilled seamen, a national identity that made it possible to
fly a flag and hence enjoy the protection of international law—to say nothing
of banking, insurance, and the maze of capitalist commercial institutions.
And the functional dependence of the private trader on shipboard or on shore
meant an ultimate political subordination that was very hard to escape, even
though the metropolis found it hard to exercise continuous control over its
subjects in Africa beyond the official trade enclaves.

The trade castles were kept under metropolitan control, either directly
through the Crown bureaucracy or indirectly through a chartered company
with explicit authority to act for the Crown. The European political presence
was one aspect of a striking contrast between the African juula communities
and those from overseas. Where the African juula made a sharp distinction
between the clerical-mercantile and the political-military callings, and sought
political independence or at least autonomy for themselves, the juula from
overseas combined political and commercial roles, or else brought along
political and military specialists in the form of royal governors and garrisons.

But the Europeans made their own kind of social distinction between
commercial and politico-military occupations. Military officers and royal

92

officials tended to be drawn from the nobility or gentry and to have higher status in Europe than merchants had, and the European traders lacked the access to high status and prestige that came to the African juula from his association with Islam and all it implied in religious knowledge, literacy as a rare technique, and possible control over the supernatural world.

In this sense, war was thought of as more honorable in Europe than in Senegambia, and trade less honorable, but European culture had a special category for trade beyond the seas as opposed to trade in and around Europe itself. From the Portuguese outburst of the fifteenth century and the Spanish invasions of the Americas in the sixteenth, war and commerce were often alternate occupations for a single group of men; and the close overseas association of war and commerce continued in the late sixteenth and early seventeenth centuries when the French, Dutch, and English tried to fight their way into the Hispanic zones of commerce and control in the Indian Ocean and the tropical Americas. This union of war and commerce, rather than religion and commerce, was a far cry from the juula tradition of neutrality in war and politics, further still from the outright pacifism of the Jahaanke. War and trade beyond the seas remained joined in European thought into the eighteenth century, so that overseas trade or the service of a trading company remained a respectable occupation for a nobleman in a way that trade at home would not have been. The line between distant trade, warfare, and piracy remained narrow, and many switched easily from one to the other, their action justified most often by appeal to the higher cause of national triumph in the competition of European states. It was, after all, a mercantilist age where wealth was national power, and national power was wealth.

This peculiar European sense of ethnic solidarity was, of course, quite alien to the Senegambian way of looking at things. The Senegambian juula had his first links of solidarity with his kinship group, followed by more distant solidarity with clusters of associated lineages (like the Jahaanke or the Gajaaga clerics), next by professional loyalties to other juula. Loyalties to people of the same language and culture were far down the list, well below loyalties to co-religionists in Islam, and the secular state was treated with aversion. The Europeans, on the other hand, had only weak kinship ties, and their families stayed in Europe. They had a strong sense of solidarity with people of the same language and culture who served the same king, but this was sharply limited by social class. The "gentlemen" who ran the trade forts showed very little concern for the well-being of the working-class soldiers or artisans, while the trade rivalry between the French and English "gentlemen" in command was always close to warfare in the eighteenth century. As an ethical ideal, loyalty to the Crown came first, then loyalty to the Company or other economic associates, third, loyalty to fellow-subjects.

But these were beliefs about what men *should* do, and these beliefs fell away overseas, especially in dangerous or difficult situations like those of West Africa. Many of the "gentlemen" came to Africa after scandal or failure in Europe; many soldiers in the enlisted ranks were sent out as punishment for crime. The European communities of the trade enclaves were thus demoralized from the beginning, and demoralization redoubled in a disease environment that killed newcomers in such fantastic numbers. Out of every ten servants sent to West Africa by the Royal African Company between 1680 and 1780, approximately six died during their first year in Africa, two more died before the three-year enlistment was up, one returned home, and the last met an unknown fate that might have included reenlistment or desertion.[1] In these circumstances, it is hardly surprising that most of the upper ranks tried to build a private fortune by embezzlement or private trade, while the rest tended to take what consolation they could find in the small pleasures of alcohol.

Cross-cultural misunderstanding would have been a problem in any event, but it was made worse by the fact that few Europeans stayed alive long enough to learn much about Africa or the Africans around them. They came from a society where men of African race were the only class of permanent slaves, where Negro was synonymous with slave in the American plantations. But in the eighteenth century the level of xenophobic distrust in Senegambia was no higher than it was among overseas Europeans elsewhere in the world. It was only in the early nineteenth century that a new element was added, partly an exaggerated pride in European achievements and European power growing out of the industrial revolution and partly a belief in European racial superiority, encouraged by errors of biological science. After the Napoleonic Wars and especially from the 1840's, talk about "white man's prestige" and the properly subordinate role of Africans was sometimes heard, but the really serious impact of pseudoscientific racism on European behavior overseas was put off until the second half of the century.[2]

Under the circumstances, it may be surprising that the Europeans were able to maintain trade enclaves in Senegambia or anywhere else in West Africa, decade after decade, or that the men available could be useful agents for the mediation of cross-cultural trade. Part of the explanation lies in the fact that disease mortality was high but not invariable; exceptional men stayed alive, gained the necessary immunities to further attacks, and rounded out careers of a dozen years or more. The high death rates also applied only to Europeans

1. K. G. Davies, "The Living and the Dead," p. 16; see also Curtin, *Image of Africa*, pp. 58–87, 177–97, 343–62, and "Epidemiology and the Slave Trade," *Political Science Quarterly*, 83:190–216 (1968).

2. See Curtin, *Image of Africa*, pp. 28–57, 227–43, 363–87, for the growth of this ideology.

who came to West Africa as adults, not to those of European descent who had spent childhood in Senegambia. Finally, cross-cultural mediation was not up to the Europeans alone; Senegambians could also learn the ways of Western traders and serve as brokers, so that European ship's captains and supercargoes needed only a superficial knowledge of local conditions to enter Senegambian trade. All three groups—long-term European residents, mulattoes, and African brokers—were in fact Afro-European in culture; men and women of similar Eurafrican culture, whatever their race, were the actual and effective agents to carry on the basic purpose of the European trade diasporas in Senegambia.

The Afro-Portuguese

The Portuguese began their commerce with Senegambia from ships, not shore stations or enclaves, and they stood by that policy—at least in theory, and in spite of exceptions like the major but unsuccessful effort against Jolof in 1590, or a mid-sixteenth-century attempt to establish a post far inland near the Bambuhu gold fields.[1] Their reasoning was not from the conviction that ship trade was preferable; it was part of a broader effort to monopolize West African trade for Portugal at a time when Portuguese resources were limited. The Portuguese already had a fortified post at Arguin. They had another in the Cape Verde Islands, and, for much of the time after 1598, they had one either at Cacheu or Bissau in the "southern rivers." The government feared that if Portuguese subjects went on shore elsewhere for trade, they might well serve Portuguese commercial interests, but they were still more likely to serve the interests of French, Spanish, or English interlopers, since legitimate Portuguese interests were already served quite well enough by the existing posts.[2]

But Portuguese subjects, especially those from the Cape Verde Islands, did go on shore to trade, legally or not. Their numbers increased gradually through the sixteenth century. Called *lançados* (a contraction of *lançados em terra,* "put on shore"), they came to be important as mediators for the Cape Verde Islanders, as they were to the foreign merchants. Though they took African wives and became less Portuguese with each generation, the Portu-

1. This episode is remembered in Bambuhu oral tradition which indicates that the Portuguese evacuated after a brief stay, partly on account of their high death rate and partly because of African military opposition. Duranton to Director, Paris, 20 February 1828, ANS, 1 G 8.

2. See Boulègue, "La Sénégambie," pp. 109–38; W. Rodney, *A History of the Upper Guinea Coast 1545–1800* (Oxford, 1970), pp. 71–94; J. Barreto, *Historia da Guiné* (Lisbon, 1938).

guese authorities relented after a time and tried to see that they occasionally had the services of itinerant priests to preserve Christianity; and the descendents of the lançados themselves kept a creolized Portuguese as their home language. By the late seventeenth century, however, they were no longer physically distinguishable from their fellow Africans, though they kept the habit of wearing European clothes.[3]

Official Portuguese activity in Senegambia had dropped by the seventeenth century to occasional raids designed to suppress illicit traffic between the lançados and the foreign traders, and especially to destroy the fortifications other Europeans began to build early in the century. They attacked Gorée in 1629 and again in 1645, to destroy the Dutch fort there, which the Dutch rebuilt each time.[4] By the 1630's, the Afro-Portuguese no longer operated as scattered individuals but as a trade diaspora, with an interlocked network extending from Cape Verde into the Gambia River and working the trade of a considerable hinterland.

The political and cultural circumstances of these Afro-Portuguese communities were extremely diverse. Most were descended from lançados and considered themselves to be loyal Portuguese Christians. Alexis de Saint-Lo in 1635 found an Afro-Portuguese community of twenty-eight people waiting to be baptized in Rufisque, the principal port town for southern Kajor, another fifty at Joal in Siin, and still another community at Portudal in Bawol, though some were "New Christians" who reverted to Judaism beyond the authority of the Portuguese Crown. Nor were all Portuguese on the coast attached to the trading community. One former Cape Verde Islander served the Damel of Kajor as *Alkier,* the royal official in charge of foreign trade at the present-day site of Dakar, and he held the position as a royal slave, having been enslaved as a child.[5] Others were not descended from Portuguese at all, but joined the community by adopting the Afro-Portuguese culture and religion in the same way people could become Jahaanke by attaching themselves to a Jahaanke settlement and accepting its ways. At Sérén (Pointe Serrène) near the frontier between Bawol and Siin was an entirely Christian agricultural village, under a village head known as Padre Bernard. Some of its members had Portuguese ancestors. but most were former slaves of an Afro-Portuguese, who had given them their freedom at his death.[6]

3. La Courbe, *Premier voyage,* pp. 192–93, 204–5.

4. N. I. de Moraes, "Sur les prises de Gorée par les Portugais au xviie siècle," *BIFAN,* 31:989–1013 (1969).

5. Alexis de Saint-Lo, *Relation du voyage au Cap Verd* (Paris and Rouen, 1637), pp. 14–15. Baltasar Barreira reported a community of about one hundred Portuguese Jews in Portudal as early as 1606. ("La description de la côte de Guinée du père Baltasar Berreira," ed. Guy Thilmans and Nize Isabel de Moraes, *BIFAN,* 34:1–50 [1972].

6. Alexis de Saint-Lo, *Relation,* pp. 103–11.

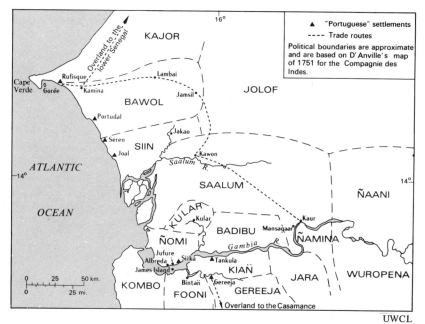

3.1 The Lower Gambia about 1750

The Afro-Portuguese settled at many different points along the Gambia, but in the 1730's their principal town was Tankula (Tankular, Tankrowall), a double town with a Portuguese and a Malinke section, in the south-bank kingdom of Kiañ. Another important point was Gereeja (Geregia, Gereges, Sangrugo), the name derived from the Portuguese *igreja* (church), and located up Bintañ Creek (Bintang Bolon) near the present village of Bwiam. It served principally as a transshipment point for the hinterland stretching south into the lower Casamance. Siika (Seaca) near James Island was still another important settlement, conveniently located for the Afro-Portuguese who served as middlemen for the trade of the Royal African Company. Siika had a church served by a priest who came twice a year from the Cape Verde Islands[7]—an indication that Portuguese culture and religion were retained over more than a century, though Afro-Portuguese trade connections were mainly with the English and hence led up the hierarchy of central places to London, while Afro-Portuguese culture was still attached to the hierarchy that went from Siika to the Cape Verde Islands to Lisbon.

Neither Wolof, Sereer, nor Malinke of the lower Gambia had a strong commercial tradition, and the trade of the far interior was left to juula from

7. Moore, *Travels*, pp. 49–50, 55.

the east. The Afro-Portuguese were therefore able to step easily into the trade of the immediate hinterland, and especially into waterborne trade. They merged the local tradition of seafaring and boatbuilding with Portuguese sails and rigging. The result was a craft the Europeans sometimes called a canoe, though it was actually a magnified version of the fishing boats used in the surf. By the late seventeenth century the ordinary capacity was more than 10 French *tonneaux*,[8] and lineal descendents of the basic design can still be seen carrying peanuts in competition with powered boats and sloops of European design.

A nodal point of transfer on the upper Gambia, from the overland juula to Portuguese waterborne carriage, came into existence early in the sixteenth century at Sutuko, and the role persisted, though it passed down through a succession of different towns. One axis of the Afro-Portuguese trade network was the river traffic from this upriver entrepôt to James Island or Albreda, but Afro-Portuguese were also involved in coastal traffic from Cape Verde, along the petite côte, calling at the lower Gambia ports, and on down through the "southern rivers" as far as Sierra Leone. Some of this north-south trade was associated with bulking for export overseas, but much of it was a waterborne equivalent of the north-south routes in the interior. Gambian iron and textiles from the Cape Verde Islands and the Senegambian mainland were shipped south in exchange for kola nuts. The source of the Senegambian iron was well inland, and many of the kola nuts were also destined for inland markets. The total water route thus formed a curve linking Sierra Leone and the upper Gambia.[9]

This waterborne trade by sea and river was attached to a wide network of Afro-Portuguese overland trade, especially in the immediate hinterland of the petite côte and the lower Gambia. Individual traders travelled the local markets buying hides, beeswax, millet, and other export products, which were bulked at the seaports for sale to European ships. At the ports, they also did some of the initial processing, like cleaning beeswax.

8. That is, 14.4 cubic meters in volume, as defined by French law in 1688—approximately 1 English deadweight ton. (F. C. Lane, "Tonnages, Medieval and Modern," *Economic History Review,* 17 [2nd ser.]: 213–33 [1964], esp. 225, 229; La Courbe, *Premier voyage,* p. 193.) See also R. Smith, "The Canoe in West African History," *JAH,* 11:515–33 (1970), for a survey of West African nautical technology.

9. A problem of terminology occurs here, since the rivers to the south of the Gambia were called the "southern rivers" at the Gambia, Gorée, and Saint Louis. In Sierra Leone, on the other hand, they were called the "northern rivers." By the nineteenth century, usage reached a compromise, so that the "southern rivers" extended only to the vicinity of the Bulama Islands near the frontier of Guinea-Bissau and Guinea-Conakry. For convenience here, however, I will follow the earlier Senegambian convention and continue the "southern rivers" as far as Sierra Leone.

See O. Dapper, *Description de l'Afrique* (Amsterdam, 1686), p. 241; [Le comte d'Estrées], "Mémoire tant sur l'arrivée des vaissaux du Roy au Cap Vert et leur sesjour

One of the most important of the Afro-Portuguese overland routes ran east from the base of the Cape Verde peninsula, then north parallel but slightly west of the present road and railway from Dakar to Saint Louis. This put them in overland touch with the trade of the Senegal mouth, and with local production in all parts of Kajor. A few Afro-Portuguese resided regularly at the Damel's court, and some of them traded into Jolof, still further east. Another important trading point of the mid-seventeenth century was Mansagaar (Mansagar, Mancugár) on the site of the present Balangar, about 6 kms below Kaur on the north bank of the Gambia. Ordinarily, the market there was nothing more than a local center for the sale of foodstuffs, since Kaur took care of the long-distance trade from the far interior. Twice a year, however, the Afro-Portuguese set up a market cross and organized a fair to serve upper Saalum.[10]

They also worked the interior markets behind the petite côte. One of the most important at this period was at Kamina on the frontier between Kajor and Bawol—a kind of market enclave, free of the direct control of either state. It was a major center for buying cotton textiles and hides, and a way-point on the important trade route leading eastward through Lambai, the capital of Bawol, and on to Jamsil, near if not precisely on the site of present-day Juurbel (Diourbel). There, it turned south to Kawon, the capital of Saalum just above Kaolak on the Saalum River, and on southeast through Saalum to the Gambia. This final leg was especially important for trade from the Saalum River salt pans toward the interior.[11]

The heyday of the Afro-Portuguese was the seventeenth century and the first third of the eighteenth, a period when the Portuguese were powerless to keep other Europeans away from the Senegambian coast, yet before either the north Europeans or local Africans could compete effectively at bulking and local trade. During the first half of this period, European factories on the Senegambian coast were so rare that the Afro-Portuguese had an effective

---

en ces rades sur le Commerce qu'on peu faire a ces costes jusques à la rivière de Gambia," BN, Mélanges Colbert, 176:224–32, f. 230; Mémoire général sur le commerce du Sénégal, ANF, C6 14; P. van den Broeck, "Voiages de Pierre van den Broeck au Cap vert, à Angola, et aux Indes orientales," in R. A. C. Renneville, ed., Recueil des voiages qui ont servi à l'établissement et aux progrès de la Compagnie des Indes Orientales, 5 vols. (Amsterdam, 1703–10), 4:306–473, pp. 308–9; Boulègue, "La Sénégambie," pp. 169 ff.

10. O. Dapper in G. Thilmans, ed., "Le Sénégal dans l'oeuvre de Olfried Dapper," BIFAN, 32:508–63 (1970), esp. pp. 523–24; J. Boulègue, "Les luso-africains de Sénégambie," mimeographed (Dakar, 1972), esp. pp. 45–48; Coelho, Duas descriçoes, p. 15.

11. Dapper in BIFAN, 32:523–24; J. Barbot, A Description of the Coasts of North and South Guinea (n.p., 1732), pp. 23, 26–27, 43. The route ran nearly parallel to the present motor road from Dakar through Thiès to Juurbel and south to Kaolak. (See map 3.1.) It would hardly take longer to pass through Jakao, the old capital of Siin, and at least a part of the traffic must have gone that way.

monopoly over the trade to the water's edge. Even after the 1660's, the newcomers lacked the personnel and even the desire to get into the trade of the interior. The Royal African Company of the late seventeenth century, for example, made a regular policy of paying higher prices to the Afro-Portuguese than to others to encourage a useful relationship.[12]

With the early eighteenth century, however, the English at James Island began pushing into the river trade. They began running their own sloops on the river, while preventing the French from going higher than James Island. A natural alliance was thus created between the French and the Afro-Portuguese, who became an extension of the French trade diaspora into the interior. When that happened, the British shifted from paying the "Portuguese" a premium to the opposite policy of offering them 25 per cent less than they paid other suppliers.[13]

The 1730's marked a peak of Afro-Portuguese wealth and power, and of prosperity for the Gambia trade as a whole. Antonio Vaz was reputed to have a fortune of more than £10,000 sterling—at a time when the Royal African Company's governor was paid only £200 a year, a factor made only £40, and an ordinary soldier drew £13. But the Afro-Portuguese were gradually supplemented and then replaced by other middlemen. Some merged with local populations, as they had been doing on a small scale all along. Others drifted off to greener pastures in the Cape Verde Islands or the southern rivers, though the Gambian community kept its identity into the twentieth century, in competition with the Europeans and other Afro-European trade diasporas.[14]

The Great Trading Companies

The seventeenth century was a major watershed in the history of European trade with the wider world. The two Hispanic powers had dominated overseas activity up to 1600. After that, it would be the turn of the northerners—France, England, the Netherlands—who had only probed the system up to that point, smuggling and stealing but avoiding direct confrontation. The first to attack was the Netherlands, in the first decades of the new century, aiming principally at the Portuguese trading post em-

12. T. Thurloe to RAC, 14 March 1677–78, quoted in E. Donnan, *Documents Illustrative of the History of the Slave Trade to America*, 4 vols. (Washington, D.C., 1930–35), 1:234.

13. R. Hull to Francis Moore, 27 May 1733, quoted in Moore, *Travels*, p. 63 (see also p. 166).

14. Moore, *Travels*, pp. 49–50; Le Brasseur, "Nouvelles reflexions sur le Gambie," 10 October 1777, ANF, C6 17; Durand, *Sénégal*, 1:129–31. For wages and salaries in Senegambia see *Supplement*, appendix 14.

pire scattered from Nagasaki to Lisbon. Since the Portuguese tried to secure their monopoly by force, the Dutch had to enter by force if they were to enter eastern trade at all. Their first agency was the Dutch East India Company, whose means were a combination of commercial competition and piracy. It was followed in 1625 by the Dutch West India Company with similar means aimed at the wealth of tropical America, especially the flow of silver from the mountain backbone and the flow of sugar from the northeast bulge of Brazil.

Africa had already entered the picture of a developing South Atlantic System as far back as the 1580's, when African slaves first began to be a substantial part of the labor force in northeast Brazil; and an intercontinental economic order began to center on the productive core of tropical plantations in the Americas. Africa's involvement was crucial. Not only was it the original source of a labor force; plantation slaves in the American tropics had a higher death rate than birth rate. The net natural decrease could only be sustained by a supply of labor from Africa.

When the Dutch entered the picture more firmly with their seizure of northeast Brazil during the 1630's and 1640's, they turned back to Africa for labor and took the main Portuguese slave-trade enclaves, Luanda in Angola and Elmina on the Gold Coast. They kept Elmina into the nineteenth century, though they lost Luanda after only a brief occupation, but the significant new pattern for other European trade diasporas into Africa was to make African trading posts a normal prize of war between European maritime powers. Senegambia had no fortified posts on the model of Luanda or Elmina Castle, and the task of cross-cultural commercial representation was performed well enough by the Afro-Portuguese. From the 1650's onward, however, European powers began building fortified factories to protect their share of the trade from European rivals.

A second consequence of the Dutch seizure of Brazil was to accelerate the spread of slave plantations in the New World. In order to increase their carrying trade, the Dutch began intentionally spreading the technology of slave-grown sugar production to other regions, especially the Caribbean. Both France and England had already seized some of the Lesser Antilles when the Dutch appeared in the 1640's offering slaves for sale, sugar masters on loan, and carrying services to take the finished product to Europe. It worked, and the French and British set up sugar plantations, first in the Lesser Antilles, then in the Greater before the end of the century. Growth and spread of planting meant increasing demand for slaves, and the average annual imports of the French and British Caribbean rose about three-fold between 1651–75 and 1676–1700.[1]

1. Curtin, *Atlantic Slave Trade,* p. 119.

Senegambia was somewhat marginal to the growing slave trade. It had once been the largest single supplier of slaves among the major regions of western Africa, but that was back in the middle decades of the sixteenth century, and Senegambia's contribution to the total probably never reached 10 per cent at any period after 1640,[2] though the proportion of slaves to nonslave exports rose steadily over the century 1690–1790. (See tables 8.2 and 8.4.) Senegambia was vulnerable, however, as the tropical African region closest to Europe.

The new fortified entrepôts began with a Dutch attempt to refortify the island of Gorée in 1647,[3] followed by the first fortification of James Island in the Gambia mouth in 1651, and the first French fortification at the mouth of the Senegal in 1659. None of these was to be continuously held by European forces, and they were curiously prone to capture by enemies. James Island (then Saint Andrew's Island) was first fortified by Kurland, but it fell to a French privateer in 1659, was recaptured by Kurland in 1660, and by England in 1661—the beginning of an English establishment on the Gambia. After 1659, three islands—Saint Louis in the mouth of the Senegal, Gorée in the lee of Cape Verde, and James Island in the mouth of the Gambia—were the points capable of dominating Senegambian maritime trade, and they held this position far into the nineteenth century, though Bathurst, with an equivalent strategic location, replaced James Island in 1816.[4]

The style of warfare among Europeans of Senegambia posts involved a dominant defender and an aggressive challenger at each stage. In the first half of the seventeenth century, the Portuguese defended against the Dutch, while France and England watched, more or less inactive, on the sidelines. Then as the Dutch became supreme in the 1660's and 1670's, English and French acted together to dislodge them, just as Holland and England were to act together against France from the 1690's to the 1710's. This game of musical trading posts centered on naval power, since none of the players would accept the loss of life necessary to maintain a permanent garrison strong enough to withstand serious attack from the sea. The typical maneuver was to send out

2. Curtin, *Atlantic Slave Trade,* pp. 216, 221.

3. The Dutch had occupied Gorée as an unfortified factory since about 1617 and their first fortification dated from the 1620's, but the Portuguese sent out an expeditionary force to destroy the fortifications in 1629 and it was left unoccupied by Europeans until 1645. N. I. de Moraes, "Sur les prises de Gorée," passim; A. de Beaulieu, "Mémoire du voyage aux Indes orientales du Général Beaulieu," in M. Thévenot, *Collection des voyages,* 4 vols. (Paris, 1664), 2:1–128 (each author's section with separate pagination), p. 128.

4. A. V. Berkis, "The Reign of Duke James of Courland (1623–1682)" (Ph.D. diss., University of Wisconsin, 1956), pp. 100–124; A. W. Lawrence, *Trade Castles and Forts of West Africa* (Stanford, 1964), pp. 250–61; R. Pasquier, "Villes de Sénégal au xixe siècle," *Revue française d'histoire d'outre-mer,* 47:387–426 (1960), pp. 389–90.

a strong fleet to sweep the trading posts all along the African coast. In the Anglo-Dutch War of 1664–67, for example, the English first captured Gorée and the Dutch Gold-Coast forts, but the Dutch then sent out their own fleet to take them all back again, with the English Gold-Coast forts to boot. In 1677, the French fleet made a similar sweep against the Dutch, taking in Gorée and some of the English forts.

This ended strong Dutch participation in Senegambian trade; the French kept Gorée most of the time thereafter, and the game settled down to a duel between England and France. England captured both Saint Louis and Gorée in 1693, though it quickly lost Saint Louis. French raiders in return swept down on James Island to capture or hold it for ransom in 1702, 1704, 1708, and 1709, when the fort was finally demolished. With that, the English abandoned the place until after the Peace of Utrecht in 1713, and they got around to rebuilding the fort only in 1717.[5] Utrecht marked the return of relative stability that was to last the next forty years—the classical era of the great trading companies in control of the overseas-European diaspora in Senegambia.

The growth of fortified trading posts was one reason Europeans began to entrust their Africa trade to single national monopolies. Forts were expensive, and war risks were especially high beyond European waters. Chartered companies could take prizes as well as risks; but they needed monopoly powers in order to pass the cost of warfare on to the consumer, since they usually found that the cost of fighting could not be met through profits on trade. Authorities at the time thought the consumer should be made to pay the full cost of his overseas imports, thus relieving the taxpayer from the burden of subsidizing distant trades that might not be especially profitable but were considered in the national interests.[6]

The model after 1602 was the Dutch East India Company, originally founded to conquer the Portuguese trading post empire of the Indian Ocean and South China Sea. Many later companies kept the object of trying to control a whole ocean, like the Dutch West India Company (1625) or the French Compagnie des Indes Occidentales (1664), with theoretical power reaching all shores of the Atlantic, but those that were to be important for Senegambia were limited to a single region, and sometimes to a narrow range of commodities.

In the 1670's, both France and Britain founded new companies that touched Senegambia. The French Compagnie du Sénégal (1673) was the first

5. For European activities in Senegambia in these years see J. M. Gray, *History of Gambia* (London, 1940), pp. 133–56; P. Cultru, *Les origines de l'Afrique occidentale: Histoire du Sénégal du xve siècle à 1870* (Paris, 1910); A. Ly, *La Compagnie du Sénégal* (Paris, 1958).

6. See K. G. Davies, *The Royal African Company* (London, 1957), pp. 16–38.

of a long series bearing similar names and designed to supply slaves for the American plantations, but neither it nor its successors were very successful. As each Senegal Company failed, a new one took over its physical plant and some of its personnel, operated a few years, and then failed in its turn. Whatever the group of stockholders being milked in France, the operations in Africa carried on like those of a single company merely passing through changes in central management. This was so even after 1720, when the current Compagnie du Sénégal became an operating division of the Compagnie des Indes, a new identity that lasted until the death of the India Company in 1758. Although its privileges and jurisdiction changed frequently, the general result was the same financial failure, since no company could bear the cost of maintaining forts and soldiers on shore in Africa and still compete with other shippers who had no such expenses.[7]

The Royal African Company (1672) had a larger operating area than the Compagnie du Sénégal, but nothing like that of the Compagnie des Indes, with its spheres in the Atlantic and Indian oceans. Its grant included a legal monopoly over the British trade from Salée to the Cape of Good Hope, though most of its business was done on the shores of the Gulf of Guinea. The history of the Royal African Company was happier than that of its contemporaries on the Senegal. It began as a mildly successful monopolist during part of the 1680's, with increasing problems thereafter from the English "interlopers." In 1698, England opened the Africa trade to all English shipping, though the interlopers, now become "separate traders," paid the Royal African a 10-per-cent duty on all exports from Africa to help defray the Company's cost of maintaining fortified posts. In 1712, even this provision expired and the trade was free and open to all. It became evident after a time that the forts could not be maintained without some kind of subsidy, and, in 1730, Parliament passed a direct annual grant to the Company for that purpose. It also continued to trade on its own account, and it did trade extensively on the Gambia during the 1730's. In the 1740's, however, Company trade dropped steeply, and in 1751 Parliament substituted a new company for the old.

The new Company of Merchants Trading to Africa began as the old Company had ended—a firm whose sole business was to maintain trading enclaves open to any British shipper who paid a low fee for membership. Its business was not trade but fortifications. It disappeared from the Gambia in 1765, when a royal "Province of Senegambia" was created, though it continued elsewhere in West Africa until 1821.

---

7. Ly, *Compagnie du Sénégal*, esp. p. 151; H. Weber, *La compagnie française des Indes (1604–1875)* (Paris, 1904), passim. See *Supplement*, appendix 2.

The theoretical era of the great chartered companies thus lasted only into the 1740's, but the actual era ended long before that. In fact, it was very short indeed. Even *de jure,* the Royal African Company held its monopoly rights only from 1672 to 1698. Its various French equivalents held theirs more sporadically through the whole period 1673–1791, though Senegal trade was legally open to all French ships after the restoration of peace in 1713, with certain partial exceptions for 1720–25 and 1789–91. For all practical purposes, the era of the great chartered companies began in the early 1670's and ended during the War of the Spanish Succession, roughly forty years later.

The gap between theoretical desirability of a national slave-trade monopoly and its practical impossibility grew from the fact that the African coast was long, foreign competition was active, and plenty of fellow-subjects were willing to violate a company's legal rights. Some special advantage might accrue to the owner of an armed post at the mouth of the Gambia or Senegal. But the rivers were alternate routes to the interior; a joint or collusive monopoly would have required Anglo-French cooperation, the help of the Afro-Portuguese, and the help of the Portuguese government to close access by way of the southern rivers. Europeans of the eighteenth century were unable to muster or to sustain that degree of international cooperation, even for the most selfish cause.

The Trade Diasporas of the Europeans

As a result, the economic focus of the great trading companies began to shift away from ocean shipping. The cost of maintaining fortifications and troops on the Senegambian coast was so great that neither company could compete effectively against private shippers who had no such expenses. The companies found, however, that their presence in Africa gave them an advantage over the competition in the strictly African part of the trade. They could use their contacts with the Afro-Portuguese or the juula from the east to buy slaves, ship them to the coast, and hold them for sale to the seaborne traders. On the Senegal River after 1716, the Compagnie des Indes put its special effort into developing the Gajaaga trade. On the Gambia, the Royal African Company began in the 1720's and even more in the 1730's to develop its own upriver posts. Independent shippers, in turn, gladly paid a handsome premium for shore-side services that promised a quick turnaround.

The companies' employees on shore duty in Africa became, in short, a new form of trade diaspora manned by Europeans and hired Africans and working closely with existing Afro-Portuguese and juula networks. Saint Louis, Gorée, and James Island each became the center of a separate network specializing in

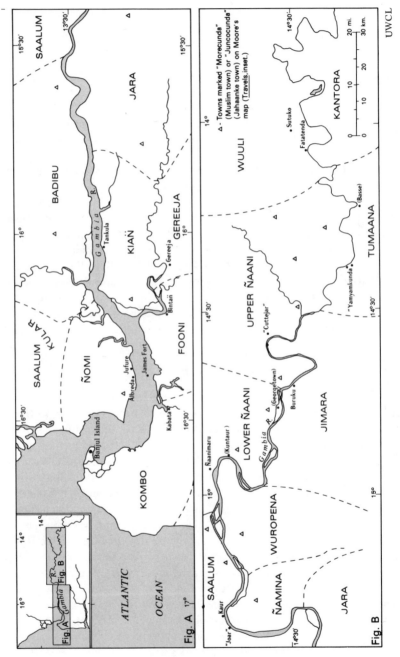

Fig. A

ATLANTIC
OCEAN

KOMBO

ÑOMI

SAALUM

SAALUM

BADIBU

KIAÑ

FOONI

GEREEJA

JARA

Banjul Island

Kabata

Bintañ

James Fort

Jufure

Albreda

Tankula

Gereeja

Gambia R.

Fig. B

SAALUM

ÑAMINA

WUROPENA

JARA

LOWER ÑAANI

UPPER ÑAANI

JIMARA

TUMAANA

WUULI

KANTORA

"Joar"

Kaur

Ñaanimaru

(Kuntaur)

"Georgetown"

Buruku

(Basse)

"Yamyamkunda"

"Cuttejar"

Fatatenda

•Sutuko

Gambia R.

△ - Towns marked "Morecunda"
(Muslim town) or "Juncoocunda"
(Jahaanke town) on Moore's
map (Travels, inset.)

0   10   20   30 km.
0   10   20 mi.

UWCL

3.2 Principal Factories on the Gambia River about 1735

waterborne trade. Each of the three islands became a multifunctional central place with a shifting group of specialized out-stations forming a hierarchy of decreasing specialization.

Gorée's network partly succeeded and partly incorporated features of the Afro-Portuguese operations of the early seventeenth century. It was originally put together by the Dutch in the 1640's and 1650's, with unfortified factories at Rufisque, Portudal, and Joal on the petite côte and customary agents, if not resident factors, on the Gambia, the Casamance, and the southern rivers. When the French captured Gorée in 1677, they kept up an equivalent group of factories, including one at Bissau during most of the early eighteenth century. The more important of these factories, like Bissau or Albreda in the Gambia, had its own subordinate out-stations, sometimes manned only on a seasonal basis or by African sub-agents—related to Bissau or Albreda in the same way each of these was related to Gorée, and Gorée was related to the Company's headquarters in Europe. But this trade diaspora was not so much French as Goréen or Franco-Wolof. Gorée itself was a connecting node between the European diaspora that conducted its business in French and a bilingual diaspora that conducted much of its business in Wolof and worked through Goréens living on the mainland. This is one reason the network was transferable from one European metropolis to another; when Gorée passed from Holland to France, and occasionally to England, the Goréen network went on working. It simply shifted to a new central place in Europe.

A largely parallel and partly competitive Gambian network normally worked the trade of the upper river as well as the coastwise trade of the petite côte and the southern rivers. Originally formed by the Afro-Portuguese, its direct political tie to Europe began with the Kurland occupation of the 1650's, which had its main base at James Island, eight riverside factories, and a battery at the present site of Banjul or Bathurst—though it is uncertain how many of these were occupied simultaneously or for how long.[1] When the Royal African Company took over, it worked the river and coastal trade with a set of five or six sloops of 34 to 45 cubic meters (30 to 40 English tons burden), large enough for the coastal trade but small enough to be useful in the upper reaches of the Gambia. Like the competing craft of the Afro-Portuguese, similar sloops are still used in the Gambia peanut trade. (See illustration.) Serving the central place at James Island was at least one factory somewhere on the petite côte, one in the southern rivers (often at Cacheu), one for each bank of the lower Gambia (often Jufure to the north

<hr/>

1. Berkis, "Duke James of Courland," pp. 102 ff.; Davies, *Royal African Company,* pp. 217–28. For European fortifications in Senegambia generally see Lawrence, *Trade Castles,* and W. Raymond Wood, "An Archaeological Appraisal of Early European Settlements in the Senegambia," *JAH,* 8:39–64 (1967).

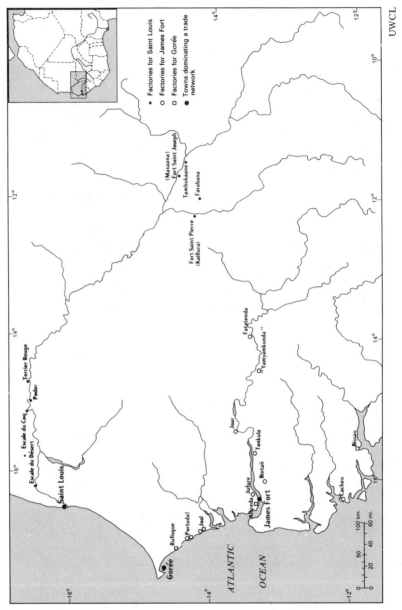

Legend:
- Factories for Saint Louis
- Factories for James Fort
- Factories for Gorée
- Towns dominating a trade network

Saint Louis
Escale du Désert
Escale du Coq
Terrier Rouge
Pedor

(Maxaana)
Fort Saint Joseph
Tambukaane
Farabana

Fort Saint Pierre
(Kaiffura)

Fatatenda
Yamyamkunda

Joar
Tankula
Bintaiŋ
Albreda Jufure
James Fort

Bissau
Cacheu

Rufisque
Portudal
Joal
Gorée

ATLANTIC
OCEAN

0   20   40   50   60 mi.
0   50   100 km.

16°   14°   12°   10°

3.3 European Trade Networks of the 1730's

108

and Gereeja or Bintañ to the south). Upriver, it was essential to have a factory somewhere on the northern bend of the river in Saalum or Ñaani–Kaur, Ñaanimaru (Nianimaru), and Kuntaui were used at various times. That region was the normal terminus for seagoing ships, as it is today, but the English tended to follow Afro-Portuguese precedent and trade still higher up. Today, the functional descendent of this highest post is Basse, but Sutuko and Fattatenda in Wuuli also served at different times.

The third trade diaspora had its coastal base at Saint Louis, looking north to the desert and inland upriver, not to the coastwise traffic. The desert was important for gum-Senegal gathered and sold on the river mainly through zwāya Moors. Some gum was also sold on the Mauritanian coast, at Portendick near present-day Nouakchott or Arguin further north in the lee of Cape Blanc; but the river was a better route to the gum forests and traders with access to the river rarely traded on the coast.

The principal points of river trade were known as *escales,* suggesting a mere stopping point rather than a permanent factory, and they were actually seasonal fairs held at customary places from February to May each year. The location of these escales was remarkably stable from the late seventeenth century onward, with the escale du Désert in Waalo and the escales du Coq and Terrier Rouge in Fuuta near Podor. All three could be reached from Saint Louis throughout the year, and the higher escales operated part of the time under the protection of a fort at Podor.[2] Higher still, beyond Fuuta, were one or more points of trade in Gajaaga and vicinity, subordinate to a fort at Maxaana in the eighteenth century or Bakel in the early nineteenth. The Gajaaga posts were thus a subsystem of the larger network based on Saint Louis.

An Era of Transition, 1750–1816

The long period of relative stability in Anglo-French affairs ended for Senegambia with a new period of active hostilities beginning in 1757. The era had ended somewhat earlier with the financial failure of the

2. The fort at Podor was first built in 1743 and used by the Compagnie des Indes until the English occupation of Saint Louis in 1758. The English experimented with various kinds of occupation but then abandoned the fort to the occupation of their interpreter, who had been the African mayor of Podor, in effect the African notable of the region who had acted for them in relations with the Futaanke. The French returned once more in the period from 1783 to 1792 but again abandoned the fort to African control until 1854. See "Mémoire du roi au sieur Schmaltz," 18 May 1816, in C. Shefer, ed., *Instructions générales données de 1763 à 1870 aux gouverneurs et ordonnateurs des établissements français en Afrique occidentale,* 2 vols. (Paris, 1921), 1:230; return dated 16 March 1765, CO 388/52.

great chartered companies, and it was obvious as early as the mid-1740's that their failure was beyond useful rescue through government subsidies and other aids. But war and financial collapse were overshadowed in Senegambia by a far more serious catastrophe. In the 1750's, drought, locusts, famine, and disease sharply reduced Senegambian population along the sahal, coming as they did on top of decades of chronic dry weather and the raids of the Ormankoobe.

It is not yet possible to trace the full ramifications of this disaster for Senegambian societies, but the crisis itself is clear from the records of the Europeans on the coast. It began with three inadequate rainy seasons in 1746, 1747, and 1748. The year 1749 brought a normal harvest along the lower Senegal, but grain reserves were not yet replenished by 1750, when the rains were again insufficient on the lower river. The famine could be relieved in part by importing grain from the upper Senegal, which had a normal harvest in 1750, but now even the Gambia was brought into the disaster area by swarms of desert locusts, which remained a danger here and there in the region during most of the next decade, with an especially severe attack on Waalo in 1758. Harvests in Wolof country were again bad in 1751 and terrible in 1752, so that people began to slaughter and eat their reserves of cattle. Slaves held in Saint Louis awaiting shipment began to die of malnutrition. Then, in 1753, water was more than plentiful; the Senegal flooded half of Saint Louis and washed away part of the curtain wall from the fort at Maxaana, but the floodwater came from distant rainfall upriver. By 1754 many people on the jeeri land in Kajor and Jolof were so close to starvation they streamed north to the river banks where food could still be grown on the waalo land in Waalo and Fuuta. Many were simply enslaved by the Futan-koobe and Waalo-Waalo, who sold them to the French at Saint Louis. The Compagnie des Indes that year shipped more slaves than it had ever done before, though slaves and traders at entrepôt had to be kept alive with food imported from France. In 1755, the harvest was again sufficient for current needs in the northern Wolof country, though reserves continued dangerously low. Saint Louis was especially hard hit when the British blockade began in 1757. The French commander finally drove some five hundred slaves out of the fort to fend for themselves, rather than let them die of starvation in captivity. Even after the British captured the island in May 1758 and the rains came again, desert locusts prolonged the famine. By the end of the year, the British themselves were forced to send a ship off to the Cape Verde Islands in hope of buying provisions that were unavailable on the mainland. After that, the worst was over, but the natural catastrophe must have been far more serious across the whole northern belt of savanna than the European records could possibly indicate.[1]

1. See *Supplement,* appendix 1 and the sources cited there.

The last years of the famine were the first years of the new phase of belligerency between English and French posts in Senegambia. The long truce had lasted with only minor infractions from 1713 down to 1757. Even when France and England went to war in Europe during 1743–48, peace was kept in Senegambia until 1745, and then the only belligerent act of importance was an English attack on the unfortified French post at Albreda. Another breach of the truce involving Albreda took place in 1750–51, but peace returned thereafter and for nearly a year after Britain and France formally went to war again in 1756. But from 1757 to 1815, Britain and France were at war more than half the time,[2] and war elsewhere meant raids and counter-raids in Senegambia as well, returning to the pre-1713 pattern of altering fortunes with the appearnce of a major naval force. Two major shifts were involved in this new phase. In May–June 1758, Britain captured both Gorée and Saint Louis, keeping Saint Louis (renamed Fort Lewis) and returning Gorée to France in the peace of 1763. Later, in 1779, France repeated the maneuver—recaptured Saint Louis and destroyed James Fort, which was left unoccupied with the return of peace, though private British merchants still kept posts on the Gambia. The new period of warfare after 1793 was less decisive, though Britain again held the upper hand. British forces captured Gorée in 1800 and held it till the end of the war, with the exception of a few months in 1804. They captured Saint Louis once more in 1809 and remained in occupation till 1817.[3] That ended the period of transition and ushered in a new period of comparative stability superficially like the situation before 1750, with a French enclave commanding the mouth of the Senegal and the British commanding the mouth of the Gambia.

From the Senegambian point of view, as before, it probably made little difference which European power controlled which posts, so long as no one power held them all and tried to monopolize the trade of the region—and that never happened. After the British sweep of 1758, Gorée and its network remained in French hands. After the French sweep of 1779, the English kept their trade contacts in the Gambia even though they lacked a fortified post. Even the levels of the slave trade remained remarkably constant, though the British carried the bulk of it in the 1760's and 1770's, while the French carried most in the 1780's.

One innovation at this time was common to the Atlantic trade and to the

2. That is, 1756–63, 1778–83, 1793–1802, 1803–15.

3. The older authorities, Gray, *Gambia*, and Cultru, *Sénégal*, are still the most convenient for the general course of military affairs of the European posts, but for more detailed and recent studies of shorter periods see L. Jore, "Les établissements français sur la côte occidentale d'Afrique de 1758 à 1809," *RHCF*, 5:3–477 (1964); F. Deroure, "La vie quotidienne à Saint-Louis par ses archives (1779–1809)," *BIFAN*, 26:397–439 (1964); H. Dodwell, "Le Sénégal sous la domination anglaise," *RHCF*, 4:267–300 (1916).

Senegambian internal trade alike; new groups of merchants began to participate. On the African side, the Jahaanke seem to have lost some of their earlier
prominence, while other juula groups became more important. On the coasts,
the French and English companies were joined by others including North
Americans, who became especially prominent during the Napoleonic Wars
when their neutral status made them welcome in the blockaded French
trading posts.[4]

After the 1750's, the Europeans drew back from some of their earlier
dreams of monopolizing Senegambian trade or exercising informal control
over Senegambian states. The 1720's and 1730's had been a period when
elaborate schemes for political and economic control had flowed back to
Europe along the communications network to the metropolis. Both French
and British officials considered seriously the possibility of trying to seize
control of the Bambuhu gold fields, as Portugal had done briefly in the
sixteenth century. Though none of the projects advanced beyond the stage of
feasibility studies,[5] after the 1750's they had even less chance of a serious
hearing in Europe. Both home governments had learned by then that monopoly was not possible in the slave trade, and both had learned the mortality
cost of trying to station Europeans on the African coast. From the 1750's to
the end of the Napoleonic Wars was an era of declining European interest in
Senegambia. Even though the peak decade of the whole Atlantic slave trade
was the 1780's, slave exports from Senegambia were generally lower in the
second half of the century than they had been in the first. In spite of brief
wartime peaks in garrison size, fewer Europeans were resident in Senegambia
during the first decade of the nineteenth century than at any equivalent
period since 1650. It was as though the European juula retracted slightly
from their Senegambian diaspora toward the end of the slave trade, only to
return in greater force with the development of "legitimate trade" in the
1820's and later.

The Afro-French Community of the Eighteenth Century

The apparent withdrawal of the Europeans was both a cause
and a result of the increasing importance of the Afro-European communities
based on the European forts but stretching into the interior with their own

4. See G. E. Brooks, Jr., *Yankee Traders, Old Coasters & African Middlemen: A
History of American Legitimate Trade with West Africa in the Nineteenth Century*
(Boston, 1970), esp. pp. 9–72.

5. The French archives are especially rich in detailed projects, especially ANF, C6 9
and 10, and many of the relevant documents are printed in Machat, *Documents*. English
plans of the 1730's are treated in Curtin, *Africa Remembered*, pp. 17–34, Grant, *The
Fortunate Slave*, pp. 159–99, and Gray, *Gambia*, pp. 198–214.

trade diaspora. The Afro-French community was formed somewhat earlier than its Gambian counterpart, as would be expected from the somewhat larger number of shore-based French throughout the eighteenth century. The garrison at James Island was usually quite small. In 1719, for example, a force of only six men unsuccessfully defended the fort against pirates. In 1721, the Company reacted by sending out 170 recruits, but a year later death and desertion had reduced their numbers to 26.[1] The total was sometimes larger for short periods, but it was rarely more than 50 for any length of time. The European population of Saint Louis, on the other hand, was 60 as early as 1685, and the Compagnie des Indes kept a staff of 100 to 200 during the 1720's and 1730's. (See *Supplement,* appendix 4.)

These differences are explained by the same geographical factors that gave the rivers their unequal advantages as arteries of trade. The Gambia's open route for oceangoing ships meant that ship's personnel could take care of many services, like bulking and storing produce on board, since there was no need to transship at the mouth of the river. Saint Louis was therefore a central place with more functions to perform in aid of river traffic than James Fort had, and the French may have simply followed precedent in making subsidiary points like Maxaana and Podor more elaborate and multifunctional than the Gambian equivalent. In any event, the British occupation of Senegal in 1758–79 dispensed altogether with the upriver forts.

Navigation on the Senegal was also more labor intensive than it was on the Gambia, which meant in turn that the French had to associate more Africans in the actual carrying trade along their network. Where a ship on the Gambia could drift with the tide, the current on the Senegal above Podor varied between 1.5 and 4 knots, with an overall average at about 3, and the river could only be used during the few months it was in flood.[2] Winds were unfavorable most of the time and rarely strong enough to overcome the force of the current. As a result, it was often possible to move upstream only by kedging, carrying an anchor forward by canoe and then pulling the boat up to the anchor with a windlass—or, more commonly, by lining or cordelling, putting part of the crew on shore or in the shallows to pull the boat ahead with a long tow line. The upstream trip was so slow that larger craft made only one trip to Gajaaga and back during a single high season, though the smallest and fastest river boats could leave in late June, get back to Saint Louis by October, and then make a second trip before December.

African boatmen had developed appropriate techniques long before the Europeans began to work the river route, and they had sizeable craft in river trade. One report of 1675 mentions "canoes" with a capacity of 15.8 cubic meters (14 English tons burden). Other boats of a similar size were sent out

1. Davies, "The Living and the Dead," passim; Gray, *Gambia,* pp. 157 ff.
2. Annual report of the post of Galam for 1827, 2 April 1828, ANF-OM. Sénégal IV 15.

from France and may have had partly French crews in the late seventeenth century, but the crews were quickly Africanized. By 1750, the typical crew was made up of about 25 sailors, called *laptots* in Senegalese French, and 2 to 4 officers who were usually free men from Saint Louis and often Christian converts.[3]

The laptots, on the other hand, were usually domestic slaves owned by the well-to-do of Saint Louis, who rented out their people in return for a half share of the wages, the other half going to the man himself. The term *laptot* is a Gallicized form of the Wolof word for sailor, and it originally had the same meaning in French. In time, however, it shifted to mean any African who worked with the Europeans, whether as sailor, soldier, clerk, or administrator.[4] In 1755, a partial occupational census of Saint Louis enumerated the African male population as 15 masters of boats, 15 mates, 36 sailors, 3 chief translators, 36 journeyman workers, 98 Company slaves, and 550 slaves belonging to the other inhabitants. Since it would have taken about 250 men to run the fifteen boats, about 200 of the private slaves and many of the Company slaves must have been sailors as well, which would have meant that about 40 per cent of the male inhabitants were rivermen.[5] By the 1780's, as many as 300 to 400 men made the annual trip to Gajaaga.

These men were Afro-French, *Saintlouisien,* or simply Senegalese. They worked with the French and adopted some of the French way of life, but they were not necessarily descendents of French fathers, and they were more often Muslim than Christian. Other Africans worked with the French company in responsible positions. In 1724, a certain Maalik Kuumba, classified as an interpreter, was the commandant of the small out-station the Compagnie des Indes maintained at Tambukaane in Gajaaga, while Ali Moodi, described simply as a laptot, ran the factory at Lani. A similar Afro-French partnership developed in the trade diaspora based on Gorée, where the captains and crews of the coasters to the petite côte and the southern rivers were either Afro-Portuguese[6] or Lebu, the Wolof-speaking fishing people of the Cape Verde coastal region.

3. Chambonneau in Carson I. A. Ritchie, ed., "Deux textes sur le Sénégal (1673–1677)," *BIFAN,* 30:289–353 (1968), p. 320; Barbot, *Guinea,* pp. 17–19; "Mémoire générale sur le commerce du Sénégal (1718), ANF, C6 14; Saint-Robert to CI, 28 December 1722, ANF C6 7; unsigned memorandum dated 1750 from the internal evidence, C6 29.

4. J. C. Nardin, "Recherches sur les 'gourmets' d'Afrique occidentale," *Revue française d'histoire d'outre-mer,* 53:215–44 (1966).

5. Conseil du Sénégal, "Reponse au memoire de Sieur Godheu de Fevrier 1754," undated, ANF, C6 14.

6. Procès verbaux de Pierre Charpentier, 25 April and 31 March 1974, ANF, C6 7; "Observations sur l'isle de Gorée," enclosed with Rastel de Rocheblave to Boniface, n.d. but 1773 on internal evidence, ANF, C6 16.

Not only the commerce but also the defense of the "European" posts was partly Africanized. The French bought slaves to be trained as soldiers, even as their African neighbors did. In order to be effective in possible local wars, they had to be foreign to the region, and so many of the French slave soldiers were from the far interior that they were all called "Bambara." On the Gambia at the same period, they were more often called "castle slaves," and the Royal African Company occasionally exchanged slaves with the Gold Coast so that the castle slaves in either post would be alien to the local culture and unlikely to escape.[7] Like the African slave armies, these men were remarkably loyal, with an apparently smaller incidence of garrison revolts than was found among the European soldiers. At least one Bambara soldier kidnapped near a fort and carried away into slavery was able to escape and return to his post, even though the return simply exchanged one kind of slavery for another.[8]

Both in Saint Louis and Gorée, the role of the Afro-French became markedly more important from the middle of the eighteenth century, as the weakening of the Compagnie des Indes gave them a larger share of general commerce. The British in 1758 found Afro-French boatmen in sole control of the Gajaaga trade, and they left it that way. They also formalized their political relations with the Afro-French community by recognizing an African official they called a mayor. The operative word here is "recognize," not "appoint" or "create," since the office paralleled the role of the Wolof *Jawdi mbul,* who represented the free-born lineages of Kajor. He was a spokesman for the lamanate and the old ruling class in dealing with the more recently created office of Damel, and equivalents were present elsewhere in Senegambia, as with the Great Jaraf of Siin. The French had probably dealt informally with local notables even before 1758. When they returned to Gorée in 1763, they continued formal recognition, simply changing the title from mayor to *maire,* and they did the same at Saint Louis in 1779.[9]

In either case, the title was something of a misnomer; the maire was more than a mere executive officer for municipal government, though he was that too. In Saint Louis, he served as intermediary between the French commander and two subordinate *chefs de quartier,* who were in turn charged with the two wards of the town, north and south of the fort at the midpoint of the

---

7. T 70/55, passim, esp. African Committee to Rogers and others, 14 September 1727.

8. Levens, Report of 10 July 1725, ANF, C6 9. A copy is also found in BN, FF, NA, 9339, f. 144.

9. For the office of mayor or maire see Colvin, "Kajor," pp. 83–88, 90, 94; Jore, "Les établissements français," p. 257; P. Lintingre, *Voyages du Sieur de Glicourt à la côte occidentale d'Afrique pendant les années 1778 et 1779 (Dakar, 1966),* esp. pp. 135–40, 165–66.

long, narrow island. In judicial affairs, the chefs de quartier had original jurisdiction in cases not involving Europeans, and the maire heard appeals. He was also responsible for raising and commanding the local militia, a matter of great power and responsibility in a place where the mortality rate of European troops was so high. Finally, he acted as a kind of minister of foreign affairs for the French governor, carrying out diplomatic negotiations with the Damel, the Brak of Waalo, and other African rulers.

With the French Revolution in 1789, the office of maire became elective, but this made little actual difference in the person who held the title. Even when the office had been appointive in theory, the governor had no practical option but to name the recognized community leader. With the reoccupation of 1817, French officials began with the misconception that they could appoint whomever they wanted, but they gave up in 1823 and accepted François Pellegrin, who remained in office until 1836 because he alone had the recognition and stature in the community. Meanwhile, the office of *Tamsir* of Saint Louis was created for the religious head of the Muslim community, with judicial functions in Muslim law and responsibility for Arabic-language correspondence between the governor and nearby states.

It was only with the 1840's that the French began seriously trying to retrieve these dispersed powers. They set up a Direction des Affaires Extérieures in 1847, as a local-level ministry of foreign affairs under a European official. By the 1850's the mayoralty had made most of the transition from the Wolof to the French institution.

Even if there had been no African institution to use as a model, the exercise of great de facto power by local notables is typical of a colonial situation where governors come for only short terms and local men stay on and on. The Afro-French community of Gorée or of Saint Louis could usually have its way when it felt strongly about an issue, so long as the issue was not fundamental to the French position. On Gorée, for example, French officials tried in the 1770's to force Goréens to sell "excess" domestic slaves for service in the Americas. The idea ran head on into Wolof law and custom, which prohibited the sale of domestic slaves without cause and judicial condemnation. One effort to force the issue almost led to a bloody insurrection, and the plan had to be dropped.[10] In Saint Louis, the principal issue of the 1770's onward was the threat to reestablish a privileged trading company, and it became a reality briefly in the late 1780's.[11] In 1802, the governor,

10. Le Brasseur, "Questions sur nos possessions de la côte d'Afrique avec les réponses de M. Le Brasseur," c. 1776, ANF, C6 17. Lajaille, "Suite au mémoire sur le commerce presenté en 1784," ANF, C6 18, says that a bloody insurrection actually did take place, but the evidence of Le Brasseur, who was commandant at Gorée in 1774–77, is preferred.
11. Petition to Castries, 26 July 1785, ANF, C6 18.

Colonel Laserre, tried to create a monopoly of the gum trade on his own authority, but Charles and François Pellegrin, the later maire, organized a coup, seized the governor and his wife, and deported them to Gorée. Since the governor had been acting illegally and the war with England began again the next year, Paris decided to overlook the incident, and the Pellegrins won their point.[12]

By the 1780's, the economic organization of the Senegal River trade was partly controlled by French firms, and partly by the Afro-French of Saint Louis. A new chartered company with varying privileges was again in operation. A second French firm, Aubry de La Fosse et Compagnie of Nantes, also worked with French capital through a French manager in Saint Louis. Although the two French firms were the largest single carriers in the river trade, the majority of the trade was in the hands of the Afro-French merchant community of the port, and the actual carriage of the goods, command of the ships, and negotiation with African trade partners along the river was done by men from Saint Louis.

They were a mixture that ran the gamut from Africans with no French ancestors, through a large group of *métis*, to a few metropolitan French. The important characteristic of this community was cultural mixture, not racial mixture, and the most effective of the traders from France were those who could cross the cultural line between Europe and Africa in their commercial relations. One career, that of Paul Benis, illustrates the point. Benis originally came to Gorée in the early 1770's as part of the human flotsam that drifted into the lower ranks of the European establishments on the African coast. He was illiterate, but he survived. He learned Wolof. When the French reoccupied Saint Louis, he came with them, but living in African style and enjoying the confidence of his African neighbors. By the mid-1780's, he had become one of the most important merchants. Cultural mixture could come from the other side as well. A certain Dubois, of purely African descent in spite of his name, also had the reputation at that time as one of the most skillful traders on the river.[13]

The distribution of the Gajaaga trade according to firms was recorded for certain years, and the records help to indicate the way economic power was distributed among the French firms and the Afro-French traders from Saint Louis (see table 3.1), at least for a brief period. Since slaves formed such an overwhelming part of the total trade, the division of slave shipments between carriers is the indicative figure. In 1786, the Company's monopoly was still effective only for gum, and its river boats were only in the middle range of size. Two of Aubry de La Fosse's vessels carried an average of 142 slaves each,

12. Jore, "Les établissements français," pp. 164–79.

13. Saugnier, *Relation de plusieurs voyages à la côte d'Afrique, à Maroc, au Sénégal, à Gorée, à Galem* . . . (Paris, 1791), pp. 175–80.

Table 3.1
River Trade, Gajaaga to Saint Louis, 1786 and 1788

Total returns

Commodity and measure	(1) Quantity		(2) Value in sterling		(3) Mean per cent of total return both years
	(a) 1786	(b) 1788	(a) 1786	(b) 1788	
Slaves, number	766	964	£20,199	£25,421	98.7
Ivory, metric tons	2.04	3.15	28	43	0.2
Gold, kgs	2.6	3.3	234	297	1.2
Total			20,461	25,761	100.0

Returns in slaves, by carrier

Carrier	(4) Number of vessels		(5) Number of slaves		(6) Slaves per vessel		(7) Per cent of tota slaves carried	
	(a) 1786	(b) 1788	(a) 1786	(b) 1788	(a) 1786	(b) 1788	(a) 1786	(b) 178
Compagnie du Sénégal	3	6	120	345	40	58	15.7	35.
Aubry de la Fosse et Cie.	3	–	296	–	99	–	38.6	–
Other European merchants								
Paul Benis	2							
Floquet	1							
Vigneux	1							
Duchesne	1							
	5	–	150	–	30	–	19.6	...
Habitants of Saint Louis	11	37	200	619	18	16	26.1	64.
Total	22	43	766	964	35	22	100.0	100.

Sources: "Sénégal 1786, voyage de Galam" and "Voyage de Galam 1788," in ANF, C6 1
Values are the average current selling prices in Saint Louis in the 1780's, from Supplement, tab
A15.6. Data for 1786 omit one royal ship which accompanied the fleet. Of vessels listed for th
habitants in 1788, no single owner had more than two.

which helps to explain why the two French companies carried 54 per cent of
the slaves shipped downriver that year. The five vessels belonging to the
overseas Europeans were again in the same size range as those of the
Compagnie du Sénégal, as were three of the eleven belonging to habitants of
Saint Louis. The remainder of the Saintlouisien craft carried only 6 to 15
slaves each.

In 1787 no fleet went to Gajaaga, because Abdul Kaader, the Almaami of
Fuuta Tooro, demanded a higher toll for passage than the Senegalese govern-

ment would agree to. When trade resumed in 1788, the Compagnie du Sénégal was ready to exercise its new monopoly right, and Aubry de La Fosse disappeared from the scene, along with other overseas Europeans who could not qualify as *habitants* of Saint Louis. The Company intended to monopolize the Gajaaga trade and planned a set of four or five out-factories dependent on Fort Saint Joseph at Maxaana, but it conceded Senegalese the right to trade as far as the mouth of the Faleme (in effect, anywhere in lower Gajaaga), though even there they hoped to keep some control over the trade through credit and price controls.[14]

The columns marked (b) in table 3.1 show the result. Though the Company now sent six vessels on its own account, only one of them brought back more than 100 slaves. The rest were in the medium range. The habitants, on the other hand, sent out thirty-seven boats, most of them small, and succeeded in bringing back nearly two-thirds of the slaves. At the heyday of the Compagnie des Indes, a half-century earlier, they had merely handled the Company's boats; they still did, but they were now capable of moving half the trade in their own boats.

Given the unsettled state of the French government after 1789, conflict between the Compagnie du Sénégal, with its legal privilege, and the habitants, with their commercial power, was not long in coming. In 1790, the habitants refused to sail under the terms offered, and the Company was not able to send any fleet to Gajaaga. In August, the Brakna Moors also forced the Company to evacuate the fort at Podor, but the strike of the Saintlouisiens ended its commercial operations on the Senegal.[15] In January 1791, the monopoly was repealed by the National Assembly.

The trade enclaves and trading posts of the Afro-French diaspora were economically dependent on the surrounding African societies as well as on the central places further up the hierarchy. In this way they were different from the juula towns, which had an agricultural component to make them self-sufficient in food. The Franco-African island enclaves were truly specialized trade centers that bought their food from the mainland, and often from a distance. Throughout the eighteenth and nineteenth centuries, Saint Louis imported a great deal of millet from Fuuta Tooro, often from as far as Bundu, beyond the Gajaaga trading posts. This specialization meant, among other things, that the Afro-French trading towns tended to be smaller than nearby African towns which included large numbers of agricultural workers. Where the larger African trading towns had as many as 3,000 to 5,000 inhabitants in the sixteenth century, Gorée in 1767 had reached only 1,000— compared to its nearby contemporaries, that would make it roughly one-third the size of Lambai, capital of Bawol, the smallest of the Wolof states. Two

14. Conseil du Sénégal to CI, 14 July 1787, ANF, C6 19.
15. Blanchot de Verly to MC, no. 29, July 1790, ANF, C6 20.

mainland towns within sight of the island had 3,000 people each, Dakar on the Cape Verde Peninsula and Rufisque at the beginning of the petite côte. Saint Louis had reached 3,000 people only in the 1760's, while Bathurst (and its predecessor at James Island) were well below that size until the 1830's. (See *Supplement*, appendix 7.)

The European trading towns were also demographically dependent on the surrounding countries. None of them even tried to establish a self-sustaining community of overseas Europeans. European women were almost totally absent, and the number of European men was always a volatile figure, as new drafts arrived from Europe and were then thinned out rapidly by disease. The result was a community with a continuous life, but sustained from three different sources—immigrant European males, immigrant African females, and the locally born, who were normally either métis or African. The strongest of these streams was that of African females. All through the eighteenth century, the non-European population of Saint Louis had highly atypical sex ratios. Expressed as males per 1,000 females, the rate was 623 in 1767, 630 in 1776, 586 in 1779. It became more normal in the nineteenth century, reaching 959 in 1832, but even then, the change came from an excess of males over females in the slave population, balancing a sex ratio of only 871 among free Africans.

This peculiar sex ratio was both a cause and a result of the fact that the Europeans tended to establish semipermanent liaisons with African women, *mariages à la mode du pays,* as they were called. This custom not only led to the growth of a métis population, it also influenced the socioeconomic status of the ladies, who were known as *signares* (or *senhoras* on the Gambia, where the same custom prevailed). They received presents from their men, and they sometimes inherited. When one man died, as often happened, or returned to France, as occasionally happened, the signare found herself free to take another husband with a similar life expectancy. As a result, she became wealthy, with most of her capital tied up in real estate or slaves who worked as laptots on the boats and paid her half their earnings. In time, income and savings of the signares became a source of further expansion for the Afro-French trade diaspora—though they also spent a good deal on show, maintaining the large entourage of slaves the French officials complained of and attracting minstrels from the mainland to serve them as they formerly served the Wolof nobility. Nevertheless, and in spite of the romantic picture sometimes painted of the gay young noblemen and the beautiful signares in the twilight of the old regime, the society was ultimately artificial. It was sustained from the outside by a continuous one-way drain of men from Europe, whose function was to support and further an even larger drain of men from Africa to America.

The people least transient or alien were the métis, the class par excellence for cross-cultural mediation—at least in the first generation, when they had close contact with an African mother, sometimes followed by a period of education in France. The most prominent members of the Franco-African merchant group were often métis, like Charles Thévenot, who served as mayor under the English from about 1764 to 1778. Other prominent families of the period were the Estouphan de Saint-Jean family, who claimed descent from a former governor of Gorée, the Le Juge, Blondin, and Pellegrin, or the family of Charles Cornier, maire of Saint Louis through the 1780's and 1790's. As early as the English occupation, however, the prominent métis families tended to marry within their own circle, producing a self-perpetuating community that tended to be progressively integrated into the dominant patterns of European culture.[16] Meanwhile, other métis, less well-to-do, were absorbed in the dominant Wolof culture of the great majority. The cultural mixture that often followed racial mixture thus showed a tendency in that social setting to move in the direction of either French or Wolof norms.

Overseas Traders and the Politics of the Neighborhood

The enclaved Europeans of the trade diasporas were in a peculiar position in relation to the African states around them. The best long-run policy for the maximum passage of trade was to maintain a strict neutrality, just as the African juula tried to do. But strict neutrality and pacifism were not possible so long as the Europeans were often at war with one another; the very fact that they armed their forts against other Europeans created a temptation to use the arms for other, more local ends. They must also have found it psychologically difficult to know that the real military power of their home countries was so much greater than any Senegambian power, yet to find themselves almost always weaker than any state in their African neighborhood.

Available military power was itself a peculiar combination of advantages and disadvantages. The Europeans were reasonably safe from African attack inside one of their stone-built forts, since they alone had effective artillery. They also had an overwhelming potential power in the fleet that might be called down from Europe, with its mobile artillery that could strike anywhere along the coast and up the rivers (though with special problems caused by the

16. Lintingre, *Voyages de Glicourt,* p. 137, printed a marriage act between Jean Jacques Thévenot and Marie Magdeleine Estoupan de Saint-Jean in 1779 at which nine of the eleven signatories signed in French, including four women. See also L. P. Raybaud, "L'administration du Sénégal de 1781 à 1784: L'affaire Dumontet," *Annales africaines,* issue from 1968, pp. 133–72, esp. p. 151. See G. Brooks, *Yankee Traders,* passim, for local trading communities of Saint Louis and Gorée.

Senegal bar). But the fleet could never stay very long because of mortality from disease, nor could European landing parties march far from the shore. This meant that the Europeans in the enclaves were capable of lightning blows of great power, even though their year-in, year-out position was one of military inferiority.

They sometimes tended to overplay their brief moments of triumph, especially in the early decades before they learned the conventions and usages of local war and politics. In 1679, for example, when Ducasse led a major French naval force down the African coast in pursuit of the Dutch, he followed his attack on Gorée with one on the mainland states of Kajor, Bawol, and Siin, forcing them to sign treaties ceding to France the entire coastline from Cape Verde to the Gambia River, *en propriété et Seigneurie,"* and reaching 25 kms into the interior.[1] It is doubtful that the African parties to those treaties had either authority to sign or the knowledge of what they agreed to, but that was beside the point. France simply lacked the ability to enforce any such concession, and to have tried seriously would have destroyed the commercial value of Gorée. The French therefore kept Gorée and waited two hundred years before trying again for equivalent territorial authority.

This is not to say that the enclaved Europeans stayed clear of local entanglements. Their normal pattern of behavior was to support whatever existing alliance of African states seemed most likely to further their cause. The Fuulbe called the chief of the French Senegal concession *Laamido Ndar,* King of Ndar, the African name for Saint Louis, and he often followed the role implied—the head of a small secular state, whose principal local interest was to prevent a large state from dominating the region. The French joined with other small secular states whenever such a threat appeared, as it did with Nasîr al-Dîn's attempt to build an Islamic empire in the 1670's. Saint Louis's garrison was not large enough to be important, but the militia could also act, and it was possible to help out with material aid like guns and powder. When Saint-Adon allied with Samba Gelaajo Jegi against Saatigi Konko Bubu Muusa in 1737, the Company had already begun to subsidize Waalo attacks on Fuuta.[2]

The most serious problem for any of the European enclave was the African state outside the walls—Waalo for Saint Louis, Ñomi for James Island and later for Bathurst. The kings of Ñomi held an especially complex position, since they were landlords of the English for the island and a post on the bank at Jufure, as they were also landlords of the French for Albreda; and the three posts were in sight of one another. The various fees for anchoring, taking on wood and water, or the passage of goods down the river became a

1. Treaty is found in ANF, C6 1.
2. Conseil du Sénégal to CI, 6 November 1736, ANF, C6 11.

major part of Ñomi's revenue, which Ñomi wanted to keep flowing in. A threat appeared in the late 1750's, when the new Company of Merchants Trading to Africa no longer performed the bulking services of the Royal African Company. British slavers therefore found it worthwhile to sail upriver and trade here and there along the banks. Ñomi wanted to go on collecting tolls regardless of the point of trade, and the shippers resented paying tolls merely for the privilege of sailing past.[3]

Up to this point, the quarrel between Ñomi and the British was the ordinary quarrel between any group of juula and a state whose territory they had to cross. Both sides wanted to maximize their own share of the profit. Britain threatened to stop "customs" payments, and Ñomi countered by threatening to stop ships from taking on extra crew and interpreters in Ñomi, as they had been doing for decades. The British had the guns of the fort, but Ñomi had a fleet of war "canoes," each carrying forty or fifty men armed with muskets. For a time it was a standoff, but quarrels of this kind rarely led to serious fighting or a long stoppage of trade, since neither side profited when trade stopped altogether.

The strategic nature of the quarrel changed, however, when a second European trade network entered the picture, as France did in 1764 with a return to the old factory at Albreda—unoccupied for the past six years and only briefly occupied since 1745. Since the British refused French ships permission to pass James Fort on their way up the Gambia, the French had to trade in Ñomi and pay Ñomi tolls, setting up a natural Franco-Ñomi congruence of interest as the British had earlier created a natural alliance between the French and the Afro-Portuguese. The British, still following the European norms of trade rivalry, decided to punish Ñomi for welcoming the French back to Albreda by cutting off payments they had been making for each ship that passed upriver. This time, the result was open war between Ñomi and James Island, and the war spread into a general commercial war.

Saalum also had an interest in the matter, since the trade that Gorée hoped to divert to Albreda formerly passed overland to the Saalum River and hence to Gorée. The British ships Ñomi was trying to hold to the lower river also did much of their trade in Saalum, so that Ñomi's actions hurt Saalum in two different ways. Saalum entered the war on the side of Britain and against Ñomi. (See map 3.1 above, p. 118.) The French then entered the war against Saalum, sending a warship up the Saalum River to do whatever damage it could do to villages along the bank. At that point, France and Britain, having just made peace in 1763 in the rest of the world, went to war by proxy in Senegambia along the chain that pitted James Fort against Ñomi against Saalum against Gorée. But the circle never quite closed with direct hostilities between France and Britain. At the metropolitan level, France refused to

3. Joseph Debat to African Committee, Gambia, 1 August 1759, T 70/30.

renew the war for the sake of an obscure trading post and ordered Gorée not to pursue Gambia trade quite so energetically. Locally, Gorée had opened its trade offensive at Albreda with an offer to raise the price paid for slaves by 10 per cent. They actually succeeded in persuading one caravan of 500 to 600 slaves to come on down along the north bank from Ñaanimaru, but then the French sailors began to die so fast that the commander at Albreda was forced to break off and return to Gorée with his main force while he still had enough men to work the ships. As it turned out, the French were only able to buy 92 of the slaves, presumably leaving the remaining 400 or 500 to be sold to the English at the old price.[4]

The crisis that began in 1764 dragged on as an Anglo-Ñomi war, lasting until 1768, and it illustrates a new stage in the changing relations between the trade enclave and its hosts. Relations had begun in the late seventeenth century, when Ñomi was locally strong and the Europeans were comparatively weak. James Fort was content enough at that stage to work through the Afro-Portuguese and the sloop trade, without sending oceangoing ships to the middle and upper reaches of the river. With time, the Ñomi ruling class fell into a parasitic relationship to the post. They had no commercial tradition of their own and few other resources, so they settled down to live on the trade that passed their doorstep. As long as the British were willing to pay off, all was well, but the crisis of the mid-1760's reflected the onset of unwillingness. A further crisis was postponed till after 1816 by the English absence from James Island,[5] but when they did return, they came with a new level of military power. As new tensions cropped up, the governors at Bathurst were constantly tempted to use that power to settle the Ñomi problem once and for all, as they did with the Anglo-Ñomi war of 1831–32. After 1832, part of Ñomi was annexed to the colony and the rest had become a de facto protectorate. Ñomi's demands were much as they had been in the eighteenth century— what the traffic would bear without completely stopping the flow of trade—but the new distribution of military power allowed the Europeans to force toll payments downward until they gradually disappeared.[6]

4. Extract of Debat to African Committee, 26 May 1764, CO 267/13; Debat to African Committee, 20 July 1764, T 70/31; Poncet de la Rivière to MC, 25 May and 10 September 1764, ANF, C6 15; Instructions for M. Boniface [as Governor of Gorée], Paris, 6 March 1772, ANF, C6 16.

5. For the further international affairs of Ñumi see Richard Evans to Charles O'Hara. 31 August 1768, CO 267/14; William Myers to Dartmouth, Gambia, 14 July 1774, CO 267/16; MacNamara to Dartmouth, 26 October 1775, CO 267/16; and "Détails sur l'establissement des français dans la rivière Gambie," unsigned and undated, but c. 1776, ANF, C6 17. For the Anglo-Ñumi war of 1765–68 see O'Hara despatch of 15 September 1768, CO 267/14, and Le Brasseur, "Questions sur nos possessions de la côte d'Afrique, avec les réponses de M. Le Brasseur, ANF, C6 17 [c. 1776].

6. Rendale to Goderich, 30 January 1832, CO 87/6. See also P. M. Mbaeyi, "The British-Barra War of 1831: A Reconsideration of its Origins and Importance," *JHSN*, 3:617–31 (June, 1967).

On the Senegal, the state whose position approximated that of Ñomi was Waalo, though Saint Louis lay near the frontier between Waalo and Kajor and could trade easily with both, just as James Island could trade with south-bank states as well as with Ñomi. But the strategy of Waalo trade was not quite the same as that of Ñomi, since Waalo had no contact with a competing European power—and no overland trade route paralleled the Senegal, as it did the Gambia. The main eighteenth-century problem for Saint Louis was to keep clear of entanglements in the internal affairs of Waalo and neutral in inter-state wars. Some of the dangers are illustrated by a sequence of events in 1719–22. The capital of Waalo was normally well to the north, near the Senegal River, which meant that Saint Louis's closest relations were often with the provincial governor, or *Beeco,* in charge of the province just across the Senegal from the fort. In the late 1710's, the kangam in office was a certain Beeco Malixuri, who was trying to build his own power, partly from the income he drew from his proximity to the fort. He also did favors for the Europeans, lending them 150 soldiers in 1719 when they were threatened by a possible pirate attack, and hoping for French help in return when he made his bid for power over the whole kingdom. The temptation to give that help must have been great, since it promised a puppet ruler in their back yard; but the French officials stood by their neutrality, and Malixuri failed.[7]

This policy was undoubtedly correct, but neutrality also had its dangers. A few years later, in 1722, the Ormankoobe moved their raiding operations to the lower Senegal, a Moroccan army operated in alliance with the Brakna Moors and the Saatigi of Fuuta Tooro against an alliance of Waalo and Kajor. This presented a dangerous situation from several points of view. If the northern alliance won, they might well devastate Waalo, which would destroy the local supply of food and might endanger the security of the enclave itself. If the Wolof won with French help, on the other hand, the French would have a hard time buying the Brakna gum or passing Fuuta Tooro on the way to Gajaaga, and might well run into troubles from the Qaïd commanding the Moroccan forces. The French commander hoped for a Wolof victory, but he remained neutral.

After the Wolof had won decisively in 1722, they were unusually strong, and they were angry at Saint Louis's standing aside in their hour of need. The Brak, Yeerim Mbañik, lorded it over the French post when he and his army visited Saint Louis later that year. He had recently cemented an alliance with the Trarza Moors by marrying a sister of the Emir, Ali Chendura (r. 1702–27), so that he had reason to think his bargaining position was extremely strong. He demanded a personal loan, a 25-per-cent increase in the price paid for slaves, and a 33-per-cent decrease in the price asked for rum. The French stood firm and

7. For the general history of Waalo at this period see Barry, "Royaume du Walo," pp. 135–62.

made only minor concessions, but the danger was real.[8] The Trarza and Waalo together could easily have blocked passage up and down the river.

In the second half of the eighteenth century, Waalo came to be involved even more closely in a competitive struggle between two neighbors, the Trarza immediately to the north and the Brakna further inland, north of Podor. Before 1758, when the French held Saint Louis and the English traded on the "gum coast" to the north, Anglo-Trarza friendship was countered to some extent by a Franco-Brakna entente. A dubious report of that period told how the Trarza helped England with military intelligence about Saint Louis, and held that the Trarza promised 700 men for the assault on Saint Louis—all this in return for an English promise not to trade with the Brakna and to demolish the fort at Podor.[9] Whether or not these plans were made, the Trarza did not participate in the assault on Saint Louis in 1758, and the English kept up the Brakna trade.

But from then onward into the nineteenth century, the Trarza were a power to be reckoned with in Waalo as well as in the desert to the north. In 1775, they made an especially damaging raid into Waalo and on south into Kajor. Reports some eight years later put the total enslavements at 9,000 to 10,000 captured and exported in the second half of 1775 and the first half of 1776.[10] Contemporaneous or nearly contemporaneous observers, however, reported the raid as serious, but said nothing about such an extraordinary number of slaves passing through the European posts. Nor does it seem likely that the English paid the Trarza to make the raid for the sake of increasing slave exports, as some French authorities were to claim a few years later.[11]

8. Julien du Bellay to CI, 28 December 1722, ANF, C6 7.

9. Rev. John Lindsay, *A Voyage to the Coast of Africa in 1758* (London, 1759), pp. 86 ff.

10. "Etat des esclaves de la côte de l'Afrique," unsigned, undated, but filed as for date in 1783, ANF, C6 18. But the error in this case seems to arise from a misreading of an earlier despatch (Ar#eny de Paradis to MC, 29 April 1777, ANF, C6 17) reporting diplomatic negotiations with Moorish ambassadors, who were very anxious to dethrone the reigning Damel. They promised that *if* the French would supply them with arms they could capture 3,000 Kajor-Kajor slaves for sale to the French and 6,000 for sale to the English. These figures tend to recur in later despatches, but assigned to the earlier and actual Moorish raid of 1775.

11. Evidence about these events is curious. B. Barry, the outstanding specialist in Waalo history and otherwise a careful historian, credits French accounts that actually date from several years after the supposed raid. (Barry, "Royaume du Walo," [thesis], pp. 188–95.) The earliest French despatch I have been able to locate reported in April 1777 that the Moors had already swept through Waalo and turned it into a desert; but it said nothing about English complicity, though it mentioned a Trarza offer to capture lots of slaves for sale if France would only supply a subsidy. (Armény de Paradis to MC, 29 April 1777, ANF, C6 17.) The next mention in the despatches from Gorée to France came in 1778, asking permission to subsidize the Moors and now claiming that the

Whether that raid was gigantic or simply large, it meant that the Trarza emir replaced the Brak of Waalo as the local authority with greatest power near Saint Louis. After the French return in 1779, they tended at first to placate the Trarza, keeping neutral when possible, paying what they had to pay so long as it was cheaper to pay than to fight. With the second return in 1817, the French found the Trarza still annoying, and the distribution of power had changed drastically as it had at the mouth of the Gambia. The French also wanted to establish plantations in Waalo, and they resented having to pay off the Trarza emir as well as the Brak. The crisis was nevertheless delayed and finally came with the same timing as the Anglo-Ñomi crisis of the 1830's. The Trarza intervened in Waalo affairs in 1833–35, and this time the French drove them out, leaving a divided and weakened Waalo which slipped, like Ñomi, into the status of informal protectorate, drifting unhappily toward full annexation by Saint Louis in 1855.[12]

"Legitimate Trade" and the French Reoccupation of Saint Louis

The era of the Napoleonic Wars was not a watershed in the history of Europe alone; it also marked real and substantial changes in the

English had done the same to encourage the Moorish raid on Waalo in 1775. (Armény de Paradis [gov. 1777–78] to MC, 5 March 1778, ANF, C6 17.) In Fort Lewis, meanwhile, Governor O'Hara, who was supposed to have instigated the raid, reported in August 1775 that the Moors had attacked some English ships on the river, threatened invasion of the island itself, and were destroying the region essential to the provisioning of the post. (O'Hara to Dartmouth, Fort Lewis, 18 August 1775, CO 267/16.) MacNamara, who took over in January 1776, immediately wrote to London with a long bill of particulars about the misconduct of his predecessor, and criticized him for quarreling with the Trarza to the detriment of trade—not for having worked with them too closely. (MacNamara to Dartmouth, 26 January 1776, CO 267/16.) The bulk of the French accusations against O'Hara date from 1783, in a series of unsigned documents advocating that France do the same and using O'Hara's supposed conduct to justify the policy. ("Mémoire sur le commerce du Sénégal," February 1783, ANF C6 18 [another copy in ANF-OM, AFC no. 69, Sénégal 2]; "Etat des escalves de la côte occidentale d'Afrique," unsigned, undated, but filed as for 1783 and wartime by internal evidence, ANF C6 18.) In 1789, the story was still current. Lamiral, a resident of Saint Louis since 1779, wrote that African states in the vicinity never went to war merely to capture slaves for sale, but he mentioned the Trarza raid into Waalo in 1775 as a single exceptional atrocity, abetted by Governor O'Hara. (*L'Affrique et le peuple affriquain* [Paris, 1789], pp. 172–76.) In the same year, John Barnes, an English merchant with a long-term connection with Gambia trade, denied before a House of Commons committee on the slave trade that Moors ever had made a practice of raiding south of the Senegal in order to capture slaves. (Great Britain, *Parliamentary Sessional Papers* [cited hereafter as PP], *Accounts and Papers*, 25 [635], p. 30.)

12. Barry, "Le royaume du Walo du traité de Ngio en 1819 à la conquête en 1855," *BIFAN*, 31:339–442 (1969).

operations of overseas Europeans in Senegambia. Before the wars, the foreign traders had accepted African trade on mainly African terms, and trade patterns were governed by long-standing custom that both sides respected. The return of the French to Saint Louis in 1817 and British to Bathurst in 1816 brought back some "old coasters," but it brought new officials, as well, who were ignorant of custom and tradition and not much inclined to respect it even if they understood it. The change was not simply a shift in relative power, though it was that too; the new men were sent out to *do something* in Africa, not just to supervise trade for a few years and go home.

The new reformism was strongest in regard to the slave trade. Once the British illegalized their own slave trade in 1808, they were intent on stopping all the rest of the Atlantic slave trade as well, and the call for "legitimate trade" had strong moral overtones. The cause of agricultural and commercial development seemed to have higher motives than mere profit, motives drawn from the morality of the antislavery movement and linked to nationalism—for Britain, a national pride in leadership of the anti-slave-trade movement, for France, a national effort to counter the loss of Saint Domingue in the Antilles by creating new plantations on the Senegal. While the new aggressive mood was still far from the imperialism of the 1880's, it was a long step beyond the masterly nonintervention in noncommercial affairs that marked the European attitude toward Senegambia in the eighteenth century.

The shift from company control to royal government over the enclaves was a significant move in that direction, though it dated back to 1758 for the French and 1764 for the English. More important still, royal officials after 1816 were bureaucrats at a time when bureaucratic efficiency was on the rise. They felt obliged to get things done, and they were less concerned than their predecessors had been if they had to intervene in the affairs of their African neighbors. In one sense, their roles reversed those of their eighteenth-century forerunners—sent out to trade, but asked to perform diplomatic and military chores on the side. The new generation were sent out to govern, and it was now the turn of the mercantile community to ask for diplomatic and military aid to commerce.

Industrial technology began to be important soon after the reoccupations of 1816–17. Steamboats were introduced on the Senegal in November 1819, and the first steam-escorted convoy to Gajaaga sailed in 1820. Steamers narrowed the advantage of the Senegal over the Gambia, and they brought every riverside village within range of waterborne artillery during the high season. The artillery was also different. The breech-loading musket (the breakthrough for infantry) was still far off in the 1860's, but explosive shells and antipersonnel projectiles like grapeshot and shrapnel had already appeared in the late eighteenth century, followed by breech-loading cannon, rifled barrels for greater range and accuracy, and improved recoil mechanisms in the first half of the nineteenth.[1]

Tropical medicine also began to reduce the horrifying death rate of new-comers from Europe, though only gradually before the 1850's. If nothing else, the Europeans learned not to use European troops in Senegambia. After losing 483 dead per thousand men per year in the Sierra Leone Command (which included the Gambia), the British disbanded the last all-European military unit in West Africa in 1829 and switched to African troops with European officers and noncoms;[2] but the isolation of quinine from cinchona bark in 1820, making possible effective prophylactic treatment of malaria, had greater long-run importance. At least some of the French in Senegambia were using it regularly by 1843,[3] and the English followed in the 1850's. The death rates of Europeans in West Africa dropped by about 80 per cent between the early and the late decades of the nineteenth century, though most of the change came in the second half of the century.[4]

A note of greater aggressiveness was also found in commercial affairs, though the number of Europeans in the Senegambia was less than it had been in the eighteenth century, at least until the 1840's. The men who went out to beat the bushes for new business were Africans and Afro-Europeans, though they often worked with commercial credit drawn from Europe. The Afro-European diasporas from Saint Louis and Bathurst began to carry more goods than ever before, though the African juula networks were still active.

In the Senegal enclaves, the new French authorities gradually formalized relations between different groups of merchants, each with its own set of functions and its own place in the hierarchy of commerce and society. The broadest term for people engaged in any form of trade was *commerçant*, and the pinnacle of the commerçant pyramid was occupied by the *négociants* who dealt in the import and export trade to the French metropolis and were themselves mainly French, not Senegalese. The next step in wealth and importance were the *marchands détaillants*, retail merchants who might import directly from France but were not engaged in the export trade. Last among those whose business was mainly in Saint Louis or Gorée were the *licenciés*, licensed retail shopkeepers, traders, cabaret operators, and the like.

1. Europeans tried to guard field artillery from African hands, though they sold muskets freely enough. The exception was Laaji Umar Taal's capture of shell-firing field guns from the French in Bundu and his subsequent use of this artillery in the conquest of Kaarta. See Y. Saint-Martin, "L'artillerie d'El Hadj Omar et d'Amadou," *BIFAN*, 27:560–72 (1965).

2. PP, 1840, xxx [c. 228], p. 6; Curtin, *Image of Africa*, pp. 177–97.

3. Raffenel, *Voyage dans l'Afrique*, p. 102.

4. Curtin, *Image of Africa*, pp. 343–62.

The men who actually moved out along the routes of the trade diaspora were classed as *traitants*. Where the négociants were either Europeans or métis and rarely counted more than a dozen firms, the other categories were African or occasionally métis, and they numbered hundreds of firms and thousands of individuals.[5] They too were divided more informally according to a social and commercial hierarchy. At the top were those who traded on their own account and with their own capital, a dozen or so big firms and a number of smaller traders. A second group traded on their own account, but with borrowed pièces de Guinées, the blue baft from India that was the main import exchanged for gum or gold along the river or in Gajaaga. A third group did not even trade on their own account but acted as agents for the négociants or marchands at the port.

Those who traded on their own account were further subdivided in prestige according to the size of their capital. The "Galam" trade to Gajaaga needed the largest capital and up to six months for repayment. It was therefore the special preserve of the largest firms, though they also worked the gum trade at the escales in competition with smaller traders and agents for the merchant houses in the town. Still another and more modest group were the *marigotiers*, who sailed their small craft into the maze of creeks (*marigots* in Senegalese French) that extended out from the main stream of the Senegal. In low water they stayed below Podor, but in high water they went further up, buying millet, some ivory, hides, and peanuts (after the 1840's) in Fuuta and Waalo.[6] Their overland counterparts for the inland trade into Kajor and the hinterland of the petite côte were peddlers who could work on even smaller capital. It was common to begin with this trade in a small way in hopes of working up the ladder toward the "Galam voyage."

The usual practice in French colonies, as in metropolitan ports, was to organize a formal relationship between the government and the merchant community through *chambres de commerce,* semiofficial organizations taken to represent the corporate interests of all merchants but usually representing only the négociants or their equivalent. The négociants of Saint Louis wanted

5. Some of these grades were regulated through license fees. Négociants paid 450 frs in 1837 and 600 frs in 1843 (£17.46 and £23.28 respectively), while marchands détaillants paid 225 frs in 1837, rising to 300 frs in 1843 (£8.73 to £11.64), and licenciés paid 300 frs in 1837 to 400 in 1843 (£11.64 to £15.51). Traitants were somewhat apart from the licensing system. They were subject to regulations and to compulsory registration, but at most times they were not required to pay a fee. They were also much more numerous than the other three categories, 187 being registered in 1842. See Arrêté no. 3, 15 May 1837, *Bulletin administratif,* 1:472–78; Arrêté no. 1, 20 January 1843, *Bulletin administratif,* 2:1–3.

6. E. Bouët-Willaumez, *Commerce et traite des noirs aux côtes occidentales d'Afrique* (Paris, 1948), pp. 27–28, 30–31; Raffenel, *Nouveau voyage,* 2:84–87; Brossard, Report of 1 January 1853, ANS, 5 B 14.

a similar privilege, but they were outmaneuvered by the governor, Baron Roger, who set up a legally constituted Comité de Commerce, in 1821, which included elected representatives of the traitants and marchands as well as the négociants.[7] With minor variations, the Comité lasted down to the Faidherbe period at mid-century.

Meanwhile, and in spite of such occasional bows to a more open organization, the Senegalese trade diaspora still had a strong tradition of privileged or monopolized trade. The earlier companies had always had trouble monopolizing the gum trade of the lower escales, but the long river route to Gajaaga held the promise of easily controlled prices, and monopoly profits at the expense of the upriver consumers or the upriver gold miners. And it was easy to argue that the distance and danger of the river route made government regulation essential, which opened the way to government price fixing. The very first Galam voyage sailed under the armed escort of royal ships and under the command of a convoy commodore who dealt with the authorities in Fuuta and Gajaaga on behalf of the whole group. From this collective bargaining through a government official, it was only a short step to a general cartel for the Gajaaga trade, though membership in the cartel was to be open to all commerçants of Saint Louis, regardless of category. The scheme was tried out in the high seasons of 1820 and 1821, and through the dry seasons that followed, since the new fort at Bakel made it possible to remain in Gajaaga and trade throughout the year. After one year of reversion to competitive trade in 1823, the monopoly was reestablished in 1824 and retained in some form or other until 1848.[8]

At first, in 1823–24, the institutional form was a company organized for the trade of a single year and automatically terminated with a full distribution of capital and dividends. Then, after 1824, the usual form was a series of companies each lasting three or four years, though they were all called Compagnie de Galam (or a close variant), and the continuity of management and ownership really made it a single enterprise, though one that changed its activity from time to time. It began with a monopoly of the gum trade in Gajaaga, but it shifted in 1823 to a general monopoly over all Gajaaga trade—although only during the dry season. Between August 1 and December 31, trade was open to anyone who had a boat and could reach Gajaaga, but after the falling water isolated the upriver factories, the Company alone had

7. See Roger to MC, 14 September 1822, *ANF-OM,* Sénégal XIII 4, and that file in general. Roger was far more pro-African than most colonial governors of the period. He wrote a study of Wolof oral literature and a long historical novel about Senegal, in which the protagonist was an African, not a European.

8. This and the following paragraphs on the Galam companies are based on E. Saulnier, *La compagnie de Galam au Sénégal* (Paris, 1921), supplemented by references indicated in the notes that follow.

the right to trade there. When there was trouble between Senegal and Fuuta, the government stopped small traders in the high season as well as the low. This had the effect of cutting them out altogether in 1839, 1841, 1843, and 1847, or nearly half the years between 1839 and 1847.

Government control and government initiative were omnipresent in the Company's affairs. Its chief executive officer was a *directeur,* appointed by the governor from a list of three names submitted to him by the board of directors. The board, in turn, was elected annually by secret ballot of stockholders, voting on a basis that was partway between the alternatives of voting by shares and voting by stockholder. In 1832, stockholders with nine shares or less had one vote, those with ten to nineteen had two, and so on by multiples of ten, but only to a maximum of three votes. This was, of course, more democratic than European forms of company organization, and in 1847 it was changed to the single principle of one stockholder, one vote.[9]

In fact, and in spite of some appearances, the companies tended to fall more and more into the hands of a few principal Wolof and Afro-French traders. Senegalese government began with regulations in the spirit of Roger's Comité de Commerce; shares originally sold at the low price of 500 frs (£12.40 sterling), or even less, with sale limited to residents of Saint Louis or Gorée and a fixed maximum number allowed to a single person. Yet a typical company was the one chartered in 1836 with a total capital of 400,000 frs (£15,520 sterling), in 2,000 shares of stock sold for 200 frs (£7.76) a share and limited to ten shares per customer. In short, the maximum individual investment was less than £100, and a total of 200 stockholders was assured, at least in the beginning. But the stock was transferable, and when the 1836 company was dissolved five years later, the entire stock belonged to ten individuals.[10]

Even though the trade of the high season was open to all, it was under tight government regulation. Boats might leave Saint Louis only between August 20 and September 15 each year—no more double round trips—and they had to arrive at Mafu in Fuuta on the way back by January 1. There, they presented the government pass they carried and had their gum officially weighed. In Gajaaga itself, the commandant of the fort set prices for food-stuffs and interpreters' salaries at the main fair at Bakel. He acted jointly with the senior representative of the Galam Company and three elected merchants as a supervisory council with power to exclude offending traders from the fair or to expel them from the upper river.[11]

Relations between the commerçants and the government of Senegal were intertwined financially as well. The fort at Bakel and the naval establishment

9. See Saulnier, *Compagnie de Galam,* pp. 62 ff.
10. See Saulnier, *Compagnie de Galam,* pp. 68–74.
11. Arrêté no. 48, 28 June 1857, *Bulletin administratif,* 4:67–70.

on the river were a form of subsidy to Gajaaga trade, while the government felt free to help itself to the monopoly profits of the Galam Company by imposing special obligations in the charters. The Company carried government mail on the river free of charge, and government officials could draw on Company stores in Gajaaga, obliged only to repay in kind. Some companies were more heavily burdened. The one founded in 1828 undertook to complete the second story of the new factory at Maxaana, to send at least one caravan into the far interior each year, to maintain a factory at Sansandiñ in Bundu, to buy a particular plantation in Waalo from the government and then operate it. That particular burden was a little heavy. The Company lost 18 per cent of its capital trying to run the plantation, before giving it up as a total loss, and it failed to carry out some of its other obligations; but the monopoly profits from three years of trade on the river were enough to repay the investors' capital (or nearly so), though the Company paid no dividends for those three years.[12]

Similar special levies fell again on the Company in the 1840's, when it was required to maintain a new and unprofitable factory at Seeju (Sédiou) on the Casamance River and another at Merinagen (Mérinaghen) on the Lac de Guiers, designed to tap the new peanut trade of eastern Waalo. Where the average profit on the Gajaaga trade of 1843–46 was 89 per cent on capital, the average dividend was only 38 per cent—the special obligations, in short, amounted to a tax on profits at the rate of 57 per cent. The government, which had created the monopoly profit in the first place, considered that it had the right to take some of it back, and the Saint Louis investor who put his money into each Galam Company in turn would have done very well for himself. (See table 3.2.)

Government regulation was also tight at the three gum escales of the lower Senegal. They had shifted slightly in location since the eighteenth century. Terrier Rouge was abandoned, and the escale du Coq now carried all the Brakna trade, while a new "escale des Daramancours" operated only 4 kms downstream from the old escale du Désert, which still served the Trarza.[13] But the commercial geography was basically unchanged; the camel caravans met the river trade at two points, one at the northernmost bend of the river, a

12. Governor Senegal to MC, no. 275, 10 August 1828, ANS, 2 B 12, and no. 60, 20 February 1832, ANS, 2 B 14.

13. The "Daramancours," also known to the eighteenth-century French as "Aladaliji," had been the principal merchants at the escale du Désert in the early eighteenth century, when Waalo still controlled the north bank of the lower Senegal. (Undated annotation to Labat, ANF, C6 29.) Their French name and location suggest that they must have been a fraction of the Banū Daymān, the principal subdivision of the Tashumsha zwāya in the Trarza area. (A. Leriche, "Tribus de Mauritanie," *BIFAN*, 17:173–203 (1955), pp. 191–97.) By the early nineteenth century, the Trarza themselves were selling gum, and a separate escale had been set up for the "Dramancours."

Table 3.2
The Rate of Profit of Successive Galam Companies

Years	Per cent profit or dividend reported
1820	247
1821–22	>60
–	–
1824–28	small
1828–32	none
1832–36	small or none
1836–37	89
1837–38	6
1838–39	28
–	–
1843–44	32
1844–45	32
1845–46	51

Source: Saulnier, *Compagnie de Galam,* pp. 42, 49, 101, 115–17, 130–31, 148–49.

second near the place the river turned south for its final run toward the sea. By long tradition, the trade with the Moors was confined to the official escales. It suited the Moorish emirs by assuring the full market tolls and payments due to them under their treaties with Senegal, and it suited the French by cutting the cost of trying to protect hundreds of traitants scattered up and down the north bank. Though the trade of the escales was open to all, it was left in the hands of African traitants, and the large number of small middlemen in this trade was a source of concern to the Senegalese government. They were hard to control, and trading on credit was a further problem. A small trader, having received a loan of so many pièces de Guinée payable in so many kgs of gum at the end of the season, was at the mercy of changing prices, and the very fact that he lacked resources to hold guinées from one season to the next made the demand for gum more inelastic than it might have been.[14]

Considerations of this kind entered into the Senegalese government efforts to fix gum prices at the escales whenever it judged that competition between traitants was likely to drive the price of gum too high. Their first device was known euphemistically as "the compromise." In fact it was simply a government declaration of the maximum price that could legally be paid for gum that year. The compromise was extremely hard to enforce, but it was used in

14. Saulnier, *Compagnie de Galam,* pp. 17–18, 45–46; Bouët-Willaumez, *Commerce et traite des noirs,* p. 11.

1833, 1837–39, and 1841.[15] By 1842, it was a recognized failure. The supply of gum depended on the incidence of rainfall, warfare in the desert, and other uncontrollable factors. With an inelastic supply and demand, the market price was erratic and unpredictable. As a result, the small-scale traitants tended to make wrong estimates so often that they fell further and further in debt to the large-scale dealers in Saint Louis. In 1842, the total debt stood at 2,500,000 frs (£97,000).

The Senegalese government first proposed to meet this crisis by setting up a second company modelled on the Galam Companies, with shares to be sold in Senegal only, and a charter to run for the next five years. This met the political decisions. Where economic determinants were weak or absent, and France. The whole object, after all, was to raise the prices to the French consumer and lower those paid to the Moorish producers, all for the profit of the body of commerçants based in Saint Louis. Metropolitan French merchants who saw themselves excluded from the gum trade were an effective opposition, and the plan died.[16]

Both the circumstances and the outcome were common enough in colonial affairs, but they also illustrate a recurrent style of decision-making in trade diasporas. The total revenue from the operations of the system was necessarily allocated to its various functions by institutional arrangements and political decisions. Where economic determinants were weak or absent, and the nodes on the network were arranged in a hierarchy of central places with increasing multifunctionality, the power to make the ultimate decision lay with the final central place—in this case Paris.

Saint Louis had less power, but it was not powerless; it had no useful appeal against Paris, but it could still manipulate the lower range of the hierarchy on its own periphery. In one sense that power had already been used in the interests of the large négociants, in allowing them to make loans to the traitants on terms extremely favorable to the lenders. But now so many of the traitants were so far in debt that their collective relation to the négociants approached that of a very large debtor whose creditors were forced to throw good money after bad or else lose the original capital. The financial plight of the traitants had thus become the financial plight of the négociants as well.[17]

15. Bouët-Willaumez, *Commerce et traite des noirs,* pp. 11–16. The season of 1834 was an exception because of the Trarza-Senegalese war along the river. In that year, the gum trade of the escales was organized through a chartered company on the model of the Compagnie de Galam.

16. Bouët-Willaumez, *Commerce et traite des noirs,* p. 16.

17. This is in line with the aphorism attributed to Lord Keynes—that if you owe your banker a thousand pounds you are in his power, but if you owe him a million, he is in yours. (C. Geertz, *Peddlers and Princes: Social Change and Economic Modernization in Two Indonesian Towns* [Chicago, 1963], p. 37.)

It was expressed through the Comité de Commerce and finally emerged through the good offices of Governor Bouët-Willaumez as a new plan for the gum trade. This plan combined tight control over the escales, tight regulation of the trade on the river, and a generous government subsidy toward the tolls payable at the escales—a subsidy that ran to nearly £1,600 a year in the early 1840's. Only registered traitants were allowed to trade at the escales, and in order to register, the individual had to be either African or métis, born in Saint Louis or Gorée, and not previously registered as a négociant or marchand, and he had to show experience of at least one expedition to the escales since 1836. Once registered, the traitant was required to trade only at the times, places, and prices specified by the Senegalese government, and 5 per cent of his investment in trade goods went into a common fund to be traded by the government itself. At the end of the trade season, the profits on government trade were distributed—but in each case, creditors had first claim on the share due to any traitant.[18] It was a neat scheme to bail out the creditors and debtors together by creating a monopoly profit, and Governor Bouët-Willaumez estimated later that the traitants had cleared all their indebtedness by the end of the 1845 season.

But the mid-1840's was a high-water mark for the old system of trade. A particular and historically determined combination of checks and balances had allocated the revenue of Senegambian trade to many different groups—to local rulers, juula in the overland trade, zwāya gum traders, and Senegalese rivermen; and to the various specialist functions performed at the central place on the coast or in the distant center of the European trade diaspora. Even before the 1840's the old order began to change, but the changes have to be seen in the perspective of a regional trade system. Saint Louis and Gorée were the chief Senegambian nodes of the trade diaspora that began in France and reached up the Senegal. In the same way, Bathurst was the chief coastal point on the lines that reached back to London, but its trade was fed from the same hinterland that supplied the French posts.

The English Return to the Gambia: Revived Competition between the Rivers

The same post-Napoleonic decades of impressive growth for the Afro-French trade diaspora saw a parallel growth for the Afro-English trade diaspora on the Gambia and a renewal of the old rivalry for the trade of the distant hinterland. One difference between Gambian and Senegalese development was a matter of metropolitan policy. The French thought they needed plantation colonies, while the British were satisfied with the planta-

18. Ordonnance of 15 November 1842, printed in Bouët-Willaumez, *Commerce et traite des noirs*, pp. 17–20. See also Raffenel, *Nouveau voyage*, 2:84–86.

tions they had. Where French were sanguine about the future of colonization in Africa, the British had the immediate background of colonial failure in Sierra Leone—or so they considered it—and they were not inclined to expect very much from other places in tropical Africa. Where the Senegal had a saleable product in Mauritanian gum, the Gambia had no such staple to offer in place of the slave trade. In fact, the only serious reason Britain had for fortifying the mouth of the Gambia was to prevent the slave trade—only secondarily to have a place to relocate the British and Afro-British merchants to be displaced from Gorée by the return of the French.[1]

An Anglo-African community had been forming on Gorée since the British acquired the island in 1800, working the familiar Goréen trade network to the southern rivers and the Gambia. The foundation of Bathurst in 1816 was little more than a shift of central place from one point in the network to another, but the Gorée merchants were far more optimistic than the London officials, though their hopes were centered on the gum trade of the Mauritanian coast, not on the hides, ivory, beeswax, and gold of their own hinterland.[2] They were also different from the usual British merchant community on the West African coast. The usual pattern was found with William C. Forster, who represented Forster and Smith of London. He moved from Gorée to Bathurst in 1816 and remained in trade there until his death in 1849. But the others had more often drifted to Gorée on other business and turned to trade as an unplanned new career. Richard Lloyd had been British commander of Gorée from 1804 to 1808. Charles Grant, a prominent merchant until he returned to Scotland in the early 1840's, was a close relative of Captain Alexander Grant, the military commander who founded Bathurst. Edward Lloyd had also served in the military forces on Gorée. Grant and Edward Lloyd both formed alliances with senhoras and left large families. So too did W. H. Goddard, who was to become the most influential single member of the merchant community after Forster's death.

Other Afro-British and Afro-Portuguese merchants were already active in the Gambia trade, and many of them moved their headquarters from upriver towns to Bathurst. One of the most interesting was Thomas Joiner, whose career illustrates once more the principle that effective cross-cultural mediation was possible to people who started from the African side, as it was to those from Europe, like Paul Bénis. Joiner began life as a Gambia Malinke of the minstrel caste. He was captured, sold off to America as a slave, where he gained his freedom, earned enough money to return, and set up shop on Gorée sometime before 1810. Along the way, he learned to read and write and gave himself a moderately good education for the time and place. He moved to Bathurst with the British, just as Paul Bénis had moved to Saint

1. For the general European expectations see G. Hardy, *La Mise en valeur du Sénégal* (Paris, 1921), passim, and Curtin, *Image of Africa*, esp. pp. 123–39.
2. Mahoney, "Government and Opinion."

Louis. His business prospered, and by the 1830's he was the most important shipowner on the Gambia. His brigantine *General Turner*, 67 tons burden, was the largest single ship in the trade of the upper river.[3]

Others who moved to Bathurst were the descendants of the English who had stayed as private traders on the Gambia after James Fort was destroyed in 1779. Robert Aynsley, for example, was the mulatto son of an older Robert Aynsley whose firm had helped Mungo Park organize his journey to the interior—and incidentally had also organized Thomas Joiner's journey to slavery in the New World. The younger Aynsley moved his business from Karantaba down to Bathurst in 1817. Still other firms were run by women, often by a surviving senhora of a departed trader or a daughter who took an interest in the business. Among the most prominent was Madam Tigh, a mulatto trader for whom Tighkunda was named, but most of the women who inherited commercial capital tended to invest it in Bathurst real estate or ships that sailed under a hired captain with a Wolof or Afro-Portuguese crew—much like the signares of Gorée or Saint Louis.[4]

Family and social connections between Senegal and the Gambia were far closer than they had been in the eighteenth century. The earliest African inhabitants of Bathurst were Wolof from Gorée, so that all shared a single language and culture on the African side. They sometimes had a common heritage on the European side as well. Many of the Saint Louis métis community had English fathers; and the most important mulatto merchant in Bathurst was Jean (later John) Pellegrin, whose family had organized the coup of 1802 in Saint Louis and later held the post of maire there.

Some Cape Verde Islanders and Afro-Portuguese from the southern rivers also moved to Bathurst as it began to prosper, and many of the mulatto community, whatever the mixture, settled in the part of Bathurst known as Portuguese Town. Gambian English had already adjusted to the new reality; by the nineteenth century "Portuguese" meant any Afro-European, whatever his origin or descent.

The final immigrant group were recaptives taken by British cruisers from slave ships captured at sea. The great majority were landed in Sierra Leone, but some were sent on to the Gambia for resettlement. Since their African culture was usually different from the local Wolof, Malinke, or Joola, and they were subject to intensive education and proselytization by Christian missionaries, they too became Afro-European in culture—often more to the European side of the scale than were other Gambians of Afro-European descent. These recaptives or "liberated Africans," as they were called in the nineteenth century, became the nucleus of the Gambian Creole community.[5]

---

3. Gray, *Gambia*, pp. 306–32; Mahoney, "Government and Opinion," pp. 38–39.
4. Mahoney, "Government and Opinion," pp. 64–66.
5. The Gambian English *Creole* and the Sengalese French *créole* are cognates, both derived from a common English, Spanish, or French term in the eighteenth-century

The Gambian trade diaspora of the nineteenth century was thus more African-controlled than the Senegalese, more informal, and less tightly controlled from the distant metropolis. The contrast is highlighted by the way each set out to establish an upriver post. The French moved first in 1818 with an expedition to Gajaaga under a *capitaine de frégate,* commanding two brigs and a smaller royal vessel in addition to the Senegalese boats that went along for trade. In 1823, the English in Bathurst finally sent their own expedition to choose an upriver satellite factory, which turned out to be the site of Georgetown on MacCarthy's Island. That party consisted of the army major commanding the forces, Thomas Joiner, representing the merchant community, a missionary, a sergeant, and twelve black soldiers.[6]

The same contrast emerges from the census figures. While the percentage of Europeans resident in Saint Louis or Gorée was about the same as the Bathurst figure of the mid-1840's, around 1.25 per cent, the absolute number was much lower in Bathurst—50 Europeans, as against 235 in Saint Louis and Gorée. The sex ratio of the European community was more telling still, 6,143 males per thousand females in Bathurst, as against only 2,423 in the French posts. In absolute figures, seven European women living in Bathurst in 1845 meant that only seven households could have both partners from Europe, and that was too few to stand aloof or try to dominate local society. (See *Supplement,* appendix 7.)

In other respects the socioeconomic operations of the two diasporas were similar. Both depended heavily on capital supplied by a few, mainly European firms centered in the local metropolis. In Bathurst as in Saint Louis, they let out trade goods on credit to African traders who went up the river and the creeks in search of gold, ivory, hides, or beeswax. The fundamental task of making the cross-cultural adjustments to keep a trade flowing was therefore in the hands of African juula, whether attached to the Afro-European diaspora or to the purely African diasporas of the interior. It is hard to estimate the relative weight of European capital in these operations. The governor estimated in 1848 that the total credit outstanding was in the neighborhood of £60,000, or roughly a third of the annual value of Gambian exports,[7] and the figure can be compared to the £97,000 arrears of the Senegambian traitants in 1842.

Caribbean, where the original meaning was simply American, or American-born—applied to people of any color, as well as sugar cane, rats, and styles of cooking, among other things. With the sea passage to Africa, the French *créole* referred to people of mixed race, while English *Creole* came to mean people of mixed culture in Sierra Leone and the Gambia, though they were of entirely African descent.

6. Marty, *Etudes sénégalaises,* pp. 91–219; Hardy, *Mise en valeur,* pp. 40–54; Gray, *Gambia,* pp. 334–36.

7. MacDonnell to Secretary of State, 20 June 1848, separate, CO 87/43, and 16 June 1849, CO 87/45.

The potential competition between the two rivers was a natural fact of the environment, and it began again with the reoccupation of the rivermouth *enclaves*. The strategic advantages and disadvantages of the two streams were much as they had been in the eighteenth century. Though steamboats came to the Senegal in 1819, they were mostly used for military purposes, and the bulk of the trade with Gajaaga was still carried by sail and human power until well after the 1850's. On the Gambia, steamboats called at the mouth from time to time and had sailed to the head of navigation and back in the 1820's, but the combination of tides and sails remained so efficient that regular use of steam began only in 1843. With this continuity from eighteenth-century conditions the Senegalese could easily slip back into the strategy of a protective screen on the line of the Faleme, while the Bathurst merchants could return to their predecessors' dream of reaching through to the source of Bambuhu gold, and beyond.[8]

Senegalese strategists could also dream of stretching their diaspora on to the Niger in direct competition with the African juula. Europeans had lacked the power to move in this direction in the early eighteenth century, but the idea began to crop up more seriously from the 1780's onward. Fear that the French might move to screen off Gambia trade was part of the background for Mungo Park's two expeditions in 1795–97 and 1805. Renewed explorations and feelers began in the late 1810's with the Peddie-Grey expedition toward the Niger, followed by the explorations of Grout de Beaufort, Duranton, and Tourette from the upper Senegal in the 1820's. Even though most of these explorers failed to reach Segu, they encouraged Saint Louis to move on from exploration to experimental trade feelers.[9]

Under government pressure, the Compagnie de Galam sent an embassy to Segu in 1828 with samples of the goods it hoped to make available there, and it followed in 1829 with a caravan carrying goods valued at the equivalent of £167, with the expectation that they could be exchanged for 3.412 kgs of gold from the upper Niger.[10] The caravan moved easily and rapidly from Dramane on the Senegal to Segu on the Niger in twenty-five days, under the leadership of a Soninke cleric from Gajaaga, but it was able to buy only about 30 per cent of the gold it wanted, taking the rest of the return in ivory, slaves

8. Maj. H. C. Cobbe to Ingram, 25 January 1844, CO 87/33.

9. For more general accounts of the Senegambian explorations by Europeans in this period see R. Hallett, *The Penetration of Africa: European Exploration in North and West Africa to 1815* (New York, 1965), pp. 217–49; C. Faure, "Le premier séjour de Duranton au Sénégal (1819–1826)," *RHCF*, 9:189–263 (1921), and "Le voyage d'exploration de Grout de Beaufort au Sénégal en 1824 et 1825,' *Comité des travaux historiques et scientifiques: Bulletin de la section de géographie*, 34:146–204 (1919); G. Hardy, "L'affaire Duranton," *CEHSAOF*, 2:413–36 (1917).

10. If they had bought the gold at the expected price, it would have had a prime-cost value of £48.90 in Segu, or roughly a third of its value in Europe.

and African cotton textiles. After paying tolls along the way, the profit remaining was not enough to encourage a second venture, and the Company dropped the effort to compete directly with the African juula.[11] The juula still found the route profitable, however, and several caravan leaders were working the trade regularly with up to two round trips a year. Some caravans originated in the east, but others formed in Gajaaga or in Bambuhu, with as many as 1,500 pack animals and 2,000 men, and some Senegalese from Saint Louis joined these eastern caravans even before 1850, as they were to do in greater numbers in the second half of the century.[12]

Though the strategy of trade competition followed old formulae,[13] the political and military realities of the upper Senegal were far from the neat blank surface imagined by the strategists in Saint Louis or Bathurst. Some of the factors at play are illustrated by the career of Ferdinand Duranton, whose activities intersected the web of interest and power that centered on the upper Senegal, stretching northeast to Kaarta and the Mbārek Moors and southwest to Bathurst. Duranton began life with a colonial background in Jérémie on what was then French Saint Domingue in the Caribbean. From 1819 to 1821, he served as a minor clerk in the Senegalese government, then as a merchant in private trade, briefly after 1822 in the service of the Compagnie de Galam. He then joined the staff of the government expedition toward Timbuktu, headed by Grout de Beaufort, who died in 1825 leaving Duranton in charge. Though Duranton never got beyond Xaaso that time, he was appointed head of a new exploring expedition into Bambuhu in 1826. This again led him to Xaaso, where he married Sajoba, daughter of the ruler, Awa Demba. With royal permission, Duranton settled down and built a small fortified factory at Madina near the head of Senegal navigation.[14]

Once established, Duranton had an opportunity to look at Senegambian

11. Compagnie de Galam, annual report, 3 April 1830, and Conseil Privé du Sénégal, meeting of 16 June 1832, ANF-OM, Sénégal XIII 7.

It may come as a surprise that a French chartered company could participate legally in the slave trade at this period, but the slave trade within Africa was not illegal to French citizens, and the slave trade in Africa continued till nearly the end of the century, with a trickle of slaves flowing more or less illegally into the port towns and overseas until at least 1848.

12. De Maricourt to MC, August 1827, ANF-OM, Sénégal IV 191; Hecquard, report dated Bakel, 30 June 1847, ANS, 13 G 165. For the later penetration of the Senegalese traders see E. Baillaud, *Sur les routes du Soudan* (Toulouse, 1902).

13. For some representative nineteenth-century versions of these strategic ideas see Gérardin to Governor Senegal, undated document 8 (about 1826), ANS, 1 G 10; Gerbidon to MC, 25 August 1827, ANS, 2 B 11; Raffenel, Report of 14 March 1844, *Revue coloniale,* 4:183, 197; Paul Holle to Governor Senegal, Bakel, 5 June 1846, ANS, 13 G 165; Laude, Report of a Mission to Bundu, 4 June 1880, ANS, 1 G 44.

14. The principal authorities on the Duranton affair are those cited in note 9 above, and Saulnier, *Compagnie de Galam,* pp. 107 ff.

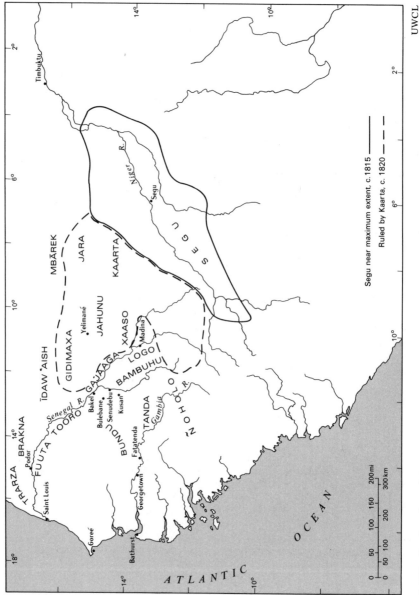

3.4 The Bambara Incursions

Segu near maximum extent, c. 1815 ——————
Ruled by Kaarta, c. 1820 — — — —

trade and politics from a new point of view. The circle of vision from Xaaso was very different from that of Saint Louis or Paris, and Duranton had an opportunity through his wife and in-laws to see the power relations on and beyond the upper Senegal from something like a Xasoonke perspective, where the central threat of the 1820's and a half-century back was the power of Kaarta. The Bambara were just as serious an external threat to eastern Senegambia of the early nineteenth century as the Moroccans had been to northern Senegambia in the first half of the eighteenth.

The Bambara outburst went back to the early eighteenth century and a military and social innovation among the Bambara near Segu. This was the tō-jō, literally "association of slaves," but in actual origins a hunting association of young men, some slave and some free. The crucial change was the transformation of this relatively peaceful association into a standing army, recruiting new membership through capture, and capable under appropriate leadership of forming new political units of imperial size. The result was a number of states that came to live by raiding and constant warfare, and the Bambara raids of the early eighteenth century were the prime source for the slaves exported westward from Senegambian ports.[15]

The Bambara move toward the eastern frontiers of Senegambia began in the middle of the eighteenth century, when a breakaway Bambara group under the leadership of the Masasi family moved north into Kaarta. They annexed Kaarta, made it their base, and went on to conquer other states in the sahal region. The new empire was not fully established until the 1780's, but its raids began to reach into Gajaaga as early as 1751, where the Bambara were known as the "black Ormankoobe." By the 1790's, they were no longer raiders from a distance but a force that threatened to conquer the whole eastern half of Senegambia. During the first half of the nineteenth century, their main armies reached as far as Fuuta, and southwest to the navigable Gambia. Their military strength forced Bundu, Gidimaxa, and parts of Gajaaga into tributary status for varying lengths of time, and they annexed the former core area of Xaaso to the north of the Senegal. Even when official Bambara armies were not on the march, raiding parties went out with small regard for official war or peace.[16]

Duranton was of course familiar with the traditional juula policy of neutrality in all possible circumstances. The European trading companies had sometimes acted militarily to punish a weak state or help an African ally, but it

15. See L. Tauxier, *Histoire des Bambara* (Paris, 1942), esp. pp. 69–158; C. Meillassoux, "Histoire et institutions du kafo de Bamako d'après la tradition des Niaré," *CEA*, 4:186–227 (1963), esp. p. 217.

16. G. Boyer, "Un peuple de l'ouest soudanais: Les Diawara," *Mémoires de l'Institut français d'Afrique noire*, no. 29 (Dakar 1953), pp. 39–52; Tauxier, *Histoire des Bambara*, pp. 114–26; Conseil du Sénégal to CI, 20 August 1751 and 24 February 1752, ANF, C6 13. See Park, *Travels*, 1:158–66, for his observations on the Bambara wars.

was crucial not to offend the powerful. Duranton came to believe that the French had to abandon strict neutrality—that neutrality which might favor trade in the short run but would surely lead to the destruction of eastern Senegambia and its capacity to trade in the longer run. He proposed that France take the lead in creating a major alliance based on the nucleus of Xaaso and Bundu (already allied against the Bambara). Gajaaga was just then split into two factions—one led by Samba Xumba Jaama of Tiyaabu (Tuabo) and anti-Bambara, the other under Samba Yaasin of Maxaana and generally pro-Bambara. Duranton hoped to make peace between them and bring Gajaaga into the fold. As a side issue, Fuuta was still making trouble for Senegalese traffic on the river, but Duranton thought the problem could be solved by backing a revolt of the remaining Deñankoobe against the alma-mate.[17]

Though Duranton could hardly have known it, his ideas had a precedent in Saint-Adon's alliance against Saatigi Konko Bubu Muusa in the late 1730's, and even earlier in the French intervention against Nasīr al-Dīn's jihad in the 1670's. In the 1820's, however, they were barely given a hearing in Saint Louis. The fact that Duranton also favored open trade and opposed the Galam Company's monopoly was enough to turn the dominant commercial interests against him. In the hierarchy of central places, Duranton had espoused the interests of Madina and of Xaaso. The Galam Company worked for the interest of Saint Louis (or at most of Bakel, 130 kms downstream from Madina). In either case, Kaarta was not an immediate threat; it could cut off trade and was treated gingerly on that account, but nothing more. A few pro-Duranton and pro-free-trade voices were heard in Saint Louis, but the strong opposition of the Galam Company was enough to hold the line. It was not until the 1850's, when Shaykh Umar had already ended the Bambara danger by his conquest of Kaarta, that Faidherbe settled the rivalry between Bakel and Madina in favor of Madina. From then on, Médine, as the French called it (and later its functional successor, Kayes, 10 kms downstream) held second place after Saint Louis in the urban hierarchy of the Senegal valley.

Once Duranton had been rebuffed in Saint Louis, he began to build the anti-Bambara alliance on his own—without France, and if necessary against France. In 1829 and contrary to orders he made the French government's artillery at Madina fort available to his father-in-law, Awa Demba, for a campaign to consolidate his position in what remained of Xaaso. That brought safety for the moment, but Awa Demba (and hence Duranton) was weak within Xaaso, and Duranton lay at the end of a long transportation route back to Saint Louis—one dominated by an unfriendly monopoly, at that. Like others so placed in the past, it was only natural to look around for

17. Duranton to Compagnie de Galam, Bakel, 2 April 1824; and report of February 1826, ANS, 1 G 8.

3.5 Xaaso and Its Vicinity

an alternate route to the sea and for a source of gum not already tapped through Gajaaga. The Gambia provided the outlet, and the Ulād Mbārek (sometimes called Ludamar by the Europeans) were the source. The Mbārek had a more substantial government than most nomadic peoples; they were unfriendly to the Bambara, and their enemies, the Īdaw 'Aish, blocked the way to Bakel. Nor could they bring their gum to Madina for shipment down the Senegal, because Samba Yaasin of Maxaana blocked the river against Senegalese trying to move further in upstream. If Duranton could only open an overland route from Xaaso to the Gambia, a combination would fall into place that was simultaneously anti-Bambara, anti-Compagnie de Galam, and profitable. Duranton's diplomatic arrangements secured the passage of trade through Xaaso and Bundu. When all was arranged, Duranton set out for Bathurst, arrived in July 1831, and went immediately to Lieutenant Governor George Rendall with the unexpected information that 300 loads (about 32 metric tons) of Mbārek gum would be delivered at Baraku near Barokunda Falls in March or April of 1832.[18]

Duranton, in short, had succeeded in breaking through the potential Senegalese shield along the line of the Faleme, and he seemed to open the whole trade of the interior to Gambian merchants. He was clever, but he was also lucky. The strategy of a screen or blockade against trade to the Gambia depended first and foremost on Bundu, which at this period was a strong and well-administered state that could enforce an embargo if it wanted to do so. Duranton's luck came mainly from a change in ruler. The Bundunke royal house, the Sisibe, were divided into two branches, one with a capital at Bulebane in northern Bundu, while the other was centered at Kusan in the south. The northern branch was closer to Bakel and contact with the Senegalese, which could sometimes make the southern branch turn to the Gambia as a counterweight. Just at this time, the office of Almaami had passed to the southern branch, to Tumaane Moodi (r. 1827–35). Even before Almaami Tumaane took office, the French wooed him with promises of subsidies and asked permission to put a fort on the upper Faleme to help stop the Gambia trade. The English not only sent agents to Bundu in 1829; they also sent a Jahaanke trader all the way to the Mbārek with the message that they would be happy to buy gum delivered overland to the upper Gambia. At first, Tumaane did what he had to do for the French subsidies, but not so much as to offend the English. Then, in 1830, he quarrelled with the French commander at Bakel and broke off all trade with the French post. The alternative was the Gambia, and it was this that opened the way for Duranton.[19] But the open route for the Mbārek gum closed almost as soon as it opened. In 1832, Bundu and Wuuli went to war, and Wuuli stopped Gambian emissaries trying to reach Bundu, with a hint that the local juula disliked the idea of an Afro-English entry into their eastern trade.[20]

That left Bathurst with the traditional juula alternative of trying to go around the trouble spot, and another possible route to the east ran from the upper Gambia through Tanda and Ñoholo to cross the Faleme well to the

18. Caille, "Notes sur les peuples de la Mauritanie et de la Nigritie, riverains du Sénégal," *Revue coloniale,* 10:1–10 (September 1846); Rendall to Hay, no. 42, Bathurst, 3 August 1831, CO 87/5.

19. Commandant Bakel to Governor, 14 July 1824, ANS, 13 G 164; A. M. Fraser to Almami of Bundu, H. M. Schooner *Sophia,* 10 December 1827, ANF-OM, Sénégal IV 15; Gerardin to Governor Senegal, undated [c. 1837] document 8, ANS, 1 G 10; Duranton to Governor Senegal, Médine, 18 July 1829, ANS, 1 G 8; Commandant Bakel to Governor Senegal, 30 August 1830 and 17 September 1830, ANS, 13 G 164.

Some gum also came from the Ferlo wilderness to the west of Bundu, and the Gambia government gave special prizes to encourage that trade. (See list of presents enclosed with Rendall to Hay, 6 December 1830, CO 87/3.)

20. Rendall to Hay, 28 April and 24 December 1823, CO 87/6.

south of Bundu and Bambuhu. Even before Duranton's dramatic appearance in 1831, Bathurst merchants had begun to organize a Tenda, or Tandah, Company in imitation of the Compagnie de Galam, though with a smaller capital. Its object was to draw the trade of the southern route to a new factory established in Tanda, but not far from the navigable Gambia. It opened a trading post in 1832 and reported success for a time, but then it collapsed and dissolved in 1834. In fact, the merchants who founded the Tenda Company wanted what the Saint Louis merchants had in the form of disguised subsidies—a fortified post maintained at government expense, government payment of tolls to the African states, and a monopoly over the trade of the upper Gambia. The Gambian government was simply not willing to do all that.[21]

In 1835, the Duranton gum route was again in operation—perhaps on an even larger scale than 1832, but in a new political setting that foreshadowed changes to come in the next decades. The diplomatic shift that opened the route this time came in Kaarta, where Gara, the new ruler, had broken with the Senegalese and wanted another outlet for his trade and the trade of the Moors to the north. In 1835 and 1836 the Moors brought caravans of pack oxen to Fatatenda on the upper river, under safe-conduct from Gara paid for by a public subscription of £120 from the Bathurst merchants. But Gara brought his army through Bundu as he brought the caravans through, and his mixed force of Xasoonke and Bambara raiders did far more damage to the trade sources among the Gambia Malinke than the value of 50 tons or so of annual trade in gum.[22] The Jahaanke contention that kings and merchants have different goals seemed to be borne out, along with their belief that caravans move better when they move in peace.

Duranton meanwhile made a last stand for his general alliance against Kaarta. In 1835, Kaarta had driven him from Xaaso, and he took refuge in Bakel, where he was soon caught up in the pro- and anti-Kaarta frictions among the Baacili of Gajaaga. In 1837, he again lent the artillery he had brought down from Xaaso, this time to Samba Xumba Jaama, the effective leader of lower Gajaaga and the anti-Kaarta faction, who used it to stop Senegalese shipping carrying supplies to his enemies of the Maxaana-Kaarta alliance. The use of

21. J. Roan, Report of 9 June 1827, CO 267/93; Charles Grant, Despatch of 24 August 1829, CO 87/2; Hutton to Hay, 18 May 1829, CO 87/2; Capt. Belcher, "Extracts from Observations on Various Points of the West Coast of Africa, Surveyed by His Majesty's Ship *Aetna* in 1830–32," *JRGS*, 2:278–304 (1832), p. 296; Rendall to Hay, 14 July 1830, CO 87/3 and 14 May 1831, CO 87/5; Petition of 20 June 1835, enclosed with Rendall to Stanley, 2 July 1834, CO 87/10; Rendall to Glenelg, no. 24A, 9 December 1835, CO 87/12.

22. Rendall to Hay, confidential, 3 September 1835 and 28 September 1835, CO 87/12; Rendall to Glenelg, confidential, 23 October 1836, CO 87/14; Commandant Bakel to Governor Senegal, 5 October, 1836, ANS, 13 G 164.

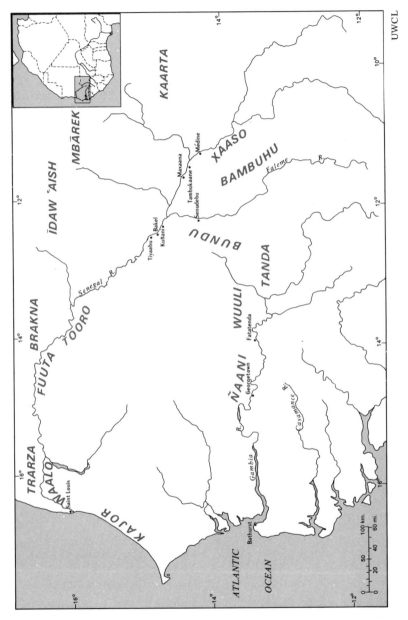

3.6 European Trade Networks of the 1830's

French artillery to threaten French shipping struck the Compagnie de Galam as nothing short of treason; its officials in Bakel arrested Duranton and sent him to Saint Louis for trial. The court cleared him of the explicit charges but the government dismissed him from its service and he died before he could act again.

With the 1840's, the tendency to settle trade disputes by force became more pronounced than ever and was associated with a general increase in raiding and counterraiding throughout Senegambia. Secular rulers made less effort to protect their own peasant villages, while simultaneously spending more energy than usual raiding peasant villages across the frontiers. The trend is not quantifiable, but the strong impression of the archival sources is that raiding and counter-raiding after the 1830's was far more serious than it had been during the era of the Atlantic slave trade. The Almaami of Bundu, for example, raided annually into Wuuli and Ñaani and the Malinke micro-states to the south, while unopposed Moorish or Bambara raiders crossed the Senegal and the Faleme to raid Bunduunke villages that had to defend themselves with little more than their own manpower and resources. Much the same pattern occurred in western Senegambia, where the ceddo military aristocracy tended more and more to raid the peasantry, even within their own state.

It is clear in retrospect that the Senegambia as a whole experienced a rising crescendo of violence against society on the part of the military, often with the connivance or participation of the traditional rulers. This was the case in Fuuta, where the religious revolution had gone sour under the great electors, as it had in Bundu, where the almamate had shifted steadily away from its clerical origins since the death of Maka Jiiba in the early 1760's. It was also the case in Kajor and Ñomi, where a clerical party was in chronic conflict with the secular state. (This tendency, however, was less pronounced if not altogether absent in the Sereer states) In retrospect, this final burst of oppression appears as a prologue to the religious revolutions that followed in the 1850's and 1860's, though the results of unbridled raiding are clearer than the causes.

The written record left by the European traders and government officials tends to show a rising sense of frustration at circumstances beyond their control, perhaps heightened by the knowledge that they now had the military power to intervene if the home government would allow it. Seen from Bathurst, the eastern route through Bundu seemed to open and close inexplicably—though the explanation would have been clear enough if Bathurst officials could have followed the intricate diplomacy between the Almaami and the French commanders in Bakel, a diplomacy where the opening of the route to the Gambia was one ploy the Almaami could use to extract better terms from the French. Fighting on the upper Gambia was also bad for trade, and the Bathurst authorities were constantly tempted to intervene, as they did in Ñaani in 1834 and 1841.[23]

The Bathurst merchant community also became frustrated by new problems and some of the old cross-cultural misunderstandings. After the failure of their attempted monopoly through government action in the early 1830's, Charles Grant organized the others who traded above MacCarthy's Island as a price-fixing ring in the early 1840's. They set a common maximum price to be paid for various kinds of African produce, and they agreed on a joint refusal to pay the customary gifts and tolls. The result was a sharp drop in trade, as the juula took their business to Bakel or the southern rivers, and the Bathurst group were forced back into open competition.[24]

For the Afro-French in Gajaaga, the equivalent source of frustration was the seemingly endless war of 1833–41 between the two Sambas, accompanied as it was by frequent raids from Bundu and Kaarta in aid of one party or the other. Until the early 1840's, however, the French kept neutral as firmly as they could, and limited their intervention to bribery, diplomatic pressure, or occasional bombardment from the river.

In the 1840's, however, they began to move with more military pressure. Part of the pressure was on Bundu, which granted France treaty rights in 1843 to build a fort at Senudebu on the Faleme and promised not to let caravans pass through toward the Gambia. The fort was not actually built until 1845, and even then Almaami Saada was able to use it as a hostage to protect his other interests. Since it could be reached by river only a few months each year and was completely surrounded by Bunduunke territory, Saada could cut off trade at any time—he could play Bakel against Bathurst, and the Afro-French traders at Senudebu against the commanders of the fort.[25] Another and firmer kind of pressure was used along the Senegal to the north. Moving on from simple bombardment, the French landed troops in 1846 and 1849 to destroy towns accused of blocking traffic on the river.

The greater military pressure came simultaneously with the rise of economic liberalism in French commercial policy. Laissez-faire economics called for the destruction of government monopolies like the Galam companies, and the last of the companies was abolished immediately after the revolution of

23. Rendall to Hay, no. 38, 14 June 1834, and no. 51, 21 August 1834, CO 87/10; Rendall to Aberdeen, no. 50, 17 June 1835, CO 87/12; Huntley to Lord John Russell, separate, 24 April 1841, CO 87/25.

24. Ingram to Stanley, separate, 30 March 1843, CO 87/30.

25. Draft treaty enclosed with Huard to Bouët, 6 January 1844, ANF-OM, Sénégal III 6; Raffenel, *Voyage dans l'Afrique,* pp. 340–41; Raffenel to MC, 8 March 1847, ANS-OM, Sénégal IV 18; Vébre to Governor, 25 October 1850, ANS, 13 G 246; Baudin to MC, no. 330, 17 July 1850, ANS, 2 B 30. In addition, the file ANS, 13 G 165, contains extensive accounts of the negotiations between Bakel and Almaami Saada of Bundu.

1848 in France. It also called for the abolition of all kinds of noneconomic tolls paid to political authorities anywhere they could be avoided. A French government commission on trading posts and the Africa trade recommended in 1851 that the whole practice of price-fixing and restricting trade to particular points like the escales be abolished.[26]

France might have enforced these policies with military force, even if Laaji Umar had not raised the cry of jihad on the upper Senegal, but the religious movement and the intense ferment among the riverain populations in the mid-1850's provided the occasion for Saint Louis to act. By the 1860's, the government was able to abolish the escales as the sole place for the gum trade of the lower Senegal. It abolished the government payments to the Moorish emirs and substituted a flat payment of 5 per cent on the value of gum traded—a payment to be made by the individual trader—and it abolished the tolls Senegalese shipping paid to African authorities up and down the river.[27] When the fort at Madina under the command of Paul Holle, a métis from Saint Louis, stood Shaykh Umar's seige in 1857, the victory belonged to Saint Louis even more than it did to France, and not just symbolically. Through the new level of European technology and European power, Saint Louis was able to establish a new degree of dominance over the lower-echelon central places in the trade network.

And the victory of Saint Louis was mainly a victory for the Franco-African participants in the trade diaspora. The capacity of the Saint-Louis-based traders increased steadily through the second quarter of the nineteenth century. Where 25 to 40 boats had gone up to Gajaaga each year at the heyday of the slave trade in the 1780's, the Saint Louis river fleet of the 1840's was about 420 vessels averaging 14.4 cubic meters in capacity (12.7 English tons burden) and employing more than 2,000 laptots. By 1845, 121 registered traitants were in the gum trade of the escales. By 1850, when a new, nonmonopolistic company had taken over the trade of the Compagnie de Galam on the same scale as the old company, it was already joined by two other Saint-Louis-based companies that were almost as large.[28] Macodé Sal had a large, permanent factory on shore at Bakel by 1851, another at Senudebu in Bundu, and a brig of 144 cubic meters (127 English tons

26. Commission des comptoirs et du commerce des côtes d'Afrique, Rapports spéciaux, June 1851, ANF-OM, Sénégal XIII 3.
27. L. L. C. Faidherbe, "Notice sur la colonie du Sénégal," *Annuaire du Sénégal et dépendances,* 1858, pp. 129 ff.; Convention with the "Doaïch Moors," 1 November 1857, *Annuaire du Sénégal et dépendances,* 1861, pp. 266–67.
28. Raffenel, *Nouveau voyage,* 2:86; Saulnier, *Compagnie de Galam,* pp. 167–70. The names of the Bakel traders signing a memorial to the government are a useful reminder of the Anglo-French-Wolof origins of the group, and of the high percentage of *métisage* among the most prominent—J. P. Audibert, François Patterson, Waly Bandia, J. Pellegrin, Macodé Sal, Victor Couder, Yama Diey, Couteau S. Ohara, Zeler, d'Erneville (fils).

burden) on the river. Waly Bandia had a less imposing establishment in Bakel, but it was valued at about £300, and a number of other Saintlouisien merchants planned to set up their own shops for the low-season trade.[29]

This short-run victory for Saint Louis, and a less impressive mid-century prosperity for Bathurst, was only a transitional stage in the demolition of the old commercial order. In the most general and schematic way, the victory of Bathurst and Saint Louis over their own hinterlands was simply a prelude to the economic dominance of Bordeaux and Marseilles over both Senegambian trade networks; but the further shift of economic predominance to firms based in metropolitan France was not immediate. It involved the shift to peanuts as the dominant export, diplomatic negotiations that ran along with the European partition of Africa, and a French decision to use the Senegal valley as their main point of entry for the conquest of the western Sudan. These developments belong to another and a very different era in Senegambian history.

29. Rey to Governor Senegal, 10 March 1851, ANF-OM, Sénégal XIII 10. Another indication of Senegalese investment in Gajaaga is the claim that they lost nearly £4,000 in trade goods to Laaji Umar's raiders in 1854, even though they had been warned to bring their goods within one of the French fortifications. (Bakel Traders to Governor, 8 February 1855, ANS, 13 G 168.)

4 | THE TRADE IN SLAVES

The abolitionists of the last century made their point very well—the slave trade was evil, and it had to be ended. Perhaps they made it too well, at least for the sake of retrospective understanding: their intense publicity for slavery and the trade alike left historians with a false sense of confidence in their understanding of both. In fact, none of the publicists had paid serious attention to the operations of the slave trade within Africa, and historians paid little until the 1950's, when the reawakening of African history brought them back to the remaining historical problems, only to find the haze and smoke left over from the heated debates of a century earlier still in the air.

As it turned out, the abolitionists had made a number of subsidiary points that were still accepted as articles of faith. For one, Africa was supposed to be a savage continent, made that way largely by the slave traders. As "savages," the Africans had been seen only as victims, never as men in command of their own destiny, having a serious role to play in their own history. To new historians of Africa it was obvious, on reexamining the evidence, that African societies had been systematically slandered during the nineteenth-century heights of racism and cultural arrogance. Yet, if they said African savagery was largely mythic, some of those who still held the old view would think they were trying to minimize the evil of the trade. If they said that African states had had real and legitimate interests, which they pursued through diplomacy and wars—that they were not mere puppets in the hands of the slave traders—the new Africanists could be accused of trying to shift the burden of guilt for the horrors of the trade from European to African heads.

It is important to recognize that most new research about the slave trade within Africa cuts at least two ways when applied to the historical issues of African or Afro-American history, and equally important to be conscious of

153

the fact that Africa (even the slave-furnishing parts of Africa) was not a single place, uniformly affected by the trade. Some African societies were destroyed, leaving hardly a trace. Others were virtually untouched, others were seriously attacked, but only over a few decades. Still others were the attackers, who may have profited, but at the price of diverting potentially creative energy to destructive ends.

One of the troubling regional differences is between most of West Africa, where the slaves sold into the trade were mainly war captives, and other source of slaves, such as the hinterland of Angola, where a much larger proportion seem to have been recruited through judicial and political processes. Judicial enslavement existed in West Africa as well, causing a constant drain of people into the slave trade, but apparently in small numbers. Part of the evidence for this comparatively low level is negative—the fact that historical sources discuss the trade as though almost all slaves began as captives, rarely mentioning judicial enslavement. A second kind of evidence is the fact that the real value of the goods received by the enslaver, in Senegambia at least, was very low—so low that no rational person with command over a slave's labor would give him up unless he showed genuine tendencies toward criminal activity or political "trouble-making." In central Africa, on the other hand, the evidence suggests that many of those sold into the trade were not war prisoners, nor yet true criminals or even political prisoners, but unfortunates who could be conveniently gotten rid of because they lacked lineage ties of the kind that might protect them against more powerful lineages and political authorities.[1]

For the moment the question has to be left open. Better understanding of the impact of the trade on Africa generally will have to wait for more careful studies of the trade inside Africa, region by region. Senegambian patterns were not necessarily those that prevailed in other parts of Africa, even other parts of West Africa. But it still seems safe to proceed with the assumption that, in Senegambia at least, the vast majority of all slaves shipped (at least 80 per cent, to give the order of magnitude) were captives, though some no doubt had "slave" status before their capture.

The Internal Trade and the Export Trade

A few general principles, however, seem to apply more broadly in West Africa. First, war prisoners (including noncombatants) were subject

1. This recruitment by threat of force or the exercise of authority by the more powerful to "draft" the less powerful into the slave trade appears to have been more common in the Congo basin than in West Africa. See, for example, Joseph C. Miller, "The Slave Trade and the Jaga of Kasanje" (unpublished paper presented at the annual meeting of the African Studies Association, Boston, October 1970).

to enslavement by the victors, for exchange or ransom at the end of hostilities or else for sale into slavery. Second, newly captured war prisoners had little or no value at the point of capture. West African societies were not equipped by custom or usage to guard prisoners on a permanent basis or to extract the kind of gang labor that might be available in prison camp conditions. New prisoners were a threat to the captor and a risk of loss by escape. If exchange or ransom was not contemplated, they were therefore normally sold into the slave trade, to be taken to a distant point where they could be sold to total strangers. This practice fitted the assimilative nature of much of West African slavery, where the slave gradually became a member of the new society and acquired rights, in normal circumstances,[1] including freedom from resale. For an unknown distance into the past, some kind of trade network had made it possible to move slaves to a distant point.

The possibility of export across the desert to the north also appeared as early as the eleventh century, and the trans-Saharan slave trade had a certain importance by the fourteenth century. Some of the prisoners found their way through Muslim North Africa to Europe, and communities of African freedmen already lived in several Spanish cities before the Portuguese reached West Africa by sea. When that happened, they began their export trade by tapping the existing trade to North Africa. Rather than trying to export slaves directly from the sub-Saharan coasts, they set up a post on the Mauritanian island of Arguin, which then attracted caravans making for Morocco. In the second half of the fifteenth century, they were able to buy 800 to 1,000 slaves a year, and for a short time they had a second post at Wadan in the Adrar, where they could deal directly with northbound caravans.[2]

This initial Portuguese entry into the trans-Sahara trade suggests that the internal slave trade before the fifteenth century was probably less important in the forest belt than it was in the open savanna to the north. In any event, comparatively few slaves were sold to the Europeans from any part of the main east-west coast bordering the Gulf of Guinea until after the middle of the seventeenth century, but Senegambia, with its combination of sahalian characteristics on the desert fringe and an opening to the Atlantic, became a major center for the sixteenth-century export trade by sea, losing its predominance first to Angola toward the end of the century and then to other West African regions through the course of the seventeenth. Senegambia was

1. For the non-salability of second-generation slaves see Moore, *Travels*, p. 43; Durand, *Sénégal* (for the Gambia Malinke); William A. Brown, "The Caliphate of Hamdullahi, ca. 1818–1864; A Study in African History and Tradition" (Ph.D. diss., University of Wisconsin, 1969), pp. 178–79 (for Maasina); Raffenel, *Nouveau voyage*, 1:441–42 (for Kaarta); Dr. Patenostre, "La captivité chez les peuples du Fouta-Djallon," *Outre-Mer*, 2:241–54, 353–72 (1930), pp. 243–48, 259 (for Fuuta Jallô and Maasina); Monteil, *Les Khassonké*, pp. 344–50 (Xaaso).

2. V. Magalhães-Godhino, *Economie de l'empire portugais au xve et xvie siècles* (Paris, 1969), pp. 181–85.

never again a major supplier in the enlarged trade that followed in the seventeenth and eighteenth centuries.

It is especially difficult to assess the relative importance of the relocation trade and the trans-Saharan exports. The relocation trade is impossible even to estimate before the mid-nineteenth century, when it grew immensely with the wars of Shaykh Umar in the 1850's, religious revolutions of the sixties, and the empire-building campaigns of Almaami Samori Ture that fed the trade into Senegambia from the southeast in the last quarter of the century. The size of the trans-Sahara trade is almost equally hard to estimate at most times, but it appears to have been especially large from about the time of Nasīr al-Dīn's unsuccessful jihad in the 1670's to the end of the Moroccan menace about the middle of the eighteenth century. The peak may well have come in the 1710's and 1720's, since Moroccan estimates place Mulai Ismā'īl's black army at a peak strength of 180,000 men, with 120,000 still enrolled at the time of his death in 1727.[3] These figures imply a total Moroccan import of at least 200,000 slaves over a fifty-year period, or about 4,000 a year—perhaps twice the number exported from Senegambia by sea at that same time. Morocco, however, drew from the whole sahal as far east as Timbuktu, and Senegambia's contribution may not have been as much as half of the total.

Enslavement and the Supply Function

The close connection between warfare and enslavement profoundly influenced the economics of the trade. For analytical purposes, two distinct models can represent the two different types of enslavement. One, an economic model, can be imagined as the circumstance in which the enslaver considered the act as an economic enterprise, allocating scarce resources according to a calculation of potential profit and loss. In this imaginary and extreme case, he would pay attention only to costs and revenues, setting the cost of waging war, organizing a raid, or kidnapping a child from a nearby village against the price he would receive from the slave dealer. A second model, a political model, can be imagined in opposite circumstances, where costs and profits had no place—where a ruler went to war for power, prestige, vengeance, or some other motive, but without considering the possible income from the sale of prisoners.

As with most analytical models of this kind, both are so extreme that neither was likely to have been a common reality, though both were possible. The conditions of the political model were fulfilled if the captor preferred to

3. James M. Matra to Lord Sydney, Tangiers, 28 March 1789, *PP, Accounts and Papers*, XXV (646), pp. 4–5.

kill all his prisoners for no ritual object rather than selling them. This is reported in a few cases where vengeance was the principal motive, but it was rare in Senegambia. The conditions of the economic model on the other hand, were met when kidnappers captured non-enemy people and sold them into the trade. This too may have happened, but even a gang of bandits would choose to raid enemies rather than friends as long as costs and risks were equal; and it would be hard for any ruler to contemplate a declaration of war without some thought of the booty that might come with victory.

Particular instances of enslavement might lie at various points along the continuum between the political and economic models, and the tendency toward one or the other was crucial in determining the initial "cost" of a slave entering the trade. As a particular case approached the political model, captives were a windfall with neglegible actual cost to the captor. He could therefore sell them at the going price in his region, and that price would be very low where captures on the political model were common. In effect, it would only cover the opportunity cost—the value of the slave put to alternative use—and a war prisoner held by enemies near his homeland would be expensive to guard and dangerous to have around. Where the economic model was dominant, however, the actual costs and risks of capturing people were part of the economic cost. In theory, then, the price elasticity of supply—the degree to which supply to the trade would respond to price changes—would be higher where the economic model was dominant and zero where political factors fed slaves into the trade regardless of cost.

This analysis suggests the theoretical possibility of assessing the importance of the political as against the economic model by reference to the price elasticity of slave supply from any part of Africa, though the possibility cannot be fully realized. Data are available to estimate elasticities of supply from coastal points only, and at those points the total cost of a slave for export had two components, the price paid to the original captor and the cost of moving the slave down the caravan routes to the coast. Whatever the motivation of the captor, that of the traders was clearly economic. They would therefore respond to higher prices by going further into the interior in search of slaves for sale, and a responsiveness in the supply of slaves on the coast might indicate nothing more than the enterprise of the juula. If, on the other hand, the supply of slaves were unresponsive to price changes, that fact would create at least the presumption that enslavement on the political model was dominant.

This hypothesis would have to be checked against the full range of evidence from several regions in Africa to be confirmed, but it is worth pursuing in an experimental way for Senegambia alone. Fortunately, slave prices are reasonably well reported, at least over the long run. (See *Supplement,* appendix 8.) Separate time series for Saint Louis and the mouth of the Gambia are

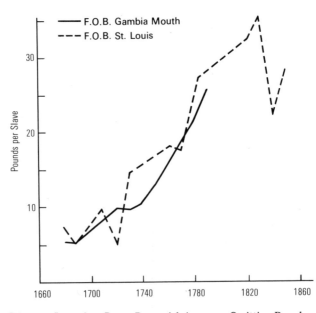

4.1 Slave Prices at Senegalese Ports, Decennial Averages, Omitting Decades with Insufficient Observations   UWCL

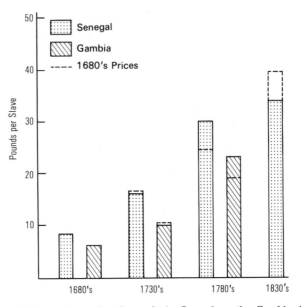

4.2 Real and Money Prices for Slaves f.o.b. Senegal or the Gambia, by Fifty-Year Intervals, 1680's–1830's   UWCL

mutually reinforcing in their evidence about the main trends. (See figure 4.1.) And the money prices can be adjusted to approximate real values. (See table 4.1 and figure 4.2.) The real prices approximately trebled between the 1680's and the 1780's, and then doubled in the half-century to the 1830's.

Similar data on the quantity of slaves exported are necessary to calculate the price elasticity of supply, and this information is more difficult to come by. Some aspects of the Senegambian slave trade, like the number passing downriver from Gajaaga to Saint Louis, were reported with some frequency— in this case twenty-nine years of the eighteenth century are covered (see table in *Supplement,* appendix 12), but the actual number exported from the Gambia in English ships is explicitly reported for only one year, 1766–67. French exports from Senegambia are reported for only fifteen individual years of the whole period 1680–1830. Though incomplete as a time series, these reports are at least a point of departure, and are given in the *Supplement* table A11.1.

More complete estimates have to be built up from other and more indirect kinds of information. One kind is the individual estimate by a contempo-

Table 4.1
Prices of Slaves in Senegambia, Decennial Averages
1680–1860

	F.o.b. prices in prime-cost value of goods paid, expressed £ sterling		F.o.b. prices expressed £ sterling at prevailing value of the 1680's	
	St. Louis	Gambia mouth	St. Louis	Gambia mouth
1680's	£8.15	£5.47	£8.15	£5.47
1690's	5.19	5.27	–	–
1700's	–	–	–	–
1710's	9.71	–	–	–
1720's	5.61	9.43	–	–
1730's	14.38	9.03	15.98	10.03
1740's	–	10.05	–	–
1750's	–	12.80	–	–
1760's	18.27	14.10	–	–
1770's	17.90	–	–	–
1780's	27.14	20.95	24.67	19.05
1790's	27.52	–	–	–
1800's	–	–	–	–
1810's	–	–	–	–
1820's	32.79	–	–	–
1830's	34.33	–	39.92	–
1840's	22.32	–	–	–
1850's	28.52	–	–	–

Source: *Supplement,* table A8.2.

raneous observer, either in Senegambia or in Europe, giving the usual level of the trade "in an ordinary year"—or occasionally predicting the level to be attained in the near future. In either case, the figure should be understood as a capacity estimate, and the real annual average trade carried will be smaller. Those who talked about "an ordinary year" were not talking about statistical annual averages. They usually thought of a recent year when nothing spectacular went wrong, taking no account of the years when the trade at sea was stopped by European wars or the years when caravans failed to arrive from "the merchants' country" because of African wars. Those who made predictions often did so as advocates of particular policies, and they were usually overoptimistic.

Whenever capacity estimates of this kind can be checked against actual, measured time series, the measured series fall short—in the slave trade of the eighteenth century by a range between 25 and 50 per cent.[1] But it is still possible to use the estimates when necessary, correcting the more grandiose where possible with harder data,[2] to come up with a table based on as many capacity estimates as the contemporaneous literature affords. In table 4.2, each individual estimate was reduced to an annual average and then assumed to stand for the approximate level of slave exports for the period between the midpoints separating it in time from the next earlier or later.

A second form of estimate from distant and indirect information gives another and predictably lower result. In this case, the total slave exports estimated for French and British shipping respectively can be subdivided according to the coastal region of origin by reference to a variety of samples. These can be port samples, such as the declared destinations of ships from Nantes or Liverpool, filled in occasionally with contemporaneous opinion where that opinion about the percentages derived from different parts of the

1. This tendency to speak nonstatistically is common still in ordinary speech. A "day's work" is the measure of an ordinary successful, fully occupied work period. It takes no account of the inevitable effect over time of accidents like sickness, snow storms, traffic tie-ups, or other vicissitudes of modern life.

In *The Atlantic Slave Trade* I collected global capacity estimates of this kind for the British slave trade. The best available measured totals (*Atlantic Slave Trade*, p. 142, revised with reference to Roger Anstey, "Volume and Profitability of the Atlantic Slave Trade, 1761–1810," in S. L. Engerman and E. D. Genovese, eds , *Race and Slavery in the Western Hemisphere: Quantitative Studies* [Princeton, 1974]), come to 56.3 per cent of the capacity estimates.

2. In this instance, one estimate for the period 1763–78 gave an annual average of 5,700 ("Etat des esclaves." in ANF, C6 18), while another for 1786 went as high as 7,450 (S. M. X. de Golberry, *Fragmens d'un voyage en Afrique, fait pendant des années, 1785, 1786, 1787, dans les contrées occidentales de ce continent, comprises entres le cap Blanc de Barbarie . . . et le cap des Palmes . . .* , 2 vols. [Paris, An X (1802)], 2:18–20, 147–51); but both of these were omitted because they were contrary to recorded exports at these or adjacent dates.

coast can fill a gap in the record. A calculation of this kind for the several regions of the West African coast is reprinted in table 4.3.[3]

Table 4.3 is inaccurate in one major way. The slave trade carried by the North Americans was especially active in Senegambia, beginning in the second half of the 1780's, and continuing through the next decades at least until the United States' abolition of its legal slave trade in 1808. The special American position as a neutral carrier during the wars of the French Revolution and Napoleon made it possible for the Americans to pick up some of the excess export capacity left by the French and English after 1793, but the extent of this pickup is uncertain. Contemporaneous reports make it highly unlikely that the total slave exports ever again reached the level of the 1780's, but they were certainly markedly higher than the figures reported for the English and French alone in those last two decades of legal trade.

Projections of French exports are not possible for the period before 1711, but the English slave trade from the Gambia can be estimated back to 1681 on the same basis as table 4.3. For 1683–88, the Gambia account books of the Royal African Company have been preserved. The Company's monopoly was nearly fully intact in the Gambia at that period, so that its trade can be treated as the total British trade, and it is possible to estimate the quantities of each commodity exported, including slaves. (See *Supplement*, appendix 11.) Unless the samples are skewed in some way not clear from the account books, the general accuracy of these estimates should be comparatively high. (See table 4.4.)

Tables 4.3 and 4.4 can be illustrated graphically, with additional estimates for the period after 1815, and this time-series can be compared with the capacity estimates from table 4.2. As figure 4.3 indicates, the capacity estimates were generally higher than those calculated from indirect projections, as expected. The rise and fall of the quantities exported is basically similar on the two curves, with the marked exception of the 1750's, 1760's, and 1770's. Each of these is explicable. The capacity estimates for the 1750's were based on estimates for the early 1750's before the recommencement of the Anglo-French war and the English capture of Saint Louis. Those for the 1760's, on the other hand, tend to overestimate the trade the English would be able to carry on with both the Senegal and Gambia in their control, and they too are based on peacetime years during a decade when the French and English were still at war until 1763. During the 1770's, the "competent

3. The proportional distribution is preferred to absolute numbers in an estimate, since absolute numbers refer to capacity rather than performance. The version I published in *The Atlantic Slave Trade*, p. 142, has since been revised on the basis of the new evidence offered in Roger Anstey, "Volume and Profitability," and republished in Curtin, "Measuring the Atlantic Slave Trade," in Engerman and Genovese, *Race and Slavery in the Western Hemisphere*.

Table 4.2

Consolidated Capacity Estimates for the Slave Exports of Senegambia
(not to be understood as the number of slaves actually exported)

Date of estimate	Distribution of slaves by embarkation point					Total annually	Applied to years	Total for period
	St. Louis	Gajaaga	Gorée	French Gambia	English Gambia			
1687[1]	100	—	500	750		1,350	1681–89	12,150
1693[2]	200	—	200	500		900	1690–1704	13,500
1716[3]		2,380			750	3,130	1705–16	32,160
1718[4]	50	600	470	400	750	2,270	1717–23	15,890
1730[5]		1,090			3,000	4,090	1724–35	49,080
1741[6]		900			2,140	3,040	1736–46	33,440
1753[7]	500	550	540		1,000	2,590	1747–60	36,260
1766[8]	1,110		425		1,511	3,050	1761–67	21,350
1769–78[9]	1,500		300		1,500	3,300	1768–78	36,300
1779–88[10]		1,716			1,050	2,800	1779–92	39,200
1795[11]		—			1,000	1,000	1793–1800	8,000
1802–10[12]		700				700	1801–10	7,000
							Total	304,330
							Total 1711–1810 only	259,900

Sources:

1. Ducasse, "Mémoire ou relation du S. du Casse sur son voyage de Guinée," (mss., ANF-OM, DFC Sénégal 1, no. 4).
2. La Courbe, "Mémoire sur le commerce de Guinée," ANF, C6 2.

3. Brue to CI, 13 February 1617, ANF, C6 5. Estimate of the French trade is a measurement of slaves actually shipped between August 15, 1715, and February 13, 1716—doubled to yield an approximate annual rate. English trade from the Gambia follows estimate for 1718 cited in note 4 below.

4. Unsigned, undated "Mémoire général sur le commerce du Sénégal," ANF, C6 14. Estimate of the French-carried exports reprinted and identified as 1718 in Postlethwayt, *Universal Dictionary* (1710), 1:845. English exports as estimated in "Mémoire sur le commerce du Sénégal," a document similar to the foregoing but different from it in certain respects. Also in ANF, C6 14.

5. An estimate of French-carried exports formed by taking the mean of the recorded exports for 1729 and 1730 (1140 and 1039 respectively) from "Etat des sommes," dated 28 July 1732, ANF, C6 10, and "Sénégal 1731 à 1740," ANF, C6 12. English export estimate is from Francis Moore, *Travels*, p. 41.

6. Estimates drawn from Conseil du Sénégal to Compagnie des Indes, 14 January 1742, ANF, C6 12; unsigned "Mémoire concernant le commerce," enclosed with Commandant Gorée to Director Saint Louis, 4 June 1741, ANF, C6 12.

7. French estimates from Conseil du Sénégal to CI, 31 July 1755, ANF, C6 14; English from Skinner to African Committee, 28 February 1752, T 70/29.

8. A composite estimate based on recorded exports at nearby dates. Saint Louis exports are adjusted from recorded sailings between 23 September 1764 and 11 August 1765 to produce an annual figure. (Return of Exports, 31 May 1766, CO 267/1.) Gorée exports are as estimated by O'Hara, the English governor of Senegal, for 1766. (Despatch of 15 September 1768, CO 267/14.) Gambia sailings are an annual figure derived from a list of ships passing James Island outbound between 4 May 1766 and 5 August 1767. (Return enclosed with Debat to Board of Trade, 21 Sept. 1767, CO 267/1).

9. Senegal and Gambia estimates are those of William Rogers, memo dated 29 August 1778, CO 267/17, giving these estimates as those of "competent judges" of the annual average purchases in the Province of Senegambia over the period approximately 1769–79. Gorée estimate is that of Le Brasseur for 1773–74, "Nouvelles reflections sur le Gambie," 10 October 1777, ANF, C6 17.

10. Gambia estimate is that of Captain Heatley, a Gambia trader at this period, from Board of Trade Report, part I. The Saint Louis and Gorée estimate is the annual average of recorded purchases in 1784 and 1786–88, reported in annual returns found in ANF C6 19.

11. French slave trade was at a very low ebb after 1793 and can be assumed to have been inactive. M. Park reported as of c. 1795 that the exports from the Gambia by all nations were less than 1,000 per year. Hence that figure is adopted as an overall estimate for the whole Senegambia.

12. An estimate for 1810 is found in J. M. Gray, *Gambia*, p. 295, on the authority of the African Institution. During the Peace of Amiens, the French succeeded in exporting 456 slaves a year from Saint Louis. (Statement for the second half of the year and the first half of the year XI [approximately 4 March 1802 to 5 March], 1803 ANF, C6 20.)

Table 4.3

Slave Exports from Senegambia, 1711–1810
(based on aggregate estimates of the French and English
slave trades derived from shipping data
and assigned to coastal regions following
a variety of samples)

Dates	French exports	British exports	Total
1711–20	10,300	20,600	30,900
1721–30	13,400	9,100	22,500
1731–40	12,300	13,900	26,200
1741–50	7,700	17,300	25,000
1751–60	6,300	16,200	22,500
1761–70	2,300	11,800	14,100
1771–80	4,000	8,100	12,100
1781–90	17,400	2,900	20,300
1791–1800	3,400	2,800	6,200
1801–1810	500	1,500	2,000
Total	77,600	104,200	181,800

Sources: Curtin, *The Atlantic Slave Trade*, pp. 221, 170, 180; Anstey, "The Volume and Profitability of the Atlantic Slave Trade 1761–1810" (unpublished mss). The French export figure for 1801–10 modified in the light of slave export during the Peace of Amiens, in statement covering the years X and XI, ANF, C6 20.

Note: For the decades 1761–70 and 1771–80, British-carried exports include most exports from both the Gambia and the Senegal, and French-carried exports are those by way of Gorée only.

judges" who supposedly knew the capacity of the Gambia and Senegal slave trade merely repeated the usual estimates of the recent past; the projected figure based on the sailings from Liverpool is therefore preferred. With the 1780's, the figures for Senegal in table 4.2 are no longer capacity estimates but the actual count of slaves exported (as given in the *Supplement,* appendix 11, table A11.1), and the confirmation of the indirect projections in table 4.3 is almost too good to be true; but the Gambia capacity estimate for that decade continues almost three times too high. In general, then, table 4.3 should be far more accurate than table 4.2, but 4.2 is still helpful in filling in the distribution of the slave trade among Senegambian ports.

With the estimates of quantity and price in hand, the problem of elasticity reemerges. It is hypothetically possible that an inelastic supply of slaves would imply enslavement mainly following the political model, while an elastic response to price would open the possibility of "economic" enslavement. The unanswered question is the relative weight to be placed on more

Table 4.4

Estimated English Slave Exports from the Gambia, 1681–1710

Year	Annual export	Period	Annual average export
		1681–90	1,200
1683	1,310		
1684	690		
1685	1,480		
1686	1,850		
1687	810		
1688	1,040		
		1691–1700	900
		1701–10	1,750

Sources: 1683–88 from Gambia Journals, RAC, T 70/546. Following the mode of calculation outlined in *Supplement*, appendix 15. Data for 1691–1710 from P. D. Curtin, *Atlantic Slave Trade*, p. 150.

active enslavement, as against more active penetration to distant sources by the slave dealers.

The issue is raised most forcefully, for the entire Atlantic basin, by correspondence between the steep eighteenth-century rise in the real prices paid for slaves and an equivalent increase in the numbers carried across the ocean. One recent line of interpretation points up the importance of rising slave prices for the planters of the American tropics. Planters generally calculated in the early eighteenth century that it was cheaper to buy new slaves from Africa than to encourage the natural growth of a creole slave population—hence heavily unbalanced sex ratios, minimal time allowed female slaves for child care, and other policies that discouraged population growth. As prices rose, however, replacement from Africa was no longer an economic alternative to seeking high fertility rates among creole slaves. The critical price level was reached at different times in different parts of the Americas, but the general result was to encourage policies designed to make slave populations capable of net natural growth, which in turn placed a limit on the long-term demand for slaves from Africa.

On the African side, rising prices increased the potential profit from slave raiding. They therefore encouraged a shift from the political model toward the economic model of enslavement. It is impossible to measure this shift, but the enormous increase in incentives suggests that it was probably significant. Not only was the export of more people an obvious atrocity against those who were shipped overseas, but it was also damaging to societies like those in West Africa which tended to be underpopulated in any event. Even if there was no increase in the rate of enslavement, only in the rate of export, the

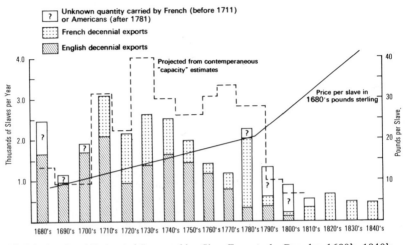

4.3 Calculated and Estimated Senegambian Slave Exports, by Decades, 1680's–1840's

UWCL

inland spread of slave traders into new parts of the continent meant that more people were diverted from the relatively benign African servitude to the more destructive plantation slavery of the New World.[4]

On the face of it, the highest price elasticity of supply to the Atlantic slave trade as a whole came at the period from the 1680's to the 1780's, being 1.2, measured by the price of slaves in Saint Louis set against the general estimates for slaves delivered to the New World. (See figure 4.4.) A similar calculation based on prices current on the Gold Coast has yielded a similar result, implying an overall elasticity of 1 or a little more.[5] That result, however, is true only for the Atlantic slave trade as a whole, not for the regional exports of Senegambia considered separately. From the 1680's to the 1730's, Sene-

---

4. See P. Bohannan and P. Curtin, *Africa and Africans,* 2nd ed. (New York, 1971), pp. 268–76; P. D. Curtin, "Epidemiology and the Slave Trade," *Political Science Quarterly,* 83:190–216 (1968), esp. pp. 207–15. Many of the implications are spelled out in greater detail in E. Phillip Le Veen, "British Slave Trade Suppression Policies 1821–1865: Impact and Implications" (Ph.D. diss., University of Chicago, 1971), and "A Quantitative Analysis of the Impact of British Suppression Policies on the Volume of the Nineteenth-Century Atlantic Slave Trade," in Engerman and Genovese, *Race and Slavery in the Western Hemisphere.*

5. Quantities exported are for the final quarter of the seventeenth century and for the twenty years 1761–80 respectively, from Curtin, *Atlantic Slave Trade,* pp. 119 and 216. Values are £8.15 for the 1680's, rising to £18.09 (the mean for the 1760's and 1770's in *Supplement* table A8.2). See also Le Veen, "Suppression Policies," esp. pp. 156–68.

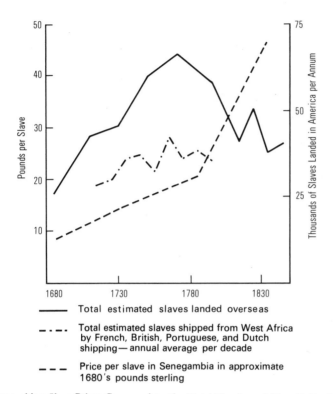

—————— Total estimated slaves landed overseas

— . —. Total estimated slaves shipped from West Africa
by French, British, Portuguese, and Dutch
shipping—annual average per decade

— — — Price per slave in Senegambia in approximate
1680's pounds sterling

4.4 Senegambian Slave Prices Compared to the Total Number of Slave Deliveries to the
New World   UWCL

gambian exports rose even more rapidly than slave prices, but after the
1730's, when the prices went on up still more rapidly, Senegambian supply
fell, indicating a negative elasticity of supply, presumably because the Senegambian supply curve shifted to the left in response to changing political and
military conditions. If the rising prices encouraged some people to work
harder kidnapping others for the trade, the net effect of these captures was
lost in the more significant regional decline.

Then, between the 1770's and the 1780's, the trend was apparently reversed by a new factor at play. With the French back in control of Saint
Louis after 1779, paying a bounty of £3.98 for each slave delivered to the
French colonies, raised to £6.37 in 1787, the demand curve shifted upward
and supply responded with a sharp increase in the French-carried trade in the

1780's. At the same time, the British trade, which paid no bounty, dropped to less than it had been at any time in the past century. (Figure 4.3.)

After the 1780's, prices paid for slaves dropped in some parts of Africa, and lowering prices brought lower deliveries and a continuing price elasticity of supply.[6] In Senegambia, however, the supply curve continued to shift to the left, and the local price rose, with no response in supply. The Senegambian price for the 1830's is based on prices in Gajaaga, which rose and remained high for seasons peculiar to the upper Senegal. In spite of the use of steam on the river, the French in Saint Louis found that they could buy slaves in Bissau on the coast for 40 per cent less than they had to pay in Bakel.[7] Regionally within Senegambia, in short, the chief region of supply to the export trade had practically priced itself out of the market. The apparent implication, then, is that the economic response to price changes was not absent, but at most times it was comparatively unimportant in this region, compared, at least, to its role elsewhere in Africa.

The Economics of Delivery to the Coast

The trade in slaves was a trade in people—people treated as a commodity but still people--and this gave them an economic character different from other commodities. To begin with, they were self-propelled. The cost of moving a gang was no more than the cost of food and the wages of guards, both required whether the slaves moved or not. To an extent, this was true of cattle as well;[1] they too needed food and herdsmen, but they could often find more food by moving than by staying in one place, and the parallel has other limits. Cattle were sold for their meat and hides, so that cattle fed for the market could increase in value; they could even multiply and produce marketable offspring within a short time. Idle people do not increase in value, and idle slaves were simply unemployed workers, whose maintenance was a dead loss to the master.

6. E. Phillip Le Veen found that Gold Coast prices declined as supply declined in the late eighteenth century, so that an elasticity of about 1.5 continued even through the downward part of the curve. (Le Veen, "Suppression Policies," esp. pp. 156–68.)

7. C. Faure, "La garnison européene du Sénégal (1819–1826)," *RHCF*, 8:5–108 (1920), pp. 70–76.

1. A similar distinction was made among the Soninke of Jahunu and its vicinity between *naabure siginto* (standing or walking property), such as cattle, slaves, or horses, and *naabure jura* (property lying down), but this distinction had to do not merely with mobility but also with visibility. The *naabure siginto* were the prestige goods signifying a rich man, because, if for no other reason, they were obvious to his neighbors in a way that gold, silver, cowries, or a store of cloth might not be. (See E. Pollet and G. Winter, *La société Soninké (Dyahunu, Mali)* [Brussels, 1972], pp. 145–48.)

Thus, while it cost comparatively little to move slaves, it cost a great deal to hold them for the market. This cost varied a good deal from year to year, depending on the rainfall, which governed the price of millet—but it was always high in comparison with the market price of slaves who needed a daily ration of up to 1 kg of millet a day, plus some allowance of other food. Millet prices at Saint Louis in the mid-1750's varied from about £2.60 a metric ton in a very good year to as much as £19.50 a ton in a very bad year if it could be found at all. In a year thought to be ordinary, millet cost about £6.80 a ton, and that can be taken as a rough annual average. At that price, it took £2.74 to keep one person in millet for one year, at a time and place where an ordinary slave cost £10 to £12. With additional costs for housing, clothing, guards, and other food (which was essential to keep a slave in good physical condition for later sale), the cost of holding slaves (in effect, the storage cost) must have been about half the purchase price per year, in an ordinary year, varying downward to a quarter in a very good year, but higher even than the purchase price in a year of famine.[2]

Storage costs were the most important part of the difference between the price paid for slaves in the interior and the f.o.b. prices on the coast. This aspect of price structure was especially striking in Gajaaga, where boats could carry the slaves through to Saint Louis only in the annual high season. Slaves bought in January just after the boats left had to be held for at least nine months, and this was reflected in the price. In the 1750's, the Compagnie des Indes paid according to a sliding scale, rising by 80 per cent from a low point

2. Food prices for the 1750's reported in memoir dated 15 May 1754, ANF, C6 14. Millet rations were reported as 1 kg per day per slave in 1718, but without a meat allotment, though Christian Africans at the same period were allowed 857 grams of millet supplemented by 245 grams of meat. ("Mémoire général sur le commerce du Sénégal," ANF, C6 14.) From all indications, neither the rations nor the range of prices were very different from those that prevailed in the 1710's or the 1720's, though the exceptional drought of the 1750's meant that there were more years of scarcity and high prices at that time. For the earlier period see Labat, *Nouvelle relation,* 4:244; Demoin, Memorandum of 7 April 1726, ANF, C6 9.

This general relationship of slave prices to the cost of food was remarkably persistent. In the early twentieth century in Xaaso a system of ideal values related millet to cloth and to slaves so that 180 *mud* of millet were considered equal to a year's support, while the standard price of a young male slave was 500 mud and that of a young girl 1,000 mud—so that the value of a young male slave was translatable at a nominal 2.75 years of support. (Monteil, *Les Khassonke,* pp. 119–22.)

Because of these storage costs, one possibility for European merchants in the enclaves was to sell slaves to local Africans in return for other commodities that could be stored more easily. The RAC officials at James fort decided at one point in 1722 that uncertainty about the arrival time of the next ship made it worthwhile exchanging their slaves for ivory. (Council Minutes, James Fort, November 12, 1722. Rawlinson Papers, Bodleian Library, Oxford).

after the departure of the annual fleet to the high point just as the last boats prepared to sail at the end of the next high season.[3]

Storage costs other than food imposed some economies and some diseconomies of scale. It was not necessary always to keep slaves waiting shipment inside the stone-built trade castles, but only adequate and properly designed *captiveries* or slave quarters could hold many slaves with few guards. Numbers too great for the planned accommodations increased the cost so much that the French in Gajaaga sometimes let exceptionally large caravans pass on to the Gambia without even trying to buy. The problem at Fort Saint Joseph was all the more severe because of the long dry season without shipping. The fort could have handled more slaves, but only at the expense of large fixed installations that might not be needed every year. Just before the English invasion of 1758, the captiverie at Fort Saint Joseph could hold only 250 slaves, which set a limit on possible dry-season purchases (though slaves arriving in the high season could usually be shipped off immediately to Saint Louis). This limitation tended to accentuate Gambia's advantage in the dry-season trade.

The European traders were at a serious disadvantage in storage costs compared to their juula trade partners and sometime competitors. Their European posts lacked an agricultural or industrial sector that could absorb labor on a temporary basis, while the juula towns always had farm work to be done in the wet season, and weaving the year round, both of which used slave labor. This meant that slaves held for later shipment could be made self-sustaining and might even produce a small surplus over their own maintenance. In Gajaaga, for example, the merchant-clerics held slaves brought in during the dry season, rather than selling immediately to the French. They could use the labor to put in the millet crop on the jeeri land early in the rainy season. When the boats actually began to arrive from Saint Louis, not only was planting over but the price of slaves also reached its annual maximum. Only then were slaves turned over to the Europeans.[4]

Similar uses of slave labor made it possible to accumulate slaves from one season to the next, or until the group was large enough to justify a trip to the ports and command the higher prices paid on bulk purchases. The possibility of delay also allowed the juula to adjust to short-run fluctuations in European demand. When Mungo Park came through to the upper Gambia with a caravan from the Bamako region in 1797, they soon began hearing reports of low demand on the Gambia. The first to drop out was a Jahaanke merchant from Bani Israela in Dentilia. His home was about halfway along the route between the Niger valley where the slaves originated and the point of sale on

---

3. A retrospective description of trade practices before the loss of Sénégal in 1758 is found in "Mémoire sur la concession du Sénégal," 2 November 1762, ANF, C6 14.

4. Levens, Report of 10 July 1725, BN, FF, NA, 9339, f. 147.

the coast, and he decided to put them to work for a year rather than risk a low market on the Gambia. Further along, in the Tanda wilderness, they met another, eastbound caravan with still more news of low demand for slaves. At that, some Gajaaga clerics who had joined the caravan partway along also broke off and made for their own home base, some 300 kms north-northeast. Once home, they could put the slaves to work during the approaching rainy season and then sell them to the Saint Louis traders before the water fell, or else hold them for the next season's dry-season trade on the Gambia.[5] Meanwhile, the Muslim Malinke from the Niger valley had no such option and kept on to the Gambia to make the best arrangement they could. One alternative still open was to rent land near the Gambia and stay over a season to grow crops for sale—the distant beginnings of the later Gambian phenomenon of "strange farmers" who came from the east to rent land for a season or so before returning home with their savings.

Even without juula account books as evidence, it seems a fair speculation that this ability to adjust the supply to the demand over the short term was one of the principal advantages the juula had over the European trade networks. On the Gambia by the second half of the eighteenth century, African traders and brokers were in fact performing the functions once performed by the Royal African Company, selling slaves to English ships along the middle Gambia on conditions that were essentially f.o.b. for bulk purchases—and, incidentally, taking the local middleman's profits that had once gone to the Company. (See *Supplement,* appendix 8.)

Juula could also profit from the fact that slaves on the march could carry a load at no extra cost. Economically, the passage of slaves was like ballast in ocean shipping, where high-bulk, low-weight cargoes (or voyages with a paying cargo in only one direction) called for an additional load of heavy cargo for the sake of seaworthy stowage. Since the cost of the voyage was paid by the regular cargo, captains or supercargoes were free to load anything that was heavy and could also bring some price at the other end. Ballast, in effect, was free cargo capacity. In much the same way, slaves had to move, and they had to be fed; their passage meant low-cost cargo capacity moving westward. In addition, the caravan leader had to have some way of taking the return cargoes eastward. The normal transport animal was the donkey, but it was simply not possible to sell slaves and buy donkeys with part of the proceeds. The Gambia was a net importer of donkeys, and even Gajaaga bought most of its donkeys from the sahal further north.[6] This meant that each westbound caravan offered "no-cost" transportation equal to the carrying capacity of the slaves plus that of the donkeys that went along.

A rough estimate of this carrying capacity is possible by looking at actual

5. Park, *Travels,* 1:527–28.
6. Raffenel, *Nouveau voyage,* 1:32.

Table 4.5
A Sample of Quantities and Weights of
Goods Exchanged for 180 Slaves,
the Gambia, 1740–41

Commodity	Quantity	Actual or estimated weight (kgs)
Silver	1,178 coins	17
Guns	164	372
Rum	119 gallons	450
Gunpowder		518
Silesias (linen cloth)	150 pieces	300
Iron bars	430 bars	4,730
Cutlasses	92	63
Gunflints	450	1
Carnelian beads ("arrangoes")	15,195 stones	30
Salt	1,162 kgs	1,162
Bafatas (Indian textile)	43 pieces	108
Glass beads		1,996
Woolen cloth, various colors	219.2 yards	219
Lead balls		16
Crystal	60,700 stones	131
Brass pans	102 pans	457
Pewter ware		301
Pistols	71 pairs	129
Long cloths (Indian textile)	20 pieces	40
Cowrie shells		17
Manchester goods (textiles)	30 pieces	130
Fringe		181
Paper	47 reams	107
Copper	2 rods	1
Total		11,476

Source: T 70/573 and 575. The sample is the total of three
representative sales of 180 slaves to the Royal African Company
in June 1740 and June 1741. The bundle of commodities received is the kind of assortment involved in most large transactions on the Gambia in the mid-eighteenth century. The indicated weight is the weight of the commodity alone, with no
allowance for packing materials.

transactions, taking some Royal African Company transactions of 1740–41 as
an example. The purchase of a large group of slaves in a single transaction
indicated a caravan coming down from the interior. The total of three large
transactions in 1740 or 1741, for 180 slaves in all, is shown in table 4.5 by
quantity and estimated weight. The returns came to 64 kgs a slave, for which
donkeys had to be provided. Since donkeys normally carried 50 to 100 kgs

each, this meant approximately one donkey making a round trip for each one-way trip by a slave in transit. Slaves themselves were usually loaded with 25 kgs for men and 15 kgs for women. At 5 men to each woman (a conservative ratio for this period), there would have been 150 men and 30 women, or a westward carrying capacity for the slaves of 4.2 metric tons or about 23 kgs per slave. Total "costless" or ballast transportation generated would then be on the order of 87 kgs per slave sold. The total is not enormous—perhaps 35 metric tons a year when the slave trade from the upper Niger to Senegambia ran at an ordinary rate of about 400 slaves a year, or 218 tons in peak years when slaves moving over that route may have been as many as 2,500—but quantities flowing in Senegambian trade were not large either. The total of ivory exported from the Gambia in 1741 was only 25 tons;[7] that much could have been carried as "ballast" with something over for other goods.

The economic consequences of this ballast effect were significant in breaking through the natural tariff of distance and high transport costs. It made possible the inland extension of elephant hunting as the coastal elephants were wiped out. Most of the slaves from the far interior came through Bundu, which allowed Bunduunke cloths to sell on the Gambia in competition with the local product and the Indian cloths imported by Europeans, even though Bunduunke cloth had to be head-loaded or carried by donkeys as far as 500 kms. The European traders also recognized the economics of the ballast effect. At least for a time in the 1690's, it was regular policy of the Royal African Company to buy slaves on the Gambia for the sole purpose of attracting other goods, even though the slaves cost more than they did elsewhere along the African coast.[8]

The European Factor

As we have seen more than once, Europeans on the coast functioned as part of the Senegalese family of trade networks, as well as intermediaries between those networks and the unacculturated Europeans. In the era of the great companies, they not only acted as middlemen for the maritime slave trade, they also sold slaves to coastal Africans[1]—acting, in

7. "Mémoire concernant le commerce," enclosed with Commandant Gorée to Director, Saint Louis, 4 June 1741, ANF, C6 12.

8. Thomas Thurloe to RAC, Gambia, 15 March 1677/78, T 70/10; Boucard, "Relation de Bambouc," June 1729, AM, mss, 50/2, f. 22–23; Davies, *Royal African Company*, p. 236. For the nineteenth-century Bunduunke cloth industry see Raffenel, *Nouveau voyage*, 1:78; Rey to Governor Senegal, 15 October 1852, ANF-OM, Sénégal XIII 54.

1. Davies, *Royal African Company*, p. 236; RAC to Thomas Whitney and others, 16 May 1721, and RAC to Anthony Rogers and others, 29 February 1727/28, T 70/55.

short, as middlemen in the internal slave trade as well—and they sold slaves to each other from time to time, even though this was contrary to the spirit of national competition. In 1740, the Royal African Company made a regular contract with the Compagnie des Indes to supply 300 good slaves a year at James Fort in return for 587 kgs of gum per slave. Even later, in the 1770's when the companies were gone, O'Hara, the English governor at Fort Lewis, sold a shipment of slaves to the French commandant on Gorée, though this appears to have been an exceptional act in time of famine.[2]

Some of these transactions, where the multiple functions normally performed by slave traders can be regarded separately, provide a rare opportunity to see how different functions were rewarded. In 1733, for example, the Royal African Company accepted a cargo of trade goods from a private trader in return for African products. The shipper was credited with a markup of 45.8 per cent over the prime cost of those same goods in England, representing the probable estimated value of his services in transporting those goods to the Gambia. The Company then sold him a cargo of slaves, ivory, and wax, where its own markup in return for bulking and transportation to James Island was about 280 per cent for slaves, 360 per cent for ivory, and 230 per cent for wax. The usual markup was somewhat lower, in the vicinity of 60 per cent, but even at that lower rate the charge for the Company's middleman role was greater than the cost of bringing trade goods from England. Over the years 1731–40, the Compagnie des Indes found that its cost for slaves f.o.b. Saint Louis over the period 1731–40 represented an advance of 76.2 per cent over the price per slave it paid to the Africans.[3]

In either case, the high markup was worthwhile to the shipper. A fast turnaround allowed him to avoid the high mortality and the high costs of keeping a ship idle waiting to purchase slaves in small quantities, and he could send ships to the Gambia or Senegal under officers only slightly acquainted with Senegambian languages and trading practices. Bulking at fortified trading posts by European personnel was extremely expensive, but it was considered to be cheaper for European shipping firms because it saved the higher costs of doing the same on shipboard.

That situation began to change on the Gambia after the 1730's, as more of the English slavers began to trade upriver, dealing directly with African middlemen. Over time, they began to pay higher prices, but these prices

2. Contract of 25 May 1750, ANF, C6 12; RAC to Anthony Rogers, 25 November 1731, T 70/55. For O'Hara's transaction see Rastel de Rocheblave to Boniface, "Observations sur l'isle de Gorée, ANF, C6 16.

3. See *Supplement*, appendix 8. For sample transactions of this kind see Gambia Journals, 16 February 1732/33, pp. 332 and 120; 8 May 1736, T 70/565; 5 May 1739, T 70/571. Comparable French data are from "Sénégal 1731 à 1740," ANF, C6 12. In 1730, the Royal African Company believed that it could have "reasonable profit" if trade goods from England were marked up 40 to 50 per cent over prime cost when sold at the Gambia. (RAC to Anthony Rogers and others. 31 July 1730, T 70/55.)

reflected the fact that Africans now fulfilled the old role of the Royal African Company. Even on the coast, at James Island and Gorée, the usual markup from the price paid to the African slave dealer on shore to that charged the European slaver at the port dropped from more than 66 per cent to about 33 per cent after the middle of the eighteenth century. Since the slave ships could not easily sail up the Senegal, the Afro-French community in Saint Louis kept a markup of about 200 per cent between Gajaaga and the port,[4] but its economic competitors on the Gambia were no longer a European company. After the 1740's they were a diverse group of juula, Afro-Europeans, and private Europeans.

Many other trade practices grew out of an interaction between the interests of the Europeans and those of their African trade partners. The age and sex distribution in the slave trade, for example, depended on African as well as American conditions. The custom of the slave trade from at least the end of the sixteenth century had been to deal in slaves in terms of a standard unit of labor power, called a *peça da Indias* in Portuguese and carried over as a *pièce d'Inde* in French or simply "one good slave" in English. In the beginning, the standard was considered to be a young male slave in good health, no more than twenty-five years of age. Slaves below standard counted as a fractional part of a peça. But the standard changed over the next century or so. Women came to count as much as men in eighteenth-century Senegambia, and the age limit slipped upward to about thirty-five—though women were occasionally at a discount over the age of thirty, while men as old as forty might be given full value.[5] From the 1680's through the first half of the eighteenth century, a specialized trade in young slaves also sprang up, with destinations principally in Spain and Portugal rather than the Americas. By the 1720's and 1730's, the Royal African Company figured to fill an annual demand for fifty to ninety young people of either sex between the ages of ten and fifteen.[6] This demand from Lisbon and Cadiz wiped out age discrimination in Senegambia, so that any slave in good health of either sex over eight or nine and under about thirty-five could be counted as a "good" slave.

In spite of nondiscriminatory prices with no regard for sex and only a

4. Average markup for 1784–99 was above 200 per cent, but occasional years had markups as high as 330 per cent, as in 1785. (Saugnier, *Voyages,* pp. 316, 321.)

5. F. Mauro, *Le Portugal et l'Atlantique au xviie siècle (1570–1670): Etude économique* (Paris, 1960), pp. 173–74; "Mémoire sur le commerce du Sénégal," 1718, ANF, C6 14; "Mémoire concernant le commerce," enclosed with Commandant Gorée to Director, Saint Louis, 4 June 1741, ANF, C6 12; Labarthe, *Voyage en Sénégal,* p. 99.

6. La Courbe, *Premier voyage,* pp. 59–60; RAC African Committee Despatches of 24 January 1722/23, 31 October 1723, 20 February 1723–24, T 70/55; Plunkett and others to RAC, 3 August 1724, T 70/7; Moore, *Travels,* p. 45. A less regular demand existed in northern Europe as well. The King of Prussia made a contract with the RAC in 1732 for ten male slaves in good condition, plus three boys about ten, "suitable for presents." (RAC to Richard Hull, 8 February 1732–33, T 70/55.)

Table 4.6
Sex Ratios among Sample Slave Groups
Exported from Senegambia

Place	Date	Size of sample	Sex ratio (males per thousand females)
Gambia	1683–88	1,190	7621
Gambia	Jan.–May 1727	1,111	9417
S. Louis	1720	325	4702
Gorée	1720	640	910

Sources: Gambia Journals T 70/456 (1683–88), T 70/550 (1727); Du Bellay to CI, 28 December 1722, ANF, C6 7.

minimal concern for age, the sex ratios of the slaves actually shipped from Senegambia strongly overrepresented males. Where the Atlantic slave trade is generally thought to have carried about two men for each woman in the eighteenth century, the sex ratios of Senegambia exports were much higher. (See table 4.6.) Fairly large Gambian samples roughly a half-century apart are on the order of eight or nine to one. The ratio for the general run of slave exports from Saint Louis had been nearly as high. Only Gorée appears to have approached a balance of the sexes.

Data available are not complete enough to establish this pattern over time, but they make sense in the light of other evidence. The North African slave market showed a consistent preference for young people and women, and so did the Senegambian hinterland. The Europeans on the coast might pay the same price for either sex, but Africans in the hinterland valued women above men. Jahaanke trading to the sahal trading towns around 1690 paid twice as much there for women and boys as they paid for men, but they kept the women and boys in their own towns and sold only the men to the Europeans. In rough terms, the markup on men bought near Ñoro in present-day Mali and sold on the Gambia was about 300 per cent, but the higher purchase price for women reduced their markup to only 50 per cent. As long as these conditions persisted, long-distance trade from the east would be mainly in men.[7] Gorée, on the other hand, drew few slaves from the far interior, and the Gorée samples of the 1720's may well be slaves of coastal origin. If so, the higher proportion of women would also be explained by the European lack of

7. Hodges to RAC, 16 September 1690, printed in Stone, "Journey of Cornelius Hodges," p. 92. Prices were reported as one ounce of gold for men, two for women, at "Tarra" near present-day Ñoro. The price paid for gold in Gajaaga around 1698 was about a quarter of its European price, or £1 per ounce. (Labat, *Nouvelle relation*, 3:338.) Thus male slaves could be bought for the equivalent of £1 on the sahal and sold for the equivalent of about £3 on the Gambia, while women cost £2 and brought no more on the Gambia than men did.

price discrimination. Even if the coastal region, like the interior, paid a premium for women (and we have no evidence either way), the premium was only realizable after the woman had been removed some distance from her old home. Under these circumstances, immediate sale to the Europeans at the same price as men might be a viable alternative.

Sources and Regional Variants: East of the Rivers

The main pattern of Senegambian slave origins is relatively simple—a small, steady, and inelastic supply of slaves from the coast, alongside a much larger, sporadic supply of slaves from the interior east of the head of navigation on the two rivers. Senegambia was the first sub-Saharan source of slaves shipped directly to Europe by sea, and it continued as a principal supply area through the sixteenth century. Slave exports can be estimated as 250 to 1,000 a year in the period 1526–1550, and two centuries later they were still in the range of 250 to 1,000 from the original coastal region of supply—the Wolof, Fuulbe, Sereer, and the Gambian Malinke. Meanwhile the whole slave trade to the Americas had grown so much that Senegambia's share dropped from about 25 per cent to less than 1 per cent of the whole.[1]

None of the evidence suggests that slaves were drawn from the interior before the middle of the seventeenth century, and one would expect an inquisitive observer like Richard Jobson in the 1620's to mention such a trade, if one existed. Instead, the first mention comes from Francisco de Lemos Coelho in 1669, noting a large category of people called *bacháres* being sold at Barokunda, just below the Gambia falls. The name is clearly a cognate of present-day Bajar, probably used at that time to designate the whole Tanda ethnic grouping, including along with the Bajaraanke and Koñagi, Basari, and Bedik or Tandanke. They appear once to have occupied the whole region from northern Guinea-Conakry through the Senegalese départment of Kedugu and north into Bundu.[2] The Malinke movement west to the sea split them in two. The northern division was then pushed out of Bundu by a combination of Malinke moving west from Bambuhu and Fuulbe moving south

---

1. Curtin, *Atlantic Slave Trade,* pp. 95–115.
2. Bunduunke traditions remember their presence there, and some of them may have been assimilated into the dominant Halpulaar culture rather than expelled. (Hammady Madi Sy, Medina Kojalaani, CC T7 [2].) See also J. J. Lamartiny, *Etudes africaines: Le Boundou et le Bambouc* (Paris, 1884), p. 7, J. Tardif, "Kédougou: Aspects de l'histoire de la situation socio-économique actuelle," *Bulletins et mémoires de la Société d'anthropologie de Paris,* 8 (11th ser.):167–230 (1965), and Capt. Bouchez, "Région de Labbé," *Revue coloniale,* 2 (n.s.):373–86 (1903), pp. 375 ff., for an early description of the Bajaraanke. Other Tanda are discussed by Monique de Lestrange, *Les Coniagui et les Bassari* (Paris, 1955), and by reports of the investigative team directed by R. Guessin and

from Fuuta. The southern group, however, is still numerous and densely settled in favorable regions like that of Yukunkun (Youkounkoun) in Guinea-Conakry, but the total is probably much reduced from past levels.

Part of the Tanda decline was no doubt caused by enemy raids, but Lemos Coelho hints at a second possibility in mentioning that Tanda slaves brought a low price in the 1660's because of their tendency to sicken and die when they reached salt water. This information suggests that the Tanda, in their relative isolation from other West Atlantic peoples, may have had a narrower range of endemic diseases than some of their neighbors, hence a narrower range of immunities. They lived apart, in compact stateless societies, with an agricultural technology superior to most in the vicinity but little contact with the outside world. It was the common African experience of the early colonial period for almost any movement away from the home disease environment to increase rates of morbidity and mortality; and the more isolated the home environment, the greater the damage from unfamiliar diseases. Isolation would also make a people peculiarly liable to epidemics imported from the outside. If strangers in search of slaves had carried new diseases into Tanda country, the resulting epidemics would help to explain how the population, presumably quite large at one time, could disappear during the era of the slave trade and yet leave no evidence of its presence among the slaves arriving in the Americas.

Whatever the cause, the Tanda phase in the Senegambian slave trade was brief. In the 1680's "Bambara" began to enter as a second interior people, first in the slave trade to Gajaaga, then dominant in that trade by the late 1690's. The Tanda, meanwhile, continued to be important in the trade to the Gambia well into the new century. In about 1725, they were mentioned as the main victims of a series of slave raids launched northward from Fuuta Jaalō, which would then have been in the midst of its early religious jihad under Karamoho Alfa. In the early 1730's, they were still the main component in the Jahaanke caravans to the Gambia,[3] but then they disappear from the historical record.

The term *Bambara* is always hard to interpret in the historical record because it has several different meanings. It could refer to the Bambara, an ethnic group very nearly identical in speech with the Malinke, generally non-Muslim, who made up the dominant people of the new kingdoms of Segu and Kaarta in the eighteenth century. But the word also meant, in Sene-

---

published in the *Cahiers du centre de recherches anthropologiques,* beginning in 1963, as supplementary volumes to the *Bulletin et mémoires de la société d'anthropologie de Paris.*

3. La Courbe, *Premier voyage,* p. lvi; Labat, *Nouvelle relation,* 3:333–36; Levens, Report of 10 July 1725, ANF, C6 9 (copy also in BN, FF, NA, 9339, and printed in Machat, *Documents*); Moore, *Travels,* p. 411.

gambian French, any slave soldier serving in Senegal, and it could be taken as a very general designation for all Malinke-speaking peoples, or even of all people from east of the rivers. The "Bambara" slaves shipped west as a result of eighteenth-century warfare or political consolidation could be dissident people who were ethnically Bambara, or they could just as well be non-Bambara victims of Bambara raiders. In any event, the first flow of "Bambara" appears to have come from the northern part of the Bambara region, being transshipped by way of Jara on the sahal. Then, from the 1720's, the flow was more clearly from the Bambara core area, and Jahaanke were the principal carriers. This new source of Bambara slaves after about 1715 seems to be associated with the rise of Mamari Kulubali (r. 1712–55) and his foundation of the kingdom of Segu. But some warfare caused a decrease in the slave trade. In 1721, for example, the Bambara factions stopped fighting one another in order to stand off the Ormankoobe, and the flow of slaves from the east was sharply cut.[4] Gajaaga again enjoyed a good year for the Bambara trade in 1733, possibly associated with the Bambara victory over Kong at about that time, but the peak of the Bambara trade came in the period 1739–44, possibly associated this time with Mamari Kulubali's consolidation of his position in Segu, which called for a good deal of sporadic civil warfare.[5]

The end of this important phase of Bambara trade to Gajaaga came as the result of a new war, illustrating once again that warfare was good for the slave trade—but not all warfare. In this case, a prolonged series of wars broke out between Gajaaga and Xaaso in the later 1740's. This made it hard to move caravans through to Gajaaga in safety, while simultaneously the decline of the Royal African Company and the rise of upriver middlemen on the Gambia meant that private shippers began to compete with one another. Soon they were paying African merchants on the middle Gambia as much as they had once paid the Company for slaves delivered to the river mouth. The Compagnie des Indes failed to enter into this price competition until 1755, and then it was too late. Most of the trade from the east was already moving through to the Gambia.[6]

Nor were all military leaders willing to sell slaves in all circumstances. In the early 1750's, the last crisis of Mamari Kulubari's reign was his struggle against Kulakoro, head of the rival branch of the Masasi dynasty with its head-

---

4. Robert to CI, 28 March 1721, ANF, C6 6; Charpentier, Memorandum of 1 April 1725, ANF, C6 9. For the general history of the Bambara see L. Tauxier, *Histoire des Bambara,* esp. pp. 60–70.

5. While no year before 1723 saw as many as 700 slaves shipped through Gajaaga to Saint Louis, several between 1739 and 1743 exceed 1,000 to 1,500. See table, appendix 11, *Supplement;* "Mémoire sur le commerce du Sénégal," 10 October 1723, ANF, C6 7.

6. "Mémoire sur la concession du Sénégal," 1763, BN, FF, NA, 9557, ff. 151–52.

quarters in Beledugu. Observers on the upper Senegal knew enough about these battles to record the names of the rivals, though the major fighting was 400 kms further east, and they also recognized that fighting of that intensity was not good for trade. The rivalry was too serious for either side to encourage slave traders; Gajaaga merchants were not welcome, and returns to Gajaaga were low. The Bambara slave trade recovered only in 1754, the year Fulakoro was defeated and killed.[7]

The supply of Bambara dropped off when Mamari Kulubali himself died in 1755. Command in Segu fell to a succession of brief reigns, dominated by the tõ jõ, the slave army which could now replace the legitimate lineage with its own candidates. Internal quarrels of this kind were hardly a return to peaceful conditions, but palace coups are a poor source of slaves in quantity. The supply of "Bambara" remained low in the 1760's and 1770's, and the declining numbers of slaves shipped from the Gambia and Senegal alike came from sources closer to the coast.[8]

In the 1780's, the Bambara source revived for one last surge in the Senegambian slave trade. That was the final decade in the long reign of Ngolo Jarra (c. 1766–90), the slave soldier who finally mastered the state and founded a new dynasty of his own descendants, who were to rule in Segu down to the Umarian conquest of the 1860's. Once in power, Ngolo Jarra led the most impressive phase of Segu's expansion, conquering down the Niger valley to Timbuktu, establishing his dominance over Jenne, the Niger port serving the juula route to Asante, and fighting wars of aggression against both the Fuulbe of Maasina and the Mossi of Yatenga.[9]

The coincidence of high prices on the coast and new raiding in the interior might appear to be cause and effect, but Ngolo Jarra's wars apparently fitted the political rather than the economic model of enslavement. For one thing, the impact of rising prices was well dissipated that distance from the coast. If the markup from Gajaaga to Saint Louis was about 200 per cent, it must have been nearly 500 per cent from Segu to the Gambia; yet the cost of waging war could hardly have been less in Segu than it was on the Atlantic.

But slave raiding approaching the economic model did exist in Bambara country, though at lower cost than open warfare against powerful opponents. To take on the Fuulbe of Maasina or the Yatenga cavalry was a courageous

7. [A. E. Pruneau de Pommegorge], *Description de la Nigritie* (Amsterdam, 1789), pp. 75–76; Conseil du Sénégal to CI, 20 August 1751, ANF, C6 13; Commander, Fort Saint Joseph to Conseil du Sénégal, 20 June 1754, ANF, C6 14.

8. Tobias Lisle to African Committee, Gambia, 18 July 1758, T 70/30; John Barnes, Evidence to the Commons Committee on the Slave Trade, 26 March 1789, PP, *Accounts and Papers,* xxv (635), pp. 17, 21.

9. Tauxier, *Histoire des Bambara,* pp. 88–96; Brown, "Caliphate of Hamdullahi," pp. 40–53; Saugnier, *Voyages,* pp. 265, 301; "Exportation du Sénégal et Gorée 1786–87," ANF, C6 19.

act and risky, while picking off women or children away from the home village was far safer and far more likely to repay the investment. Whenever the countryside was incompletely under government control, private banditry could appear. The institutional framework for Bambara banditry developed out of the same fundamental *tō* (association) that gave rise to the tō jō as a dominant political force. The tō as an association of hunters developed in one direction to become the standing army; in another it became a band of raiders. The Bambara distinguished sharply between warfare and raiding. Warfare (*kele,* from a root meaning "to call out") was an honorable affair of state, while raiding, the word for *tegereya,* came from a root implying theft, and the distinction governed such matters as the distribution of booty. Booty captured in warfare was considered to be *kele fẽ,* the property of the tō in its collective capacity, though held by its commander (*tō massa*) on behalf of the group. Booty captured in banditry, however, was considered to be *ni sōgō* (the price of life), and it remained the property of the individual raider.

Two different kinds of tegereya were common. One was a cavalry operation (*sobolila*), carried out by a group of forty or fifty men who would establish a temporary camp in an isolated spot and raid outwards from there, trying to find villagers in the fields, or lightly defended herds of cattle. The technique depended on speed and surprise, and it was especially associated with the Fuulbe of the Niger valley rather than their Bambara neighbors. The Bambara were more apt at tegereya proper, its infantry equivalent. The band or tō would be formed in secret by men from a single village or a group of nearby villages. On pretense of a few days absence, the tegereya would leave to meet in the bush, make a series of quick raids on unsuspecting neighbors, sell the product at a distance, and then return home.[10]

An operation of this kind could turn a profit with small risk and small investment whenever security forces were weak, but it was unlikely to produce sharp peaks in the number of slaves delivered. *Kelakela,* or state warriors, on the other hand, might capture whole villages or groups of villages in a short time—at far greater cost, but with a willingness to sustain losses in frontal assault for the sake of political goals. One might therefore suppose in a rough way that the usual year-in, year-out supply of slaves from the Manding region was derived mainly from tegereya and approximated the economic model of enslavement, while the peak exports in one or two contiguous years probably indicated keleya and something like the political model.

This hypothesis makes possible an estimate of the balance between the two forms of enslavement. If the normal and steady level of slave supply from the Manding culture area east of Gambia navigation, through all outlets to the

10. Park, *Travels,* 1:441–50; Meillassoux, *Kafo* de Bamako," *CEA,* 4:186–227 (1963), pp. 203–6, 215–16.

coast, is taken at about 300 slaves a year, while the peak years could turn up as many as 1,500 to 3,000 (possibilities based on the kinds of data shown in the table of Gajaaga exports in the *Supplement,* appendix 11, and occasional spot estimates) and if the peak years marked by warfare are estimated at about twenty in the eighteenth century, each producing on the average 2,000 slaves more than the normal supply, 40,000 slaves would be the century's yield from political enslavement, while 300 a year from tegereya for a full century would have yielded 30,000. In short, the totals for the two forms of enslavement would not have been far different if the speculative variables used in this calculation have any resemblance to reality. The point, however, is not so much their accuracy as the illustration that over a long period of time a small but steady drain of only a few hundred kidnapped each year can add up to an unexpectedly high total, compared to the more spectacular warfare that could pump thousands into the trade in a single year.

To say this is not to deny the probable dominance of the political model in Senegambia, but it points up the existence of a continuous flow of kid-napped prisoners, political prisoners, and others exiled by judicial condemna-tion, alongside the more spectacular flow of war prisoners. In short, though the negative correlation between supply and price seems to argue against the frequency or importance of the economic model, it has to be remembered that Senegambia apparently had a consistently upward-sloping supply curve. Political conditions and the incidence of warfare could shift the position of that curve to produce the apparent negative correlation at some times.

At first glance, the political model of enslavement looks the more benign of the two, since the slaves were people who would have been made prisoner in any event, with or without the Atlantic slave trade. But it was malignant nevertheless, since warfare exacted a price in deaths that was inevitably several times the number of captives enslaved and shipped to the coast. Kidnapping and judicial condemnation might remove people at a lower social cost to the African society concerned, but they too caused a drain of population; and that drain responded most readily to the external demand. It would therefore be a mistake to consider political enslavement comparatively benign in contrast to the economic model, though political enslavement obviously responded to African conditions while economic enslavement had its roots in the American plantations.

Sources and Regional Variants: Senegambia Proper

In contrast to the steady drain of slaves from Manding to the west, neither the middle valley of the Senegal, the valley of the Faleme, nor that of the upper Senegal supplied many slaves to the Atlantic trade at any time after the sixteenth century. The states of that region—Fuuta Tooro, Gajaaga, Bundu, and even the Malinke states in Bambuhu—made their own kind of political decision about the slave trade: while they were willing at times to profit from the passage of slaves or to allow some of their people to participate as traders, they consistently opposed the export of slaves from their own territory. And the effort was generally successful, in spite of enforcement problems and occasional lapses.

The Ormankoobe raids from the 1680's to the 1750's were a major exception which probably carried an unknown number of tens of thousands away to the north. Even later, Moors from the steppe raided the river valley and south into Bundu and Bambuhu. A few of the slaves captured in this way were carried west by desert caravans and sold at Saint Louis, but this was never a significant source of Senegalese exports by sea. Most of those captured by the Moors or the Moroccans were either absorbed into Mauritanian society or sent north across the Sahara.

French merchants were otherwise unanimous in reporting the scarcity of people from Gajaaga, Bundu, or Fuuta as trade slaves. In Gajaaga it was sometimes government policy, but it was even more a custom not to sell free men captured in the numerous Gajaaga civil wars, and behind that was the religious prohibition against the enslavement of fellow Muslims. The French recognized the fact, but their explanation was pure xenophobia—one official thought the Soninke were fine merchants but too lazy for field work and too ugly to command a good price.[1] In Fuuta, custom and government policy combined to oppose the sale of slaves. In the middle of the Ormaanke troubles of the 1720's, a French merchant complained that Jolof and Fuuta together furnished fewer than sixty slaves a year (and Jolof followed an anti-enslavement policy like that of Fuuta).[2] The Futaanke, moreover, had leverage they could apply to the Europeans in Saint Louis, simply by closing the river trade. In 1775, for example, Governor O'Hara of English Senegambia acquired some Futaanke prisoners and sent them off to the West Indies, with the result that Fuuta closed the route to Gajaaga, and the British lacked the power to open it again by force.[3] Later, after the return of the French and the foundation of the almamate, the export of Futaanke as slaves was forbidden by treaty, and the Almaami could enforce its terms even when the French failed to do so. In 1788, he ordered the convoy from Gajaaga stopped and searched, and his soldiers removed by force the eighty or ninety

1. Charpentier, Memorandum ot 1 April 1725, ANF, C6 9. See also Saugnier, *Voyages*, p. 216.
2. Rubault, in Durand, "Voyage du Sénégal à Galam par terre, 1786" ANF, C6 19. See also Labat, *Nouvelle relation*, 3:262; Saint-Robert to CI, 18 July 1725, ANF, C6 9; Prélong, "Mémoires sur les iles de Gorée et du Sénégal," *Annales de chimie*, 18:241–303 (1793), pp. 292–93; Saugnier, *Voyages*, pp. 265–66.
3. McNamara to Dartmouth, 26 January 1776, CO 267/1.

Table 4.7

Slave Exports from Wolof and Sereer Coastal States

1675–76	A very large and unusual export of slaves resulting from the jihad of Nasîr al-Dîn.[1]
1678	Exports from Gorée about 500.[2]
1687	Exports from Gorée about 500.[3]
1693	Exports from Gorée about 200.[4]
1714	Royal African Company managed to buy more than 266 slaves on the petite côte.[5]
c. 1715	Although Kajor normally sold only 200 to 300 slaves a year, it sold 500 in an exceptional year.[6]
1718	Joal (Siin) normally sells about 120 slaves annually, brought by the Jahaanke from the interior, and Gorée total including these supplies from Joal was about 470.[7]
1734	Saint Louis traders bought no more than 80 to 100 slaves a year in Kajor, Walo, and lower Fuuta.[8]
1740's	Slave exports of the whole petite côte were less than 150 slaves a year.[9]
1741	Saint Louis exports of slaves drawn from Kajor and Waalo were 60 a year.[10]
1745	Gorée exports 250 in a "normal year."[11]
1753	Serious famine in Kajor, where the Damel enslaved and sold almost 400 slaves.[12]
1754–55	Famine continued, with resultant increase in the rate of enslavement.[13]
1758	Three hundred slaves exported from the entire petite côte.[14]
1762	Whole petite côte exported about 150 to 200 slaves in a normal year.[15]
1762–64	French purchases of slaves from Kajor over 2.5 recent years came to an annual average of 24.[16]
1765	Kajor is "capable of" furnishing 100 to 150 slaves. (Not an estimate of performance.)[17]
1767	Joal (Siin) is expected to supply about 80 slaves a year. Portudal (Baol) is expected to supply about 100 to 120.[18]
1768	French buy an estimated 350 to 500 slaves a year in Kajor and Baol. (Note that this is an English estimate from Fort Lewis.)[19]
1773	Portudal expected to furnish about 100 slaves a year. Joal expected to furnish 100.[20]
1776	Moors brought 60 slaves overland for sale in Gorée, which also bought less than 100 each in Portudal and Joal.[21]
1775–76	Trarza sweep into Waalo and Kajor brought an estimated enslavement of 9,000 to 10,000 people in these two states in late 1775 and 1776, but the validity of the account is doubtful. (See pp. 126–27 above.)[22]
c. 1779	Slave export of Kajor was about 80 a year—20 to Gorée and 60 to Fort Lewis. Siin was exporting about 80 to 100 slaves a year through Joal.[23]
1789	Siin has recently been exporting fewer than 50 slaves per year.[24]

Sources:

1. Chambonneau, "Histoire de Toubenan," p. 351.
2. Thurlow to RAC, 14 March 1678, Donnan, *Documents,* 1:234.
3. Ducasse, "Memoire," ANF-OM, DFC Sénégal 1, no. 4.

Futaanke they found on board.[4] Not even the warfare that came with the jihad of the 1770's and after increased the shipment of slaves from Fuuta.

In the range of coastal states from Waalo on the north through Kajor, Baol, and Siin to Saalum and Ñomi, none was as clearly and consistently against the slave trade as Fuuta, but annual contribution by any of them was small, barring exceptional circumstances. Table 4.7 assembles a number of opinions about the size of the trade in a variety of years, and incidentally indicates the kinds of circumstances that could increase the trade—political crisis, civil war, famine, raids by the Moors.

The table may also obscure real differences between Wolof and Sereer society and geography. Waalo and Kajor were located where no important overland routes reached into the interior. Their slave exports were therefore either war prisoners or, very often, their own people. The rulers of Waalo, Kajor, and Bawol alike claimed a royal monopoly in dealing with the Europeans, and they were responsible for most enslavement of their own subjects, either by intent or by their inability to control ceddo slave-soldiers. As the Europeans in the posts saw it, the ceddo were allowed to plunder the peasantry any time the ruler felt the need for foreign exchange to buy European goods, or whenever the ceddo themselves became greedy for booty.

4. Prélong, Mémoires, pp. 292–93.

Source notes to table 4.7, continued:

4. La Courbe, Mémoire sur le commerce, ANF, C6 2.

5. W. Cook to RAC, 5 April 1714, T 70/3.

6. Labat, *Relation,* 4:232.

7. "Mémoir général sur le commerce du Sénégal," ZN C6 14.

8. Anon., "Nouvel arrangement touchant la concession du Sénégal," BN FF NA 9341, ff. 67–68.

9. Unsigned, undated annotation to a Labat mss., in ANF, C6 29.

10. Conseil du Sénégal to CI, 30 July 1741, ANF, C6 12.

11. "Commerce du Sénégal," ANF, C6 12.

12. Conseil du Sénégal to CI, 20 June 1753, ANF, C6 14.

13. Debat to Worge, James Fort [1762], T 70/30.

14. M. Adanson, quoted in Machat, *Documents,* p. 81.

15. Debat to Worge [1762], James Fort, T 70/30.

16. Doumet, "Mémoire historique . . . sur Gorée," ANF, C6 29.

17. J. Barnes to African Committee, 17 February 1765, T 70/37.

18. Mémoire du roi pour sieur de Gastière, 27 Feb. 1767, Shefer, Inst. 1:21–29. Reprinted in subsequent Instructions of 1772–74.

19. C. O'Hara, despatch of 15 Sept. 1768, CO 267/14.

20. Doumet, "Extrait des mémoires sur l'isle de Gorée, 1773," AN C6 16.

21. Le Brasseur, "Extrait de la mémoire relativement à Gorée," 1776, AN C6 17.

22. "Etat . . . des esclaves . . . de la côte occidentale de l'Afrique," unsigned, undated, but filed as 1783, ANF, C6 18.

23. "Details historiques . . . de la côte d'Afrique," ANF, C6 29, pp. 95–96.

24. Commandant Gorée to MC, 24 July 1787, ANF, C6 19.

The permission to go on internal raids, however, was even more closely associated with internal politics; victims were rarely chosen at random. Whether for politics or greed, however, the rise of the ceddo and their raids on the peasantry were one cause of the religious revolutions that were to come in the second half of the century, and the Europeans sometimes played along to the extent of withholding arms sales from individual Wolof so as to reduce the rulers' cost for internal slave-raiding and thus increase the yield in slaves.[5]

Further south, in Siin, Saalum, and the kingdoms of the Gambia Malinke, kidnapping sometimes took place, but not in quite the organized form of the Bambara tegereya or the legalized pillage of the Wolof ceddo. Local enslavement was therefore mainly from judicial condemnation or interstate warfare. The Gambia states had a military class, often of slave origin like the ceddo, yet not quite so prone to pillage their own people—at least until the middle of the nineteenth century on the eve of the religious wars. The two Sereer states did better still. They had an institution equivalent to the Wolof ceddo, but the military were kept under control. The greater number of slaves shipped from the lower Gambia and Saalum Rivers can be counted as having come from further east.[6]

That situation was ideal for the European traders. They recognized warfare as a source of slaves for sale, but warfare near the trade enclaves was likely to do more harm than good. It was detrimental to the trade in wax, gum, ivory, and hides—all products that would not bear the cost of long overland transportation. Slaves could come from much further inland; the juula networks had the flexibility to detour around troubled areas or to zero in on crucial centers of violence where captives were likely to be available. A steady and predictable supply was most desirable so that the merchants could make rational fixed investments in facilities like fortifications and slave pens.[7]

The only exception to this basic strategic attitude was a train of suggestion that began on Gorée in the late 1770's and continued in Saint Louis into the 1780's. The idea began with the massive Moorish raid into Waalo in 1775, which the officials on Gorée took to have been a major source of slaves for

5. See Colvin, "Kajor," passim; Pruneau de Pommegorge, *Nigritie,* p. 20; Doumet, "Mémoires historiques sur . . . Gorée," ANF, C6 29; "Détailes historiques . . . de la côte d'Afrique," ANF, C6 29; Rastel de Rocheblave to Boniface, "Observations sur l'isle de Gorée," 1773, ANF, C6 16.

6. "Mémoire servant de réponse à . . . M. de Sartine sur la reduction de Gorée en simple comptoir," 1776, ANF, C6 17; De Repetigny to MC, 11 June 1785, ANF, C6 18; Commandant Gorée to MC, 24 July 1787, C6 19; Beudet, Memoir of 30 October 1772, ANF, C6 16.

7. A long tradition of strategic thought about the relationship between warfare and the slave trade runs through the despatches from the European enclaves. See as examples Du Bellay to CI, 18 June 1724, ANF, C6 8; Levens, Report of 10 July 1725, BN, FF, NA, 9339, p. 145.

the English at Fort Lewis. Having assumed that the English had instigated the raid, they began petitioning the home government to let them do the same. One official in 1783 predicted that the immediate hinterland could yield 2,000 slaves a year on a regular basis, simply by using the Moors as paid slave raiders, though he himself recognized that the project was "un peu barbare."[8] As far as the evidence goes, the idea was rejected in Paris, but it remains important as an example of possible enslavement following the economic model, and one that was recognized as exceptional at the time.[9]

That is not to say that the political model was dominant in Wolof territory, to the exclusion of the other. The internal plunderings of the ceddo have obvious economic implications, but these were not important enough to affect the supply over time. Here on the coast, where the full force of rising prices should have been felt most strongly, the supply of local slaves continued at about the same rate established in the early century. Even the brief peak in the 1780's came mainly from the interior beyond Gajaaga, not from the coast. (Compare *Supplement* table A11.1 and appendix 9.)

A final way of looking at the ethnic distribution of the Senegambian slave trade is to assemble a number of different samples of contemporaneous opinion at different dates. These are available only from French sources, but table 4.8 shows six sample opinions broken down for comparability into the percentage of total French exports derived from each source. The dominance of the Gajaaga trade and of the "Bambara" is clear. So is the reciprocal relationship between the Gambia and Senegal routes; exports by way of the Gambia rose when the Senegal was cut off, and the reverse. Thus the deviation from one sample to the next is much less than it appears to be at first glance. The total for the upriver Senegal plus the Gambia actually varied from a minimum of 45 per cent to a maximum of 85 per cent. Even if half the Gambia trade (for both England and France) is assigned to the lower river, about two-thirds of all slaves exported in the eighteenth century seem to have come from east of the heads of navigation—about one-third by way of Gajaaga and two-thirds by way of the Gambia.

The Nineteenth-Century Twilight of the Export Trade

The overseas slave trade was never again as important after 1816 as it had been during most of the previous two centuries, but persisted and was sometimes an important branch of commerce. Various European

---

8. "Mémoire sur le commerce du Sénégal en faveur des Compagnies," unsigned, 1783, and "Etat ou appreçu des esclaves que peuvent retirer les nations de l'Europe de la côte occidentale d'Afrique," unsigned and undated, but filed as of 1783, both in ANF, C6 18. Another copy of the first is found in ANF-OM, DFC, no. 69, Sénégal 2, dated February 1783.

9. Lamiral, *L'Affrique*, p. 172.

Table 4.8
Distribution of French Slave Exports from Senegambia
by Origin: A Set of Samples

Ethnic Group and State	1722	1733	1738	1745	1762	1763–78	Mean of all Samples
Wolof							
Waalo	–			5.9%			
Kajor	17.2%	17.3%	12.7%		2.0%	5.7%	16.3%
Bawol	19.3				5.9	3.0	8.5
Sereer							
Siin	3.9	–	–				
Saalum	–	–	–	3.9	2.0	5.7	2.6
Fuulbe							
Fuuta	–	–	–	–	21.7	5.7	4.6
Moors	2.8	–	–	–	–	–	.5
Non-ethnic							
Gajaaga	49.1	82.4	2.5	62.7	63.3	51.4	51.9
Gambia	7.7	0.3	76.0	21.6	8.0	22.9	22.8
Bissau	–	–	8.8	–	–	–	1.5
Total	100.0%	100.0%	100.0%	100.0%	100.0%	100.0%	100.0%
Size of sample	564	1,363	789	2,550	3,000	3,500	

Sources

1722: Du Bellay to CI, 28 Dec. 1722, ANF, C6 7. Original totals covered last four months of the year only. For Gajaaga, these would be the only months slaves were shipped to Saint Louis. Therefore the other figures are adjusted to an annual basis by multiplying by three.

1733: Devaulx to CI, 28 May 1733, ANF, C6 10.

1738: Conseil de Gorée to Conseil du Sénégal, 4 July 1738, and Conseil du Sénégal to CI, 1 August 1738, ANF, C6 11.

1745: Estimate for a "normal year" in unsigned "Commerce de la Concession . . . la traite des noirs," ANF, C6 12.

1762: A prediction of future possibilities, therefore less reliable than the others. "Mémoire concernant la concession générale du Sénégal," 1762, ANF, C6 14.

1763–78: Also an estimate, but this time of past performance. "Etat des esclaves de la côte d'Afrique," filed as 1783 in ANF, C6 18. Some aggregated data in 1745 and 1762 have been disaggregated in proportion to the data for 1763–78.

powers made the maritime slave trade illegal for their subjects at various dates scattered through the first half of the nineteenth century, but the date of illegality made less difference than the date of willingness or ability to enforce the prohibition. Illegality for the British Empire began on the first of January 1808, but it made little difference on the Gambia until the British had a working gun battery at Bathurst. French abolition of the slave trade was imposed at the peace of 1815, but effective enforcement was postponed until 1831, and even then various subterfuges were used to continue the trade in fact if not in theory.

Leakage through the net of prohibition operated in a number of different ways. Although the foundation of Bathurst cut off open use of the Gambia, some slaves were landed at Albreda and marched overland to the petite côte. Even more commonly, juula from the interior ferried their slaves across the Gambia from Wuuli or Ñaani, to continue their march to the Casamance, Geba, or Cacheu.[1] This route was competitive with the Gambia route in any case, since the distance from Barokunda Falls to the navigable Geba is only about half the distance from Barokunda westward to the petite côte; but it seems to have carried only moderate numbers after 1816, and it was gradually blocked by British cruisers at sea, so that it must have dwindled to a mere trickle by the 1840's.[2]

Until 1831, the Senegal route to Saint Louis would have been easier and probably cheaper, at least for slaves who originated near Gajaaga or passed by on the way to the coast. The French at first regarded abolition as an onerous condition of peace, imposed by the British and honorably avoided if possible. As a result, the French slave trade at large revived and even flourished between 1814 and 1831; 612 probable slavers sailing from French ports have been identified, including 10 from Senegal.[3] Most of the slaves shipped in this period came from other parts of Africa, but the numbers from Senegambia may have reached 1,000 a year in the first five years or so, dropping to perhaps 500 a year on the average through the 1820's.[4] Then, in 1831, the

1. See Fox, *Brief History*, p. 477, for a firsthand report of this diversion.

2. One reason why it was not more important was price. In spite of the long overland haul from the upper Senegal to the navigable Geba, prices on the Geba were often lower than those in Bakel; so that French officials in Saint Louis found it cheaper to send down to the Portuguese posts on the southern rivers for slave soldiers than to buy them in Gajaaga. See Faure, "Garnison européene," pp. 70–80. By the 1840's, the British cruisers were increasingly effective in catching slavers in the southern rivers, so that exports by sea were no longer as safe as they had once been.

3. The principal historical investigation is the ongoing work of Serge Daget. Taking his total sailings of 612 ships over 1814–31 at an average cargo of 250 slaves per ship (a usual figure at the eighteenth-century height of the French trade), the total French exports from all parts of Africa would have been an average of 5,500 a year. This estimate is consonant with estimates based on demographic data from the French West Indies, indicating an import of about 5,500 a year during the fourteen years 1816–30. (Curtin, *Atlantic Slave Trade*, pp. 80–84.) This figure becomes significant in the light of past French exports during the eighteenth century—as low as 7,000 or 8,000 a year in low decades, and only 27,200 a year in the peak decade of the 1780's. (*Atlantic Slave Trade*, p. 171.) See Daget, "L'abolition de la traite des noirs en France de 1814 à 1831," *CEA*, 11:14–58 (1971).

4. Daget, "L'abolition de la traite," p. 31, quotes Abbé Guidicelly's evidence that 900 slaves were held for shipment in Saint Louis in May 1818, and 1,500 in November. Enforcement by the early governors up to late 1820 was notoriously lax. (Marty, *Etudes*

Table 4.9
Ethnic Origins of Slaves Sold in Bakel, 1846
(based on a sample of 73 slaves of known origin,
unknown origins disregarded)

Ethnic group or district	Number	Per cent	Number	Per cent
Bambara			47	64.4
Segu	17	23.3		
Kaarta	14	19.2		
Bambara (undifferentiated)	16	21.9		
Moors	6	8.2	6	8.2
Soninke			10	13.7
Gajaaga	5	6.8		
Kamera	2	2.7		
Goi	1	1.4		
Jawara	1	1.4		
Gidimaxa	1	1.4		
Halpulaar			5	6.8
Fuuta Jaalō	3	4.1		
Bundu	1	1.4		
Maasina	1	1.4		
Malinke			5	6.8
Bambuhu	1	1.4		
Xaaso	1	1.4		
Wasulu	2	2.7		
Gāgarā	1	1.4		
Total	73	100.0	73	100.0

Source: Bakel traders to Governor Sénégal, 12 November 1846, ANS, K 8.

French Chambre passed an anti-slave-trade law, with penal sanctions and intent to see them enforced. That ended the open illegal trade.

Meanwhile, the internal relocation trade went on with no evidence of diminution. The "Bambara" were still the most important source of slaves sold on the upper Senegal, but these victims of the Bambara now came from closer to home, as Kaarta became a more important military aggressor. In 1821, Major Gray saw a caravan of 400 slaves captured by Kaarta in Fuladugu pass through the town where he was staying, and these were only part of the reported 1,200 captives taken in that campaign.[5] Later in the 1820's, the

---

sénégalaises, p. 157.) The evidence for lower estimates for the 1820's is chiefly negative—partly the fact that reports of illicit trade decreased and partly the fact that the government itself had a hard time buying as many slaves for military service as it wanted and at a price it considered to be reasonable. (Faure, "Garnison européene," pp. 70–80.)

5. Gray, *Western Africa,* pp. 318–19.

Xasoonke began to be especially numerous among the captives; many were sold and resettled in Fuuta Tooro.[6] After the mid-century, the number of enslavements appears to have risen sharply, even though the Atlantic slave trade was finished. Shaykh Umar's wars were a major source of slaves for the internal trade, and the wars of Samori after the 1870's may have been even more important. The French campaigns in the second half of the century also added to the traffic, since the French followed the African rules of warfare and enslaved captives, though these captives were usually distributed as part of the booty due to African allies rather than sold directly.[7]

This meant that the main center of enslavement near Senegambia was still the region east of the rivers, and the internal slave trade still ran from east to west as it had done in earlier centuries. Bakel came to fill the old role of Fort Saint Joseph as the main point of exchange in Gajaaga, while Genoto near Barokunda became the main point of transfer to river traffic on the upper Gambia. As late as the 1890's traders from the west went to Kayes in Xaaso to buy slaves from still further east, and the Jahaanke of Bundu still remember the last great spurt of the slave trade as their grandfathers followed the armies of Samori to buy slaves for the repopulation of Bundu after the Umarian fergo, and for sale to Fuuta as well.[8] But the nineteenth-century routes were cut at the middle Senegal, and the trade from the east weakened as it moved on toward the coast. A substantial sample of the slave population of Saint Louis in the mid-1840's shows far fewer Bambara or Xasoonke than was normal in the eighteenth century, and more than half were drawn from within a 200-km radius of the town. (Table 4.10.) One sample cargo shipped as early as 1818 showed a similar ethnic distribution, suggesting that the slaves available in Saint Louis were already more local in origin than they had been in the 1780's. This is in striking contrast to Bakel (table 4.9), where the earlier pattern persisted.

These sample tabulations are important evidence, but they say nothing about the complexity of the individual experience of enslavement, sale into the trade, transfer again and again to new masters, until the ultimate resettle-

6. Gerardin to Governor, undated, doc. 8, ANS, 1 G 10.

7. See for example Horney to Governor, Bakel. 16 April 1857, and Flize to Governor, Bakel, 10 March 1856, ANS, 13 G 167; Faidherbe to MC, 16 December 1857, no. 686, ANS, 2 B 32.

8. Gerardin to Governor, undated, doc. no. 8, ANS, 1 G 10; Guillet, "Notes de l'ordonnateur sur l'affranchissement des captifs." 29 January 1826, ANS, K 7; P. Holle to Governor, Bakel, 7 November 1845, ANS, 13 G 164; De Pineau to Governor, Matam, 8 February 1862, ANS, 13 G 168; Humbert, Order no. 163, Kayes, ANS, K 19; Deherme, "L'esclavage en AOF," ANS, K 25 passim; "Etude en execution de la circulaire du 18 janvier 1902," Kayes, 27 January 1904, ANS, K 17; Hammady Mady Sy, CC T 7 (1); Tamban Dindiata, CC, T 16 (1); Baku Kaba, Tambura, CC, T 13 (2).

Table 4.10
Ethnic Origins of Sample Slave Populations from
Coastal Senegal, 1818 and 1843–48

Ethnic group	Slaves found on board *Le Postillon* in the illegal slave trade, 1818			Slaves emancipated in St. Louis and Gorée, 1843–48		
	Number	Number	Per cent	Number	Number	Per cent
Moors		18	22.5		8	4.2
Trarza	13					
Brakna	4					
Idaw 'Aish	1					
Wolof		28	35.0		77	40.7
Jolof	5			8		
Kajor	13			26		
Waalo	2			14		
Bawol	8			29		
Sereer		17	21.3		18	9.5
Siin	3			9		
Saalum	13			3		
(undifferentiated)	1			6		
Halpulaar		6	7.5		23	12.2
Fuuta Tooro	3			16		
Bundu	1			1		
Fuuta Jaalō	2			–		
(undifferentiated)	–			6		
Soninke (all Gajaaga)		–	–		26	13.8
Xaaso		–	–		2	1.1
Malinke		4	5.0		17	9.0
Gambia	2			3		
Bambuhu	1			10		
Kaabu	1			1		
Gāgarā	–			1		
(undifferentiated)	–			2		
Bambara		7	8.7		18	9.5
Segu	–			3		
Kaarta	–			1		
(undifferentiated)	7			14		
Total	80	80	100.0	189	189	100.0

Sources: Data for 1818, ANS, K 2. Data for 1848, emancipations in either Saint Louis or Gorée 1843 through 23 June 1848, tabulated from the *arrêtés* promulgated in the *Bulletin administratif*, disregarding those born in Saint Louis or Gorée itself.

ment in a different society. Even a single individual narrative is a useful antidote to patterned generalization, and one that found its way into the record was that of the travels of "William Landay."[9] He was originally Temne from near Port Loko in present-day Sierra Leone. There he was captured as a youth and shipped off toward America in about 1810. A British cruiser captured his ship and landed him at Freetown, barely 60 kms west of his original homeland. He nevertheless stayed in the Sierra Leone colony, where he settled in the village of Gloucester, took the name William Landay, learned Krio and some English, and served an enlistment in the British army. After discharge, he worked as a canoeman for William Tendah, a Creole trader into the Temne country.

Sometime about 1828, on a commercial trip to the Scarcies River, his master sold Landay into slavery once more—this time to a certain Ali Jankona, a Puulo from Fuuta Jaalō, in return for a ton and a half of rice. Ali Jankona took him home, near Labe, where they stayed for a year before Ali again sold him to a Soninke merchant headed west toward the Gambia with three other slaves intended for the export trade. On reaching Albreda, they found the French and Franco-African merchants still occupying their enclave and still actively buying slaves. One of them bought Landay's three fellow slaves, but they refused to pay the fifty dollars (£12.50) asked for Landay himself.[10]

Because he knew the British in Sierra Leone gave refuge to escaped slaves, Landay decided to make a break at Albreda; but he miscalculated and took refuge in the compound of a certain Jacques Panet, who promptly returned him to his Soninke owner. When the owner had finished his other business in Ñomi, he retraced his steps up the Gambia valley, selling Landay once more in Jokadu to a Malinke named Bukari. After two months, Landay managed to escape once more with one of his fellow slaves. They made their way back down to Ñomi, where they profited from his earlier error and avoided Albreda. Instead, they went to the Malinke town of Jufure next door, stole a

9. Deposition of William Landay, Bathurst, 10 August 1830, CO 87/3.

10. Both of the prices mentioned in Landay's account appear to be low for the time and place, but explicable. The value of one and a half tons of rice would be highly variable from season to season and place to place. At the average Gambia price over the period 1829–32 (Gambia Blue Books, CO 90/6) it would be roughly £12.50—or exactly the price asked for Landay at Albreda. Neither price would be equivalent to an f.o.b. price, however, especially when the British in Bathurst prevented Albreda from serving as a seaport for slave ships, but both are nevertheless lower than usual for the time and place. The probable explanation is that Landay was a liability on the coast near Sierra Leone, but he might be sold at a low price for transportation to the interior. Once brought down to the lower Gambia, he was again likely to be able to escape, and his knowledge of English and service in the British armed forces might endanger those who tried to export him illegally.

canoe from the beach, and paddled out to James Island, where the British trade fort had once stood. As luck had it, the island was again temporarily occupied by a small British force sent to watch the French in Albreda. The soldiers sent Landay and his companion down to Bathurst, where they told their story, and Landay presumably found a way to get home by sea.

Aside from their intrinsic interest, Landay's travels illustrate some of the general patterns of the slave trade. One example appeared in his initial sale to a Puulo and his march toward the interior at a time when most slaves marched toward the coast. As a Sierra Leonian of Temne origins, Landay would have had far too many possibilities of escape and refuge around the Scarcies River, hence the immediate removal to a distant point. The second sale is less explicable, since Landay would seem as much of a liability near Bathurst as he was near Freetown, but the possibility of his being a British subject may not have occurred to the Soninke buyer, who came from as far away as Gajaaga and perhaps even further east in the sahal. The fact that the new master had come so far and followed such an indirect route toward the Gambia illustrates the way juula could pass along the trade networks regardless of ethnic origin.

Aside from the open-but-illegal slave trade, which ended in 1831, the French continued to buy slaves on the upper Senegal and elsewhere for incorporation into the Senegalese community, as slaves in fact if not in law. The use of slave soldiers was an African practice, taken up by the French and now continued after the slave trade itself had ended. In the days of the Compagnie des Indes, African soldiers were essential, if only because European soldiers died in such numbers. After 1817, the only difference from past practice was that slaves bought to be soldiers were emancipated on enlistment for a ten- to fourteen-year term—as long a period as they were likely to be useful soldiers, in any case. The Senegalese government never succeeded in buying as many men as it wanted, but it did build up an African force of about 100 in the early 1830's, rising to 200 by 1845, and an intended 450 after 1854. Other soldiers recruited by purchase in Senegal were sent to serve overseas, in effect continuing the overseas slave trade. One hundred and ninety-eight were shipped to Madagascar in 1828, and 100 to French Guiana in 1831. One hundred more were ordered for Guiana in 1839, 50 in 1850, and 300 for various overseas posts in 1854.[11] A rough estimate of slave soldiers purchased for export over the whole period 1818–56 would be on the order of 500, with another 1,000 for use in Senegal itself—or a rough average of 40 a year for the period.[12]

11. Faure, "Garnison européene," passim.

12. The government of Senegal gave up such overt recruitment by purchase in 1857 with the foundation of the Tirailleurs sénégalais as an elite military unit. The new troops served for only a four-year enlistment, and they were comparatively well paid and well

A similar legalized slave trade persisted in the civilian sector, but only from the hinterland to the enclaves, not for export. At the outset of the new administration, Senegalese government officials found the labor force of the port towns insufficient for the economic development, and the town workers were inexperienced at the kind of intensive agriculture planned for a series of plantations in Waalo. At first, labor could come in through the local slave trade, which remained legal until 1823, but then a new system was instituted. It worked on the same principle as forced enlistment in the army. A slave bought in the interior came to Saint Louis or Gorée through the ordinary slave trade. On arrival, he was "emancipated" but tied to his owner by a fourteen-year indenture (called *engagement à temps*), which was enforced with penal sanctions and transferable by sale to a third party. It was equivalent to slavery for a stated period, and Senegalese practice made little or no distinction between *engagés* and domestic slaves. In spite of occasional efforts to end the practice, *engagement* lasted until 1848, when it was ended along with slavery itself in the French enclaves.[13]

The *engagements* were theoretically registered, but most authorities at the time and later believed that registrations far understated the facts. Over the period 1823–44, registrations totaled 3,077, or about 140 a year; but an official report in 1844 put the actual flow of new engagés into the two enclaves at 400 a year, half private and half in government service.[14] If this last is a fair estimate, the total flow of engagés and slave soldiers together would have been in the vicinity of 400 a year during the 1830's and early 1840's. The number may not be high in absolute terms, but it is nevertheless about 25 per cent of French-carried slave exports from Senegambia in the 1780's—the peak decade for the French trade—and several decennial averages in the "era of the slave trade" before the Revolution were lower still. The slave trade was far from ended with the formal acts of abolition.

armed, but they still received a recruitment subsidy approximately equal to the market value of a slave in the hinterland—and this subsidy was often paid to a notable who claimed the recruit as his son or dependent, rather than to the man himself. In fact, most recruits appear to have been of slave status into the 1880's and beyond, though an increasing number volunteered, as a few had done even earlier in the century. (Faure, "Garnison européene," pp. 101–8; F. Zuccarelli. "Le régime des engagés à temps au Sénégal, 1817–48," *CEA*, 7:420–61 [1962], p. 459.)

13. Zuccarelli, "Régime des engagés," passim.
It should, perhaps, be kept in mind that involuntary labor contracts, enforceable with penal sanctions, existed in the Gambia as well, where Africans recaptured from slave ships taken at sea by the British navy were assigned as "apprentices" to the inhabitants. The number of "apprentices" per capita was smaller than that of engagés, the period of apprenticeship was shorter, and the apprentices were not purchased from the usual suppliers of slaves.
14. Breghat de Polignac, "Rapport sur la question des engagés à temps," 22 January 1846, ANS, K 8.

From the point of view of Senegambian commerce, it made little difference whether a slave was taken to Saint Louis and liberated at the end of fourteen years, whether he was sent across the Atlantic, or whether he was relocated in a different African society: he still served as a commodity in a trade pattern that lasted to the end of the nineteenth century and even into the early colonial period.[15] The crucial change in the second half of the nineteenth century was not the fact that the slave trade had ended, since only the export trade had ended; it was the fact that slave exports became insignificant compared to other forms of commerce in Senegambia. In the western Sudan as a whole the slave trade, counting relocation as well as the export trade, may have been as large as ever, perhaps even larger at times during the wars of Shaykh Umar and Almaami Samori Ture. Even for Senegambia, the shift from an eighteenth-century dominance of the slave trade to a nineteenth-century era of "legitimate" trade can be overstated, since the slave trade had not been the only trade, even at its peak.

15. In 1852–62, the French government returned to the use of *engagés à temps* for work in the American colonies. The men were purchased through the usual sources of the slave trade, liberated under forced engagement, and shipped to the Antilles under conditions that reproduced those of the slave trade, though their service was now limited to a period of years. Imports into the French Antilles over these years are usually estimated at about 15,000, the great majority shipped from ports near the mouth of the Congo River. (B. Schnapper, *La politique et le commerce français dans le Golfe de Guinée de 1838 à 1871* [Paris, 1961], pp. 159–61.) In 1852 through 1854, the French government recruited some of these people by purchase at Bakel—14 in 1852, 64 in 1853, and 75 in 1854. (ANS, 13 G 166, various despatches from commandant Bakel to Governor.) In 1855, however, the purchase of engagés at Bakel was stopped in order to buy more slaves for military use.

1. St. Louis and the mouth of the Senegal. Photograph by the author

2. Ruins of the trade fort, James Island, in the mouth of the Gambia. Photograph by the author

4. Senegal River craft at Kayes. Photograph by the author

3. The Senegal River and ruins of the French fort at Bakel. Photograph by the author

5. Felu Falls, on the Senegal. Photograph by the author

6. Guina Falls, on the Senegal. Photograph by the author

7. The Faleme River, from the air. Photograph by the author

8. The Faleme at Tombura, fordable at low water. Photograph by the author

9. Dry savanna woodland with laterized soil, Bundu. Photograph by the author

10. Savanna woodland, southern Bundu. Photograph by the author

11. Peanut sloop, the Gambia. Photograph by the author

12. Boatyard at Barra Point, Nomi, on the north bank of the Gambia. Photograph by the author

13. Camel loaded with Saharan salt. Courtesy Documentation française

14. Pack ox in southern Mauritania. Courtesy Documentation française

15. Pack ox in the land north of Gao. Courtesy Documentation française

16. Madina, capital of Wuuli, 1820. From Gray, *Travels in Western Africa*

17. Bulebane, capital of Bundu, 1820. From Gray, *Travels in Western Africa*

18. Mosque and place of assembly at Dramane, in Gajaaga, 1820. From Gray, *Travels in Western Africa*

19. A part of the town of Tiyaabu today. Photograph by the author

20. Bantaba at Kusan, Bundu—the village meeting place. Photograph by the author

21. Village mosque in the Jahaanke village of Tombura, Bundu. Photograph by the author

22. Village mosque, Bundu. Photograph by the author

23. Salt workings at Taodeni, in the Sahara. Photograph by the author

24. Salt merchant in a Manding market. Photograph by the author

25. Salt packed for shipment, Fajuut (Fadiout), on the petite côte. Photograph by the author

26. Fish drying on the Faleme. Photograph by the author

27. Iron working, Bundu. Photograph by the author

28. Weaver, Bundu. Photograph by the author

29. Samani Sy, a traditionalist, recording the history of Bakel

30. A Puulo aristocrat, Bundu. Photograph by the author

31. Village head of Tiyaabu, Gajaaga. Photograph by the author

32. Illa Tall, A Bundunke cleric and direct descendent of Shaykh Umar. Photograph by the author

33. A Malinke cleric.
From Boilat,
Esquisses sénégalaises

34. A Malinke woman.
From Boilat,
Esquisses sénégalaises

35. A Bambara woman.
From Boilat,
Esquisses sénégalaises

36. A Bambara man.
From Boilat,
Esquisses sénégalaises

37. A Soninke man.
From Boilat,
Esquisses sénégalaises

38. A Puulo woman.
From Boilat,
Esquisses sénégalaises

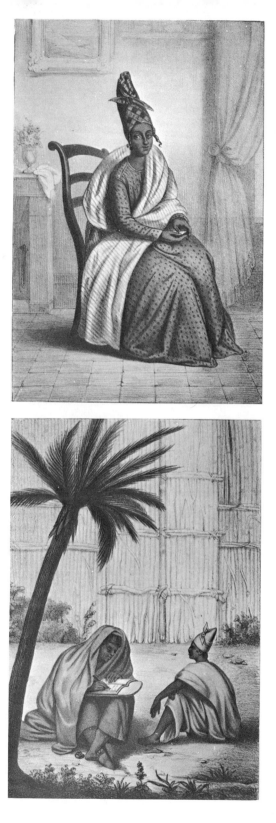

39. A *signare*.
From Boilat,
Esquisses sénégalaises

40. A Futaanke cleric making a charm.
From Boilat,
Esquisses sénégalaises

41. A Wolof aristocrat of Waalo.
From Boilat,
Esquisses sénégalaises

42. A Wolof merchant.
From Boilat,
Esquisses sénégalaises

43. A Wolof *ceddo.*
From Boilat,
Esquisses sénégalaises

5 | PRODUCTION FOR THE MARKET

Perhaps the most durable of all myths about precolonial Africa is the belief that it contained myriad, isolated economic units—"subsistence economies," where the village group if not each individual family actually produced all it consumed. The myth survived partly because former economies were more self-sufficient than their present-day successors, but it was even more useful as an imaginary model of production without exchange beyond the household. Imaginary models are a useful analytical tool, and this one served all too often as a substitute for empirical investigation. Development economists in particular have been led by their concern with the future to ignore the present and imagine the past. One is tempted to doubt that this makes for good economics and it certainly makes for bad economic anthropology and economic history. In point of fact, it is doubtful that *any* African economy of recent centuries was absolutely self-contained, without trade of any kind, even in the most isolated parts of the continent.

Senegambia, where the sahal of the desert meets the shore of the sea, has had a monetized exchange and a network of interconnected markets for centuries. Most people produced most of the food they ate, but that was a general condition of pre-industrial life; and many Senegambian towns were far from self-sufficient. Hundreds of tons of foodstuffs were marketed each year to supply incipient urban centers. Thousands of tons of foodstuffs were exchanged on the desert fringe, where both the value and quantity of the cereals exchanged for animal products were far greater than the gum trade that figures so largely in European accounts. Millet was also shipped regularly up or down the Senegal in response to local shortages, while meat, fish, shea butter, and salt were only the most important of the other food products entering trade. If these food products are slighted in the discussion that follows, it is no reflection on their importance to the Senegambian economy.

197

The fault lies with lack of data in the historical record kept by Europeans and with emphasizing products exported by sea.

Gold

In spite of the fact that slaves were the most important export in the late seventeenth and the eighteenth centuries, Europeans were usually more interested in the gold trade—not the actual gold trade but the gold trade that might be made to flow if it were properly tapped or if the mines could be exploited with European technology. As it turned out, the expectation was wrong. Part of the error was the bullionist fallacy that ran through Western economic thought in various guises for centuries. In fact, all gold is not wealth, nor are gold miners necessarily rich; but the fact that this particular eldorado turned out to be a dry hole takes nothing from its importance as a lure to Europeans. It therefore took on inordinate importance in European-Senegambian relations.

Although some of the gold exported by way of Senegambian posts may have come from Bure, most at most periods came from the gold fields of Bambuhu, the "Bambuk" of the French records. This Malinke-speaking region to the east of the Faleme River has a long history of independence and political fragmentation. Even the great empires like Ghana, Soṅrai, and Mali exploited the gold fields by controlling access rather than production. According to at least one tradition, the three regions known today as Bambuhu, Konkadugu, and Gāgarā were part of a large province that broke away as a unit from the declining power of Mali, but even the breakaway unit had disappeared by the eighteenth century. None of the three regions was then more than a geographical expression taking in a number of smaller political units. Bambuhu proper was the region bounded on the west by the Faleme, on the east by the crest of the hills overlooking the Senegal valley, and extending southward to include the small states of Tambaura, Nacaga, and Ñambia.[1] (Europeans, however, have sometimes used "Bambuk" as the name of the single small kingdom in its northeast corner, otherwise called Farabana, and sometimes to cover a much wider region including everything between the Faleme and the Bafing right down to the present Mali-Guinea frontier.)[2]

Although Gāgarā and Konkadugu both exported gold, the narrower Bambuhu was the center of production and of European interest over the

1. Boucard, "Relation de Bambouc" ff. 11–12.
2. See, for example, L. Flize, "Le Bambouk," *Moniteur du Sénégal et dépendances,* no. 51–52, 24 March 1857, part 2, p. 3; Lamartiny, *Le Bondu et le Bambouc,* p. 58; G. Colin, "Le Bambouk (Soudan occidental)," *Bulletin de la Société languedocienne de géographie,* 8:640–45 (1885); Vallière, "Notice sur le Bambouk," ANS, 1 G 85.

centuries. It was the lure of gold that led the Portuguese down the Saharan coast in the first place, and the first direct export of slaves was merely a by-product. In the late fifteenth century, it was gold that led the Portuguese to their major, if unsuccessful, effort to seat Bumi Jelen as ruler of greater Jolof. In the sixteenth, it was gold that led the Portuguese into Bambuhu itself, to the establishment of the first European post in the interior of West Africa. In the seventeenth, the Gambia was advertised in England as source of "the golden trade," and French plans on the Senegal were focused on gold at least as much as on slaves.

In the next century, the French inherited the hope for riches in the interior, and they, even more than the Gambian English, held the gold mines of Bambuhu as a central theme in their strategic plans and projects. Their pet idea of cutting off Gambia trade with line posts along the Faleme fitted neatly into the prospect of using these same posts to control the gold field that lay just east of that river. One flurry of especially elaborate planning emerged about 1719, and ran on into the 1730's. The chief official spokesman was André de La Bruë, and its chief publicist was Father Labat.[3] The more ambitious projects of this period called for such expenditure as an expeditionary force of 3,000 men or more, and the Compagnie des Indes actually established two fortified posts near the gold fields and held them from 1725 to 1734. By 1732, however, the Company found that the gold trade had not matched the dream, while the cost of posts in Bambuhu and Gajaaga came to 78,866 livres a year (£2,445), or more than the annual cost of the island fortress at Gorée and almost as much as that of Saint Louis itself. The Company therefore dropped the idea of controlling the gold fields, though Fort Saint Joseph in Gajaaga remained as an upriver post reduced to a modest level of staff and garrison.[4]

But the scheme was not forgotten. Sieur Aussenac revived it once more in the 1750's in connection with a bold new forward policy that was never put into effect. The Crown returned to it once more in the mid-1780's, when Bambuhu gold figured as one of the objectives outlined in the instructions to Governor de Boufflers. At the close of the Napoleonic Wars, the first expedition to Gajaaga included a mining engineer, and a series of official exploring expeditions in the early nineteenth century always included the

3. Labat, *Nouvelle relation*, was compiled in some measure as a device for interesting the public in La Bruë's projects.

4. Delcourt, *La France au Sénégal* (Dakar, 1952), pp. 165–66; Machat, *Documents*, esp. pp. 22–23; Labat, *Nouvelle relation*, esp. 2:3–4, 4:18–21; La Bruë, "Mémoire sur le Sénégal," 7 April 1723, enclosed with despatch of 17 October 1723, ANF, col., C6 10; Levens, report of 10 July 1725, BN, FF, NA, no. 9339, f. 141; Charpentier, Memorandum of 1 April 1725, ANF, col., C6 9; Devaux to Compagnie des Indes, 22 March 1733, ANF, col., C6 10.

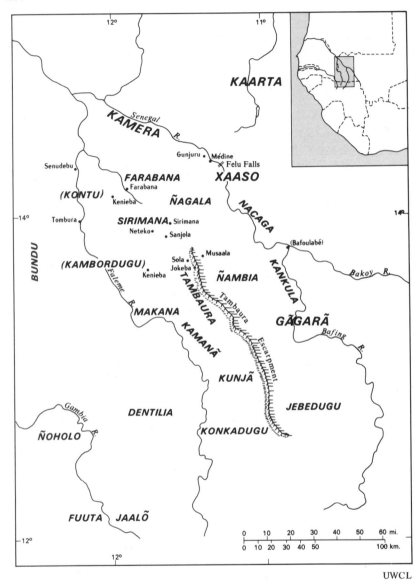

5.1 Bambuhu

UWCL

mines of Bambuhu as at least a subordinate objective.[5] General Faidherbe finally took the decisive action in this, as in other aspects of French policy on

5. Marty, *Etudes sénégalaises,* pp. 95–104; Hardy, *Mise en valeur,* passim; papers on the Grout de Beaufort expedition, ANS, 1 G 7.

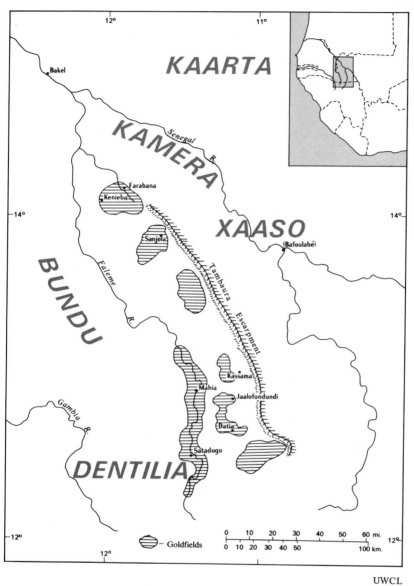

5.2 Bambuhu Gold-Producing Regions (Source: Meniaud, *Haut-Sénégal-Niger,* 2:179)

the Senegal. One of his first acts after his defeat of Shāykh Umar was to take personal command of an expedition from Bakel to Kenieba in 1858. Since Kenieba was in that part of Bambuhu claimed by Bundu and Farabana alike, Faidherbe secured treaties from both, ceding the town to France and protecting French access. He installed a garrison and a mining expert, and France had finally achieved the goal of nearly two centuries of planning and effort.[6] Two years later, in 1860, the French withdrew the post and stopped mining operations; the mortality of the European staff was too high and the yield in gold was too low to be worth the cost.

The chimera was to reappear once more in the early colonial period; once more the prospect of immense wealth was held out only to disappear into nothing.[7] By the 1960's, the gold production of the Republic of Mali was too small to figure as a separate item in official statistics of Malian mineral production or appear on the list of exports.

During all these centuries, Bambuhu gold was mined and exported, even though it failed to reach the quantities Europeans hoped for. In approximate terms, the gold exported by way of Senegambia came to about 35 kgs a year in the sixteenth and seventeenth centuries, though this figure has to be treated as a capacity estimate for "a good year," not an annual average. Gold exports then rose to about 60 kgs in the best years of the eighteenth century, and on to a bit more than 100 kgs in the early nineteenth. It may have been as high as 200 kgs in the early twentieth century, and the peak all-time record for gold exports from the French Sudan (now Republic of Mali) was 320 kgs in 1940.[8]

The explanation of small returns after such expectations begins with the physical makeup of the region. All gold found in the basin of the Faleme came ultimately from ores that once existed in quartz pipe veins scattered here and there along the ridge line of the Tambaura escarpment and its extensions to the south-southeast—in effect, along the watershed between Bafing and Faleme drainage. The pipes themselves have mainly eroded away, contributing little or nothing to recent gold production, but they were the source of alluvial ores now found in three different types of deposit between the ridge of the escarpment and the Faleme River. One form, and the oldest, was laid down in the Upper Tertiary period and the Pleistocene epoch when the landforms were quite different from those of the present. These deposits are now found in the high plateau region. A second type came later, but are now either higher or lower than the present level of the flood plain. Some of these are found up valley sides, where they formed terraces as erosion deepened the valley in which they were first laid down. Others are found

6. For treaties see *Annuaire du Sénégal,* 1882, p. 54. See also Rançon, Le Bondou," pp. 454–55; Morney to Governor, 20 March 1858, ANS, 13 G 167.

7. P. D. Curtin, "The Lure of Bambuk Gold," *JAH,* 14:623–31 (1973).

8. See *Supplement,* appendix 12, and V. Magalhães-Godinho, *L'économie de l'empire portugais aux xve et xvie siècles* (Paris, 1969), p. 216; H. Labouret, J. Canus J. Fournier, and G. Bonmarchand, *Le commerce extra-européene jusqu'aux temps modernes* (Paris, 1953), p. 57

aligned with present streams and depression, but deeper than the present flood plain and buried under later alluvia. A third form is found in present valley and stream beds and represents the erosion and redeposit of the earlier alluvial beds. Some of these deposits are still being laid down, so that a stretch of beach or riverbank panned for gold in one dry season could be panned again after only one year's flood.[9]

In the light of modern mining technology, these deposits suffer from a low average gold content per ton of ore, and even more from an erratic distribution of high- and low-grade ores. Some small sectors are very rich, and occasional nuggets of 40 to 50 grams have been recovered. But the gold content of the ores varies from 0.6 grams to 8.4 grams per cubic meter. The general character of the older alluvial deposits is a lateritic clay, spread over an immense area at a depth of one to twenty meters. The ore tends to be richest at the bottom of the alluvial layer. The erosion that brought it there was a washing process that acted a little like a miner's pan, where the lighter dirt swirls to the top and the gold sinks to the bottom. The surface itself is generally sterile, either a sandy topsoil or more commonly a lateritic crust partly decomposed into a field of boulders and small stones

The problem with ore deposits of this kind is that deposits rich enough for treatment by a recovery plant are too small and too scattered to justify the capital cost. The old African techniques, on the other hand, were suited to searching out and exploiting the richest ores. Since the alluvial layer was rarely deeper than 20 meters, no really deep mining was required. Some ores could be dug from a simple surface excavation of less than 2 meters, and the recent alluvia along the Faleme could be taken directly from the sand banks that stood out each dry season.

Most mining, however, had to pass through the relatively sterile lateritic crust and topsoil to get down to the better ores just above bed rock. The typical excavation was a vertical well, about 75 cm square. As the hole went deeper, it was reinforced with sills at intervals, and at least one side was protected by a grate of horizontal sticks that could serve as a ladder for climbing up and down. Miners usually dug to bedrock before sending out horizontal tunnels in each direction as far as they dared without risk of a cave-in. A vertical shaft 20 meters deep was no great problem, since the people of the region dug wells that were often deeper still to provide water in the dry season.[10]

9. For recent gold mining in Bambuhu and region see J. Meniaud, *Haut-Sénégal-Niger: Géographie économique*, 2 vols. (Paris, 1912), 2:171–75; G. Lasserre, "L'or du Soudan," *Cahiers d'outre-mer*, 1:368–74 (1948); A. Belan, "L'or dans le cercle de Kédougou," *Notes africaines*, no. 31, pp. 9–12 (July 1946).

10. For traditional gold-mining techniques see especially Ballieu, "Rapport sur Bambuk," part 3, ANS, 1 G 212; Belan, "L'or"; H. Hubert, "Coutumes indigènes en matière

The work organization and political control over mining operations provide another kind of clue to the relation of gold-working to the local economy. The largest political units in Bambuhu of the eighteenth or nineteenth centuries were small states that were in effect confederations of villages corresponding to the kafu found in other parts of the Manding culture area. The head of state was the Saatigi, who was also village head of a particular village. Other village heads, called Farin, had nearly as much authority within their own villages. The Saatigi had the right to collect tolls on the gold trade, as he had a right to collect tolls on all trade, but control over gold deposits belonged neither to the Saatigi nor to the Farin. It rested instead with a different kind of official called the *Jala nila.* He and he alone had the right to allocate land for gold prospecting or mining, and his authority was hereditary in a particular lineage, different from the ruling lineages. It was also exercised over a territory that was not necessarily coterminous with that of the village or the state. The Jala nila, in short, appears to represent a separate and probably more ancient level of local authority, similar to that of the lamanate in western Senegambia or the earth priests of the Voltaic region.

The similarity went further still, since the Jala nila was not so much the owner of the subsoil as its custodian on behalf of the whole community, and subsoil rights were treated as a virtually free good, just as farming rights over unoccupied parts of the countryside were assigned without exacting a market price. The Jala nila's main functions were religious. Gold was thought of as a living thing, guarded by more or less benevolent spirits, but it had to be extracted from the ground without offending the spirit world. This required appropriate rituals. The Jala nila chose the site for the season's mining, performed the necessary rituals, and received a fee from those who wanted to mine; but the fee was a payment for his knowledge of where gold might be found and for his ritual intervention, not for the right to mine as such. Some Bambuhu villages moved en masse for the whole of the mining season, but permission to mine was not restricted to a single village. Others from beyond Bambuhu could come to mine for a season, sometimes from several hundred kilometers away.

Gold mining was a dry-season occupation, but it could not begin as soon as the rains stopped; the ground had to dry out and the water table had to drop before many of the deposits could be reached. The main season therefore began only in late January or early February and continued until May. This fitted into the agricultural cycle, since agricultural labor was finished by November, leaving two to three months for well digging, house building and

d'exploitation des gîtes aurifères en Afrique occidentale," *Annuaire et mémoires du comité d'études historiques et scientifiques de l'A.O.F.,* 2:226–43 (1917); Meniaud, *Haut-Sénégal-Niger,* 2:175–79.

repair, and other such dry-season tasks before the gold mining season. By January, underemployment was chronic, and the opportunity cost of labor was at the lowest point of the year.

Once work began, mining was directed by the *Sanukutigi* or *Duratigi* (chief of the works or chief of the goldfield), who also inherited his office. He assigned particular spots to individual digging groups or teams and preserved order during the season. In return, he too received gifts from the miners, and he was entitled to a percentage cut on all provisions sold in the mining camp. The actual work was done by a mining group under a *Damatigi* (or chief of the mine), who recruited his team from his own patrilineage and their wives. He had to maintain a balance of the sexes between excavation, which was men's work, and the extraction of gold from the ore, which was women's. The usual team was of one or two men plus three or four women; but it might be no more than the Damatigi and his wives. However the team was made up, the gold was divided into two equal shares, one share subdivided equally among all the men and the other among all the women.[11]

This method yielded a maximum normal return of only about 2.25 to 2.50 grams of gold dust per person per day in the early colonial period, and there is no reason to think that it may have been higher in earlier times. At the eighteenth-century European price of gold, about £141 a kg, a daily wage of £.35 would have been munificent, but the gold was not mined in Europe. In the mid-eighteenth century Bambuhu gold was sold in Gajaaga for a bundle of trade goods whose English value would have been £40 to £50 a kg. If the markup between Gajaaga and Bambuhu was about 50 per cent (as it was in the late nineteenth century), the value of gold in English goods payable in Bambuhu itself would have been £25 a kg or a bit less. A day's maximum wage was therefore more nearly £.06 in English value, and most people probably made less.[12]

If this calculation is only roughly correct, it helps to explain why the people of Bambuhu could treat gold ore as a free good. In fact, the ordinary day's winnings were less than the cost of subsistence for the worker for one day, and this was still true in the early colonial period.[13] The activity was so close to margin that it bore no rent—in Marxian terms, there was no surplus to be expropriated. The evidence from the seventeenth and eighteenth cen-

11. Hubert, "Coutumes indigènes," pp. 237–38; Meniaud, *Haut-Sénégal-Niger*, 2: 175–79.

12. The estimated per-person daily yield in gold is that of Méniaud, *Haut-Sénégal-Niger*, 2:181, for the early colonial period, but Méniaud points out that this is a maximum normal expectation in a situation where the average would be substantially lower, though an occasional lucky find was also possible.

13. Méniaud, *Haut-Sénégal-Niger*, 2:181.

turies indicates that at some periods Bambuhu gold was mined only in very small quantities, and what was offered for sale and export was too expensive to be competitive in the world market. Especially in the 1760's and 1770's, Europeans on the coast and the two rivers were unwilling to buy gold because of the high price. Earlier, in the mid-seventeenth century, the Portuguese found the price of gold on the Gambia so high they preferred to invest their trade goods in other commodities.[14]

Given the scanty evidence from Bambuhu itself in either period, it is always possible that gold was mined in quantity and exported to Europe or the Muslim world by some other route. More likely still, mining did not repay the miner's cost, and two other incentives may have made it economically feasible to mine the gold at all. One of these is the "Klondike" principle. As every professional gambler knows, people will place bets even when they know that the house makes a regular profit. In the same way, a miner might be unwilling to work for a wage representing the average return from a day's mining, but he would nevertheless work for that same income if it also included a chance to make a lucky find, and the Bambuhu goldfields held out that possibility in the form of the occasional large nugget. The second incentive was in the seasonal nature of mining. Whatever the cost of subsistence, people in Bambuhu and vicinity had little else to do with their time at that latter part of the dry season, when the opportunity cost of labor might well be lower than the cost of subsistence.

In the seventeenth and eighteenth centuries, therefore, gold production was not a function of the market price of gold. It depended rather on how many of the normally agricultural population had an opportunity to dig for gold and lacked an opportunity to do something more profitable. When the region around Bambuhu was relatively peaceful, people could come from a distance to mine gold in the late dry season. When the roads were dangerous, it was wiser to stay at home. The lack of gold for export after the 1750's may be explained by the military disturbances involving Xaaso and the Bambara of Segu and Kaarta, the same disturbances that drove the caravan routes southward and threatened to close the Senegal as a through route for east-west trade. Thus the Senegambian production of gold for export, like its production of slaves for export, was caught up in a web of local political conditions that made it comparatively unresponsive to changes in the market price.

14. John Barnes, Evidence to House of Commons Committee on the Slave Trade, 26 March 1789, PP, *Accounts and Papers,* xxv (635), p. 24; Captain Heatley, Evidence in Great Britain, Privy Council, *Report of the Lords of the Committee of Council for . . . Trade and Plantations. . . Concerning the Present State of Trade to Africa, and Particularly the Trade in Slaves* . . . (London, 1789), part 1; De Capellis, "Mémoire sur un établissement dans la rivière de Gambie," May 1779, ANF, col., C6 17; "Détails historiques . . . de la côte d'Afrique," ANF, col., C6 29, ff. 93–94; Coelho, *Duas descriçoes,* p. 131.

Iron

Unlike gold, found only in localized deposits, iron ore was available almost everywhere in West Africa. The lateritic crust that covers so much of the savanna country between 10° and 15° north latitude often contains from 40 to 60 per cent iron. Charcoal for smelting was also available almost everywhere, because West African savannas are more often open dry woodland than grassy plains devoid of trees. The knowledge of iron-making had also been available in West Africa since well before the Christian era. But iron production was nevertheless concentrated—first of all, in the hands of a separate and specialized "caste," though smiths were not barred from growing crops as well during the wet season, and secondly in the most favored regions. Most iron produced in Africa therefore entered trade.

The most efficient types of furnace and the highest quality of iron or steel at the beginning of the colonial period were found in the savanna country from Fuuta Jaalõ, Bundu, and Fuuta Tooro eastward to the lower Niger valley in present-day Nigeria. The dominant furnace type was the high clay furnace, using natural draft. This furnace is also found in central Africa, especially in the region between Katanga, Lake Malawi, and the bend of the Kafue River in central Zambia, and more sporadically here and there along the southern fringe of the Sahara and in the Horn of Africa.[1] But the western Sudan had apparently been a major iron-producing region for many centuries.

Even within West Africa, the style and appearance of the high furnace could vary from place to place, though the basic technology was the same. The building material was clay, usually mixed with material from a "live" termite hill, which made the clay water resistant. The standard shape was a truncated cone, which might be several meters in diameter and no more than 1.5 meters high, or could be comparatively narrow and as high as 4 or even 5 meters. Some furnaces were temporary, built for use in a single dry season near a convenient source of iron or charcoal or both. Others had a permanent site, where a new furnace had to be constructed for each firing. Still others were a permanent installation, sometimes lasting a century or more in the same place, though minor repairs were necessary each new season. Furnaces also used different forms of forced draft. Some had human labor working bag bellows (see illustration), but the more common design used the natural draft of the fire itself, pulling in the outside air through a series of clay tubes that stuck out from the furnace in all directions and angled downward toward

---

1. The most useful general studies of iron metallurgy in Africa are Walter Cline, *Mining and Metallurgy in Negro Africa* (Menasha, Wis., 1937); C. Francis-Beuf, "L'industrie autochtone du fer en Afrique occidentale française," *CEHSAOF,* 20:403–64 (1937); H. Sasoon, "Early Sources of Iron in Africa," *South African Archaeological Bulletin,* 18:176–80 (1963).

the base of the fire. The relationship between the diameter of the flue at the top of the furnace and the combined diameters of the vent tubes is a critical factor, at the proportion 9 to 3, though the master smith who controlled the operation could also control the entry of the air by blocking one or more of the vents as circumstances required.

The basic smelting process diffused from the Middle East to West Africa (as it had to northwest Europe) during the last half-millennium before the Christian era. The fundamental operation was the chemical reduction of a mixture of iron ore and charcoal. That is, the furnace was charged with a mixture of ore and fuel—in West Africa, with about an equal weight of each in alternate layers until the inner cavity of the furnace was full. When the charcoal began to burn, the combustion was incomplete, so that one of the gaseous products was carbon monoxide rather than the usual carbon dioxide produced by an open fire. As the hot carbon monoxide passed upward through and around the heated ore, it picked up the extra carbon atom, becoming carbon dioxide and deoxidizing the ore in the process. The desirable temperature for reducing ore in this way was about $250°$ to $300°$ centigrade, high enough to allow molten slag to be drawn off, yet low enough to inhibit the harmful absorption of too much carbon in the iron. It was important to stay far below the melting point of iron at $1539°C$, since the ore could begin to absorb carbon at temperatures as low as $730°C$, which would, in turn, begin to reduce the melting point of the carbon-iron amalgam to something like $1130°C$. If the temperature crept this high, the result was a brittle cast iron, completely useless for tool-making.

The African product of 24 to 36 hours of smelting was a pasty mass at the bottom of the furnace, called a bloom, which had to be reduced to hard iron by heating and hammering to expel remaining slag. Even the finished product was not completely homogeneous, since it contained minute bits of slag, particles of steel, and iron of several different chemical compositions in different parts of the mass. Whether steel or wrought iron, both of these were distinguished from cast iron or pig iron by having less than about 1.7 per cent carbon, and carbon content is critical to the iron's malleability. Too much carbon made the product brittle. Low carbon content made for wrought iron, which is malleable but lacking the small amount of carbon necessary to give it a firm edge when tempered. If the smelting temperature was high enough but still short of the critical shift to cast iron, the result was steel—malleable when hot, but extremely hard when cooled suddenly.

West African iron and steel technology was little different from that available in northwest Europe before the fourteenth-century introduction of forced-air draft powered by water wheel. Even with this new European technique the result was cast iron, but it was cheaper and more plentiful than iron had ever been before. Its very availability was an incentive to experiment in order to make it more useful, and by the mid-seventeenth century cast iron could be used efficiently even in cannon. The next important changes in Europe came in the eighteenth century, first with the substitution of coal for charcoal, and second with puddling and rolling processes that could change brittle pig iron into malleable wrought iron—at a price. The final step into the age of steel came with the Bessemer converter, invented in the 1850's but not applied on a large scale until the 1870's. With that, steel became as cheap and readily available as pig iron had been a century earlier.[2]

African iron technology changed, too, during these centuries, but West African societies were functionally nonliterate. They had a class of literate scribes in the form of the Muslim clerics, but they lacked printing and a wide diffusion of literacy to other groups in society. Smithing was often regarded as an esoteric if not a dangerous art, where the master smiths worked by rule of thumb and kept their discoveries within their own kinship group. The best technology was very good, but it was not widely known to the mass of smiths.

One of the most refined methods on record was still practiced in 1903 by smiths of the forest-savanna fringe in Yorubaland, near new Oyo, and described by C. V. Bellamy, a European visitor who understood metallurgy. The crucial innovation in this case was the use of slag from a previous smelt as flux fed into the furnace along with the iron ore and charcoal. This material, a ferrous silicate, helped to decarbonize the iron and absorb other impurities, thus increasing both the quantity and the quality of the yield. When this cinder flux was used at low furnace temperatures, for example, it helped to reduce the phosphorous content of the iron. If the same ore had been put through an ordinary European blast furnace of the period, it would have produced pig iron of .06 per cent phosphorous. With the African process, phosphorous was kept to .01 per cent and the finished product after puddling was a good steel of .22 per cent carbon.[3]

While many European travelers described African smelting in the nineteenth century and earlier, few of them knew anything about metallurgy. Several reports state that the African blacksmiths drew the molten metal from a hole at the base of the furnace. Smelting at such a high temperature was probably impossible, given the type of furnace. If possible, it was undesirable, yielding cast iron that was worthless in African circumstances. None of the Senegambian accounts are as careful as Bellamy's description of steel production near Oyo, but several travelers identified samples of the Senegambian product

2. For a convenient summary of these changes see D. S. Landes, *The Unbound Prometheus: Technological Change and Industrial Development in Western Europe from 1750 to the Present* (Cambridge, 1969), pp. 89–95, 215–19, 249–69.

3. C. V. Bellamy, "A West African Smelting House," *Journal of the Iron and Steel Institute,* no. 11, pp. 99–126 (1904), p. 112.

as steel rather than wrought iron and praised the quality of the tempered blades.[4] One sample sent back to France for analysis in 1818 was described by a metallurgist as being " . . . of excellent quality, and exactly like our iron from the department of Arriège, which is manufactured by the Catalonian method, and which is always mixed with grains and small veins of steel."[5]

One puzzle of Senegambian iron production is the fact that smelting seems to have been confined to the interior. Many visitors described the high furnaces of Bambuhu, Gajaaga, Fuuta Tooro, and Bundu, but the reports of smiths' work nearer the coast are either silent about the source of the iron or say explicitly that it was imported.[6] The Wolof, Sereer, and Gambia Malinke may once have made their own, but it must have been in the distant past, if ever. By the sixteenth century, the coastal states imported iron from their own hinterland as well as buying it from the Europeans. None of the evidence suggests that the coast once produced iron but was then driven out of business by the cheaper European product.

African iron production appears, in fact, to have held its own relatively well in the face of European competition. While the iron imports into Senegambia rose from about 150 tons a year in the 1680's to 410 tons a year for the period 1836–40, the value of iron among Senegambian imports dropped from about 25 per cent of the total in the 1680's, to 20 per cent in the 1730's, to 3 per cent in the 1830's.[7] These figures imply a slow penetration of European iron, an implication supported by other evidence. Before the 1720's, iron was not usually sold to the juula for shipment inland, but coastal merchants noticed a change about that time as the Jahaanke began to buy iron.[8] Bundu and other upriver states on the Senegal, however, still manufactured their own iron in competition with the European product as late as the 1890's, and the quantities were substantial until well after 1850.[9] Still further inland, in

4. See, for example, Moore, *Travels,* p. 41, or Park, *Travels,* 1:431–34.

5. Mollien, *Travels,* appendix by M. Berthier, p. 350.

6. See Alvares, *Tratado breve,* p. 29; Jobson, *Golden Trade,* pp. 164, 199; Chambonneau to CI, July 1688, printed in H. Froidveaux, "La découverte de la chute du Félou, 1687," *Bulletin de géographie historique et descriptive,* 13:300–321 (1898), 310; Labat, *Nouvelle relation,* 3:305–7; John Barnes, Evidence to Commons Committee on the Slave Trade, 26 March 1789, PP, *Accounts and Papers,* xxv (635), p. 35; Durand, *Sénégal,* 1:151, 2:227–28; Mollien, *Travels,* p. 189; Gray, *Western Africa,* p. 122; Tourette, Report of 14 August 1829, ANS, 1 G 12; Raffenel, *Nouveau voyage,* 1:56–57.

7. See below, table 8.11.

8. De la Bruë to CI, 12 June 1720, ANF, C6 6.

9. Raffenel, *Voyage dans l'Afrique,* p. 306; Roux, "Tournées dans le cercle de Bakel, 1 April 1892, ANS, 1 G 135. Rey; "Voyage à Farabana (Haute Sénégambie)," *Revue coloniale,* 12 (2nd ser.):34–62 (1854), p. 52, and "Rapport au gouverneur du Sénégal sur un voyage dans le Kasso, en juin et juillet 1851," *Revue coloniale,* 9 (2nd ser.):241–75 (October 1852), p. 262; Rançon, *La haute Gambie,* pp. 499–500.

Yatenga, the northernmost of the Mossi states, about 1,500 high furnaces were in production as late as 1904, with an estimated capacity of around 540 tons of iron or steel a year.[10] Since this single regional center produced more iron each year than had been imported by way of Senegambia in the 1830's, it seems probable that the westernmost Sudan as a whole must have produced more iron than it imported, at least until after 1850, and the excess of domestic production over imports must have been substantial in the seventeenth and eighteenth centuries.

The general trend is confirmed by prices, which in turn reflect the changing European iron and steel technology. In the 1680's, the Royal African Company paid an average of £16.14 in England per metric ton of iron for export to Africa. By 1846–50, the average price of bar iron was down to £7.60. That 50-per-cent drop over a period of 160 years is a measure of a gradually changing technology. Then came the Bessemer converter to bring the price of steel down to £7 by the 1860's, and the price of pig iron dropped to about £3 a ton by the end of the century. As against these prices, the fine steel produced near Oyo in 1903 sold on the local market for the equivalent of £18.70 a ton.[11] Steel at £18 far in the interior would have been competitive with steel at £7 a ton, f.o.b. London, as long as high-cost transportation kept the interior markets isolated. If the Oyo price represents the level of costs elsewhere in West Africa, it would explain why the African iron industry remained competitive until the coming of railroads and motor roads.

Cotton Textiles

At least six different species of cotton were known in West Africa, suitable to a variety of different environmental conditions, though Senegambia depended mainly on *Gossypium punctatus,* introduced from the Americas in the sixteenth century, grown and made into cloth almost everywhere. It was thus theoretically possible for a village to meet its own textile

10. Francis-Beuf, "L'industrie du fer," pp. 450–59.
11. Prices for 1680's from Gambia Journals, RAC, in T 70/546; 1840's from T. Tooke, *A History of Prices and of the State of Circulation from 1792 to 1856,* 6 vols. (New York, 1928; first published 1838–57), 2:406 and 3:397; later nineteenth century from Landes, *Unbound Prometheus,* p. 255, and Bellamy "Smelting House," p. 118.
Here and below in this chapter, where money prices in England are quoted, it is possible that the changes noted are merely a reflection of changes in the general price level rather than changes in real values. In the century and a half from the 1680's to the 1830's, however, the European price index of Senegambian imports was nearly steady over the long term. (See *Supplement,* appendix 15.) The money prices can therefore be taken to be close enough to real prices for the purposes at hand.

needs, but textiles were not part of the "subsistence" economy. Some regions were better suited to cotton growing than others, and regional specialization was even more a matter of skill and taste. A caravan carrying one type and quality of cloth might well meet another carrying a different type and quality in the opposite direction.

Bundu, for example, was a center of cotton production, a center of weaving, and a net exporter of raw and woven cotton, but the Bundunke also imported the specialty cloth of other regions. From the east came *kasa* (pl. *kasaaji*), a woolen cloth made at several points up and down the Niger valley but thought of in Bundu as a Segu cloth, since the juula from Bundu bought their supplies at Segu market. Other currents of trade turned on specialized dyeing. In the late nineteenth century, Bundu exported undyed cloths to Gajaaga and imported in return the dyed cottons (*guude Gajaaga*) for which Gajaaga was famous, along with other Soninke cloths brought from Jahunu to the northeast by the Gajaaga merchants. The cloth trade intersected with other trades, since cloth was a currency throughout Senegambia, as well as a commodity. The fact that Bundu was a net exporter of cloth was therefore a considerable advantage to the Bunduunke position in foreign trade. The cloth could either go west, where it was universally acceptable, or it could go east to Bambuhu, which imported textiles and exported gold, a valuable medium of exchange in long-distance trade anywhere to the east and northeast.[1]

Fuuta Tooro was also a net exporter of cotton textiles. As early as 1068 A.D., al-Bekri reported that the people of Silla (the present-day upper Fuuta and Gajaaga) traded in millet, salt, copper rings, and "cloths of fine cotton which are called *sheggiyyāt*," which came from the nearby country of Taranqa. These were about 4 empans (90 cm) wide and the same in length. He added: "There is much cotton in this country, and almost every house had its cotton bush."[2] In the sixteenth century, Fuuta was still exporting cloth to the lower Senegal and Gambia, and the Portuguese tied into this trade by buying cloth on the Senegambian coast for export by sea to the Gulf of Guinea. At their own base in the Cape Verde Islands, the Portuguese began to import slaves to manufacture the African styles of cloth from locally grown cotton. As a result, Senegambian textile technology and even the Senegambian monetary system of cloth currency were carried a short distance overseas and assimilated by a European colony.[3]

The westward export of Futaanke cloth had its counterpart on the Gambia,

1. Hammady Mady Sy, Medina Kajolaani, CC, T 7 (2); Ali N'Diaye, CC, T 15 (2); Boucard, "Relation de Bambouc," June 1729, AM, Mss. 50/2, ff. 14, 22–23.

2. V. Monteil translation, *BIFAN*, 30:108 (1968).

3. Alvares, *Tratado breve*, p. 14; C. Monteil, "Le coton chez les noirs," *CEHSAOF*, 11:585–684 (1926), pp. 260–61. See also A. Carreira, *Panaria cabo-verdiano-guineense: Aspectos históricos e sócio-económicos* (Lisbon, 1968).

where the coastal region was also a net importer of textiles. This was an ancient trade, where differences in resource endowment led to specialized production. It was not that Mali had better land for growing cotton; the Malinke needed salt. To get salt from the lower Gambia and Saalum rivers, they had to sell something in return, and what they sold was cloth. In this sense, the east-west trade in salt for cloth was a counterpart to the north-south trade in gold for salt from the desert. Production that may have begun as a necessity became in time a virtue; Malinke cloth was so low in price and high in quality that the Europeans often found it more profitable to export cloth than gold.[4]

Specialized cloth production thus built up patterns of skill in the interior and habits of consumption on the coast. European merchants found that they could make up to 100 per cent gross profit on the shipment of cloths from the upper course of either river to the coast, and they entered the internal textile trade as well as the export trade. About 1678, for example, the Royal African Company found that it needed to buy one to two thousand "country cloths" (*pagnes* in French, from the Portuguese *pano*) on the upper Gambia simply for use as currency to buy provisions on the lower river. Of the Company's cloth purchases on the upper Gambia, about half were resold in Senegambia, while half were exported by sea to other parts of West Africa. The French had a similar trade on the Senegal, where their exports of finished cloth ran as high as 10,000 pieces in some years before the great famine of the 1710's. After that, the local price of Senegambian cloth trebled, and it stayed at the higher level through the first half of the eighteenth century. Europeans never again found cloth export quite as profitable as it had once been, though cloth continued as a minor export. Even in the early nineteenth century, the Gambia still exported about 1,500 pieces in a good year.[5]

Textile production was a normal household task with no specialization beyond spinning for women and weaving for men. Only the Fuulbe considered weaving a "caste" craft to be left to an endogamous group called *maabube* (sing. *maabo*), but its separation grew from the fact that the maabube were minstrels as well. Other Senegambian societies considered weaving a suitable occupation for either free men or domestic slaves. The Jahaanke, in particular, left weaving to the servile class, since slaves for growing and weaving cotton were a useful reinvestment of trading profits.

Other weavers were free and semimigratory. Some of the maabube from Fuuta went out looking for work in other cotton-growing areas over the dry

---

4. Jobson, *Golden Trade*, p. 120; Lemos Coelho, *Duas descriçoes*, p. 131.

5. T. Thurloe to RAC, 15 March 1677/78, T 70/10; Gambia Accounts, 1683-88, T 50/546; La Courbe, "Mémoire sur le commerce," 26 March 1693, ANF, C6 3; Gambia Blue Books, CO 272; Saint-Robert to CI, 28 March 1721, ANF, C6 6; "Mémoire générale sur le commerce du Sénégal," ANS, C6 15.

season. They were common in Bundu, where they were known as *companaaɓe* (sing. *campanaagal,* from a root meaning "to settle"). In recent years, they were lodged and fed by the master weaver, who took them into his establishment and paid at the end of the season with a share of the cloth produced. They sometimes asked for an assignment of land and stayed over the wet season, and, like other migratory workers, some never went home at all but settled down with Bunduunke wives and became, in time, Bundunkoobe.[6] While the campanaagal phenomenon may not have existed on a very large scale, it is evidence of labor mobility, a market for nonservile labor, and specialized production for export—all contrary to the myth of the African "subsistence" economy.

The technology of weaving differed little within Senegambia, where only the horizontal, narrow-band, treadle loom was used.[7] The operator usually sat under shelter or in the open shade, with one end of the warp fastened to a weight which was gradually pulled closer as the weaving progressed. The most common style was a cotton cloth about 15 to 18 cm wide and 16 meters long. In its undyed, unfinished form this was the standard "piece" of cloth (in Pulaar, *soro,* pl. *sorooji; bande de sor* in Senegalese French). In actual use, however, strips were sewn together, so that the full 16-meter length was used in the form of eight strips, 15 cm wide each, to make a cloth about 1.2 meters wide and 2 meters long. On the upper Senegal, parts of the full soro were used as fractional currency. The smallest unit was the *lefol* (pl. *leppi*), a single width 2 meters long, in effect one of the eight strips necessary to the full cloth. The half-soro or *haafere* was a unit of currency, and it was also the usual size for a woman's cloth, just as the full soro was the usual size for making man's pantaloons. In other regions, both size and nomenclature of the cloth currency could be quite different. The Soninke *tama* of Jahunu, for example, was made of the same eight strips, but they were only about 10 cm wide and 10 meters long, so that the full tama was less than half the size of the full soro.[8]

A great variety of other cloths were produced, some woven with threads dyed in different colors, others with varying degrees of fineness, still others with design imposed in the dye process, usually through tie-dye techniques.

6. Hammady Mady Sy, Medina Kojalaani, CC, T 7 (1); personal communication from Hammady Amadou Sy, July 1966. See also Monteil, "Coton chez les noirs," pp. 637–44.

7. The other two types found in precolonial West Africa were the vertical mat loom of preforest and south-savanna settings in West Africa and Central Africa alike, and the vertical cotton loom used both in Algeria and in the tropical forest of present-day Nigeria. (H. Ling Roth, "Studies in Primitive Looms," *Journal of the Royal Anthropological Institute,* 46:285–308; 47:113–50; 48:103–45 [1916–18]; 46:284–91 and 47:113–45 apply to Africa.)

8. Monteil, "Coton chez les noirs," pp. 44–46; Roux, "Tournée dans le cercle de Bakel," 1 April 1892, ANS, 1 G 135: Pollet and Winter, *La société soninké,* p. 218.

The range of colors came from three basic dyes. Indigo provided blue and purple, both from the wild plant (*Lonchocarpus cynescens*) and from the cultivated form (*Indigofera tinctoria*). A black dye came from the fruit of the *Acacia Adansonii*, while a yellow dye was prepared from the leaves of the bush *Combretum glotinosum*, whose wood ashes could also be used to fix indigo dyes.[9]

With this amount of manufacture and internal trade, it may seem curious that Senegambia never exported significant amounts of raw cotton. The stereotypes of underdevelopment suggest that raw cotton was a more likely export than finished cloth. In fact, the Europeans tried to encourage cotton-growing for export. In the 1720's, the Royal African Company sent back two slaves from Jamaica who were skilled in cleaning cotton, with the hope that they could train others; but the effort was unprofitable, though the Company made a little money selling uncleaned cotton in Britain. Other flurries of interest in cotton export followed in the 1780's, again in the 1820's, and yet again in the 1850's, but none of the plans worked out. The closest approach to success came with the French plan to make Senegal into a plantation colony, and in 1824 they actually exported 22 metric tons of raw cotton. In proving that it could be done, however, they also proved its financial impracticability.[10]

Gum

Gum arabic, gum acacia, or gum Senegal was one of the earliest of exotics to be imported regularly into Europe. It first came from Arabia and the Nilotic Sudan, by way of the Red Sea and Egypt into the Mediterranean world of classical times, and Europeans have used it when they could get it from then on, for papermaking, candy and confectionary, and the textile industry. West African gum began to replace eastern gum in the sixteenth century, and Senegambia gradually supplied more and more of the market until, in the eighteenth century, it had become the only significant

9. Monteil, "Coton chez les noirs," pp. 116 ff.; Raffenel, *Nouveau voyage*, 1:407–10; Dr. Lasnet, "Les races du Sénégal," in Lasnet and others, eds., *Une mission au Sénégal* (Paris, 1900), p. 94; Rançon, *La haute Gambie*, pp. 408–9.

10. Council Minutes, James Fort, March 15, 1722/23, Rawlinson Papers, Rhodes House, Oxford; RAC to Anthony Rogers, 25 November 1731, T 70/55; Charles O'Hara to Duke of Richmond, Fort Lewis, 1 September 1766, CO 267/13; John Barnes, Evidence to Commons Committee on the Slave Trade, 26 March 1789, PP, *Accounts and Papers*, xxv (635), p. 13; L. Faidherbe, *Le Sénégal: La France dans l'Afrique occidentale* (Paris, 1889), p. 102; Audibert, "Rapport adressé à la commission de l'Exposition universelle réunie à Saint-Louis (Sénégal)," *Revue coloniale*, 14 (2nd ser.):177–211 (1855), p. 202.

supplier to Europe. That alone indicates why the Europeans were so concerned about some aspects of Senegambian trade.[1]

But gum was produced only in a restricted part of Senegambia. It comes from several different species of acacia, the most important of which is the *Acacia Senegal,* growing along the whole southern fringe of the Sahara. The ideal environment has a rainfall of about 400 mm, or about the limit of possible rainfall agriculture. The 400-mm isohyet touches the Atlantic coast today a little to the south of Saint Louis and runs due east, leaving lower Fuuta to the north and upper Fuuta to the south. The best of the Senegambian gum from the true *Acacia Senegal* came from north of Fuuta; other acacia trees in Gidimaxa eastward produced a gum that was less desirable because it crumbled at the touch. This friable gum was usually only marketable at a low price and in seasons when the price of hard gum was exceptionally high and its supply exceptionally low. In either case, the actual gathering was done by slaves belonging to the Moors, mainly of the zwāya, but occasionally of the Hasanīya as well.[2]

Gum trees were not cultivated, but they grew more thickly in some regions than in others, so that it was customary to refer to a "gum forest." During the wet season, *Acacia Senegal* picks up water from the ground, and the bark expands. Then, with the dry season, the bark contracts and the gum is extruded through any small natural opening. It is possible to increase the yield by cutting the bark with a knife, but careless tapping of this kind can also kill the tree. Care is also necessary to pick the small, transparent, yellowish balls the size of a hickory nut at exactly the right time. Taken too soon, they will be too small; left too late they are spoiled by the adhesion of wind-blown sand. The harvest can begin in a small way with the first of the dry, easterly winds in November, but the main harvest comes in March after the vigorous and arid harmattan has blown for several months, and it continues until the beginning of the new rains in June or July.

Up to the middle of the eighteenth century, European consumption of gum was thought to have been less than 500 metric tons a year, and the price was low, with the result that the gum trade was locally important for the middle and lower Senegal River and the Mauritanian coast, but it rarely came to as much as 10 per cent of the value of Senegambian exports. (See tables 8.6 and 8.7 below.) Then, in the 1740's, Senegambian gum became suddenly important. Even though European annual consumption was still taken to be less

1. P. Bellouard, "La gomme arabique en A.O.F.," *Bois et forêts des tropiques,* no. 9, 3–18 (1947), pp. 4–5.

2. The most authoritative study of the recent gum trade is G. M. Désiré-Vuillemin, *Essai sur le gommier et le commerce de gomme dans les escales du Sénégal* (mimeographed *thèse complimentaire,* Dakar, Clairafrique, n.d. [c. 1963]). For earlier periods see Bellouard, "La gomme arabique," and Audibert, "Rapport à l'exposition universelle."

than 600 tons a year, the Compagnie des Indes shipped more than 1,000 tons in 1743 and again in 1746. These peaks were caused, however, by unusual supply conditions bringing Moors from greater distances rather than by rising prices or higher demand in Europe. In the 1750's, the trade again fell off to about 500 tons a year or less, shipped from the Senegal River, though somewhat greater quantities seem to have come from the Mauritanian gum coast,[3] and these supply conditions lasted until the end of the Napoleonic Wars.

Meanwhile, European demand began to shift in the 1770's, demonstrated first by a sharp rise in price to about five times the price prevailing in the early eighteenth century—then to ten times the old price by the 1780's and on to fifteen times by the period 1823–27, continuing at these levels to the mid-century and later.[4] The Moorish response to the price rise was slow. Deliveries hardly grew at all before 1817, but production in the 1820's was twice the prewar level. It doubled again in the 1830's and continued through the 1840's at an annual average of more than 2,000 metric tons (though with great annual variation), but that was to be the limit for the old gum forests. By the 1840's, high prices brought other sources into the market, especially from the Egyptian Sudan, and gum gathering spread into the Ferlo south of the Senegal River. By the early twentieth century, Senegal and Mauritania together had reached an annual average in the neighborhood of 4,000 tons, but the increase came mainly from the Ferlo.[5]

Senegal's gum prosperity of the 1820's through the 1840's was real enough. At £70 per metric ton (the prevalent price of 1823–27), even 1,000 tons a year was more valuable than the slave trade had ever been for a comparable period of time. The Afro-French traders based on Saint Louis thus had no trouble making the switch from the slave trade to "legitimate trade," especially when they drew some profit from slaves as well—until 1831. But gum

3. "Extrait relatif au commerce de la gomme," undated [c. 1757], ANF, C6 14. See also *Supplement,* appendix 12, for quantities exported.

4. Gum prices quoted for Saint Louis have the same problem as slave prices; it is very hard to distinguish prices paid the African supplier from the price f.o.b. Nevertheless, some representative eighteenth-century quotations were as follows, in sterling equivalent per metric ton:

1718	£3.40	1776	£23.31
1723	5.45	1783	44.62
1739	6.06	1788	30.36
1745	3.46	1823–27	69.57 (annual average)

See "Mémoire générale sur le commerce du Sénégal [1718 on internal evidence], ANF, C6 14; Memorandum of 11 October 1723, ANF, C6 7; "Mémoire sur le prix de la gomme," 1739, ANF, C6 12; "La Commerce de la concession . . ." 1745, ANF, C6 12. Price from 1823 onward from *Statistiques coloniales* listing quantity and value of gum exported.

5. Bellouard, "La gomme arabique," pp. 4–6.

production was inelastic, and gum did little for the economy of Senegambia as a whole; it raised the incomes of gum traders and the masters of gum production, but significant change affecting a large part of the agricultural sector had to wait until the peanut boom after 1850.

Cattle and Cowhides

The export trade in cowhides was an obvious by-product of domestic meat production, and the cattle trade was probably the most important branch of Senegambian commerce before the nineteenth-century peanut boom. Although cattle could be raised almost anywhere in Senegambia, some environments gave a comparative advantage to regional specialization. On the Mauritanian steppe to the north, cereal production was barely possible, and the nomads expected to buy grain from the Senegal valley in return for their animal products. Judging by later performance, at least half the annual caloric intake on the steppe must have come through trade. Even the farmers of the jeeri and waalo were specialists who produced food partly for the market and partly for their own consumption. Those who owned cattle turned them over to the pastoral Fuulbe during the wet season, and the Fuulbe, who raised some grain, normally had to fill out their diet by selling meat and milk in return for cereals.[1]

A second web of comparative advantage was caused by the tsetse fly— actually by several different flies. *Glossina palpalis* was and is the most widespread, encountered occasionally as far north as the latitude of the Cape Verde peninsula, but it is not very common north of the Gambia and not especially dangerous to animals. The crucial fly for cattle was *Glossina morsitans*, which required permanent thick brush as a habitat. Its northward limit therefore runs along the line of the Gambia and on to the east wherever rainfall is sufficient to produce a gallery forest along streams. *Glossina morsitans* carries the parasite *Trypanosoma rhodesiense*, which is extremely dangerous to cattle. It is dangerous to man too, but the fly stays so close to thick brush that even the normal clearing around villages protects the human population from frequent bites. Cattle are also protected by clearing, which

1. Investigations in Fuuta Tooro during the 1950's indicated that 70 per cent of agricultural production was consumed by the producers, but the sedentary people tended at that time to produce about 25 kgs of millet per capita per year above their own consumption, while the pastoral Fuulbe consumed about 53 kgs of millet per capita above their own production. (Boutillier and others, *Vallée du Sénégal*, pp. 141–43.)

Another index of the probable size of the meat-for-millet trade at the desert edge is the level of trade at the beginning of the colonial period. In 1898, the annual quantity of sorghum moving north through Ñoro on the sahal of present-day Mali was 796 metric tons, valued at more than £2,200 sterling. (Baillaud, *Sur les routes du Soudan*, p. 41.)

meant that open, cleared areas of derived savanna could be safe well to the south of the danger area. Thus the Fuuta Jaalō highlands were a virtually fly-free island, extending westward into the plateau region of Fuuladu, south of the Gambia in upper Casamance. Other regions south of the Gambia raise cattle even though *Glossina morsitans* may be present. The large zebu cattle of the north cannot live there, however, and the people have to make do with the smaller *ndama* breeds, which are resistant to the trypanosomes. The change in breed also marks a social change, since the specialized pastoralists stayed clear of places dangerous to their large cattle.[2]

The combination of aridity and tsetse fly thus produced three different zones—the steppe where only pastoralism was possible, the fly-free savanna where pastoralism tended to be a specialized occupation, and the fly-infested savanna where ndama cattle were raised as part of mixed farming. The major exception was the Sereer country, where cattle were kept penned, even in the wet season, and zebu cattle could be used in mixed farming. Thus, though cattle (and hence cowhides) could be produced anywhere in Senegambia, most cattle production was in the hands of specialists who had to market a large part of their product in return for other food.

The seasonal pattern of rainfall also tended to push cattle off to the south at the end of each wet season. As the herdsmen looked ahead to limited food over the coming dry season, they began to thin the herd, and prices reached their annual low point. In these circumstances, it was only natural to capitalize on the mobility of the cattle and move them south where rainfall was greater and end-of-season prices were higher. A visitor to the Gambia in 1787 described a herd of 400 head being swum south across the river near Albreda.[3] At that point the Moorish herdsmen who drove those cattle were more than 700 kms south of their normal grazing lands and had not yet reached the market. By the early nineteenth century, hides for export by way of the Gambia also came from some of the fly-free pockets south of the river, especially from Fuuladu, where pastoral Fuulbe were pushing into the old Malinke kingdom of Kaabu.[4]

Some cattle were also sold to provision ships in the slave trade, and other ships were provisioned with dried meat. In 1718 or so, the Compagnie des Indes bought some 300 head of cattle and 400 head of sheep a year from the

2. E. Roubaud, "Les mouches tse-tse en Afrique occidentale française," *CEHSAOF,* 3:257–300 (1920), esp. 270–92; Pélissier, *Paysans du Sénégal,* pp. 394–95. See for trypanosomes in general F. L. Lambrecht, "Aspects of Evolution and Ecology of Tse-tse Flies and Trypanosomiasis in Prehistoric African Environment," *JAH,* 5:1–24 (1964), and for the most important, sophisticated, and recent study with a broad ecological approach (though not specifically about Senegambia) see J. Ford, *The Role of Trypanosomiasis in African Ecology: A Study of the Tsetse Fly Problem* (Oxford, 1971).

3. Golberry, *Travels,* 1:239–44.

4. Charles Grant to J. Rowan, Bathurst, 30 June 1826, CO 267/93.

Moors at the gum escales, in addition to other purchases closer to Saint Louis to feed the population of the town itself. And Saint Louis had a high per capita meat consumption. The French reckoned on about 1 kg per day for the habitants and 500 grams for Christian African workers of the town. If this accurately represented the per capita consumption in the region, it would have been higher than that of Europe at the time.[5]

The hide exports are one index of the cattle trade (at least of the annual number of cattle slaughtered), and cowhides played a curious and checkered role in the Senegambian export economy. As long as people slaughtered cattle for food, hides were available. Supply was diminished only by such internal events as warfare or a sequence of years with low rainfall. Overseas demand, on the other hand, was more variable. It began to be important in the sixteenth century, when the rate of export rose to 6,000 or 7,000 in the final third of the century. The first peak, however, came in the early seventeenth century, when the hide trade became more valuable than the slave trade, and exports may have reached 150,000 by the 1660's.[6] This swing grew out of a general increase in the European demand for leather. The long period from 1400 to 1750 was one of a shifting European diet from meat to grains and vegetables. One study shows a drop in German per capita consumption of meat from about 100 kgs a year in the fifteenth century to only 14 kgs in the nineteenth.[7] As a result, European leather production fell off, and the Europeans had to look overseas for hides. In the early seventeenth century, they offered good prices, the standard iron bar for one and a half or two hides.[8] At the price of iron prevalent in the 1680's (the first period with secure data), that would have been the value of about £7.40 sterling per hundred hides. By the 1680's, the price offered had dropped to less than half that figure, and it stabilized at about £2 per hundred through the early eighteenth century. At that price, the export of hides was negligible, and it remained so for the rest of the century.[9]

Then, in the early nineteenth century, leather prices recovered. In spite of

5. Mémoire générale sur le commerce du Sénégal, [1718], ANF, C6 14. From this the habitant would have to feed a substantial establishment of his wives, children, domestic slaves, and the like. And the head of a Christian African family would have perhaps a total of five individuals to feed, implying about 100 grams a day per person or about 37 kgs a year.

6. G. Thilmans and J. P. Rossie, "Le 'Flambeau de Navigation' de Dierick Ruiters," *BIFAN*, 31:106–19 (1969); G. Thilmans, "Le Sénégal dans l'oeuvre de Olfried Dapper," *BIFAN*, 32:508–63 (1970). See Boulègue, "Luso-africains," pp. 41–43.

7. F. P. Braudel and F. Spooner, "Prices in Europe from 1450 to 1750," in E. E. Rich and C. H. Wilson, *The Cambridge Economic History of Europe*, vol. 4 (Cambridge, 1967), pp. 374–86, 414–15.

8. G. Thilmans, "Dapper," pp. 538–40.

9. Data for 1680's from Gambia Journals, T 70/546. See *Supplement*, appendix 12, for quantities exported.

competition from new overseas sources like Argentina, the Senegambian price climbed to £12.50 per hundred in the 1820's and on to about £20 per hundred during the 1830's and 1840's, and hide exports rose to an annual average of 176,000, or more than the seventeenth-century peak. Hides made up only about 8 per cent of the value of Senegambian exports in the 1830's, but 176,000 hides exported implies 176,000 cattle slaughtered at a value of about £1 sterling on the hoof—an annual cattle production worth approximately half the annual value of all Senegambian exports.[10]

Horses and Transport Animals

The position of the horse in Senegambia was different from that of any other animal. Horses pulled no plows, no carts, nor even carried ordinary people. They were reserved strictly for military use, which incidentally made them a symbol of power and status. These military and status associations were close to the chivalric tradition in Europe, but the bond between the fighting man and his horse was even closer in Senegambian traditions than it was in Europe. In the historical traditions still sung by Senegambian minstrels, each hero, like Samba Gelaajo Jegi, had an equally famous horse; even the horses ridden by minor characters are remembered by name.[1] This special respect for horses and horsemanship reflected the military reality, since cavalry was the dominant force far into the nineteenth century. A middle-sized Senegambian state could put one to five thousand mounted men into the field, even if it was not in the horse-breeding zone.

Horses are much more delicate than cattle in the face of trypanosomiasis and other tropical diseases, though it is easier to keep them alive and healthy than it is to breed them. Breeding can be done only to the north of a line running from about Cape Verde to the confluence of the Faleme and Senegal rivers. The division into a horse-breeding and a horse-importing zone, however, was not absolute, and the line was not permanent through time. Even Fuuta could be a horse-importing region at certain periods, though the Mauritanian steppe was consistently a net exporter of horses, and the Gambia valley was consistently a net importer, a pattern reinforced by the fact that the supply regions would only sell stallions. After five years' residence on the Gambia, Francis Moore saw only one mare, imported in that case from the Cape Verdes.[2]

It is hardly surprising that horses from Europe were important from the

10. Prices from Gambia Blue Books, annual series, CO 90. See below, table 8.7, and *Supplement,* appendix 12.
1. This inordinate respect for the horse caught the attention of several of the early European visitors as well. See, for example, Barreira, "Côte de Guinée," p. 30.
2. Moore, *Travels,* p. 63.

beginning of maritime contact, and they continued as the principal import until nearly the end of the sixteenth century. Prices were especially favorable to the Europeans in the fifteenth century, when horses were said to have sold for fourteen or fifteen slaves each. By the early sixteenth century, however, the price had dropped to six or seven slaves, and the Cape Verde Islands became the main source of maritime imports. Meanwhile the price kept dropping. Visitors still published stories of horses exchanged for fifteen or twenty slaves, but that was simply a sign that the Senegambian love of horses sometimes led people to pay a ridiculous price for an exceptional animal, just as Europeans do. Ordinary horses exchanged for a single slave in the 1670's, and two slaves would buy three horses by the 1680's. At these prices, even the import trade from the Cape Verde Islands became unprofitable, and the Gambia got most of its horses from the Senegal valley. Before the end of the eighteenth century, Mungo Park was able to buy a horse that served him well on his first journey for less than half the price of a slave.[3]

Imported horses also had the same epidemiological problems as imported people. Trypanosomiasis would kill any horse, but locally bred horses had acquired other immunities either genetically or when young. Twice in the colonial period, in 1884 and again in 1921, the French lost heavily from "horse sickness." The second attack took 97 per cent of the French-bred horses belonging to the French army in Senegal, only a few of the Algerian mules, and none at all of the local animals. Europeans had come to realize by then that the most resistant animals available were the large ponies called *mbaiar,* bred in the dry lands of eastern Bawol, though they still preferred the Barbs from Fuuta Tooro or the steppe.[4]

The animals of real economic importance were the pack oxen of the desert edge, the camels of the desert itself, and the donkeys that served as the main transport animal of the savanna down to the tsetse line and beyond. Camels and pack oxen were bred in the regions they served, but donkeys, like horses, tended to be bred in the north, principally in Fuuta near Podor. They were then exported to other parts of Senegambia. Although their carrying capacity was less than that of pack oxen, donkeys cost two to five times as much, and

3. Boulègue, "La Sénégambie," p. 161 ff.; Chambonneau, in C. I. A. Ritchie, "Deux textes," pp. 332–33; Gambia Journals, 1683–88, T 70/456; Gambia Journals, entry of Sept. 8, 1727, T 70/555; Consiel du Sénégal to CI, 15 June 1736, ANF, C6 11; Hull "Voyage to Bundo," p. 30; Gray, *Western Africa,* p. 156; Park, *Travels,* 1:43.

4. A. Cligny, "Faune du Sénégal et de la Casamance," in Lasnet and others, *Une Mission au Sénégal,* pp. 278–79; M. Leger and L. Teppaz, "Le 'Horse-Sickness' au Sénégal et au Soudan français," *CEHSAOF,* 5:219–40 (1922); L. Teppaz, *Contribution à l'étude de la horse-sickness au Sénégal* (Paris, 1931). At least some of the Europeans in Senegambia recognized the influence of changing disease environments on animal health. See Levens, Report of 10 July, 1725, AN, FF, NA, f. 141.

the price on the Gambia in 1741 was around £1 sterling in the prime-cost value of the goods exchanged.[5]

Beeswax

The flow of Senegambian beeswax to overseas traders was much like that of hides—a small peak in the seventeenth century followed by decline in the eighteenth and a rise to a higher peak in the early nineteenth. Exports were 10 to 35 metric tons a year in the seventeenth century, at the favorable price of £42 sterling a ton in the 1680's. With the eighteenth century, the price slipped to about £29 in the early 1730's, and the quantities dropped as well. Then, with the rise of European demand in the early nineteenth century, the price climbed back to well over £100 by the 1840's, and the quantities jumped to the range of 250 to 400 tons a year.[1]

Wax and hides were also similar in their relation to local trade. Both were by-products of food production, of honey and meat. Like pastoralism, apiculture was practiced throughout Senegambia, and wild honey could also be found in the woods. But some regions specialized in beekeeping, and their surplus honey and wax entered trade. The latitude of the Gambia was especially favored, and the Gambia Malinke were the most prominent specialists. Their beehive was made of straw sides mounted on a wooden board. To harvest the hive, they first squeezed the honey out of the comb, then melted the wax in boiling water, pressed it through a cloth, and shaped it into cakes weighing 10 to 60 kgs each.[2] The local price of rough wax varied greatly, depending on the impurities it contained, but juula and occasionally one of the European trading companies would buy rough wax, reprocess it, and sell it for export at a higher price. It is impossible to estimate total Senegambian honey production, but it was the main source of sugar for the whole region, and it has held its own in many places until the present in spite of competition from imported cane sugar. There is no more reason to suppose that bees were kept mainly for the wax than there is to assume that cattle were raised for the value of the hide.

5. Cligny, "Faune du Sénégal," p. 281; Raffenel, *Nouveau voyage,* 1:32 and 457. The Gambia accounts in T 70/575 show a donkey bought at James Fort for the prime-cost value of £1.09. Camel prices were not often reported, but Golberry reported buying an eight-year-old dromedary near Saint Louis for the equivalent of £8.60. (Golberry, *Travels,* 1:266.)

1. For quantities exported see *Supplement,* appendix 12. For prices in the 1680's see T 70/546; the 1730's, T 70/553–71; the early nineteenth century, Gambia Blue Books, CO 90, and *Statistiques coloniales* (both annual series).

2. Moore, *Travels,* p. 44; Raffenel, *Nouveau voyage,* 1:20.

Ivory

Elephants once roamed near the Atlantic coast, but those herds had been killed off long before the mid-seventeenth century. By the second half of the century, some ivory came from the Tanda peoples south and east of Barokunda Falls. Some came from Wuuli and the unpopulated no-mans-land west and south of Bundu, but after the 1720's, ivory shipped from Senegambia came almost entirely from the "merchants' country" to the east.

The disappearance of the western elephant herds meant declining exports through the seventeenth and eighteenth centuries. Then, in the early nineteenth, the price shot up, as it did for so many other tropical commodities—a ten-fold increase between the 1780's and the 1830's—but this time the response was weak. Annual average exports for 1836–40 were barely more than the Royal African Company alone had shipped in a comparable period of the 1680's. The higher price simply made it economic to bring in ivory from a greater distance.[1]

Salt

Salt was crucial to the Senegambian economy, not only because Senegambian salt was cheap and accessible, but also because the savanna country to the east had none at all. Salt consumed throughout the vast interior of West Africa came mainly from the desert or one of the coasts, though small quantities could be extracted from certain vegetation if the external sources failed. Historically, desert salt had the first importance, but Senegambian sea salt was second, while salt from the Guinea coast was far behind, and vegetable salt came last of all.

The competing types came in two basic forms, rock salt and granular. The crystalline deposits of the desert were mined by cutting out large bars, the usual size at Taodeni about 1 meter long, 40 cm wide, and 3 cm thick. These bars were impervious to light rain and were convenient to store or to ship, while the granular salt from the coast had to be packed in baskets or barrels and was far more liable to damage from rain and dirt. Rock salt also varied in quality from one deposit to another. At any time after the late sixteenth century, it came from one of two places, Ijil in the west or Taodeni further north and east. (See figure 5.3.) The Taodeni salt was purer, whiter in color,

1. Lemos Coelho, *Duas descriçoes,* pp. 24, 135; Hodges to RAC, 16 Sept. 1690, in Stone, "Journey of Cornelius Hodges," p. 91; Saint-Robert to CI, 28 March 1721, ANF, C6 6; Hull, "Voyage to Bundo," p. 14; Moore, *Travels,* p. 44; Raffenel, *Nouveau voyage,* 1:78. For quantities exported see *Supplement,* appendix 12.

and was customarily cut into large bars weighing 35 to 40 kgs. Ijil salt was cut into smaller bars weighing only about 25 kgs; it was darker, more breakable, and contained more magnesium, which gave it a slightly bitter taste.[1]

The Taodeni deposits were controlled by the rulers of Arawan in the desert, but merchants from Timbuktu managed the trade by caravan from Taodeni to their own city, and controlled further shipment up the Niger by boat. The Ijil salt belonged to the Kunta, a zwāya tribe of Arab origin, but they chose not to manage the trade themselves. Instead they sold the salt at Ijil or at the oasis town of Chingetti, where merchants, usually desert people, bought it and carried it to the sahal. Ijil salt was a little more plentiful in the nineteenth century, but competition between the two rock salts was large decided by habitual taste preferences.[2]

Two competing forms of granular salt were also available. A Saharan form occurred where wet-weather streams flowed into shallow, land-locked ponds or lakes, leaving a small annual deposit as the water evaporated. The rock salt was probably first laid down in a similar way, but it had crystalized, while the other deposits had not. These uncrystalized deposits are found scattered widely in the desert, but especially in coastal Mauritania, where dunes prevent surface water from flowing to the sea. The Trarza gathered some of this salt for their own use and exported some, but it competed badly with the sea salt south of the Senegal. They therefore shipped it east by camel, where it could be landed on the sahal near Ñoro in competition with Ijil rock salt, and they carried some to the Senegal, where the Afro-French picked it up for eastward shipment by water.[3]

The second type of granular salt was derived from seawater where the tide rose over the flat shore and evaporated naturally—or where the same effect was produced by controlling the flow of water artificially. Both natural and artificial salt pans were found near the Senegambian coast. One at Maka, on the Senegal just north of Saint Louis, was the property of the Brak of Waalo. Another group of deposits near Ganjool, south of Saint Louis, belonged to the royal house of Kajor. Fajuut, near Joal in Siin, was another center on the coast, while large quantities were manufactured alongside the tidal stretches of the Gambia and Saalum Rivers—especially at the Bantanto Bolon near Kaur on the Gambia and on the Saalum near Kaolak. Enormous natural

1. Ballien, "Notice du Soudan," ANS Q 48.

2. Al-Shinquiti, *El-Wasit,* pp. 115–16; Baillaud, *Sur les routes du Soudan,* pp. 43, 113–15.

3. The large salt deposits at Nterert, Mauritania, which have been worked commercially in recent decades, were not part of the older pattern, since they were discovered only in 1910. See also G. Mère, "Les salines du Trarza," *Renseignements coloniaux,* no. 7, pp. 161–67 (1911); L. Pales, *Les sels alimentaires. Sels minéraux. Problème des sels alimentaires en A.O.F.* (Dakar, 1950), pp. 11–14, 39–40.

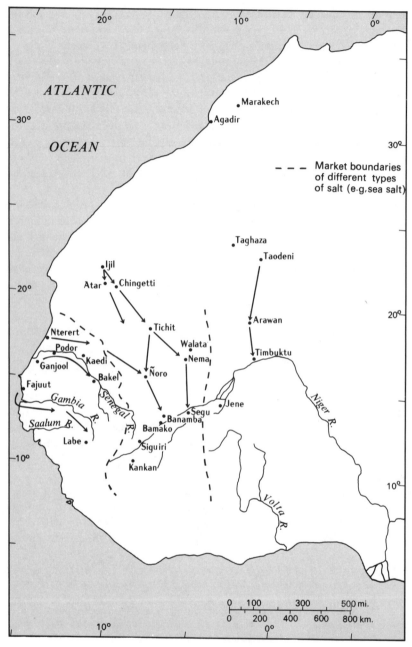

5.3 Nineteenth-Century Salt Routes to the Western Sudan

deposits of the same type were also found in the Cape Verde Islands. Whatever the origin, most of the salt entering trade moved inland up the Senegal or Gambia or southward in the coastal trade for transshipment at the southern rivers, all bound ultimately for the salt-starved interior.[4]

The best quantity estimates for the salt trade or salt production date from the late nineteenth century. They are only a rough indication of probable levels before 1850, but they are better than no indication at all. One survey of salt passing through Kayes, for example, showed about 3,000 tons of rock salt moving southward each year, about 60 per cent from Ijil and 40 per cent from Taodeni. Another 715 tons of granular salt also reached Kayes by way of the Senegal. Taking account of the probable amounts of sea salt also shipped inland by way of the Gambia, these figures suggest 500 to 1,000 metric tons of sea salt annually—or one-fourth of all salt reaching the interior.[5] Since contemporaries thought that about half the coastal salt was consumed there and half exported inland, this implies total Senegambian production of 1,000 to 2,000 tons a year. This figure is hardly more than a guess, but it is at least congruent with occasional reports on the productivity of particular deposits. The Ganjool complex, for example, sold 798 tons a year at the time of the French conquest in 1861, when it was the largest single source on the Senegal.[6]

The value was not overwhelming compared to those of other Senegambian industries of the period. Fifteen hundred metric tons at the price prevalent in 1828 implied an annual value of £1,310 at the pithead, but the price in Gajaaga was much higher, a minimum of £3.41 a ton in 1824. At that price, the estimated 750 tons a year sold in the interior would have paid for £2,500 in return goods—a significant part of the Gajaaga trade, though pièces de Guinée were far more important.[7]

This situation of the early nineteenth century was the culmination of a long

4. La Courbe, *Premier voyage*, p. 13; "Mémoire générale sur le commerce du Sénégal," [1718], ANF, C6 14; Labat, *Nouvelle relation*, 3:80, 4:247; Durand, *Sénégal*, 1:100–101, 125–26; Conseil d'administration du Sénégal, 20 April 1861, ANF-OM, Sénégal XIII 58; "Mémoire concernant le commerce," enclosed with Commander Gorée to Director Saint Louis, 4 June 1741, ANF, C6 12; T. Bentley Duncan, *Atlantic Islands: Madeira, the Azores and the Cape Verdes in Seventeenth-Century Commerce and Navigation* (Chicago, 1972), pp. 188–91; Moore, *Travels*, pp. 48–49.

5. Ballien, "Notice du Soudan," ANS, Q 48. These figures are confirmed by Baillaud, *Sur les routes du Soudan*, p. 43, as of 1899, where the imports into the *Soudan* from Ijil were estimated at about 2,250 metric tons a year. Léon Pales estimated Taodeni production at the beginning of this century at about 1,000 tons. (Pales, *Sels alimentaires*, p. 57.)

6. Conseil d'administration du Sénégal, 20 April 1861, ANF-OM, Sénégal XIII 58.

7. Duranton to Governor, 7 August 1828, ANS, 1 G 8. The Gajaaga price for 1824 was the support level set by the Senegalese government to prevent undercutting by individual Saint Louis traders. Saulnier, *Compagnie de Galam*, p. 69.

trend of lowering prices and increasing sales. As the price of granular sea salt in the interior moved closer and closer to the price on the coast, it won an increasing share of the interior market, even though rock salt was still preferred on grounds of taste. In 1729, for example, Bambuhu still bought mainly desert salt, either the granular or rock variety, but by 1796, the Afro-French sea salt could be sold in competition with rock salt as far inland as Siguiri. Though desert salt continued to be available all along the sahal, in Fuuta as well as Gidimaxa and Kaarta, it lost ground to sea salt—even in Kaarta, where Wolof traders were established in Ñoro by 1878.[8] In the early eighteenth century, people looked back to a distant past when 1 volume of salt brought 20 equal volumes of millet in Gajaaga. But regular boat trade on the Senegal with the Afro-French "Galam voyage" brought the price down to 1 salt for 6 millet in the early eighteenth century, about 1 for 4 by 1820, and 1 for 3 by the end of the nineteenth century.[9] This convergence of prices implies an extension of regional markets, and suggests for Senegambia a diffusion of localized resources and increasing gross national product.

Kola Nuts

Just as cattle, horses, and gum were exotics from the northern fringes of Senegambia, kola was the major exotic imported from the south. The *kola nitida* was grown in the tropical forest of southern Guinea-Conakry and Sierra Leone, and largely exported to the north, where chewing kola nuts as a stimulant had long been more popular with savanna people than it was in the forest where the nuts grew. Both the custom and the kola trade that made it possible were present by the sixteenth century, when demand along the Gambia and Senegal was enough to justify coastwise maritime trade from Sierra Leone. By the middle of the seventeenth century, Sierra Leone exports northward by sea were as much as 225 metric tons a year, though much of this trade may have stopped short of the Gambia.[1]

8. Boucard, "Relation de Bambouc," p. 81; Park, *Travels*, 1:455; Renseignements laissé, July 1827, ANS, 13 G 164, ff. 3–4; P. Holle to Governor, Bakel, 3 October 1845, ANS, 13 G 164; P. Solliet, Report dated 10 April 1879, ANS, 1 G 46.

9. The ratios of exchange given here are merely the idea people held as to what was normal. Actual ratios fluctuated from year to year or even within the year. See Boucard to Cl, 1 April 1732, ANF, C6 10; Bruë to Collé, 9 December 1716, ANF, C6 5; Du Pont to Governor, 8 July 1819; ANS, 1 G 2; Ali N'Diaye, CC, T15 (2).

1. For a more general treatment of the kola trade in the history of the Senegambian hinterland see Person, *Samori*, 1:89–129, and Alvares, *Tratado breve*, p. 31. The estimate derives from Lemos Coelho, who mentioned 10,000 "loads" a year, each load being about 3,000 nuts, assuming that the load would be what a man could actually carry, or about 23 kgs. See W. Rodney, *Upper Guinea Coast*, pp. 206–7.

The coastal route for kola imports competed with a still more ancient overland route. Occasional mention by European observers make it possible to trace a gradual shift in the breaking point between seaborne and overland kola. In 1620, for example, Jobson reported the price of kola at the mouth of the Gambia as the highest on the river, and it declined gradually as he moved inland. At least as early as 1716, kola traders from Fuuta Jaalō came through to Gajaaga in a single journey, rather than passing the kola nuts through intermediaries on the way. The foundation of the almamates of Bundu and Fuuta Jaalō helped this north-south trade in the eighteenth century by eliminating a multiplicity of small jurisdictions, and Jahaanke, among others, began to trade more actively to the south in the nineteenth century, reaching the coast at Sierra Leone and the other river-mouth ports to the northwest.[2] As late as the 1890's, overland kola still dominated the market at Kayes, in spite of steamships at sea and steamboats on the Senegal; but the Gambia had already been taken over by the seaborne trade, and the zone of competition between the two routes had moved east and south into Demantan and the Koñagi country along today's Senegal-Guinea-Conakry border.

By 1910, world kola production was estimated at about 20,000 tons, of which 15,000 were *kola nitida,* and Senegambian consumption was 1,450 tons.[3]

Minor Products

Some products have to be classified as minor through sheer ignorance—they were important but not much is known about them. Millet is one of these, though substantial amounts undoubtedly entered trade. Surplus millet from Fuuta Tooro was traded to the nomads for animal products. It figured in Futaanke trade with the coast for salt. All of the European trade enclaves kept themselves alive by buying millet on the market, often at some distance. Saint Louis depended normally on Fuuta, but sometimes bought food as far away as Bundu. In 1756, 200 metric tons of grain were shipped

2. Jobson, *Golden Trade,* pp. 183–85; Bruë to Collé, 9 December 1716, BN, FF, NA, 9341; Mollien, *Travels,* p. 195; Companie du Galam, Annual report dated 3 April 1831, ANF-OM, Sénégal III 7; P. Guébhard, *Au Fouta Jallon: Elevage, agriculture, commerce, régime foncier, religion* (Paris, 1910), p. 79; René Caillié, *Journal d'un voyage à Tombouctou et à Jenné dans l'Afrique centrale,* 5 vols. (Paris, 1830), 1:279–80; Raffenel, *Nouveau voyage,* 1:444, 2:205–6.

3. Hequard, report on travels, n.d. but c. 1841, ANS, 1 G 22; Rançon, *La haute Gambie,* pp. 457–58; Roux, Tournée dans le cercle de Bakel, ANS, 1 G 185; L'Orza de Reichenberg, "De Kayes au Bambouk," *Revue de géographie,* 30:101–12, 161–71 (1892). For production and trade in kola generally see A. Chevalier and E. Perrot, *Les kolatiers et les noix de kola* (Paris, 1911).

from Gajaaga to Saint Louis. The high cost of holding slaves has already been pointed out, and locally purchased food supplies were a large part of the overhead cost of maintaining the garrisons. A large sample of purchases on the Gambia by the Royal African Company over the five-year period 1684–88 shows that the purchase price of the slaves themselves was only about 80 per cent of the total cost of holding and shipping slaves. The other 20 per cent went for agricultural provisions to feed slaves waiting shipment and to store ships for the Atlantic crossing.[1]

Most other food products were genuinely minor, though many different foods entered trade in small quantities. The shea butter tree (*Butyrospernum parkii*) did not grow at all in western Senegambia, but shea butter formed a regular part of the trade from the east. In 1892, André Rançon met a westbound caravan of ninety-three people in Dentilia (now in southeast Senegal), of whom seventy-nine were carrying shea butter, nearly two metric tons in all, from Konkadugu for sale at MacCarthy's Island on the Gambia.[2] Another, smaller current in the food trade was palm oil, mainly originating in the more humid region along the Gambia and southward. Dates, on the other hand, grew far better in Gajaaga than elsewhere, and they were exported in some quantity to other regions. Tobacco was grown everywhere in small quantities, with Fuuta a specializing subregion, and Senegambian tobacco held its own against imports till the end of the eighteenth century. Peanuts were also found almost everywhere. By the 1720's they were grown as far east as Bundu and Bambuhu, though they came originally from America, like maize and manioc.[3]

Peanuts were first exported from the Gambia in small quantities in 1834, while the Senegal began a little later, exporting more than one metric ton for the first time in 1841. After that, peanuts grew rapidly in importance, though the full peanut revolution came only in the second half of the century. Meanwhile, almost from the beginning, commercial peanut cultivation grafted itself to an existing form of labor migration. As far back as the 1780's and probably earlier still, a few inland farmers from countries like Bundu would go down to the Gambia for a period of farming near the salt water markets. The initial impulse was as much commercial as agricultural. since these early labor migrants used their labor over the wet seasons to build a stake in trade goods to be carried inland at the end of the rains.

They were the first of the free "strange farmers" that were to be so important in the Gambian economy from then on, though another kind of "strange farmer" was found in the period of the slave trade. Since land could

1. Calculation based on Gambia Journals, T 70/546.
2. Rançon, *La haute Gambie,* p. 546.
3. Raffenel, *Nouveau voyage,* 1:195; Pruneau de Pommegorge, *Nigritie,* pp. 6–63; Curtin, ed., *Africa Remembered,* p. 47; Boucard, "Relation de Bambouc," f. 52.

even then be rented during the wet season, some slave caravan leaders from the interior would rent land for the season as a way of putting their trade slaves to work, thus holding them cheaply until ships appeared or the price improved. Karfa Ture, the caravan leader from Manding who brought Mungo Park to the Gambia in 1797, rented land and huts from a village head near the present town of Karantaba so as to hold his slaves till the next dry season. The rise of peanut exports changed this minor incurrent of labor migration into a major institution. Far more land was available close to the Gambia than could be worked by the existing population, and it was more efficient to move the labor close to cheap transportation than it was to move the crop overland. Migrants from the east flocked to the banks of the Gambia to grow peanuts. As early as 1849, the governor of the Gambia estimated that more than half of the exported peanuts were produced by these "strange farmers" rather than by long-term residents.[4]

Fishing communities had much in common with pastoralists. Many produced nothing but the fish they caught and sent to market. Some, like the Lebu of Cape Verde, worked the rich and cold south-flowing ocean current that passed by on its way from Europe. Others, like the *subaalbe* of Fuuta, were specialists in river fishing, though they also owned some of the best waalo land in Fuuta, which they either worked themselves on a part-time basis or rented out to others. Equivalent fishing groups were found on the upper Senegal and the Faleme. In spite of the rapid spoilage of fresh fish in a hot climate, salt fish or dried fish could be preserved for several weeks and shipped to distant points. Moors, for example, brought caravans of donkeys all the way to Cape Verde, 300 kms from home, to buy Lebu fish, even though there was good fishing on the Mauritanian coast and the Senegal River was much closer.[5] Some of the dried fish was not so much a food as a condiment to give flavor to other dishes; fish for this purpose turn up on the provision lists of the Royal African Company as "stinking fish."

Nor were cloth and iron the only manufactures entering the market. Woven mats were widely sold for sleeping, sitting, and for privacy fencing around the perimeter of a compound and the interior space of the compound assigned to bathing and the latrine. They were so generally useful that they sometimes served, along with cloths, as a form of currency, especially on the Gambia. Pottery was not so often the work of specialists, but some pottery and tobacco pipes entered trade. All kinds of utensils made from iron, silver, or gold were considered smiths' work and left strictly to that "caste," which removed metalwork from the "subsistence" to the "market" sector of the economy.

4. MacDonnell to Gray, 16 June 1849, CO 87/45.
5. Adanson, *Voyage to Senegal*, pp. 121–23.

In spite of an active market in all of these goods, the market sector of the eighteenth-century Senegambian economy was smaller than the self-subsistence sector. Most goods and services were produced and consumed within the household, usually a not very extended family. Distribution of goods within the household was no doubt based on currents of reciprocity and redistribution reflecting social patterns rather than allocation of scarce resources.

But it is not simply the bias of the sources that makes the Senegambian economy of two hundred years ago appear more market oriented than some other African economies, more so, for example, than those of the pre-forest zone of the twentieth century—the Tiv described by Laura and Paul Bohannan or the Gouro described by Claude Meillassoux.[6] It *was* more market oriented. Labor could be hired, land could be rented, commercial capital could be borrowed, all for a price. The fact that factors of production had a market value, even if they were not widely marketed, brings the Senegambian economy closer to the usual model of formal Western economic theory than it is to the model of "primitive economy" used by some economic anthropologists.[7] But the principles of the formal theory do not apply until they are reinterpreted to fit Senegambian circumstances. The Senegambian monetary system is a notable example of the gap between Western and West African practices at this period.

6. P. and L. Bohannan, *Tiv Economy* (London, 1968); C. Meillassoux, *De l'économie d'auto-subsistance à l'agriculture commerciale en pays gouro (Côte d'Ivoire)* (Paris-La Haye, 1964).

7. For example, M. D. Sahlins, "On the Sociology of Primitive Exchange," in M. Banton, ed., *The Relevance of Models for Social Anthropology* (Garden City, N.Y., 1967).

6 | CURRENCY AND EXCHANGE

Money is a troublesome subject, even for bankers, and the Western tradition of considering gold and silver to be intrinsically different from other commodities is both old and persistent. The troublesome point for economic anthropologists, however, is in definition—especially in distinguishing between non-money, "primitive money," and "modern all-purpose money." Some have tended to see barter, not monetary exchange, whenever the exchange token had an intrinsic value of its own. Others, like Paul Einzig, gave a liberal breadth to "primitive money" as against mere barter. For Einzig, money was " . . . a unit or object conforming to a reasonable degree to some standard of uniformity which is employed for reckoning or for making a large proportion of the payments customary in the community concerned, which is accepted for payment largely with the intention of employing it for making payments."[1] But Einzig was a strict constructionist when it came to "modern money," which he limited to coins that circulate by count rather than weight, or other objects, such as paper money, that receive their value by the fiat of the state.

Another distinction sometimes made between "primitive" and "modern" money turns on assertion that modern money is general-purpose currency, capable of effecting any and all transfers of value within that society. But this distinction is actually a matter of degree alone. No currency is absolutely all-purpose in any society, simply because no society makes payments for all the purposes payments can be made. In the West, no currency can be used to pay bridewealth because bridewealth is not paid. In some parts of West Africa, no currency could be used to buy land because land was not sold. In the West, some payments still have to be made in something of value other than the all-purpose medium. Many girls would still regard a check as an

1. P. Einzig, *Primitive Money* (London, 1949), p. 326.

unsuitable substitute for an engagement ring. The business man who offers a legislator a gift in cash is suspected of bribery, but less so if the gift takes the form of free transportation in a corporate airplane.

Many African societies had spheres of exchange still more clearly delineated—often one sphere for prestige or power goods that were exchanged within a restricted social group, while other goods were freely exchangeable with anyone. But the crucial factor is not so much the existence of separate spheres as convertibility from one to the other. Even in those parts of precolonial West Africa with separate spheres of exchange, convertibility was usually possible, though it was harder to exchange food products for prestige goods than it is today. In the same sense, Senegambian currencies were not special-purpose or general-purpose, but more-general-purpose or less-general-purpose. Here is where the static picture found in most twentieth-century ethnography is especially deceptive. Currency systems were far from static. They shifted elusively with the passage of time, and they could be very different in different Senegambian societies. The juula culture was commercial by definition, while the people among whom the juula lived and traded followed another tradition. In a changing and various setting of this kind, the distinction based on generality of purpose has little analytical value.[2]

Nor is Einzig's distinction between coinage and commodity money very useful; silver coins, in Senegambian usage up to the mid-eighteenth century, were imported in large quantities, but they were destined to be melted down for jewelry. They may have been coined, but they were not money. Some West African iron currencies like the *sōmpe* or Kissi penny of northern Ivory Coast and Liberia and northeastern Guinea-Conakry were, in effect, "coined" by manufacture in symbolic stylized models of actual tools, specifically so that they could serve as a unit of value that could pass by count rather than by weight.[3] The sōmpe was an iron stick about 24 cm long, with a spoonlike

2. For recent discussions of money in non-Western societies see T. S. Epstein, *Capitalism, Primitive and Modern: Some Aspects of Tolai Economic Growth* (Canberra, 1968), pp. 19–26; G. Dalton, "Primitive Money," *American Anthropologist*, 67:44–65 (1965); A. H. Quiggin, *A Survey of Primitive Money* (London, 1949); R. Thurnwald, *Economics in Primitive Communities* (London, 1932), pp. 252–65. And for different points of view about money in precolonial West Africa see the Introduction in P. J. Bohannan and G. Dalton, *Markets in Africa* (Evanston, Ill., 1962), pp. 1–26; R. Cohen, "Some Aspects of Institutionalized Exchange: A Kanuri Example," *CEA*, 5:353–69 (1965); G. I. Jones, "Native and Trade Currencies in Southern Nigeria during the Eighteenth and Nineteenth Centuries, *Africa*, 28:43–54 (1958); C. Meillassoux, *Anthropologie économique des Gouro de Côte d'Ivoire* (Paris, 1964), esp. pp. 263–90; P. and L. Bohannan, *Tiv Economy.*

3. Einzig, *Primitive Money*, p. 326; R. Portères, "La monnaie de fer dans l'ouest africain au xxe siècle," *Journal d'agriculture tropicale et de botanique appliquée,* 7:97–109 (1960), and also in *Recherches africaines,* 4:3–13 (1960).

shape at one end and two little flat wings at the other. Yet no useful purpose is served by calling these modern money while the ordinary iron bar of Senegambian international trade would count as primitive money.

Nor is analysis served by the more general tendency of past economic thought to consider commodity money as somehow more primitive than coins and bank notes. The underlying assumption seems to be that money is more "monetary" if it has no alternate use, but the cowrie shells used in much of West Africa are not necessarily better than gold and silver simply because they have fewer nonmonetary uses; nor are gold and silver better than cartons of cigarettes, bottles of gin, or slabs of rock salt in every circumstance. It seems preferable to recognize that anything can be money as long as the people who use it accept it as a recognized medium of exchange and standard of value.

Karl Polanyi raised a broader issue a few years ago when he made a similar distinction between "primitive," "archaic," and "modern" economies.[4] He was concerned with exchange, not simply with money, and his main point was that economists made a fundamental error in basing their science on the study of economizing—on the way men allocate scarce and desirable goods and services. Formal economic theory begins with the proposition that the allocation of goods and services will depend on value, that value in turn will depend on supply and demand and will normally be established through the influence of the market—that is, through a process of bargaining between buyers and sellers. Polanyi held, to the contrary, that the economic process is often "imbedded" in noneconomic institutions—essentially that goods in most societies outside the West and before the nineteenth century were allocated within a household according to social values. Exchanges between individuals or households also reflected social or political patterns, not the play of market forces. One important mode of exchange was "reciprocity," such as mutual gift-giving where the equivalence of value is not bargained. Another was "redistribution," where goods were passed to a central authority who then apportioned them again, without strict equivalence or the influence of supply and demand.

Following out the implications, Polanyi held that economists should study the way people make their living, the ways in which material culture is imbedded in social patterns, not the formal theory based on the assumption that people will try to economize in their allocation of scarce resources. The result was a debate in economic anthropology between Polanyi and his school

4. K. Polanyi, "The Economy as Instituted Process," in K. Polanyi, C. M. Arensberg, and W. Pearson, *Trade and Markets in the Early Empires* (Glencoe, N.Y., 1957), pp. 243–70.

(the "substantivists") and those who followed the main tradition of Western economic theory (the "formalists").[5]

The debate now seems to be finished without total victory for either side, but with general recognition that economic theory developed with reference to Western examples alone is too narrow, while the substantivist tendency to accentuate the differences in human behavior at the expense of common elements seems to deny the possibility of an economic science.

The substantivist position was also strongly antihistorical, though Polanyi and his school took many of their examples from past societies. They were not concerned with the process of change in human societies. They tended therefore to ignore exceptional or minor aspects of an economy that might be unimportant at a particular time but were nevertheless capable of growth or development. One of the principal substantivist assertions about precolonial African economies was that means of production—land, labor, and capital—were rarely bought or sold. If they were not marketed, their value could not depend on supply and demand but rested on other factors. In fact, a static ethnographic study of, say, the Gambia Malinke of Ñaani in about 1800 would have shown that land was rarely sold, that slaves were held for reasons more clearly rooted in social prestige than need for labor, that the labor of free men was mostly allocated by the family head, not hired, that loans at interest were forbidden by Islam, the dominant religion. An exceptional arrangement, like the renting of land to support a caravan of slaves until the market improved, would be overlooked—though this is what the leader of the Ture caravan from Kamalia in distant Manding did in 1797 after he brought Mungo Park through to the navigable Gambia.

In a static description it would have been a minor irregularity in the system, hardly worth reporting, yet less than a century later, most Gambian agricultural exports would be grown on land allocated in much the same way to strange farmers who had come hundreds of miles in search of economic opportunity. The point is that labor *could* be hired, land *could* be rented, workers *could* be mobilized and directed to new industries by market forces— even though those forces might seem unimportant to the functioning of the economy at the time observed. One of the factors that made possible this change in Gambian agriculture was the existence of currencies and mecha-

5. See K. Polanyi, *Primitive, Archaic and Modern Economies: Essays of Karl Polanyi*, ed. George Dalton (New York, 1968); N. Smelser, "A Comparative View of Exchange Systems," *Economic Development and Cultural Change*, 7:173–82 (1959); E. E. Lampard, "The Price System and Economic Change: A Commentary on Theory and History," *Journal of Economic History*, 20:617–37 (1960). E. E. LeClair, Jr., and Harold K. Schneider, *Economic Anthropology: Readings in Theory and Analysis* (New York, 1968), reprint selections from the debate between formalists and substantivists.

nisms for exchange already functioning in a market sector of the Senegambian economy.

Cloth Currencies and Systematic Equivalents

In the geography of precolonial currencies in West Africa,
Senegambia was nearly the core of a cloth-currency area already old by the
seventeenth century and still expanding. To the north, the monetary system
of the Moors had been based on cattle, with a head of cattle as the currency
of account and an elaborate vocabulary for dealing with variations from this
basic value. Dates were also used on the northern fringes of the Sahara, and
millet on the southern fringes, simply because these were the products most
often bought from the sedentary populations. Bars of salt were used at
certain times because of their general importance in the commerce to the
south. But, for Mauritania at least, the eighteenth century saw the gradual
replacement of all these others by a cloth currency, based in time on a
standard piece of Indian cloth from Pondichéry, usually known in the French
literature as a *pièce de Guinée* or simply *guinée.*[1]

But the northward spread of the guinée as a monetary unit was actually a
substitution of one cloth for another and much more ancient unit already
used in the Senegal valley and off to the south and east. This unit was a piece
of locally made cloth—*pagne* in Senegalese French, *country cloth* in Gambian
English, *soro* in Pulaar, *tama* in Soninke—which varied somewhat from place
to place but tended to approximate the soro of Fuuta Tooro, an unfinished
band about 16 meters long and 15 to 18 cm wide. That length was appropriate for sewing together eight strips, each two meters long, to make a rectangle
about 2 meters long and 1.5 meters wide. It was the dominant currency
eastward along the sahal as far as Nara and beyond, more than half the
distance from Bakel to Timbuktu. It also reached into the Manding culture
area, carried by Fuulbe emigrants from Fuuta, though it circulated there in
competition with the cowrie shells that were otherwise the most common
money of the upper Niger valley. The soro area stretched south into the
Fuuta Jaalō highlands, where the Fuulbe made it dominant, and it spread
overseas to the Cape Verde Islands in the fifteenth century, where the variant
called *barafula* became the standard currency in the islands and their trading
zone stretching south of the Gambia toward Sierra Leone.[2]

1. P. Dubie, "La vie materielle des Maures," in *Mélanges ethnologiques* (Dakar, 1953),
pp. 220–21.
2. Raffenel, Report of 22 August 1848, *Revue coloniale,* 3 (2nd ser.):264; C. Meillassoux, "Le commerce pré-colonial de le développement de l'esclavage à Gūbu du Sahel
(Mali)," in Meillassoux, ed., *Indigenous Trade and Markets,* p. 185; Pollet and Winter, *La*

The use of cowries was also spreading outward from the Niger bend in the eighteenth and nineteenth centuries—eastward into present-day Nigeria, which began to use the shells much more intensively in the course of the nineteenth century, and westward up the Niger valley,[3] though silver coins were sometimes used as well along the Niger. In the southern part of the savanna, however, particularly in the preforest zone of today's upper Guinea-Conakry and central Ivory Coast, the traditional currency was iron, where the sōmpe dominated a region centered on Ojene (Odienné). Further west, among the Lainé, Lola, and Nzo of upper Guinea, the shape was a flat piece of iron that may have prefigured the iron bar currency later introduced by Europeans for international trade on the coast.[4] These various currency zones interpenetrated at the fringes, and Senegambian trade dealt with currencies that were not truly monetized in Senegambia itself. Cowries, for example, were often imported at the coast and shipped eastward to the Niger valley. Silver coins were first imported mainly as a raw material for the jewelry trade, but some were no doubt shipped east as well, and gold dust was sometimes used by weight in long-distance trade.

Wherever these different currencies met, they were usually integrated by a recognized exchange rate or equivalence, but these rates of equivalence were not true market prices. They were, rather, part of a more complex set of equivalents that began with the cloth itself, taking fractional parts of the whole cloth as fractional units of currency. In Saalum, for example, the individual strip of cloth, the width of the narrow loom and about 2 meters long, was the basic unit, and multiples of 2, 8, and 16 had individual names. Each multiple then had equivalents in the world of marketable commodities. A goat rated 1 sixteen-strip unit (xopa), while an ox was 15 xopa, a prime slave 20, and a horse was rated at 50. Similar sets of equivalents were found throughout the region. They were often at variance with one another, but they opened the possibility of having, in effect, currency units of smaller and larger denominations than the cloth units themselves. Thus the guinée in use along the Senegal could be counted as 10 soro, while 10 guinées in turn were equal to a "slave," so that high prices could be quoted in slaves—a horse or an ordinary house was thought to be worth a slave, and important fines were levied in slaves, though all these items expressed in slaves were actually paid in cloth.[5]

---

société soninké, p. 120; Duncan, Atlantic Islands, pp. 218–19; A. Carreira, Panaria cabo-verdiano-guineense, passim.

3. For the cowrie zones see M. Johnson, "Cowrie Currencies in West Africa," JAH, 11:17–49, 331–53 (1970).

4. R. Portères, "Monnaie de fer"; Meillassoux, Anthropologie économique des Gouro, pp. 267–73; Rodney, Upper Guinea Coast, p. 194.

5. D. Ames, "The Rural Wolof of the Gambia," in Bohannan and Dalton, Markets in Africa, pp. 37–43, on evidence gathered in 1950 from old men reporting on the distant past. Commandant Bakel to Governor, 30 November 1850, ANS, 13 G 176.

Taken as a whole, these systems of equivalence contained a suggestion of numerology, since the steps were almost always multiples of 2 and 10, but each was also a system of comparative values that linked food, labor, and social values. The tama, the standard cloth of Xaaso, was equated to 5 *mud* of millet, which was in turn considered to be cereal enough for ten days' food (at a bit more than 1 kg per day), hence the labor value incorporated in the tama; while at the upper end of the scale 1,000 *mud* of millet might translate to the value of one prime girl slave, two male slaves, or the ordinary bride wealth. These values came to be so established that bride wealth in Xaaso at the end of the nineteenth century was still expressed in the standard cloths of tradition even though these cloths had long since given way to the imported guinées, and the actual payment would take place in guinées—not at the traditional equivalence of 10 tama to the guinée but at the market rate then prevalent.[6]

It is important to insist that these equivalences are not true prices, though they are sometimes mistaken for prices. They are, rather, ideal values, to which the actual exchanges of the market place may or may not conform. A price, in any strict sense, expresses the terms of an exchange, either offered (as in an asking price) or actual. It involves specific quantities of specific commodities, with specific timing and other terms of payment. Normative equivalents, on the other hand, were used in Senegambia in two different senses, and they can be illustrated by the Gajaaga notion that a slave was worth 10 guinées. In one sense a slave was simply a multiple of one guinée, in the same sense that a "grand" in the United States is a multiple of one dollar. Thus a bargain arrived at in slaves would be paid in guinées. In the second sense, slave represented an idealized value, and as an ideal it may have had a tendency to stabilize prices, but the actual prices paid for slaves in Gajaaga in about 1850 varied between 6 and 20 guinées.[7]

Still another form of exchange extremely common in precolonial West Africa was to honor the ideal equivalent by paying the traditional number of measures, but varying the quantity actually paid per measure. After a good harvest, the container used for measuring grain, for example, would be full to overflowing (in the same way a skillful bartender always lets the measure overflow as a sign of his generosity), while in the hungry season before the harvest is in, the container might not be even one-third full. As a result, the

6. A. S. Kane, "Du régime des terres chez les populations du Fouta sénégalais," *CEHSAOF*, 18:449–61 (1935), p. 543; C. Montail, *Les Khassonke*, p. 121; C. Montail, "Coton chez les noirs," p. 653; C. Monteil, "Fin de siècle à Médine (1898–1899)," *BIFAN*, 28:106–9 (1966). The *mud* or *muul*, of Arabic origin, was widely used in the Western Sudan, where it was supposed to be 44 handfuls of grain, or a weight of about 2.25 kgs of sorghum. (Labouret and others, *Commerce*, p. 109.)

7. Commandant Bakel to Governor, 30 November 1850, ANS, 13 G 176.

bargaining between buyer and seller, which might take the form of argument over the number of measures, shifts to the size of the measure.[8] This type of quantity bargaining to allow for market price adjustments on a seasonal or daily basis was so common in precolonial West Africa that it can be taken as the dominant system in local markets,[9] and it quite naturally influenced the exchange mechanisms that developed for dealing with maritime trade in the fifteenth and sixteenth centuries and later.

Iron Bars and Bar Prices

Where trade consists of one principal commodity exchanged for another principal commodity moving in the opposite direction, the clearest way to express the real terms of the transaction is to quote one in return for the other. This practice was common in Senegambia for long-distance trade or trade between regions of differing production, alongside the local use of general-purpose cloth currency. On the upper Gambia, these barter prices were quoted as so many cloths per *mud* of salt. On the fringes of

8. Karl Polanyi created a good deal of difficulty for himself and his followers by the terminology he adopted. He sought to distinguish between "price" defined as the terms of exchange arrived at through supply and demand of sellers and buyers in a competitive, market setting, as distinct from an "equivalency" arrived at by some other social process. (*Trade and Markets,* p. 91.) As used here the "equivalence" means only the idealized terms of exchange, as opposed to the actual terms, which in Senegambia were formed under market influences in most recognizably commercial circumstances.

Polanyi, however, changed the definition at a later point in this work, writing that "... equivalencies are set once and for all. But since to meet changing circumstances adjustments cannot be avoided, higgling-haggling is practiced only on *other items than price,* such as measures, quality, or means of payment." (His italics.) Since price in the economists' ordinary sense of the term must include the number and size and quality of units to be exchanged, as well as the terms of payment, Polanyi's special definition explains much of the heat of the criticism. To translate Polanyi into the terms I am using, that sentence would read: "... equivalencies are set once and for all. But since to meet changing circumstances adjustments cannot be avoided, prices must fluctuate with the market." But Polanyi did not, unfortunately, stay within that meaning; otherwise, there would have been no controversy. As he remarked at one point, "Language itself betrays us here." (*Trade and Markets,* p. 91.)

9. See Labouret and others, *Commerce,* p. 110; G. Vieillard, *Notes sur les coutumes des Peuls au Fouta-Djallon* (Paris, 1939); M. Dupire, *Peuls nomades: Etude descriptive des Wodaabe du sahel nigérien* (Paris, 1962), pp. 135–36; C. and C. Tardits, "Traditional Market Economy in South Dahomey," Bohannan and Dalton, *Markets in Africa,* p. 101; M. G. Smith, "Exchange and Marketing among the Hausa," Bohannan and Dalton, *Markets in Africa,* p. 321; Bohannan and Bohannan, *Tiv Economy,* or, for earlier Fuuta Tooro, Labat, *Nouvelle relation,* 7:356.

Bambuhu, it was salt or cloths per *mithqal* of gold, and along the sahal it was meat-for-millet, or, later on, guinée-for-gum.[1]

When trade with the Europeans first became important in the sixteenth century, prices were sometimes quoted in slaves-per-horse. By the seventeenth century, iron was the most important import, making up roughly half the total value of imports, while hides were the most important export. It was simply a continuation of longstanding practice in Senegambian international trade to quote prices in hides-per-bar of iron. In 1620, for example, Jobson found prices on the upper Gambia quoted in salt-for-cloth, while iron was used on the lower Gambia—not only for hides but as a general standard. He had to hire a local smith to cut his iron into appropriate units, but the iron bar was already "in."

By 1635, a standard bar weighing about 15 kgs was mentioned by Samuel Bloomaert, and Dapper referred to a slightly heavier bar at 17 kg as current about mid-century. By the 1660's, the bar was fully established as a piece of flat wrought iron about 3 meters long, 5 cm wide, and 9 mm thick, weighing about 13 kgs. It was often notched for convenient subdivision into smaller pieces, each about 20 cm long and the proper shape and weight for making a hoe blade. But the size and weight of the bar itself came from the shape and weight common in the iron trade of the lower Rhine and Maas, the original source for the Dutch trade with Africa. (The Portuguese had failed to set the fashion in this trade, as they had done in so much else, because they tried to keep their trade with Africa in goods they could furnish from Portugal itself. At certain times they prohibited the export of iron to Africa.)

By the 1660's, every commodity entering international trade had a price in bars of iron, but unlike the hides-for-iron prices which fluctuated with supply and demand, the bar prices were unchanging. They were not, in fact, price quotations so much as a system of equivalents for translating the value of other imported commodities into a certain quantity of iron, so that the current iron-for-hides barter price could be applied to a wider range of commodities. These equivalent values in bars probably represented the actual comparative values at some period in the early seventeenth century, but then they stabilized.

On the Gambia, a period of mild readjustment took place between the 1660's and the 1680's, perhaps occasioned by the greater importance of the French and by the English replacing the Dutch as maritime carriers. After that, bar prices were for the most part stable; when they did shift, as the price of red cloth did in 1693, the change was apt to be substantial (20 per cent in this instance) and the new price would again be stable for decades.

1. Jobson, *Golden Trade,* pp. 164, 121–22; Sundström, *Trade of Guinea,* p. 195; Dapper in *BIFAN,* 32:508–63 (1970), p. 538.

Table 6.1 shows the more rigid bar prices, but some were less rigid than others. Coral was one of these, largely because its European price was changing rapidly. In the 1680's, it fluctuated in England between £7 and £8 per kg. At this price, coral was already expensive in relation to its bar value in Africa. (See table 6.2.) But the price in England then rose further to about £12 per kg in the period 1721–23 and on up to more than £17 per kg in 1735–38. If the bar price had remained unchanged, the prime cost or English cost of a bar's worth of coral would have been several times that of any other import. Presumably to avoid this situation, the bar price adjusted in a series of leaps, from 1 bar an ounce in the 1660's through the 1680's to 1.5 bars an ounce in 1692, 2 bars an ounce in 1693, and finally 3 bars an ounce by the

Table 6.1
Selected Gambia Bar Prices, 1660–1760

Commodity	Price
Iron bars	1 bar per bar with the exception of 1734 and 1735, when the price went to 2 bars per bar
Amber	8 bars per lb. for large stones, shifting to .5 bar per stone about 1728
Brandy and rum	1 bar per gallon (or for 4 French *pintes*)
Glass beads	.5 bars per lb.
Swords (trade) and cutlasses	3 bars in 1666, dropping to 1 bar from 1683 onward
Brass pans ("Guinea pans")	.33 bar each in 1666, but steady at .5 bar each from 1699
Copper rods	.5 bar each (weight variable, but about 1 lb.)
Silesian linens (platilles)	3 bars each
Gunpowder	.5 bar per lb.
Flints	1 bar per 100
Red cloth	2.5 bars in 1688, then steady at 3 bars from 1693 onward
Crystal	Slight variations in the seventeenth century because of differing qualities, but settling at 10 bars per 1,000 beads of no. 22 crystal and of undifferentiated crystal after 1720's
Carnelian beads ("arrangoes")	Began to be imported in quantity only after 1718, at a steady price of 5 bars per 100
Fringe	1 bar per lb.
Cowries	.33 bar per lb. in 1666, becoming a stable .5 bar per lb. from at least 1683 onward
Long cloths	10 bars each from the 1730's onward, when they became an important import.
Silver coins	.5 bar each, whether Dutch .28 stiver pieces ("zealots") or Spanish dollars
Lead shot	.33 per lb. in 1666, but stable at .5 per lb. after 1683

Source: Gambian account books in T 70 series, Public Record Office, London.

Table 6.2
European Prime Costs of Senegambian Imports, 1685, 1731, 1785

	Cost per bar in £ sterling			
Commodity	(1) 1685	(2) 1731	(3) 1785	Commodity (at French prices converted to sterling)
Coral	.225	.200	.188	Silesian linen
Iron bars	.200	.175	.158	Trade swords
Brass pans	–	.200	.145	Double guns
Cutlasses/trade swords	.167	.088	.140	Blue bafts (guinées)
Silver coins	.164	.100	.140	Silver bells (grélots)
Copper rods	.153	.117	.105	Pistols
Crystal	.140	.175	.105	Brandy
Brandy	.123	.062	.088	Red wool
Silesian linen	.119	.108	.070	Lead balls
Glass beads	.116	.083	.056	Scarlet cloth
Long cloth	–	.120	.052	Fine guns
Fringe	–	.120	.049	Paper
Red cloth	.108	.085	.044	Trade guns
Pewter ware	.091	.125	.042	Blanc-de-niège beads
Trade guns	.084	.090	.035	Gun flints
Paper	.081	.092	.025	Tobacco
Gunpowder	.045	.048	.023	Beads (galets)
Gun flints	–	.038	.018	Gunpowder
Mean (unweighted)	.130	.113	.0824	
Standard deviation (unweighted)	.0490	.0490	.0530	
Coefficient of variation (standard deviation/mean, unweighted)	.377	.434	.643	

Sources: Data for 1685 and 1731 from T 70/456 and 558. Data for 1785 are from Saugnier, *Voyages,* (pp. 316–19, supplemented by some prices from "Etat des Coutumes," 1783, ANS 13 G 13.

1750's. Even after these changes, coral remained one of the most expensive of all imports; its price behavior seems to indicate that while bar prices were theoretically rigid over time, changes were allowed if European price alterations threatened to remove a product from the range of other prime costs for a bar's worth—wide as this range already was.

Another form of adjustment was in quantity per unit—a little like the West African market practice. Iron bars, for example, slipped from the standard size and weight of the 1680's in response to rising prices. Like coral, iron was near the top of the scale in prime cost per bar. The annual average weight of bars imported by the Royal African Company varied between about 13.8 kgs and 13.2 kgs in the years 1683–88, but the weight dropped to 12.1 kgs in 1704, 10.9 kgs in 1721, and 10.3 kgs in 1737. In effect, it was gradually devaluated by 24 per cent over the half-century. The price of iron in bars was thus partly cut loose from the prime cost of iron sold by weight in Europe. This devaluation apparently took care of long-term adjustment, but the bar price of iron occasionally had to adjust to brief short-term changes. In 1734 and 1735, for example, the price of the physical iron bar jumped briefly to two bars in most of the Gambian transactions of the Royal African Company, and then returned to one.[2]

By the 1770's, the situation had become still more unsettled, with further depreciation of the iron currency and a variety of different bars in use. After the weight of the bar had dropped as low as 8.2 kgs in 1756, British on the Gambia tried in 1771–73 to return to a high-cost and high-quality Swedish bar weighing 19.2 kgs—more than twice the lightweight devalued bar—but the effort was only temporary. Similar diversity appeared on the Senegal where the weight of bars in the late 1770's varied from 11.5 to 16.6 kgs. These bars were heavier than those in English use on the Gambia, but they were soon devalued as well; in 1786, the Saint Louis government defined the bar legally as a unit weighing between 7.3 and 7.8 kgs, now divided into only four subdivisions 24 cms long rather than the fifteen smaller subdivisions of the seventeenth century. Finally, during the Napoleonic Wars, the rising price of iron again made itself felt, and the legal standard for Senegal dropped to only two subdivisions. By this time, the bar was giving way to the dollar, though the government still tried to stabilize the bar-to-silver ratio by manipulating the size of the bar.[3]

Given these changes in the metallic content of the bar currency, bar prices might well have fluctuated widely, but in fact most stayed rigid or adjusted slowly in a single direction, like coral. Only a few commodities changed frequently in bar value. The trade gun was one of these, beginning at 3 bars in 1664, and later settling down to an alternation between 5 and 6 bars, in apparent response to the changing cost of guns in Europe. Perhaps the fact that guns themselves changed somewhat over time contributed to the relative looseness of these prices, but guns had something else in common with commodities like paper and pewterware, whose bar prices also fluctuated: all

---

2. The French in Senegambia were still ordering bars from Europe that were very nearly the old 13-kg size as late as 1736—with the claim that a bar 2.92 meters long, 5.1 cm wide, and 1.1 cm thick was the ideal size for the trade. ("Nouvelles observations sur la qualité des marchandises, 10 June 1736, ANF, C6 11.) But we have no way of knowing whether bars of that size were actually delivered and used.

3. T 70/928; "Réponse aux plaintes de M. de Paradis, 1777," ANF, C6 17: Réglement de 14 Feb. 1786, ANF, C6 19; Labarthe, *Voyage en Sénégal,* p. 187.

three were at the lower end of the scale of European cost per bar of African value. They would therefore have been subject to downward pressure on their bar prices from African merchants, just as iron and coral at the opposite end of the scale were subject to upward pressure from European traders.[4]

These goods with low £/bar ratios, however, were not the lowest on the scale. Gunpowder and gun flints were consistently even lower, yet they had stable bar prices. One possible explanation is that European merchants were more attuned than their African counterparts to European costs. They were successful both in forcing the adjustment of the highest £/bar ratios and in withstanding similar pressures on the lowest of the £/bar ratios. But the European market and the coastal market were not the only markets to be considered. The juula from the interior also had a set of market conditions to consider. The range of prices in the far hinterland is not well known for all periods, but Mungo Park left a price list in cowries for Sansanding on the Niger in 1805 and in mithqals for Kamalia (west of Bamako) in 1796, and the two show a similar pattern. (See table 6.3.) In the interior, flints were often one of the most valuable products in terms of their coastal value. The juula was therefore unlikely to be concerned with the inordinate markup in the price of flints between London and the Gambia, since he was likely to enjoy an equally high gross profit when he finally reached the Niger valley.

Exports also had traditional bar prices, and they too were rigid, though less rigid than those of imports. (See table 6.4.) Most remained steady over the first half-century, from the 1680's to the 1730's, moving upwards only for slaves and downwards only for country clothes. But the long-term changes shown in table 6.4 obscure a marked difference between import and export bar prices. Where the books of the Royal African Company record identical import prices transaction after transaction, the bar prices actually paid for exports were not necessarily the conventional value. In a sample of nine transactions of 1685, for example, for the purchase of 270 slaves in all, the actual prices paid varied from 22 to 30 bars, with a mean at 23.7 bars. Though the prices of other exports moved less widely from the conventional price, they too deviated.

4. The movement of trade gun prices was as follows, in bars-Gambia:

1664	3	1725–33	5
1683	5	1734–35	6
1686–88	6	1736–41	5
1718	6	1754–57	5
1723	6		

Pewter was depressed from .5 bars a pound in the 1680's to .33 bars from the 1720's onward, passing through a period of sharp fluctuations in 1730–33 before it stabilized again. Paper changed back and forth over a range of 2 to 4 bars a ream.

Table 6.3
Prices in the Niger Valley and Europe c. 1800, Compared

Commodity and unit	Approximate prime cost in Europe (£ Sterling)	Price in Sansanding on the Niger 1805 (cowrie shells)	Price in Kamalia (west of Bamako) in 1796 (mithqals of gold)	Cowries/sterling	Mithqal/sterling
Prime slave (1)	0.1365	65,000	10.5	4,250	1.40
Gold (gram)	0.55	580	0.193	12,000	6.00
Musket (1)	0.175	6,500	3.5	10,000	5.70
Cutlass (1)	0.035	1,750	1.0	44,000	14.70
Gunpowder (lb.)	0.060	1,500	0.5	67,000	93.30
Flints (100)		4,000	5.6		
Short carnelian beads (100)	0.45	4,000	—	8,900	—
Indian baft (piece)	1.50	20,000	—	13,300	—
Scarlet cloth (piece)	0.54	8,700	—	16,100	—
Paper (ream)	0.38	20,000	—	52,600	—
Silver dollar (1)	0.21	9,000	—	42,900	—

Source: Park, *Travels*, 1:464, 2:218–21.

Table 6.4
Conventional Bar Prices of Gambian Exports

	1680's	1730's	1780's
Slaves, adult	30	50	100–140
Slaves, children	20	40	–
Ivory, large tusk (per English cwt. of			–
50.8 kgs or French quintal of			
48.95 kgs)	18	18	–
Ivory, small tusk (cwt. or quintal)	9	9	–
Beeswax (cwt. or quintal)	16	16	9
Gum (cwt. or quintal)	3	3	12
Gold (English dram of 1.772 grams,	1	1	1
French gros of 3.824 grams)	2	2	2
"Country cloths" (African-made textiles)	0.25	0.125	–
Hides, each	0.25	0.25	–
Slaughter cattle, per head	4.0	4.0	–

Source: Gambia, RAC account books in T 70 series.

By the 1720's, even this relative stability had begun to crumble, and it was so far gone by the 1780's that conventional bar prices no longer appear regularly in the historical record—hence the blanks in the column for that decade. In the twenties, a sample consisting of all Royal African Company purchases in the first six months of 1729 already shows a variation in bar price from a high of 67.7 bars per slave, paid for a large shipment of 173 slaves brought by a single caravan from the interior, to a low of 30 bars paid for one young boy purchased locally near James Fort.

A number of special circumstances influenced prices. A futures market, for example, was already in operation, and the Company regularly paid 35 bars for the future delivery of "one good slave"—a price that reflected a discount below the market price, in lieu of interest. Prices also reflected a premium for assembling a large body of slaves for shipment. This premium not only accounted for the high price the Company paid for the caravan of 1729; it was also reflected in the Company's own operations. By this time, it had fallen into the middleman's role, buying slaves piecemeal for 35 to 45 bars until a cargo could be accumulated and sold to a separate trader for 65 bars a head.[5]

Assortment Bargaining

The structure of bar prices and relation of those prices to European costs looks improbable, at least in theory and on the surface. In a century of increased competition among the Europeans—when both the

5. T 70/558; RAC to Anthony Rogers et al., 30 July 1730, T 70/55.

Compagnie des Indes and the Royal African Company were bankrupted competing with a multitude of private traders—this deviant price structure should have converged with the nascent web of worldwide price relationships, but no such thing happened. Rather than falling gradually into line with the European costs, bar prices were so rigid that the spread of £/bar ratios increased progressively, becoming greater with each succeeding half-century. The indicator in this case is the coefficient of variation (standard deviation/ mean). At .337 in the 1680's, the jump to the 1730's carried it to .434, while the jump onward to the 1780's brought it still higher, to .643. (See table 6.2.)[1]

This phenomenon appears at first glance to be a clear exception to the expectations of neoclassical economic theory and to the trend of prices elsewhere in the world. It operated as though each commodity was imported at a different rate of exchange between sterling and bars-Gambia—not merely for a short period but over the long run, with no sign of movement toward a single rate or a narrower spread of rates. Western economic theory would hold that a multiple exchange rate could exist only as an act of political administration or in the presence of a significant monopoly element, though Polanyi and his school claim that constant and "administered" prices are to be expected at transfer points of intercultural trade like the Senegambian trade enclaves.

On closer examination, however, prices in Senegambia were neither fixed nor administered, and formal theory can be adjusted for the cultural differences between Senegambia and the West. It is true that bar prices were traditional, were imbedded in the social and political institutions of cross-cultural exchange, and were only slightly susceptible to change by market forces, but they were not prices. A price is a measure of value, but a bar price was not a measure of value unless the price agreement also stipulated the commodity or commodities in which it was to be paid. Both the African and the European merchants trading on the Gambia recognized this fact, but the bar prices served well enough in a situation where the African merchant had

---

1. These figures would be more significant if the data permitted the use of a mean £/bar ratio weighted according to the importance of each commodity, and for each of the three dates, but the unweighted means indicate a 15-per-cent drop between 1685 and 1731, followed by a 25-per-cent drop between 1731 and 1785. If the weighted means available for the first two dates are used, the drop from 1685 to 1731 is only about 11 per cent.

Not only was this kind of variance true of ratios between pounds and bar prices in Senegambia, it also appeared in a similar form with gold ounce prices on the Gold Coast and cloth prices in Benin. A published assortment of goods to buy slaves in Benin at an unidentified date in the eighteenth century, for example, shows an SD/mean ratio of .382. (A. F. C. Ryder, *Benin and the Europeans 1485–1897* [London, 1969]), pp. 210, 335.)

normally come from a distance with an assortment of goods for sale and intended to return with an assortment of goods for sale at the other end of his route. The same was functionally true for the Europeans. Bargaining between men who are both buying and selling normally involves two agreements, one on the price of the items being sold and one on the price of those bought in return. A Senegambian dealing with Europeans also involved two agreements. The first established the price of the export goods in bars—so many bars per slave, per quintal of ivory or wax, and so on. A second then established the assortment of goods in which those bars were to be paid. The whole transaction shares some aspects of a barter, but simple barter is the exchange of one commodity for another. These exchanges were rarely a single export against a single import. Even when slaves were sold alone, for example, the return goods always included an assortment of ten to fifty commodities. This practice opened the way to assortment bargaining.

The Europeans knew the prime cost of the goods and tried to maximize the quantities of cheap goods included in the assortment. The African merchants knew the market conditions they would meet when they came to resell the imports, either locally or at a distance. They therefore tried to maximize the quantities of those goods that would bring them the highest profit. Bar prices provided a convenient measure for translating the agreed price of the export goods into specific quantities of a variety of different imports. At this stage, a bar price was not so much a price as a quantity statement. That is, the merchants might agree that 5 bars of a 100-bar assortment should be rum. In so agreeing, both knew that a "bar" in rum was one English wine gallon (3.785 liters) or, in dealing with the French, nearly the same quantity in the form of four Paris *pintes* (3.725 liters). Having all import commodities translatable into bars was a convenient accounting device for working out the proportions that each would be in the final assortment. It simplified the mental arithmetic, and the equivalents were reasonably accurate for this purpose.

Assortment bargaining in this form had something in common with the older West African system of accepting a fixed price at a conventional number of units, varying the amount to be counted as a unit. Indeed, the devaluation of the iron bar by making it smaller was not very different from giving only a half-full *mud* of grain at a time of scarcity. But the overall system was quite different in its final way of equating supply and demand, and certain aspects seem to echo European as well as African traditions of economic culture. On the African side was the custom of honoring a traditional equivalence, if only as a fiction, while the practice of striking bargains in fictitious currencies of account was a long-established custom in Europe from the Middle Ages onward. There, virtually all accounting systems and all contracts before the eighteenth century were stated in terms of a coin or else of accounting unit that did not necessarily represent any existing coin. The actual payments were therefore made in a variety of circulating coins taken to be equivalent to the currency of account—sometimes by government fiat, most often by agreement of the parties.[2] In drawing a contract in the currency of account, the parties made an agreement parallel to the Senegambian practice of setting the number of bars to be paid for the export commodities. In agreeing on the actual type and weight of coins in which the price would be paid, the parties were making a second engagement parallel to assortment bargaining—though far simpler because Europeans understood within narrow tolerances the values of the different coins in circulation. The Senegambians in the same way knew very well which commodity was undervalued and which was overvalued by the bar-price system.

Various conventions helped to deal with the complexities of assortment bargaining. One was to group high-cost goods (in terms of prime cost per bar), middle-cost, and low-cost. This made it easier for the merchants on either side to think rationally about an intricate transaction. On the Gambia of the early 1730's, for example, merchants distinguished certain high-cost commodities as "heads of goods"—spread-eagle dollars (at £/bar of .270), crystal beads (at .175), iron bars (at .175), brass pans (at .200), and carnelian beads (at .250). Some bargaining might go into the differential values even of those commodities, and also into that of the lesser goods, but a gross approximation of the final price could be expressed in terms such as "80 bars plus 8 heads."[3]

On the upper Senegal, a similar distinction was often made between *barres plaines* and *petites barres*, and bargains were struck for so many of each kind. But the natural terminus of movement in this direction was for one of the *barres plaines* or heads of goods to replace the iron bar as the true *numéraire* of the transaction. In local circumstances, this came about remarkably early. For a time in the 1730's, silver had the position of primacy on the upper Senegal.[4] Later in the century, the place of silver was taken, this time permanently, by the pièce de Guinée.

Assortment bargaining had certain apparent disadvantages for the juula. His European trade partner was both seller of imports and buyer of exports; the juula was forced to make a single complex bargain with no opportunity to shop around for the best deal from a number of potential buyers or sellers—as he might have done, for example, if he had been paid in a general purpose medium and left free to look elsewhere for the cheapest goods to take back into the interior. But the disadvantage was not the fault of assortment bargaining; it followed from the fact that competition at the coastal enclaves

---

2. Braudel and Spooner, in *Cambridge Economic History of Europe*, 4:378–91.

3. Moore, *Travels*, p. 45.

4. See for example Conseil du Sénégal to Directors of Compagnie des Indes, 28 January 1738, ANF, C6 11.

was imperfect in any case. The Compagnie des Indes and the Royal African Company were frankly monopolistic when they had the opportunity. Even when the companies were not in existence, the Afro-European and European traders at a single trading point tried to act in collusion in order to improve their bargaining position. The competitive element came from the juula's freedom to choose between the Gambia, Gajaaga, the southern rivers, and perhaps the petite côte. Once the point of trade was chosen, it was a foregone conclusion that the juula might have to deal with a single firm, which meant that a single complex bargain had to be struck in any case. In that situation, assortment bargaining served well enough, and the fact that it served African as well as European interests can be shown from the books of the European firms themselves.

The most forceful argument that bar prices were a mere façade for assortment bargaining is the relationship between the £/bar ratio of a particular commodity and the quantity of that commodity imported. European merchants knew that their economic interest lay in selling goods with the lowest possible £/bar ratios—those that were cheapest in Europe. If African buyers accepted the reality of bar prices, their purchases would have been chosen from among the goods the Europeans tried to push. In fact, the Africans refused to accept those goods, and the Europeans had to comply. In 1685, for example, gunpowder had the lowest cost per bar of any major import, but it made up only 1.2 per cent of Gambian imports, while iron, which cost four times as much per bar in Europe, was 25 per cent of imports.

As the price schedules from the Niger valley indicate (table 6.3), the trade partners on the coast were actually working with a three-market situation, where the markets were imperfectly integrated by the flow of trade. The European traders had an explicit cost schedule, a knowledge of prime costs in Europe (and the companies distributed such lists to the men who did the actual trading).[5] The juula had a background schedule of implicit prices he could obtain in the hinterland, and the two were mediated by the device of bar prices and assortment bargaining. Although the African scale of prices is unavailable for most dates in the seventeenth and eighteenth centuries, its shadow can still be seen in the extent to which African bargaining forced European traders into patterns of imports contrary to their economic interest.

In table 6.5, the percentage distribution of major imports is shown for the 1680's and the 1730's, representative of the pattern found in two decades a half-century apart. Columns 1 and 2 show the effective total assortments that emerged in those years from all of the individual assortment bargains made by

5. To the best of my knowledge, no complete tariffs have survived, though commercial correspondence between Europeans refers to them frequently. See, for example, Brue to Collé, 9 December 1716, BN, FF, NA, 9341.

Table 6.5
Bar Values and Import Quantities Compared, 1680's and 1730's

Major imports into Senegambia	I Per cent of all major imports		II £/bar values expressed as an index number (weighted mean for the year equals 100)	
	(1) 1680's	(2) 1730's	(3) 1680's	(4) 1730's
Iron bars	24.9	8.5	126	151
Brandy	14.1	4.4	78	54
Beads, glass	13.9	11.7	73	72
Amber	11.4	–	119	–
Long cloths	–	5.4	–	104
Brass pans/brass ware	1.7	7.9	57	173
Crystal	7.6	8.8	89	151
Carnelian beads	–	4.1	–	30
Coral	7.0	2.0	142	173
Swords/cutlasses	5.4	–	106	–
Silver coin	4.2	16.9	104	86
Pewter ware	1.9	1.8	58	108
Fringe	–	5.6	–	104
Tapseels	1.6	–	70	–
Fowling pieces/trade guns	1.5	9.2	53	78
Red cloth	1.4	3.2	68	73
Gunpowder	1.2	5.1	28	42
Copper rods	1.0	0.8	97	101
Silesian cloths	1.0	4.6	75	93
Total	100.0	100.0		
Weighted mean, £/bar values			.158	.116
Unweighted mean, £/bar values			.133	.115

Sources: Import percentages from table 8.1, modified to remove certain commodities of small value or insufficient price data. These therefore represent averages over periods longer than one year, while the price data are those for 1685 and 1731 from table 6.2

individual merchants. The comparative European cost of this merchandise is shown in columns 3 and 4, as an index number with the base 100 equal to the mean £/bar ratio for all the commodities traded in an average year, weighted according to the propostions of each in the total of major imports. The result is a set of index numbers that can be interpreted in several different ways.

One point again obvious in this table is that the range of £/bar ratios is no narrower in the 1730's than it had been in the 1680's. The numerical evidence is the rising coefficient of variation from .377 in the 1680's to .434 in the 1730's (table 6.2).

While the range of £/bar relationships was not converging, the assortments traded were changing in other ways. One index of advantage to the African or European side in assortment bargaining is the European cost of the commodities incorporated in the average bar. If an equal value of each commodity listed in table 6.5 were imported each year, the weighted mean £/bar ratio would equal the unweighted ratio and would represent the average European cost of a bar's worth of Senegambian goods. If the Africans insisted on high-value goods, they could force the Europeans to pay more than the unweighted mean value of a bar. In the 1680's, they forced the foreigners to pay £.158 for each bar's worth of merchandise, while an evenly distributed assortment of these same goods would have come to only £.133 a bar. By the 1730's, the bargaining had shifted in this respect; the weighted and unweighted mean value of a bar's worth of merchandise were nearly the same. And the cause is obvious from columns 2 and 4 of table 6.5, which show lower percentages of high-cost imports (like iron) and higher percentages of low-cost imports (like gunpowder and guns).

In this context, however, it is important to remember that a shift in favor of the Europeans is not necessarily a shift against the Africans. It simply means that the Europeans got more bars in 1731 for the same expenditure in pounds sterling. It would be equally possible—though unknowable with present data—that the Africans also ended on the Niger with more mithqals or cowries for each bar's worth of goods sold to the Europeans on the Gambia. The European advantage came from their being able to economize on highest-cost imports (like iron) and to increase the proportion of lower-cost imports (like silver). In fact, the pressure to import silver came from Africans in the interior trade, while the imported iron was mainly consumed near the coast. It is quite possible that the development of the juula trade from the interior brought the Europeans a windfall advantage in their cost per bar. If so, it was not an important windfall, since all through the eighteenth century the slow inflation in the bar value of imports was matched by a much more rapid inflation in the bar value of exports. (See chapter 8.)

Export Prices and Their Fluctuations

European traders found it hard to describe the Senegambian monetary and trade system to others in Europe, and their superficial explanations tended to gloss over the complexities rather than trying to explain all.

They also used various shorthand methods for dealing approximately with the system, to the great confusion of all concerned. They knew, for example, that a bar's-worth of merchandise could vary enormously in European cost, but they used a shorthand conventional value for translating most bar prices into sterling. For the English of the 1680's, the conventional bar was worth six English shillings (£.30), and each shipment of goods arriving from Europe was entered in the account books twice—once at the actual invoice cost in England for each commodity in the shipment, and then at its value in bars. But these bars were not the bar values used in dealing with African merchants, they were simply the sterling divided by £.30 and entered in the books as so many bars. Most European off-the-top-of-the-head calculations, however, were made on the basis of prime cost, as shown on invoices from Europe.

Both prime costs and prices translated into conventional bars had their uses, but both also had their failings. The prime-cost value paid per slave by the Royal African Company in the period 1683–88 was £3.41, and the Company's officials sometimes wrote as though this were the actual cost of slaves. In fact, this price took no account of the fact that the Company had to transport the goods to Africa and operate its shore stations there. In 1730, it reckoned separately that goods had to be sold on the Gambia for at least 40 to 50 per cent over prime cost in order to break even.[1] At that rate, the Company was actually paying about £4.94 a slave, which is in line with the f.o.b. price of £5.50 calculated for the 1680's (see *Supplement,* appendix 8). The use of prime-cost as a normal rule of thumb was nevertheless essential to prevent more serious errors of calculation that might have come from complete dependence on bar prices.

At the same time, the actual prime cost of the goods traded was not £.30 per bar or nearly so. Taking the prime cost of goods received by the Royal African Company for the period 1683–88, the average came to only £.139 per bar—not even half of the conventional value. (See table 6.6.) But this, too, had its uses. It was one way of assuring against bargaining errors in a complex situation of assortment bargaining and multiple exchange rates. If a Company servant received goods for a trading voyage up the Gambia in the 1680's, for example, these goods were charged on the books at the conventional rate in bars, which concealed a markup of 100 per cent or a bit more. This markup was high enough to cover any reasonable cost in transportation or overhead, thus serving as a guide to the returns the Company had a right to expect.

This Gambian practice of overvaluing the bar paralleled the Gold Coast "trade ounce." In the gold trade of the 1730's, an ounce of gold was worth

1. RAC to Anthony Rogers, 31 July 1730, T 70/55.

£4 in Britain, but merchants trading to the Gold Coast used a fictitious unit know as the trade ounce—actually the value of goods having a prime cost of about £2 in England. If they gave one trade ounce worth of goods for one actual ounce of gold, or other goods in proportion, they were assured of a 100-per-cent markup to cover all expenses and even allow for errors in dealing with the complexities of assortment bargaining (which prevailed on the Gold Coast as well.)[2] The Gambian system of the 1730's was very similar. By that time, the conventional value of the bar had slipped from £.30 to £.25, but the actual value of the average bar had also dropped to the range of £.100 to £.125. It allowed, in short, the same markup as the trade ounce. Thus, the European trader on the Gambia buying gold for 16 bars per avoirdupois ounce paid exactly the English value of £4 per ounce, at the conventional value of the bar, but he paid something less than £2 in the actual value of the bar.

This is not to say that the Europeans met the complexities of African bargaining simply by such grossly inaccurate devices as the 100-per-cent markup. The records of the Royal African Company show a careful allowance for assortment bargaining, apparent in column 1 of table 6.6. Over the six years 1683–88, the Company's average cost for a bar's worth of merchandise was £.139, with a standard deviation of only .0054. Such consistency indicates a close attention to the combination of African demand and European costs. It is especially striking, given the standard deviation of £/bar ratios of

Table 6.6
Overall Sterling/Bar Ratios and Slave Prices for
Royal African Company Operations in the Gambia,
1683–88

	£/bar	Price paid African slave dealer for slaves
1683	£.138	3.61
1684	.146	3.81
1685	.130	3.08
1686	.141	3.30
1687	.141	3.52
1688	.136	3.17
Annual average	.139	3.41
Standard deviation	.0054	.30

Source: T 70/546.

2. M. Johnson, "The Ounce in Eighteenth-Century West African Trade," *JAH,* 7: 179–214 (1966).

Table 6.7
Sample Transactions for Slaves,
Royal African Company, the Gambia, 1731, 1740

	Slaves purchased			(1) Bar price each	(2) Exchange rate for transaction (£/bars)	(3) Value or price in prime cost, each
	Adults	Children	Total			
September–December, 1731 (4 months)						
1)	2	–	2	41.0	.131	£5.37
2)	19	4	23	37.9	.115	4.35
3)	5	10	15	38.8	.096	3.74
4)	8	1	9	37.7	.105	3.98
5)	8	–	8	39.0	.079	3.06
6)	6	2	8	32.6	.108	3.51
	Mean		65	37.7	.104	3.93
	Standard deviation			2.02	.0127	.50
	Coefficient of variation			.054	.122	.127
May–June 1740 (2 months)						
7)	1	–	1	55.0	.147	8.07
	(future delivery)					
8)	1	–	1	51.5	.134	6.91
9)	81	–	81	64.31	.119	7.66
10)	72	–	72	58.8	.121	7.07
	Mean		155	61.6	.121	7.38
	Standard deviation			2.91	.0026	.301
	Coefficient of variation			.047	.022	.041

Source: T 70/558 and 573.

their assortment of imports in 1685 at .049—more than nine times as much. (Table 6.2, col. 1.)

Another perspective on export prices is possible in the 1730's, a period when the Gambian accounts of the Royal African Company were well kept and it is possible to follow a number of sample transactions for the purchase of a single export product. Samples for the purchase of slaves in 1731 and 1740 are summarized in table 6.7. In each instance, the actual prime cost of each article in the assortment could be calculated, to arrive at the actual prime-cost value of the bar-price paid. The price was the same for men and women (as was normal in the Senegambia), and boys and girls commanded nearly as much as adults.[3] The influence of age and sex on price can therefore be considered negligible. The Polanyi school tended to insist that West African trade was nonmarket trade, where prices were administered and never fluctuated. As table 6.7 indicates, the bar prices paid for slaves fluctuated (though bar prices of imports were unchanging), and the actual values represented by the prime cost of the assortment fluctuated even more. These prime-cost values in column 3 are in fact the result of two separate types of price fluctuation—changing bar prices and changing assortments—which sometimes reinforced and sometimes counteracted one another.[4]

The individual transactions reported in the table also illustrate particular patterns in the Senegambian slave trade. Transaction 7, for example, was the purchase of a slave for future delivery by one Emmanuel Vas, an Afro-Portuguese trader who did a lot of business with the Company and knew market conditions well. It seems likely that his special position accounts for the combination of a moderately high bar price on top of a generous assortment of goods—for nothing more than a promise of future delivery. In contrast, transaction 8 covered a slave actually delivered by a certain Fode Kante of Siika (a town in Ñomi and within sight of James Island). If Kante was what he appears to have been from the sparse record—simply a local and part-time petty trader—the lower price he received was in line with the Company's policy of paying higher prices to traders who were capable of bringing in goods from more distant markets, that is, to the Afro-Portuguese and the juula.

Transactions 9 and 10 are examples of the "merchant" trade. The number of slaves indicates that juula had made themselves responsible for bulking, and they probably came from beyond the navigable Gambia. Their willingness to accept cheaper assortments of goods than those demanded by the Gambian merchants probably reflects an ultimate destination in the far interior, where market conditions were different from those nearer the coast.

Subdivisions of the Senegambian Market

Senegambia was no more a single market than contemporaneous Europe was a single market. Each semidetached region had its own supplies and demands, most obviously in the far-interior region of gold

3. Moore, *Travels,* p. 45.

4. Although the number of transactions is far too small to have statistical meaning, it may be some indication, at least, that the correlation coefficient between bar prices and £/bar ratios in the six 1731 cases is .114. The similar correlation coefficient for all ten transactions is .538. Simple inspection can convey the same impression. It is clear that some transactions were high in both bar price and £/bar ratio. Others were high in one and low in the other, while still others were low in both.

mithqal and cowrie currency, but the same was true of iron-currency regions nearer the coast. To this point, the bar-Gambia has served to illustrate the general nature of bar prices and assortment bargaining, but each section of the coast had its own set of bar prices, originally quite different from each other. In the late seventeenth and early eighteenth centuries, however, they converged gradually until the values of the bar-Gambia became the dominant scale. Table 6.8 illustrates the extent of convergence by 1718, when all but Saint Louis (in effect the lower Senegal) had fallen into line.

Saint Louis was an exception, and it remained one. Later in the century, it pulled Gajaaga with it into a separate system of bar values. (See below, table

Table 6.8
Variation in Bar Prices within Senegambia, 1718

Commodity and Unit	Price in bars at:					
	St. Louis	Gajaaga	Gorée	Joal	Gambia	Bissau
Rix dollars	.66	.66	–	1.0	.5	–
Buccaneer guns	8.33	–	7.5	–	–	8.0
Curved sabers	1.0	1.0	1.0	–	1.0	1.0
Amber (livre marc)	8.0	12.0	–	–	10.0	10.0
Bassins, copper 1 1/2 liv. marc	.5	–	–	–	.5	–
Bassins, copper 1 liv. marc	.33	.5	1.0	–	.5	.5
Iron bars	1.0	–	1.0	1.0	1.0	1.0
Carnelians, round (per 100 stones)	1.0	.5	–	–	.5	–
Kettles, copper 12 liv. marc	2.0	–	–	–	–	–
Kettles, copper 6 liv. marc	1.0	–	–	–	–	–
Flemish knives, doz.	.79	–	–	–	1.0	1.0
Cloth, scarlet, aune	5.33	8.0	8.0	8.0	8.0	8.0
Cloth, berry, aune	2.66	4.0	–	–	4.0	–
Brandy, pinte	.5	–	.3	.3	.25	.33
Cloves, liv. marc	5.33	–	7.5	–	–	8.0
Lead balls, liv. marc	.167	–	.25	.25	.2	.2
Paper, ream	1.66	2.0	–	–	2.0	2.0
Gunpowder, liv. marc	.33	–	.5	.5	.5	.5
Flints (100)	.83	–	1.0	–	1.0	1.0
Silesian linen (platille) aune	.33	.54	.22	.22	–	.22
Rouen cloth, 100 aunes	–	–	.5	–	1.0	1.0
"Galets" (beads), mass	.66	1.0	1.25	.5	.5	–
Beads, ordinary, liv. marc	.33	.5	.5	.5	.5	.5

Source: "Mémoire général sur le commerce du Sénégal," AN col. C6 14.

Table 6.9
Assortments Paid in the Trade
of the Compagnie Des Indes
Escale du Désert
(near present-day Dieuk, Mauritania)
3 April to 4 June 1724

Gum purchased with:	Per cent of purchase price:
Blue bafts	71.3
Iron bars	8.3
Silver coins	7.0
50-pound kettles	5.7
Other	7.8
Total	100.0

Slaves purchased with:

Silver coins	35.6
Assorted textiles	28.1
Guns, powder, and shot	22.1
Beads of all kinds	4.2
Brandy	3.2
Iron bars	3.2
Other	3.6
Total	100.0

Source: "Extrait de la traite de gomme, de captifs, et autres marchandises faitte à l'escalle du Désert . . . par le Sieur Jean Demion," August 10, 1724, ANF, col. C6 8. Also printed version in Delcourt, *La France au Sénégal,* pp. 382–87.

6.10.) The French dealt with the difference by treating the bar-Saint-Louis as a separate currency with a conventional value of 6 livres tournois in the early eighteenth century, as against only 4 livres for the bar-Gambia.[1] Data are too incomplete to follow the relationship of different bars through the eighteenth century, but much of Saint Louis's special position came from its location on the edge of the desert, dealing along the river with two different ecological zones. The Moors wanted to buy textiles and millet, and they wanted to sell cattle, horses, and gum. Other regions within reach of Senegal trade produced their own textiles, and they had other products to sell—hides and a few slaves from Waalo and Kajor, millet and meat from Fuuta Tooro, slaves from Segu, gold from Bambuhu, and ivory from Bundu.

1. These French values in livres, translated at the average market rate of exchange for that year, come to £.20 for the bar-Gambia and £.30 for the bar-Saint-Louis. The conventional English value for the bar-Gambia at this period was £.25.

The differences between the markets north and south of the river appear very clearly in the few trade accounts that have survived. Table 6.9 illustrates the results of a single season of trade at the escale du désert in Waalo, where the gum from Mauritania was paid for with a drastically different assortment of goods from that used to buy the slaves. Even earlier in the eighteenth century, the Afro-French trade with the Moors was 70 per cent or more in blue bafts, the lengths of cloth that were later to be called pièces de Guinée, though the change was not simply one in terminology. The guinées originated from a much more general type of course Indian cloth called *bafata*, hence *bafts* in English. They were originally manufactured in Gujerat in western India, but the Gujerat famine of 1630 made them scarce, and they began to be imitated all over the subcontinent. By the late seventeenth century, the type used for the Africa trade with the name baft attached to it was a particular variety manufactured on the Coromandel coast.[2] And it became more and more specifically modified to suit the African trade. The Conseil du Sénégal of the Compagnie des Indes specified in 1736 that "these cloths must be very dark blue or black, with a sheen of red or violet resulting from their being very heavily charged with dye. It is absolutely necessary not to send any light blue, or even black if they lack the sheen. . . . Their length should be 12 to 12 and a half aunes [about 14.6 meters]. . . . They should also be treated so as to give them a stiff handle."[3]

It is uncertain just when in the eighteenth century the type manufactured for Senegal at the French entrepôt of Pondichéry to the south of Madras became differentiated from the type made in nearby British India, but the difference was recognizable in the early nineteenth century.[4] By then, the guinée was both specific and standardized enough to serve as an effective currency on the Senegal, each piece measuring 15 to 17 meters long, a little more than a meter wide, very heavily dyed with indigo, and stiffened with an impregnation of rice-water starch. The weight per piece was 2 to 3 kgs, and

2. John Irwin and P. R. Schwartz, *Studies in Indo-European Textile History* (Ahmedabad, India, 1966), p. 59; J. P. Duchon-Doris, Jr., *Commerce des toiles bleues, dit Guinées* (Paris, 1842), pp. 3–5.

3. Conseil du Sénégal to CI, "Nouvelles observations sur la qualité des marchandises," 10 June 1736, ANF, C6 11.

4. Although pièces de Guinée and blue bafts were not absolutely interchangeable, the English and French traders respectively used them in the same way for the gum trade. There is no suitable translation of *pièce de Guinée* in English. A literal translation is preempted by the fact that English already has a term *Guinea cloth* or *Guinea stuff*, widely used in the seventeenth and eighteenth centuries to refer to any of a range of cheap, brightly colored calicoes produced in western India and thought suitable for the African trade, though few of these were ever sold in Senegambia. (Irwin and Schwartz, *Indo-European Textile Industry*, p. 65.)

the standard package shipped from India consisted of 20 such pieces in a bundle or bale, which could itself pass as currency of a higher denomination.[5]

The transition of the guinée from a mere commodity to a major currency was gradual. The Royal African Company imported blue bafts as early as the 1680's, and they were already the main commodity used to buy gum in the years immediately following the Anglo-French peace of 1713. It was not until the 1750's, however, that European records began to quote prices in guinées rather than bars or livres tournois. By 1756, it was said of the goods exchanged for gum, "This merchandise can replace all others, but none can replace it."[6]

In that situation, the natural European reaction was to begin looking for a cheaper substitute, preferably one that could be made in Europe. The English made an imitation baft in Manchester in the 1750's, but the Moors rejected it. Other English then tried bringing undyed bafts to Holland for finishing. That device worked better, but the Moors still refused the Dutch-dyed cloths if the Indian product was available. The French tried to make an imitation guinée in Rouen in the 1780's, but it was no more acceptable than the English product. As a result, the Pondichéry guinée remained the currency all through the Napoleonic Wars, in spite of blockade and counter-blockade. In 1821, a governor of Senegal was still suggesting that France find a way to manufacture a substitute, just as his predecessor had done a half-century earlier.[7]

Although the pièce de Guinée became currency by the same route iron bars had taken—a dominant import that then became a standard of value and a medium of exchange—it never quite followed iron into the pattern of fixed "prices" and assortment bargaining. One likely reason is that the numeraire in the gum trade in the early eighteenth century was gum, not iron or guinées. (See table 6.10.) Europeans sometimes quoted prices of gum or other exports as a schedule of direct exchange; one quintal of gum was equal to so many iron bars, or so much brandy, and so on,[8] a system that must have been extremely cumbersome when several exports had to be balanced against several different imports. In the gum trade, however, gum far outweighed other exportable commodities, and the practice continued far into the eighteenth century. As guinées established and held their place as the dominant

5. Duchon-Doris, *Toiles bleues*, p. 3–4.

6. Conseil du Sénégal to CI, 15 March 1756, ANF, C6 14; Duranger, "Journal du sieur Duranger, employé de la Compagnie des Indes, au Sénégal, du 9 mai au 19 octobre 1758," (manuscript, ANF, C6 14), entry of 8 July 1758.

7. Worge to Egremont, Fort Lewis, 16 November 1762, CO 267/21; John Barnes to African Committee, Fort Lewis, 9 July 1764, T 70/37; Saugnier, *Relation*, p. 287; Duchon-Doris, *Toiles bleues*, pp. 9–14; Governor Senegal to MC, 8 August 1821, ANS, 2B 6.

8. Labat, *Nouvelle relation*, 4:436–37.

Table 6.10
Prime Costs and Gum Values for Certain Commodities
Imported to Senegal, 1718

Commodity	Quantity required to purchase one Moorish kantar of gum (220 kgs)	Estimated per cent of all commodities used by gum each year	Ratio of gum value to prime-cost value in £ sterling/kantar
Amber	122 grams	1.2	.563
Copper basins	4 basins	2.5	.576
6-pound kettles	2 kettles	10.0	.793
Country cloths	6 cloths	4.0	.716
Iron bars	2 bars	10.0	.396
Bafatas, 14.9 meters each	1 cloth	70.0	.566
Other		1.3	
Mean			.571
Standard deviation			.115
Coefficient of variation			.201

Source: "Mémoire général sur le commerce du Sénégal," ANF, C6 14.

import in the steppe region, it was simple enough to shift the numéraire from gum to guinées, and this happened as early as 1733.[9] Over the next half-century, prices of gum (and then of other commodities) were more and more frequently quoted in guinées, possibly because the *kantar* or unit of volume used to measure gum at the escales inflated rapidly from the equivalent of 200 kgs in about 1700 to more than 1,000 kgs by the 1780's (See *Supplement,* appendix 11.)

The guinées, however, were never frozen into a fictitious set of unchangeable prices and assortment bargaining after the manner of the bar-price system. Guinée prices never reflected European values perfectly, but they were closer to doing so than bar prices were. The coefficient of deviation for a sample assortment in the gum trade in 1718 was only .20, compared to .38 for the bar prices of the 1680's, .41 for those of the 1730's, and .64 for those of the 1780's. (See tables 6.10, 6.2, and 6.5.) Part of the reason may be the fact that the cost of guinées fluctuated far more rapidly than the cost of iron, or that guinées held their dominant place among imports where iron lost out, or simply that the relationships between Senegambian and European markets were much closer in the eighteenth century than they had been in the mid to late seventeenth, when the bar prices froze once and for all.

Meanwhile, the guinée functioned as a prominent commodity in the bar-

9. Devaulx to CI, 21 March 1733, ANF, C6 10.

Table 6.11

Price Variation within Senegambia, 1785

Commodity and unit	(1) Prime cost, France, livres	(2) St. Louis bars	(3) Galam bars	(4) Liv./bars-S.L.	(5) Liv./bars-Galam	(6) Bars-Galam/bars-S.L.
Pièces de Guinée	40	10	8	4.0	5.0	.80
Double gun	82.80	20	16	4.14	5.16	.80
Fine gun	15	10	8	1.50	1.88	.80
Trade gun	7.50	6	8	1.25	.94	1.33
Pistols, pair	18.00	6	8	3.00	2.25	1.33
Gunpowder, livre marc	.50	1	4	.50	.13	4.00
Swords, trade, each	4.50	1	2	4.50	2.25	2.00
Flints, 100	1.0	1	2	1.00	2.00	2.00
Lead balls, 100 (weighing 6.25 liv. marc)	2.0	1	2	2.00	1.00	2.00
Salt (barique of 226.2 lt)	3.0	1	6	3.00	.50	6.00
Paper, ream	7.00	5	5	1.40	1.40	1.00
Tobacco, Va., liv. marc	.35	.5	1.5	.70	.23	3.00
Scarlet cloth, piece	4.8	3	6	1.60	.80	2.00
Silesian linen, piece	10.75	2	4	5.38	2.69	2.00
Red wool, lb. marc	10.00	4	16	2.50	.63	4.00
Brandy, pinte	.75	.25	1	3.00	.75	4.00
Blanc-de-neige beads, cord	.10	.083	.33	1.20	.30	3.98
White beads (galets), doz. cords	.50	.75	1	.67	.50	1.33
Silver bells (grelots), each	1.00	.25	.33	4.00	3.03	1.32

Source: Saugnier, *Voyages*; some French prices from "Etat des Coutumes," 1783. ANS, 13 G 13, pp. 316–19, 299.

price system as well as a currency in its own right along the Senegal. (See table 6.11.) The two systems were easy to relate, because guinées were among the "heavy bars" in the bar-price schedule, and assortment bargaining tended to begin at the top of the scale. That is, the bargainers would begin with the numbers of heavy bars to enter the assortment. At various times, silver coins and guinées served as the prime heavy bar in Gajaaga trade in the eighteenth century, and it was to be silver coin that displaced the bar currency on the coast, just as guinées replaced the bar currency along the Senegal. But the transition was not sudden; the pattern of market isolation, stable "prices," and assortment bargaining continued through the late eighteenth century and into the nineteenth in relations between the coast and the hinterlands.

New Currencies of the Nineteenth Century

On the coast, new currencies came gradually over the half century between 1770 and 1820, bringing flexible prices that converged with increased contact between markets. It has sometimes been tempting to associate the new currencies with the new burst of foreign trade in the early nineteenth century, with the end of the slave trade and the patterns of commercial revolution throughout West Africa, but this would be a mistake. The new monetary and exchange system came with the collapse of the old, not the beginning of the new. It came especially during the period of chronic trade depression during the Napoleonic Wars, when war at sea restricted access to Europe and wartime inflation made for rapid shifts in price levels and the comparative prices of particular commodities. The discrepancy between prime costs and bar values had been increasing all along; in the depression of the 1790's and 1810's, the old system simply collapsed.

Meanwhile, an alternate system was already taking shape, with origins that go well back in the eighteenth century. Just as it was logical to place greatest emphasis on the number of heavy bars, in any assortment, it was only a short step to a form of assortment bargaining where one kind of heavy bar so dominated the transaction that the rest of the assortment were treated as bagatelles of no real consequence in the transaction. One more step, and the choice heavy bar became an all-purpose currency in a flexible price system. The first of these steps was already taken by the mid-eighteenth century, with silver dollars often playing the same role on the Gambia as the guinée played on the Senegal. Dollars had circulated in the Gambia-Gorée trade region from at least the 1720's, partly a currency and partly a commodity. About the same time, silver coins were not merely heavy bars on the upper Senegal; it was essential to include at least a few in any assortment for the purchase of slaves. By 1738, the firm of De Beaunais et frères of Saint Malo was importing dollars wholesale from Spain, with 140,000 in a single shipment destined for the Senegal division of the Compagnie des Indes, among others; but the Dutch 28-stuiver piece was used even more by the English, and the French were importing up to 25,000 of these coins each year for the Gajaaga trade of the early 1750's.

During the next few decades, the Dutch coins gradually went out of circulation, while the Spanish dollars came into more general use, and increasingly as a currency as well as a commodity. The English made them an official medium of exchange for their occupation of Saint Louis in the 1760's and 1770's, and the French accepted the silver medium in principle on their reoccupation of 1779, though the transition from bars to silver was gradual. It was not until 1783 that 40,000 livres in new coins, especially minted, arrived in Senegal, followed by another 25,000 livres in 1788, and the colonial government began paying its officials in silver coin from 1785— replacing the payments in merchandise that prevailed in the days of the Compagnie des Indes.[1]

In the first instance, the shift to silver coinage failed. The value of 65,000 livres, apparently the only coinage imported during the whole of the 1780's, amounted to only £2,587 sterling in a market that had treated silver as a commodity and imported about £1,500 *each year* in the last years of the Compagnie des Indes.[2] Local governments in Saint Louis and Gorée tried a bimetallic solution, keeping some kind of parity between silver and iron, but with limited success. By the 1780's iron came in many weights, shapes and qualities, while a variety of silver and other metallic coins from Europe circulated alongside the official coinage. Traders did what merchants had done for centuries in Europe. They used a currency of account, the livre (currency) as opposed to the official livre tournois of France, and other coins could be equated with values measured in the fictitious currency of account. This practice went back to the 1730's for some purposes, when the currency livre was thought to be about 10 per cent less valuable than the French livre.[3]

1. Du Belay to CI, Saint Louis, 28 March 1724, ANF, C6 8; De Beaunais et frères to Marine du Ponant, Saint-Malo, 7 December 1738, ANF, B3 388, ff. 365–66; African Committee to Anthony Rogers et al., 30 July 1730, T 70/55; Rogers and Harrison to Roberts and Moore, 22 January 1732, quoted in Moore, *Travels,* appendix, p. 7; Boucard to CI, 1 April 1732, ANF, C6 10; Jore, *Etablissements français,* pp. 275–76, 278.

2. "Notes prises avec M. de la Brüe," 18 July 1751, ANF, C6 13.

3. Levens, Memorandum of 16 August 1733, ANF, C6 10; Labarthe, *Voyage en Sénégal,* pp. 185 ff.; Golberry, *Voyage en Afrique,* 1:124. Still another form of accounting was used by the Compagnie du Sénégal in 1791. It kept its book in bars, abbreviated "B.," and the bars were still quite close to the unchanging values of the past. It translated livres to bars, however, at the rate of 4.80 livres currency per bar (as against the conventional 5 livres per bar of the 1780's). But the beginning of the end of the bar currency system can be seen in the fact that the company also carried steel bars at 5 B. each, round iron at 10B. per 100 livres *poid de marc* (49 kgs), and flat or "Portuguese" iron at 15 B. per 100 livres weight.

By the 1780's, the general estimation put the French livre at twice the value of currency, while the bar was conventionally taken as 5 livres currency—giving it a sterling value of about £.087, while the bar-Gambia had also inflated by nearly the same amount, being taken at £.10 in 1795, down from £.30 a century earlier.[4]

In France, the government gave up trying to supply French coinage to Senegal in 1790 and shifted to the Spanish dollar that already passed current in all of Senegambia. In 1791, they bought coins in Spain and shipped more than 35,000 pesos duros to Senegal,[5] where the Spanish dollar soon became the currency of account and remained so until the end of the Napoleonic Wars. Then, with the return of peace and the French presence, the French franc became a real coin as well as the normal currency of account. The most important circulating medium was the gourde, a five-franc silver coin worth £.1955 sterling at par, though bars were still occasionally referred to as a measure of value, and the bar system continued in Gajaaga and eastward into the 1820's and later.[6]

The traders based on Bathurst also resumed the silver standard after the foundation of the town in 1816, again using the Spanish dollar, at least for accounting and as a circulating medium in the town. (Up-country and along the river, the ordinary cloth currency continued as ever.) Bathurst merchants could choose to keep their accounts in either one of three different ways. Some, including the government, used pounds sterling as a currency of account. That is, they used silver dollars, but they wrote down pounds, shillings, and pence, figuring the dollar at its official value of 52 pence (£.2167). Or, as a second possibility, they could keep the accounts in "pounds currency" by assuming 4 dollars to the pound currency, which gave the dollar a more convenient value of 5 shillings (£.25). Finally, they could forget about pounds and shillings and simply keep accounts in the dollars that

---

4. In fact, the value of currency was generally a little higher than an exact 50 per cent of metropolitan livres. Lamiral (*L'Affrique,* pp. 65–66) calculated that 60 per cent (or £.108 sterling per bar) was more accurate, and Saugnier worked out the actual French cost of a typical bundle of goods used to purchase a slave in Gajaaga at 3 livres 3 sous in France for each bar–Saint Louis (or £.11 sterling at the exchange rate prevalent in 1785). (Saugnier, *Voyages,* pp. 316–19.)

5. The peso duro (called piastre fort in French) had a silver content of £.2123. In the colony, however, it was officially revalued at 5.4 livres tournois (equivalent to £.2245 in silver content) to bring it into line with the conventional equivalents in bars, which were at that time 1.25 bars for each six-livre French coin (the écu or couronne de France) and 1.125 bars for the piastre fort. (Jore, *Etablissements français,* pp. 277–78, 281; H. Doursther, *Dictionnaire universel des poids et mesures anciens et moderne* (1840; reprint edition, Amsterdam, 1965), passim; Maxwell, "Answers to H. M. Commissioners," 1 January 1811, CO 267/29.

6. Gray, *Western Africa,* pp. 347–48.

were actually the circulating medium.[7] Dollars also served as fractional currency by physical division into halves, quarters, and eighths, while other coins were assimilated to the standard, doubloons passing for 16 dollars, the Portuguese 10-rei piece for 1 penny currency. In 1834, the government gave the whole system a semblance of order by defining the "Spanish dollar" so as to include a variety of Spanish American dollars in actual circulation and making it legal tender at the rate of £.2167.[8]

This apparent rationalization had some hidden dangers. Britain was then on a gold standard; it was impossible to maintain a fixed parity between gold and silver; and in the mid-century silver gradually began to lose value in terms of gold. By making silver dollars legal tender, the Gambia government in effect left the gold standard and tied pounds currency to silver, though the consequences were slight at first. In the early 1840's, British coin exchanged for Spanish silver at 4 per cent over the official rate. Since the same problem existed elsewhere in West Africa, a British order-in-council of 1843 dropped the official value of the dollar from 52 to 50 pence (to £.2083). This act stabilized the dollar, because it meant that the Gambia government and other British West African governments would pay sterling for dollars at that rate. In effect, this move in 1843 put the Gambia back on the gold standard by giving dollars a gold value. But convertibility into sterling did not apply to all silver coins in local circulation. The five-franc French gourde still had only its intrinsic value to sustain it, and it dropped from its former parity with the dollar (£.2083) to only 1 shilling 10 1/2 pence (£.1938) from 1844 to the end of the decade. Treasury bills in sterling could be bought with five-franc coins if they were discounted by 3 per cent, while other coins could be used to buy Treasury bills at par.[9]

The fine points of these monetary shifts and charges were not very important for the Senegambian economy in general, but they take on significance as a measure of the new sensitivity government officials showed for the worldwide monetary system. Bathurst was part of the broader current by the 1840's, though the rest of the Gambia valley remained a series of semiconnected markets. Imports from Europe still passed through a sequence of price

7. Even this alternative was not quite so simple as it appears. The ordinary Spanish peso, worth £.2107 in silver, circulated as equal to the peso duro worth £.2123, the Mexican dollar (£.2102), the United States dollar (£.2090), and even the French gourde of five francs (£.1955). (Doursther, *Dictionaire universel,* passim.; *Gambia Blue Books,* annual series, CO 90.)

8. Gambia proclamation of 11 June 1834, enclosed with Rendall to Hay, no. 65, 16 October 1834, CO 87/10.

9. *Gambia Blue Books,* CO 90/14 (1841), p. 49; CO 90/16 (1842), p. 14b; CO 90/22 (1848), pp. 130–31; Johnson, "Cowrie Currencies," p. 337; Ingram to Stanley, no. 58, 15 May 1844, CO 87/33.

zones, insulated from one another by the high cost of doing business in Africa. (Farmers near Kaur in 1950 could still remember the old, fixed set of equivalents that once prevailed in that part of Saalum.) One Bathurst merchant in 1829 calculated that a typical bundle of commodities with a prime-cost value of £30 in Britain would be worth £43.33 (or 44 per cent more) in Bathurst and around £200 in Wuuli on the upper river, a further markup of 360 per cent.[10] Given these differences, the precision of monetary responses in Bathurst was hardly more than a façade for much looser monetary relations in the region as a whole.

This fact was more obvious and more official on the Senegal than it was on the Gambia, simply because of the enormous importance of the pièce de Guinée in the trade along the river; and guinées became more important because gum became more important. By 1820, gum exports had greater value than slaves had ever had, and gum was paid for in guinées, whereas slaves had sold for a variety of imports. Assortment bargaining was therefore dead, even if people had wanted to preserve it. The price of the guinée was quoted in gum—so much weight for each piece of cloth—and the guinée became the all-purpose currency along the river. Trading firms and the government itself paid salaries and made contracts in terms of pièces de Guinée, but the scarcity of gum and the scarcity of cloth both changed rapidly from year to year; and the guinée prices of the nineteenth century shook off any tendency to freeze in the manner of bar prices.[11]

Guinées had some advantages even over iron bars. They were lighter, and

10. W. Hutton to R. W. Hay, 18 May 1829, CO 87/2.

11. See table 6.10. Though the guinée was the numéraire for assortments of goods well into the nineteenth century, the value in guinées was close to the value in francs in Saint Louis. In 1829, for example, the French official Duranton needed to ransom one of his agents captured by the king of Kaarta. The ransom was set at 10 P. (pièces de Guinée), but it was paid in the following assortment:

Commodity and quantity	Value in P.	Saint Louis value in francs (where known)	Fr./P.
2 actual pièces de Guinée	2	46.00	23.00
1 double-barrelled gun	3	66.25	22.08
8 beads of no. 2 amber	1	–	–
2 pistols, high quality	2	45.36	22.68
2 pieces scarlet cloth	2	–	–

Source: Duranton to Gerardin, Médine, 13 December 1829, ANS, 1 G 8. The most useful list of Saint Louis prices at that period is the *Tableau détaillé des coutumes 1829* (ANS, 13 G 16), which gives the average Saint Louis price over the period 1826–29.

they could be used with less elaborate prior intervention by smith or tailor. They were also hard to counterfeit, but the limitation to a single source could also be a problem, since supply could fluctuate in response to local conditions at the source. In 1838, for example, the Dutch in Indonesia tried to restrict the import of cloths from India. Since Indonesia was a major market for Indian cottons, the result was a sharp drop in the price of guinées, along with those of other textiles. Later on, the cotton famine of the American civil war doubled the price of guinées for a time. Groups of merchants could also try to corner the market. The general result of all this was a series of sharp price fluctuations—a 31-per-cent drop from 1828 to 1832, one of 40 per cent from 1849 to 1850, or a jump of 25 per cent during the course of 1855.[12]

The government of Senegal nevertheless accepted guinées as a de facto circulating medium. In the 1840's, it went further and attempted to monetize them. First, the French government established quality standards. Each cloth was inspected in Pondichéry before export, and stamped with a seal of quality if it met certain standards, including the dimension of 16.5 meters by 1 meter wide and the weight of 2.3 kgs. At the Senegal end, it was illegal to import or trade in unstamped guinées, and these initial regulations of 1843 were followed by the outright demonetization of silver and gold coins in 1847. Silver remained the circulating medium in Saint Louis and Gorée, but the coins were outlawed as a medium for the purchase of gum or any other produce along the Senegal River.[13]

These regulations, however, had no very obvious influence. In practice, the Moors had higher standards than those of the government inspectors and frequently rejected stamped guinées that were not up to quality. In fact, the guinées became a circulating medium because people along the desert-savanna border would accept them as such, partly because these cloths were a major article of consumption and partly because this was a cloth currency region to begin with. By the 1840's, the guinée was in use as currency far to the east, into Kaarta and beyond, but not very far to the south of the Senegal valley—not in places where cloth currency had not been in recent use and not in places that preferred other kinds of cloth. On the Senegal, for example, guinées passed current as far as Xaaso, but they were not acceptable on the river above Médine; and even in Médine a double system of pricing was used,

12. Duchon-Doris, *Toiles bleus,* pp. 9–14; Saulnier, *Compagnie de Galam,* p. 74; D'Erneville to Governor, Senudebu, 7 January 1855, 13 G 247.

13. Ordonnance du roi, no. 66, 18 May 1843, and Sénégal arrêté no. 65, 11 July 1843, *Bulletin d'administration,* 2:87–88; Arrêté no. 14, 17 February 1847, and no. 16, 19 February 1847, *Bulletin d'administration,* 4:16–19; Direction des colonies, "Commerce du Sénégal," 7 December 1850, ANF-OM, Sénégal, XIII 2; Commission des comptoirs et du commerce . . . , "Rapports spéciaux," June 1851, ANF-OM, Sénégal XIII 3.

gum from the north and northeast being quoted in guinées, while gold from the south and west was quoted in barrels of salt per gros.[14]

The steps from the bar prices and iron currency of the eighteenth century, to coined metallic currency and flexible prices, and on toward full incorporation in the Europe-centered world banking system of the twentieth century were only gradual, and they were far from completed by the 1850's. Cloth currencies continued to circulate in local markets. The guinées were remarkably persistent, even though Europeans finally learned to make reasonable imitations at half to three quarters of the Indian cost. By 1875, several different qualities and weights were available, supplied about one-third each by India, Belgium, and Britain, but the standard guinée continued to serve as currency—in some places through the first quarter of the twentieth century—and very similar textiles are still in demand.[15] The peanut revolution in the second half of the nineteenth century may well have speeded up the pace of economic change, but the Senegambian monetary system had been changing constantly to meet new conditions for at least two centuries before 1850—and the monetary system was only one aspect of a broader commercial culture that changed with it.

14. Raffenel, "Rapport de 22 Août 1848," *Revue coloniale,* 3 (2nd ser.):264; Brossard to Governor, Médine, 29 October 1854, ANF-OM, Sénégal IV 18.

15. Anon., *Le Sénégal et les guinées de Pondichéry: Note presenté à la commission supérieure des colonies par les négotiants sénégalais* (Bordeaux, 1879); J. H. Saint-Père, *Les Sarakollé de Guidimakha* (Paris, 1925), p. 25; Dubie, "Vie matérielle des Maures," p. 207.

7 | THE WAYS OF COMMERCE

The changing institutions of Senegambian commercial life are sometimes obscure as they appear episodically through the written record left largely by Europeans on the coast, but the record is rich enough, for all that, to show commercial institutions that were no more static than the economy they served.

Caravans and Caravaners

The key institution for moving goods overland was the caravan, called *cáfila* in Portuguese creole, *coffle* in Gambian English, *chemin* in Senegalese French, and *saate* in Jahaanke. In fact, it was a highly variable institution, since the simplest form was nothing but a crowd of people travelling together in the same direction for the sake of companionship and safety. But the crowd usually travelled in an organized way that could become both tight and disciplined. All caravans had a single leader called a *saatigi, silatigi, or saate feredi* in Malinke,[1] and the larger ones required a complex organization with a number of subordinate officials.

1. The derivation of the term is questionable. The root *tigi* clearly means master of. *Silate* in Malinke, *saate* in Jahaanke, means road or caravan, hence a *silatigi* or *saatigi* is a master of the road or of a caravan. The term *saatigi* also turns up in Manding as a title for a political office, including the rulership over Fuuta Tooro at the time of the Deñankoobe. (Coelho, *Duas descrições,* p. 131; Hull, "Voyage to Bundo," p. 1.) In some uses *saatigi* carries the sense of pathfinder or guide during a migration, so that as a title it can be equated with the Pulaar *aarðo* (leader of a migration or nomadic band), while the Malinke title, *mansa,* should be equated with the Pulaar *laamido,* the ruler of a place, from a village on up to a large territorial state.

271

Some of the eighteenth-century slave caravans were very large indeed, bringing as many as 600 to 800 slaves through from the Niger valley to the navigable waterways leading to the Atlantic coast. This implied nearly as many more people to act as guards, porters, or donkey drivers for the return trip; the unit in motion could therefore be as many as 2,000 people, though it was normally much smaller. Even the smaller caravans were subdivided. Slave caravans broke down into units of 30 to 40 slaves fastened together by leather cords tieing each by the neck to the persons ahead and behind. Each group of slaves and guards constituted a sub-unit of the caravan. Other caravans were often subdivided according to the commodity carried or the form of transportation, so that the cords of slaves were kept separate from the people driving donkeys, and they from cattle drovers. In time of suspected danger, the caravan might be made up of three equal units, an advance force, a center, and a rear guard.[2]

It was customary to spend seven to seven and a half hours on the road each day, leaving after early prayers in the morning just after light and marching steadily until one or two in the afternoon, so as to stop just before the hottest part of the day. Since either donkeys or pack oxen could make about 4 to 4 1/2 kms an hour under good conditions, the maximum rate of advance was about 30 kms a day.[3]

The initiative to form a caravan could come from several sources. Sometimes a prominent merchant announced that he would lead a caravan on a particular route at a particular time, inviting others from neighboring villages to join him. In that case, it was understood that the initiator would be saatigi. Other caravans, however, were formed on the initiative of a village head or other official who had no intention of travelling himself. In that case, those who intended to travel chose the saatigi once they had assembled. Many caravans of this sort were seasonal, and assembled almost automatically. The Jahaanke of southern Bundu, for example, used to send large caravans south to Fuuta Jaalō for kola. As the season approached, merchants from many different villages began to drift in to Cipi on the southern frontier of the almamate, where they formed a single unit, selected saatigi. and moved off to the south.[4]

In cases of this kind, the selection of saatigi was not a matter of open voting but of prolonged discussion leading to a sense of the meeting—no doubt in

2. See Saint-Robert to CI, 18 July 1725, ANF, C6 9; Levens, Report of 10 July 1725, BN, FF, NA, 9339, f. 157; Conseil du Sénégal to CI, 15 July 1743, ANF, C6 12; Moore, *Travels,* pp. 41–42.

3. Hammady Mady Sy, Madina Kojalaani, CC, T 7 (2); A. Raffenel, "Divers itinéraires de la Sénégambie et du Soudan, pour servir à l'intelligence de la carte ci-contre," *Revue coloniale,* 3 (2nd ser.):277–305 (1849).

4. Mammady Mady Sy, Madina Kojalaani, CC, T 7 (2).

circumstances where some opinions weighed more than others. Another device, sometimes used by the Soninke of Gajaaga, was a form of manipulable lottery. A prominent cleric, usually the imam of the Friday mosque, would stand with a koran in the center of a circle made up of those who were about to travel. The koran then moved about of its own accord until it pointed to a particular individual, and that man had the right to name the saatigi.[5]

Some saatigi were entrepreneurs in transportation, but others were simply leaders for the defense and good order of the group. With the Jahaanke of Bundu, the firm was an individual or a family, so that each merchant who joined had his own group of donkeys and his own paid porters or other attendants. He was responsible for feeding them on the road, paying any tolls or fees along the way, and dealing with potential customers at the end of the journey. The other alternative, the entrepreneurial saatigi, was common in the east-west trade to the Gambia in the 1780's. Under this system, each merchant who joined the caravan brought goods he intended to trade on his own account, but he also entered into an informal contract with the saatigi for services along the way. In return for 20 to 30 per cent of the final sale price of the goods carried, the saatigi promised to see the owner and his goods through to the coast, to pay the duties and cost of provisions along the way, and to act as broker in dealing with the Europeans.[6]

The number of saatigi was comparatively small. Moore estimated in 1730 that only one hundred merchants worked the long-distance slave trade to the Gambia, and those who were regularly saatigi were even fewer. Most of them were apparently known by name to the Europeans, and many were certainly among those who had regular credit relationships with the Europeans. In Mungo Park's time, however, the saatigi as a class were generally reputed to be wealthy enough to trade on their own capital, while the more humble juula had to borrow from the Europeans, often at very high rates of interest.[7]

Park's experience with an actual caravan from Kamalia to the Gambia in 1797 illustrates the degree to which a caravan could depart from the general pattern. In general, long dry-season trips like this one were supposed to begin in December or January, but the clerical merchants of Kamalia had first to wait for the end of the rains. Then they had to go to Kangaba on the Niger to buy slaves—that being one of the regular slave outlets for the Segu government. They then had to wait once more for the end of Ramadan, since Muslims had to fast and abstain from water from sunup to sundown during Ramadan, and the hottest time of the year was approaching. It was not until April 19th that the small caravan finally left Kamalia for the Gambia under Karfa Ture as saatigi, with four other Malinke juula and their retainers,

5. Interview with the leading men of Jawara in Gajaaga, CC, T4 (2).
6. Captain Heatley, Board of Trade Report, part 1.
7. Moore, *Travels*, pp. 41, 200; Park, *Travels*, 2:57–58.

Mungo Park as a kind of passenger, and a total of twenty-seven slaves. Two other merchants with small groups of slaves joined the caravan for a part of the journey, and a number of other free people joined simply for safety in travel—including, among others, six minstrels and a Muslim cleric travelling with eight of his *taalibe* or pupils. In this way, the caravan grew to a maximum of thirty-nine free people and thirty-five slaves, and then declined again. What with delays of a day or so here and there, the actual elapsed time from Kamalia to Pisania on the Gambia, a distance of 530 kms, was fifty-one days at an average of only 10 kms a day, although 30 or more a day were theoretically possible.[8]

This pattern of joining caravans for part of a journey was common at all times, since the desirable size of the caravan varied directly with the danger. In the nineteenth century, for example, the politically fragmented region south of Bundu was always one of considerable risk. People about to cross it tended to pause until a larger group had gathered, and once the danger was passed, those who could travel faster than the rest pushed ahead, while some lagged behind.[9]

The efficiency of juula movement was governed in part by the accuracy, detail, and speed of commercial information. The assumption that African merchants simply wandered around until they found someone to buy their goods is part of the myth of a stagnant economy in precolonial Africa. Information traveled surprisingly far and fast. Some African sellers could, in effect, place orders. When the Bur of Saalum had slaves to sell in the 1720's, for example, he sent down to the Gambia suggesting that the Royal African Company send a sloop around by sea to the Saalum River and up to Kawon, even specifying what he wanted in return. In one case, at least, the Company knew that the Bur wanted guns. Having none in stock, it had in turn to buy from a separate trader before it could send a sloop. Other African authorities hundreds of kilometers from the European posts could pass messages, and they had good sources of information about the Europeans. In the period 1714–16, a certain Corniet, the French Company's commander in Gajaaga, made a reputation for tricking Jahaanke traders and for other sharp practices; and the Jahaanke, along with the Tunka of Gajaaga, were able to see that their complaints reached Saint Louis. Or in the opposite direction a century later, in 1818, the Almaami of Bundu knew about the expedition the English

8. Park, *Travels,* 1:491–546.
9. Hequard, Report of 30 July 1857, ANS, 13 G 165, pp. 7–8; Guillet, "Mémoire de la remise de service," 24 September 1837, ANS, 13 G 22. In the mid-nineteenth century, Cipi in southern Bundu was the point of rendezvous for southbound caravans, while Bulebane was the meeting place for merchants from Gajaaga or the Gambia who were headed east across Bambuhu toward the Niger. Those coming the other way formed larger groups at Tamba before leaving for Senegambia. Other points, however, served this purpose at earlier periods. See Conseil du Sénégal to CI, 28 April 1744, ANF, C6 12.

intended to send through his country and about the projected French reoccupation of a post in Gajaaga, before either expedition had actually left Saint Louis. Strictly commercial information passed rapidly up and down the main trade routes, so that the Europeans at the trade enclaves knew which caravans under which saatigi were on their way, and the Africans knew within a few weeks which posts were low on goods, had been recently restocked, or were paying high or low prices. Some African negotiators knew more about European market conditions than one might assume. In 1785, for example, Ahmad Maktar, the emir of the Brakna, argued the new privileges granted to the Compagnie du Sénégal by France as a justification for increasing his prices.[10]

At the same time, the juula lacked the full freedom and flexibility this wealth of information might suggest. At the best of times, the safe areas for the movement of a small group or a single trader were few. Major wars could make particular trade routes unusable for decades on end. The uncertainty of overland travel was one factor that made it worthwhile to take a combination of goods from the interior to a particular point on the coast, trade them for another combination of imports, and return. The greatest theoretical profit might have gone to the juula who could buy each commodity in its cheapest market and sell each where it was dearest, but it was safer to deal with an assortment of goods and hope to maximize the profits on the whole assortment.

The European traders recognized as much. If they could give an especially good price for one commodity, they were likely to attract the business of the whole caravan. In the early nineteenth century, the Gambia had an advantage over Gajaaga in cheaper and better gunpowder, and the Gambian price for ivory was also higher than the Senegalese price. The French considered simply subsidizing gunpowder as a kind of loss leader. Both Gambians and Senegalese worried that the continued slave trade of the southern rivers might be attracting a whole range of goods away from their own rivers. By the nineteenth century, however, the increased flexibility of the spreading silver coinage opened new possibilities. At mid-century, many of the "strange farmers" who worked on the Gambia took some of their returns in English goods available on that river, while they carried the rest in silver to spend in Gajaaga on their way east.[11]

10. Minutes of Council, James Fort, November 2, 1722, Rawlinson Papers, Bodleian Library, Oxford; Brüe to Collé, 9 December 1716, BN, FF, NA. 9341, f. 41; Gray, *Western Africa,* p. 169; Thomas Hull, "Voyage to Bundo" (unpublished mss. in the library of the Duke of Buccleuch, which I was able to see through the courtesy of the late Douglas Grant), p. 16; De Repetigny to MC, Saint Louis, 30 May 1785, ANF, C6 18.
11. Governor to MC, no. 30, 20 February 1832, ANS, 2 B 14; Findlay to Hay, Gambia, 1 March 1829, CO 87/2; Mahoney, "Government and Opinion," pp. 119–20.

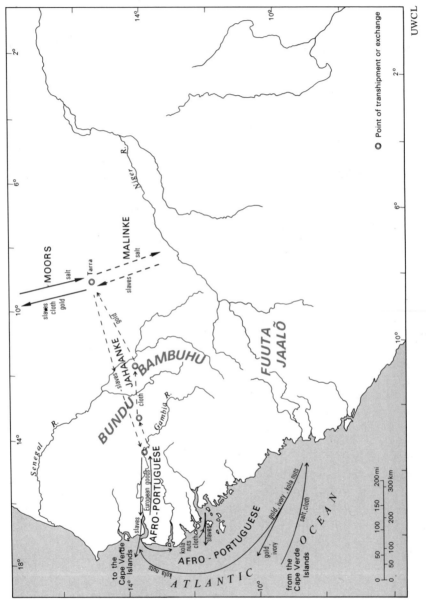

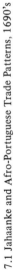

7.1 Jahaanke and Afro-Portuguese Trade Patterns, 1690's

Similar arbitrage was sometimes possible at earlier times, playing with different prices of goods at different markets. What information we have about the actual movements of particular merchants suggests that many followed a complex pattern of three- or four-sided voyages rather than plying back and forth on a familiar route. The Afro-Portuguese had long been doing this in the coastal trade. As early as the 1620's, it was usual to take a cargo of salt from the Cape Verde Islands to Sierra Leone, where African merchants took over and sent it inland in return for ivory, gold, and kola nuts. The Afro-Portuguese took the ivory and gold for ultimate shipment to Europe, but the kola went to the Gambia to be sold for sorooji. The cloths then went to the southern rivers to be sold for slaves, and the whole cycle could begin over again.[12]

In 1690, Cornelius Hodges reported an inland variant that interlocked with the coastal trade. It began in Bundu with Jahaanke merchants and cloth. They could have taken cloth directly to the coast in exchange for salt or overseas imports, but they preferred a roundabout set of price differentials. They first took the cloth to Bambuhu, where they sold it for gold. With the gold, they went northeast to the sahal city of "Tarra" not far from Jaara in Jawara. There they sold the gold for slaves, partly to help their home villages to make more cloth and partly for sale on the coast to the Europeans in return for exotic imports. They consumed some of the imports in their home villages and used the rest in Bambuhu to buy gold for the next round. The crucial factor, as they explained it to Hodges, was not merely the high markup on slaves between Tarra and the Gambia; the use of gold in Tarra made it possible to buy rapidly and cut down their turnaround time. In effect, they argued, to sell overseas imports in Tarra forced a trader to turn retailer in order to obtain the general purpose currency of that region, the locally made cloth, which in turn had to be converted into slaves. All this took so much time that it became unprofitable. By stopping in Bambuhu for gold, they came with a currency suitable for the wholesale operations of interregional trade.[13]

A little later, in the 1710's, some of the juula practiced a similar arbitrage between Gajaaga and the Gambia to alleviate the problem of having to choose a single market and sell everything there. As they came through from the east with gold and slaves, they sold the gold in Gajaaga for French imports. Using the slaves to carry the French products on to the Gambia, they could take advantage of the higher Gambian prices for slaves and make a second profit unloading a selection of French goods that were either better or cheaper than

12. D. Ruiters in G. Thilmans and J. P. Rossie, " 'Flambeau de Navigation' de Derick Ruiters," *BIFAN*, 31:108.
13. Hodges to RAC, 16 September 1690, in Stone, "Journey of Cornelius Hodges," p. 92.

the competing English products.[14] Still later, in the early nineteenth century, other arbitrage opportunities existed between Kaarta and Gajaaga, based on differences between the European structure of prices then becoming dominant in Gajaaga and the older price structure of the Sudan that persisted in Kaarta.[15] The distance between the two points was not great, but chronic warfare made it especially difficult for juula to travel back and forth, hence the persistence of separate markets.

The Economics of Transportation and the Pattern of Routes

The historical record is remarkably deficient on cost of transportation within Africa. The occasional hints about the markup between purchase price in the interior and selling price on the coast are not very useful, since they include all costs of doing business, not just transportation. One really detailed accounting of pre-steamboat navigational costs on the Senegal is provided by Saugnier from his own experience of a Galam voyage in 1785, but it is a single account and one intended to prove a point about the potential value of the Senegal trade. It is therefore somewhat suspect, though it seems to be in line with other data.

Saugnier's basic calculation gave the costs of outfitting a ship large enough to carry the goods required to buy 100 slaves. The fact that the crew were paid partly in the right to carry freight on their own account provides the only opening for calculating the cost of transportation on a ton-kilometer basis. Each crew member was allowed so many barrels of salt on the upstream leg of the voyage, from 4 barrels for the captain down to 1/2 barrel each for the washerwomen and the female cooks. Taking these as standard Bordeaux wine barrels of 226.2 liters each, they would have weighed about 150 kgs each and the total would have been about 6 tons—a significant amount, and one that Saugnier estimated would cost the owners the prime-cost value of about 60 livres per barrel or a total of £84 for salt transported on the crew's account. Because the return trip with gold and slaves was effectively in ballast, and because the limiting factor for the whole voyage was the carrying capacity for the upstream trip only, the full round-trip carrying capacity would have to be charged against the crew's salt—a point to point distance of

14. Bruë to Collé, 9 December 1716, BN, FF, NA, 9341.
15. Major Gray calculated, for example, that a prime slave could be bought in Kaarta for £7.40 worth of properly selected European goods, but in Gajaaga that same slave could be sold for a second assortment of goods, which when transported to Kaarta would now be enough to pay for more than four slaves. (Gray, *Western Africa*, pp. 347–48.)

Table 7.1
Typical Estimated Transportation Costs for Five-month
Voyage from Saint Louis to Maxaana and Return, for One Hundred Slaves, c. 1785

	Value in livres tournois	Per cent of total cost
Crew wages	3,775	32.3
Crew rations	2,175	18.6
Rations for slaves (2 months)	1,000	8.6
Tolls	3,729	31.9
Captain's commission	1,000	8.6
Total	11,679 (equivalent to £408.75 sterling)	100.0

Source: Saugnier, *Voyages,* p. 303, with alterations to correct apparent arithmetic error.

510 kms from Saint Louis to Maxaana, or 1,020 kms round trip, for 6 tons of cargo. The result would be a freight rate equivalent to £13.72 sterling per 1,000 ton-kilometers, which can be compared with the rate of £2.55 per 1,000 ton-kilometers by steamer over the route between Saint Louis and Kayes at the beginning of this century.

The distribution of this total cost tells something about the economics of river transportation. More than a quarter of the total went for provisions, another indication of the extent to which the slave trade required a marketed agricultural surplus for moving and holding slaves within Africa and storing ships for the Atlantic crossing. Tolls were also significant, and 84 percent in this case was the large payment to Fuuta Tooro, reflecting the power of the Almaami Abdul Kader after his victory in the religious revolution of the 1770's. The wages of the crew were also more than might have been anticipated, given the fact that the ordinary sailors or laptots were slaves rented from their masters (though they received half of the wage for their own use). A laptot's pay for the five-month voyage came to more than half the cost of a slave bought in Gajaaga. At the equivalent of £.95 sterling a month, the wage was not completely out of the range of the usual monthly rate of £1.50 for an ordinary seaman in the British slave trade.[1]

Comparable cost accounts for caravans are even harder to come by, but something of the possible levels are indicated by conditions at the beginning of the colonial period, when the technology of overland transportation was still much as it had been. In 1896, the *commandants de cercle* in the French

1. Saugnier, *Voyages,* pp. 303–4. For twentieth-century comparisons see Meniaud, *Haut-Sénégal-Niger,* 1:71.

Sudan were instructed to keep a record of caravan movement. The totals, admittedly incomplete, indicated that 4,600 donkeys, 1,500 pack oxen, and 17,000 camels were used that year for transporting 12,500 tons of goods. Measured in numbers of loadings, regardless of the distance travelled, this meant that about 74 per cent of pack freight was carried by camel, 6 per cent by pack ox, and 20 per cent by donkey.[2] Though these figures are certainly not precise, they can be taken as broadly indicative. The heavy use of camels is explicable; they were the preferred beast of burden all along the sahal. In the dry season they could sometimes be used safely as far south as Bamako or the Gambia River, though both were risky because of tsetse-borne disease. At the beginning of this century, camels cost about five times as much as donkeys, but they could carry about three times as much, and they could carry it a little faster—an estimated 35 kms a day as against 30 for donkey caravans. The greater saving was in human labor: since one driver was required for every five donkeys but for every four camels, the carrying capacity per driver of camels was more than double the rate for donkeys.[3] Part of the advantage, however, was environmental, since camels were used where fewer streams had to be crossed, and human labor was not required for off-loading and repacking at each crossing. The cost of camel freight on the sahal or across the desert near the end of the nineteenth century was estimated at about £10 per 1,000 ton-kilometers.[4] The rate for donkey caravans must have been higher and variable according to the difficulty of the route, increasing also with movement toward the south, where the animals' mortality rates would be higher.

These estimated freight rates have to be understood as approximate only, but they are consonant with routes taken by European or North African goods bound for the western Sudan. At any time from the mid-seventeenth century onward, the Atlantic route was preferred over the Sahara route for Senegambia itself. During the eighteenth and early nineteenth centuries, the breaking point between imports that came through Senegambia and those that came from the north lay somewhere between the upper Senegal and the upper Niger. When Paul Solliet visited Segu and Maasina in 1879, he found that most of the European and Indian textiles in use there had been imported by way of North Africa, even though *some* goods had reached this region from the Atlantic coast ever since the middle of the eighteenth century.[5]

2. Ballien, "Notice sur le Soudan," ANS, Q 48, pt. 5.

3. Meniaud, *Haut-Sénégal-Niger,* 1:118–19.

4. The data and estimates are those of Baillaud, *Routes du Soudan,* p. 110, by far the most accurate economic commentator on the western Sudan in the nineteenth century. For others see H. Stucklé, *Le commerce de la France avec le Soudan* (Paris, 1864), pp. 31–32.

5. Solliet, Report of 10 April 1879, ANS, 1 G 46. See Baillaud, *Routes,* pp. 106–10, for the change by the 1890's.

Map 7.2 shows the situation of the Niger valley above Timbuktu. Taking the 15th parallel as the rough indicator of the sahal region, a point due north of the important trading town of Sokolo would be roughly 1,200 kms from the tip of Cape Verde or almost any other coastal point between there to the Gold Coast. Even though it was 50 to 70 per cent further from there to North Africa, the desert routes were dominant until the beginning of the colonial period; which suggests that camel transportation was at least 50 to 70 per cent cheaper than the combination of boats on the Senegal and donkey caravans from Gajaaga eastward. The east-west route of sahal or savanna, however, was vastly superior to the route through the forest from the Gulf of

A circle with a radius of approximately 1,200 kms., centered on 15° N., the latitude of Cape Verde, and due north from Sokolo, shows that point to be nearly equidistant from any coastal point of entry between Cape Blanc and Cape Three Points.

UWCL

7.2 The Strategy of Access to the Western Sudan

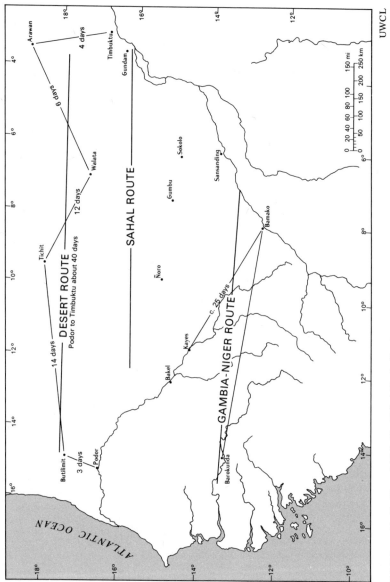

7.3 Schematic Outline of Main East-West Trade Routes

Guinea—not because the forest itself was a barrier, but only because donkeys on that route gave way to human porterage. Paul Solliet explained the greater efficiency of camels by their smaller need for human labor, but political factors also enter the picture, such as the need to pay higher and more frequent tolls in the densely populated Sudan than was necessary in the desert.

The eastward routes from the Atlantic coast to the Niger valley shifted through time, but they can be seen schematically as three that persisted over long periods, even though the exact itinerary might have changed slightly. These three routes had a certain symmetry, since the northernmost was through the desert usable by camels only; the middle lay along the sahal, usable by either camels or pack oxen or even donkeys; and the southern one, the Gambia-Niger connection, was for donkeys alone. Technically, the two northerly routes should have been more efficient, simply because they could use the more efficient beast of burden, but the Gambia-Niger route had an overland passage of only about 650 kms from Barokunda to Bamako, while the shortest practicable all-camel route from the Mauritanian coast to, say, Sansanding on the Niger is more than 1,100 kms as the crow flies. Political factors therefore played a major role in determining which would carry the heaviest traffic at any particular time.

The desert route between the Atlantic coast and the Niger bend was probably only sporadically important, and it was closely integrated with the trans-Sahara trade itself. Moors could carry Mauritanian salt (or even salt from Waalo or Kajor) to Gajaaga to be exchanged for Bambuhu gold, which in turn moved north to Morocco in exchange for manufactured products in a form of triangular trade. Many traders worked only one segment of the east-west route north of the sahal. In the 1720's and 1730's, for example, Moors from the desert furnished the greater part of the slaves purchased at Fort Saint Joseph in Gajaaga, having acquired them on the sahal further east. By the nineteenth century, some Moorish merchants used the desert route in combination with the waterborne facilities of the river trade. One Sidi al-Hājj Ahmad, for example, brought thirty camels as far as Podor in 1828 and left them there while he continued downriver to Saint Louis to sell gold dust worth nearly £1,200.[6] In any case, the desert route was not simply an east-west line barely north of the sahal but consisted of oasis-hops that carried the caravans far out into the desert. In the late 1850's, the common route from Podor to Timbuktu began by running nearly due north for about 100 kms before turning eastward to Tichit (eleven days), Walata (twelve

6. P. Charpentier, Mémoire of 1 April 1725, ANF, C6 10; Doumet, "Mémoire historique . . . sur Gorée," ANF, C6 29; Durand, *Sénégal,* 2:109–10; Solliet, Report of 10 April 1879, ANS, 1 G 46; Governor to MC, 19 April 1828, ANS, 2 B 12.

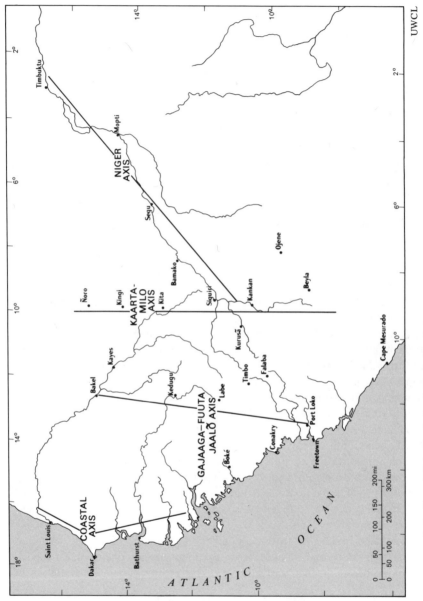

7.4 Schematic Outline of Main North-South Trade Routes

days), and Arawan (six days). From there, it was possible to drop south to the Niger bend or to continue on north to Morocco.[7]

The middle east-west route lay along the northernmost part of the savanna where rainfall agriculture was possible, but it deviated to meet the advantages or disadvantages of natural features. From the west, it followed the Senegal valley, which meant a continuous supply of water in the dry season, but it jogged north again from Gajaaga to pick up its "normal" range between 15 and 16 degrees north latitude. Approaching the Niger, it forked so that one branch swung south through Sokolo to Sansanding or Ja, while the other swung north and followed the north edge of the Niger flood plain to Gundam and Timbuktu.

The southernmost route ran between the 12th and 13th parallels, though its western sector was pulled north to follow the north bank of the Gambia. This, too, had an environmental reason for being where it was. It was a short passage from the Gambia to the Niger just north of *glossina morsitans,* hence the southernmost route donkeys could use with safety all year round. This was the route of the Jahaanke and the Mandinke Moori, just as the middle route was that of the Soninke clerics.

Since these two routes were both suitable for donkeys and both lay within the network of juula villages, it was easy to cross back and forth between them using a variety of diagonals. A westbound caravan along the sahal, for example, might drop down to Gajaaga and make a diagonal through Bundu to the Gambia, while one from the Bamako region might cross northward to make for Gajaaga. Eastbound caravans along either route might swing a little north or south to strike the Niger at an intermediate latitude, say that of Segu. Or a westbound caravan might swing south of the Gambia to make for the southern rivers.

Still another set of commonly used routes lay on a north-south axis. The most westerly of these was in reality more of a network of commerce stretching from Waalo southward through the Wolof and Sereer states to the hinterland of the southern rivers. East of Jolof, north-south trade was comparatively rare because of the difficulty of crossing the Ferlo wilderness, but a new axis ran directly south from Gidimaxa through Gajaaga and Bundu to Fuuta Jaalō. This came to be an important route for the northward movement of kola nuts, which could move either east or west along the sahal route once they reached Gajaaga. A third axis ran south from Ñoro through Kita and Siguiri to Kankan. This too was a kola route, but it carried a good deal more than kola, including rock salt from the Sahara, as opposed to the sea salt that dominated trade further west. Finally, the fourth and perhaps most important of these north-south routes was the valley of the Niger with

7. G. Lejean, "Le Sénégal en 1859 et les routes commerciales du Sahara," *Revue contemporaine,* 11:368–403 (1859), p. 388.

its waterborne transportation reaching from the pre-forest region of upper Guinea through into the desert. At its southern end, it reached the Bure gold fields as well as the maze of kola routes stretching southward from Kankan into the forest.

Since the southernmost part of the kola routes running through Kankan or through Fuuta Jaalō lay beyond the range of donkey caravans, human porters were necessary, and they were often used further north as well. While human porterage other than slaves in transit was rare on the east-west routes, less wealthy juula working north from the kola zones often carried their goods on their own backs, and even the wealthy used hired porters more often than slaves.[8]

Political Authorities and the Control of Trade

Relations between juula networks and political authorities fell in with the broader Senegambian dichotomy between politico-military and commercial-religious spheres. Juula and clerics generally sought autonomy for their communities, neutrality in wartime, and free passage for trade. Political authorities, on the other hand, regarded trade as less noble than ruling or fighting but a convenient source of wealth and power for all that. This meant that trade was controlled and taxed, while other special privileges, such as autonomy for merchant communities, were favors to be sold, not simply granted.

This is not to say that relations between kings and merchants could not be cordial. Courtiers respected the juula for their religious knowledge and prestige, while merchants respected military prowess. Nor were tolls and other charges merely a matter of autocratic whim. In Senegambian thought and practice the state was entitled to about one-tenth of all passing merchandise, just as it was entitled to about one-tenth of the agricultural produce. Either form of tax could often be paid in kind. The French had regularly paid 16 hides per hundred exported from Kajor in the mid-seventeenth century, though the Portuguese even then were allowed to get by with a payment of only 10 per hundred. In overland transportation, the rate-payment was sometimes a percentage of the goods in transit, sometimes a sum in currency. In Bundu of 1795, the rate in one instance was set in two currencies

8. The Jahaankoobe of Bundu are unanimous and strong in their insistence that their ancestors used hired porters, not slaves or free men recruited through kinship ties, for their commercial ventures to the kola regions. Hear especially Baaku Kaba, Tumbura, CC, T13 (2), and Mammady Mady Sy, Madina Kojalaani, CC, T 6 (1). Some of the juula further to the south, however, apparently used slave porters alongside hired porters. (Person, *Samori*, 1:112 ff.)

simultaneously—6 sorooji per donkey[1] if paid in cloth currency, or 1 mithqal of gold.

In addition to regular tolls governed by the volume of trade, merchants and political authorities were bound into an elaborate etiquette of reciprocal gift-giving. Details differed from one society to the next; but the practice was universal in Senegambia, and it was closely tied to the value system of the secular leadership. The politico-military sector and the mercantile-clerical sector saw wealth and its uses in somewhat different terms. Both wanted goods, and goods carried prestige as well as the pleasure of consumption for its own sake. The difference came in the way goods could be used to bring in more goods. Political leaders were at the peak of a redistributive network, receiving taxes and tolls and the product of raids against neighbors or of work by slaves in the fields. But this wealth was the result of power; it could only keep flowing if some of it were diverted to the acquisition of more power. This was accomplished through redistribution of the goods in public and semiceremonial circumstances, where gifts could cement the bonds between the political leader and his clients. This meant regular and systematic gift-giving to clerics, minstrels, subordinate kinfolk, and military followers like the leaders of the slave armies.

Clerics and merchants were in a somewhat different position. They had no automatic flow of wealth from power but lived instead from teaching, the gifts of the faithful, the sale of charms, or from trade. Some gift-giving was essential. Charity was, after all, one of the pillars of Islam. A really important cleric also had to live expensively, if only to show off his success in coping with the supernatural, but here conspicuous consumption and charity were a form of advertising, not a direct source of power or further income. Further wealth came from direct investment—in commerce, in cattle, in slaves—much as the secular authorities invested in political power.

But the secular leaders were not free to give or withhold gifts at will. Social inferiors had the right to demand presents on particular festival occasions. In many places, as in Bundu until the recent past, one of the salient marks of social status was the right to ask for gifts, which could only be done of one's superiors. The resultant ranking was far more complex than the three-fold "caste" division of free people, craftsmen, and "slaves." It subdivided these groups into a ranked order with upwards of twenty categories,[2] and the importance of the gift was not just the value of the goods changing hands,

---

1. Park, *Travels*, 1:87. For the seventeenth-century precedents in hide trade see Dapper in *BIFAN*, 32:524; Coelho, *Duas descrições*, p. 11. See also Raffenel, *Nouveau voyage*, 1:387; S. L. Pascal, "Voyage d'exploration dans le Bambouk, Haut-Sénégal," *Revue algérienne et coloniale*, 3:137–64 (1860), p. 152; Gray, *Western Africa*, pp. 115–16, 182.

2. Interview with Hammady Amadou Sy, Dakar, June 20 and July 15, 1966.

though this value could be considerable for important people at the head of the redistribution network. It was, instead, the gift's function as a symbol of social status and social solidarity. Like reciprocal gift-giving in the West, the value of the gift was supposed to reflect the wealth of the giver and to represent his prestige. But the symbolic value was not the strict market value. The form of giving and the assortment of the gift were also important, recalling the importance of assortment in market operations. The highest prestige attached to the gifts made up of the greatest possible number of different goods. Senegambian epics, for example, often record gifts from important kings to notable heroes in such terms as "one hundred of everything God created." The important point was to include everything, or sometimes "one of each" or "ten of each," where "each" meant each valuable item a man might happen to own. Even the multiplier had a certain ritual significance, since it was often divisible by either two or ten, and the value of the multiple gift has extended down to the present, where a Senegambian gift consisting of two silver coins, two robes, two kola nuts, and two sarooji will carry much more weight than the same value in cash.[3]

The special importance of variety in gifts and transactions was very widespread in West Africa, and it may help account for wide extension of assortment bargaining in market exchange up and down the coast. Some recorded transactions from Mauritania to Cameroon show the "one of each" pattern in the eighteenth and nineteenth centuries;[4] but the Senegambian practice tended to restrict this kind of payment to ceremonial gifts. It appears not only in the redistributive network of person-to-person giving, but in other gifts that were part of the constitutional order. In Waalo, for example, an electoral council chose a new Brak from among the qualified candidates. The

---

3. This tendency to emphasize the style and form of gift-giving is common to many societies, perhaps to separate the role of a gift from that of an exchange. The Western Christmas gift, for example, is surrounded by a subtle protocol. Money has lower prestige than a gift in kind, and a tendency is discernible for the prestige of the gift to vary inversely with its utility to the recipient. Hence the gift for "the man who has everything," where the gift's prestige rests on the fact that no sane and well-to-do person would buy such a thing for himself.

4. A transaction on the Mauritanian coast in 1773, for example, involved 700 pounds (343 kgs) of gum, exchanged for 3 scissors, 3 knives, 3 hides, and then 1 pound of gunpowder, 1 bar of iron, 1 padlock, 1 aulne of cloth, 1 gun, 1 ounce of cloves, and 1 pound of lead balls—clearly a mixture of "three of each" and "one of each." Another transaction in Cameroon in the late nineteenth century, two centuries and more than 3,000 kms away, involved 50 pounds of ivory sold for 36 different commodities, with the quantity 8 or 80 in 44 per cent of the items. (Capt. Charles Guillaume Hiacinthe Costé, Extract from Journal, March 1733, Portendik, ANF, C6 16; Sundstrøm, *Trade of Guinea*, p. 90.)

new king then presented each councilor with "ten of everything" as a symbol that he had now taken office.[5]

Since mutual gift-giving was a way of creating a social alliance between two people, it was also a way of creating a social alliance between a trade community and the ruler of the state. In addition to gift exchanges, the African juula could use other forms of alliance that were common in Senegambian society. With the Fuulbe, the relationship of cross-cousins (*dendiraaɓe*) was extremely close on grounds of kinship, but the same term was used as an alternate for the jõñu lineage alliance based on historical occurrence. The jõñu relationship could be further generalized to create an alliance between groups larger than a lineage. The Jahaanke of Bundu, for example, had a jõñu relation to the ruling Sisibe, which gave their trade communities autonomy within the state. They remember that one of their ancestors, Kabā Maadi Satā made a powerful talisman for Eliman Bubu Maalik Sii (c. 1701–23)—so powerful that it brought him victory over Gajaaga. That event began a relationship that has lasted down to the present. Jahaanke automomy in their own affairs became sacred; it was bida or forbidden for an Almaami even to enter Diide, the first Jahaanke village. In addition, the Jahaanke acquired a role in the state itself, including control over the main judicial and religious offices. Their pacifist tradition was honored by exemption from active military service, though they were expected to pray for victory and to help build fortifications.[6] Similar alliances, though different in detail (and no doubt changing through time) seem to have existed between other clerical communities and their host state.

When the Europeans appeared on the coast, they partly assimilated the position of the other, African juula communities. They were readily allowed autonomy in return for a series of payments in the tradition of the ceremonial gift exchanges, and other payments in the tradition of the tolls collected on the volume of trade, though they rarely recognized the local meaning of the payments. For that matter, African rulers were sometimes able to confuse the issue so that a traditional annual gift could grow into a substantial source of revenue without an equivalent gift in return. The Europeans also lacked the special claim to Islamic religious prestige which was so helpful to the African juula. Thus while their position was similar, it was not identical to that of their African counterparts.

5. Carrère et Holle, *Sénégambie*, p. 107. Like the repetitive quantities in commercial transactions, this pattern recurs elsewhere in West Africa. The Bundukas of Sierra Leone were supposedly rewarded by their Temne and Loko neighbors for help against the Limba by a gift of "one hundred of everything" and a piece of territory to rule as their own. (Wurie, "The Bundukas of Sierra Leone," p. 16.)

6. CC, Kadialé Diakité, T 1 (2); Ibramima Diassiki, Suututa, T 10 (2).

As the new relationships settled down in the late seventeenth century, each kingdom developed a set of officials to deal with trade under the title of Alkaati or the like in the Wolof states and along the Senegal, or Tubabmansa ("king of the European") along the Gambia. This official's main function was to facilitate trade and collect whatever might be due the king, though they came in time to collect a series of small gifts for themselves. The schedule of fees at Portudal in Bawol can illustrate the range. Each ship presented a gift worth about £.70 to the Alkaati, another worth £.42 to his assistant, an anchorage fee, a charge of about £.56 for watering, a further payment to the port captain, and small gifts to minor officials. About £.17 worth of brandy was customarily passed out, and a final parting present worth £2.50 was required by the three principal shore-based officials. Only after all these petty payments came the real tariffs, amounting to 10 hides (worth about £.30) for each sloopload of cargo put on board ship.[7] It was this payment, amounting to an export tax of 10 to 20 per cent, that had real economic consequences.

Once the Europeans had their permanent fortified stations the relationship to the state changed, though private traders still paid the regular tolls to the king. Formal treaties appeared, setting forth the mutual rights and obligations of the two parties. As they did so, they moved toward explicit contracts and away from the mutual exchange of gifts. The annual customs or *coutumes* (as opposed to the tolls paid on goods shipped) came to be a payment specified as, among other things, ground rent, the foreign community's right to autonomy, sometimes ancient regalian privileges foregone at European request—for example, the right to pillage wrecked ships or the right to inherit from any foreigner who died outside the merchants' enclave. The treaties also specified the amount of other payments, such as indemnities paid the African state for the return of escaped slaves, or the rate of toll payments to be charged for individual shipments.[8]

The toll payments remained the most expensive part of the bargain. In the Franco-Ñomi treaty of 1785, the French annual payments for the right to maintain an unfortified enclave at Albreda were at the modest rate of 120 bars (with a total prime-cost value of £13.23 sterling), plus another £5.51 for the Alkaati of Albreda. But each individual French ship had to pay £5.51 to the king and £2.54 to the Alkaati.[9]

The social function of the annual gift is even clearer in the example of Saint Louis, where the French officials were drawn into the general Wolof pattern

7. Barbot, *Guinea*, p. 32.

8. Salvage was especially important in Saint Louis, where ships were often wrecked trying to cross the bar into the Senegal, while the royal inheritance from strangers was crucial at Albreda. Ñomi gave up its right to inherit from French residents in the Mansa's treaty with the French, 31 March 1785. (Labarthe, *Voyage en Sénégal*, pp. 230–31.)

9. Lajaille to MC, 11 August 1785, ANF, C6 18.

Table 7.2
Senegalese Government Payments in Gifts and Duties
to African Governments and Individuals, 1786

Recipient	Total in livres tournois	Equivalent of £ sterling
Kajor	3,270	112
Waalo	4,568	157
Fuuta Tooro	5,013	172
Gajaaga (various princes)	3,574	123
Cost of keeping Gajaaga hostages in Saint Louis	181	6
Trarza Moors	11,300	389
Brakna Moors	6,134	211
Hospitality for visitors to St. Louis	4,078	140
Religious festivities, Saint Louis		
Christian	481	17
Muslim	213	7
Total payments made from Gorée	2,484	85
Totals (£ column will not add because of rounding)	41,296	1,421

Source: "Etat des dépenses au Sénégal, 1786," ANF, C6 19. The total in livres were apparently calculated by taking the total number of bars paid and multiplying by the conventional value of 5 livres per bar. This would not be an inaccurate representation of the value of the goods at the point of delivery, but the prime-cost value of the goods represented would be about 60 per cent higher.

of giving *ndewenel,* the ceremonial gifts that coincided with the three major Muslim holidays. At that season, the head of the family gave presents to everyone in the household, to the neighbors, and to the poor. This was a time during which people had a special right to demand gifts from their social superiors. The governor at Saint Louis fell into line and distributed brandy to the Muslim community—just as he also sent brandy to the Christian community—at Christmas time—and he sent brandy as well to the Damel of Kajor for distribution among his own people. The quantities were small, and the cost was low; the real importance was symbolic, though fifteen gallons of brandy must have contributed something to the gaiety of the season among the Damel's entourage.[10]

The year 1786 was near the peak of success for French operations in eighteenth-century Senegal. Payments for that year shown in table 7.2 therefore illustrate the pattern of distribution. Forty-one thousand livres was not a large sum for the time and place—only about 8.4 per cent of the total cost of maintaining the French posts and not twice the governor's annual salary. For

10. Colvin, "Kajor," pp. 113–15.

that matter, nearly 5,000 livres went for hospitality and other expenses of doing business that were not treaty obligations.

These obligations, however, became more and more specific with the passage of time. After the French return to Senegal in 1779, treaties no longer specified the payment in bars, but listed the articles to be turned over. This was no doubt necessary to avoid misunderstanding when the value of a bar varied so greatly from one commodity to another, but the treaty lists also underline the ceremonial character of the gifts and the importance of variety for its own sake. The Trarza treaty of 1785, for example, began with the substantial items, like 200 pièces de Guinée (worth about £280), 2 double guns (£3), and 15 meters of scarlet cloth (£11), but then dribbled off into a listing of 10 mirrors, 10 combs, 10 padlocks, and so on, through eight different minor commodities. The treaty also specified the payments owing to twenty-three specified individuals other than the emir, each individual listed by name or title along with the goods due him. Important people received four or five units of each major commodity; lesser folk got one or two of each.[11]

Treaties with Fuuta Tooro were still more complex, especially after the rise of Abdul Kader, when Fuuta had the power to close the river to French trade at will. The new treaty signed in 1785 not only specified the goods to be delivered but also had clauses covering the date the fleet would sail each year, the protocol to be followed in making payment, and the rates of toll to be exacted from the individual ships. These individual rates frankly discriminated in favor of the Afro-French. Residents of Saint Louis paid "two of each" in guinées, trade guns, barrels of gunpowder, salt, paper, lead balls, flints, and cloth for the right to pass through Fuuta with a river boat, while merchants from Europe paid "ten of each" from a different and slightly longer list. The Senegalese government's cost was modest compared to tolls levied on the merchants. In 1789, it paid only £110, which included the right of passage for the royal ships sent with the convoy, while six ships belonging to the revived Compagnie du Sénégal paid a total of £766.[12] Further inland the government payments were still less, a prime-cost value of only £55 to the various princes of Gajaaga and £18 more to the Almaami of Bundu. Even though the European officials complained constantly about the "exactions" of the African rulers, it was tolls, not gifts, that hurt.

Fuuta, moreover, was able to enforce other regulations on the pattern of trade. Abdul Kader regularized his own administration of Senegalese trade by appointing his cousin, Tapsir Sawa Kudi Kan as Alkaati, to reside in Salde and collect from the passing ships (and the office became hereditary with Sawa

11. Treaty of 20 July 1785, ANF, C6 18.
12. Treaty of 31 March 1785, ANS, 13 G 2; untitled report on Gajaaga customs for 1789, file folder no. 5, ANS, 13 G 13.

Kudi's descendents). The presence of a regular official made it possible to enforce the old prohibition against the enslavement of Futankoobe or the enslavement of clerics. After some unpleasant experience of Futaanke seizing slaves on board French ships, the French finally promised in 1806 to allow the Almaami's officials to inspect the slaves bought in any Futaanke village, so as to identify any who might be in the prohibited categories. It is hard to know how well this worked in practice, but the pressure of the juula to prevent the sale of Muslims was a recurrent theme.[13]

In addition to the payments properly considered reciprocal gifts in the Senegambian tradition, the Europeans at times also tried to institute payments for services rendered. In Gajaaga of the 1750's, the toll had been at the modest rate of 1 bar per slave, paid to the Baacili, the secular rulers, and 1/5 bar per slave to the heads of the clerical towns. With slaves selling at 30 bars each, the rate worked out to only 4 per cent ad valorem. In 1755, the Company decided on its own initiative to lay aside 5 additional bars per slave as bribe to be paid to any saatigi who brought his caravan to Gajaaga rather than going through to the Gambia. The Company itself thus raised the rate to nearly 18 per cent, but without practical result.[14] The Company men decided, on second thought, that they were bribing the wrong group. If the caravan leaders failed to respond, it must be on account of the raiding by the Xasoonke chiefs. The 5-bar premium was therefore divided between Xasoonke, who were to receive 3 bars, and the saatigi of each caravan, who was still to receive his 2-bar premium for every slave delivered to Gajaaga. As it turned out, the French lost Saint Louis before the plan had a chance to prove itself. The English after 1758 let the trade come through to the Gambia rather than reestablishing an upper-Senegal post.[15]

In the nineteenth century when the Europeans returned in force to Senegambia, they first resumed the old ways of tolls and gifts. The rates were no higher, but the Europeans became restive, sensing a new differential in physical power between their own and African governments, or, even more, affected by the new cultural arrogance of industrial Europe. Their moves came to the two rivers with different tactics and timing, but they had a common element of trying to lower or abolish dues, just as the new commercial policy showed a common search for monopoly. On the Gambia in 1835,

13. Franco-Fuuta treaty of 4 June 1806, ANS, 13 G 2. Pressure against the sale of Muslims went back at least as far as the 1730's, when Yuuba Jaalo of Bundu persuaded the Royal African Company to ransom all Muslims in return for two other slaves to be exported in their stead. (Grant, *Fortunate Slave*, p. 108.)

14. That is, 6.2 bars, in all, for slaves that were then sold for 35 bars each.

15. Undated, untitled tariff list c. 1740, ANF, C6 23; Conseil du Sénégal to CI, 15 March 1756, and "Mémoire sur la concession du Sénégal," 2 November 1762, ANF, C6 14.

Table 7.3
Tolls Paid to African Authorities by Private Merchants
in the Senegal Gum Trade, 1852

Place of trade	Tons of gum purchased	Tolls per ton in pièces de Guinée	Tolls as per cent of value, with gum at £54 per ton and guinées at £.8192 each, representing the annual average values for 1836–40
Gajaaga			
"High season" trade	380	1.32	2.0
"Low season" trade	501	4.57	6.9
Lower Senegal other			
than the official *escales*	215	1.40	2.1
The Escales			
Du Coq	647	2.01	3.6
Trarza (Désert)	645	2.51	3.8
Des Daramancours	215	2.00	3.0
Total or mean	2,562	2.70	4.1

Source: Brossard, Annual Report for 1852, 1 January 1853, ANS, 5 B 14, prices from *Statistiques coloniales.*

the first serious effort of the Bathurst merchants to lower tolls was joined to the project of a Tenda Company and a monopoly over the trade of the upper river. They had been paying the juula in long-distance trade a commission of 10 per cent ad valorem to meet tolls incurred while bringing goods through to the Gambia. Now, they tried to get government support for a conspiracy to lower the commission to 5 per cent on gold, ivory, wax, hides, and gum, and to abolish it altogether on country cloths, kola, dates, butter, and horses. In this instance they failed to get government support, but they returned to the attack in 1843 with a private agreement to lower the prices paid for Gambia produce and to stop paying the customary gifts.[16] The juula simply took their trade elsewhere; Bathurst gave in, and the customary payments continued on into the second half of the century.

The nineteenth-century tolls on the Senegal were somewhat lower than the eighteenth-century rates, but Senegalese merchants began to resent payments that seemed unjustified. The important merchants who stayed over the low season in Gajaaga were charged more than the lesser men who came out to

16. Memorial from Gambia merchants to Lt.-Gov. Rendall, 24 October 1835, enclosed with Rendall to Glenelg, 9 December 1835, no. 24A, CO 87/12; Ingram to Stanley, 2 February 1843, no. 8, and 30 March 1843, separate, CO 87/30.

work the river traffic only during high water. In 1853, for example, the government paid Fuuta only £79, while large private vessels paid £20 to £178 each, and smaller ones paid £4 to £20 each. As table 7.3 indicates, this meant that the ad valorem rate paid by the small traders was less than half that paid by the big operators. The total dues paid in the gum trade of the early 1850's was also divided unequally among African rulers. Of the total paid in the gum trade at Bakel, the Moors collected 52 per cent, Fuuta 31 per cent, and the princes of Gajaaga and Bundu the remainder,[17] so that the largest payments went to those who supplied the least in active aid or service.

The end came in the 1850's, when the French, having concentrated their power to oppose Shaykh Umar Taal, found it ready at hand for other purposes. Faidherbe simply refused to pay what the Africans asked. For Fuuta, Gajaaga, and Bundu, he refused to pay anything at all, and that decision was incorporated in a series of treaties signed in 1858 and 1859. For the Moorish emirates, he forced a shift from the old combination of government-to-government payments, plus tolls on private merchants, to a single export tax on gum, set at 3 per cent ad valorem for the Ïdaw 'Aish and at a similar level for the Trarza and Brakna, though expressed in different terms.[18]

On the lower river, economic as well as power relations changed rapidly in the 1850's with the rise of peanut cultivation in Kajor. Thousands grew peanuts, while the old hides, slaves, or ivory passed through only a few hands. The number of middlemen increased, as peasants sold their crops on the spot, usually to Moors who came in the dry season to carry them to the river or the shore by camel. After some experimental lump-sum payments to the Damel in lieu of tolls, Senegal in 1850 allowed a straightforward export tax of about 5 per cent, payable in peanuts directly to the Damel's officials; but in 1857 Faidherbe arbitrarily reduced the rate to 3 per cent. The power of African rulers to impose conditions on foreign trade and traders had finally ended. They might collect an export tax for a time, but the level of that tax was set by the colonial government of Senegal.[19]

Markets and Brokers

Trade diasporas first came into existence to meet the need for brokers—in a broad sense of that term, men who understood the differing ways of life of disparate trade partners as well as the intricacies of the market. This brokerage function could be independent of other commercial functions and discharged by a separate group of practitioners, or it could be joined to

17. L. L. C. Faidherbe, "Notice sur la colonie, du Sènégal" *Annuaire du Sénégal de Dèpendences,* 1858, p. 104.

18. Brossard, Annual Report for 1862, 1 January 1853, ANS, 5 B 14.

19. Colvin, "Kajor," p. 273.

the occupation of the entrepreneurial merchant. The combination could also change rapidly over a period of time. Trade on the lower Gambia can serve as an example. When the Royal African Company first entered that river, its local officials were mainly buying agents for the Atlantic trade, and cross-cultural brokerage was done by the Afro-Portuguese intermediaries between the fort and the local markets. With the passage of time, however, the Royal African Company became less involved in ocean shipping, and its local servants were better acquainted with Gambian conditions. Over the period 1680–1730, it gradually took the brokerage function away from the Afro-Portuguese and began buying slaves on its own, selling them afterward to independent shippers.

With still more time, however, the Royal African Company declined and then disappeared, and the brokerage function passed to local Africans who had come to specialize in dealing with the Europeans. By the 1770's, an independent slaver could arrive at the Gambia with some assurance of finding people who understood his culture and could guide him through the problems of trade in that setting. This was one reason why the British simply abandoned the site of the fort on James Island after its capture by the French in 1779; the functions of brokerage and bulking that the fort had once performed could now be done competently and at lower cost by a variety of African specialists.

This new pattern can be illustrated by the hypothetical experience of a typical English ship entering the Gambia in the 1780's or so. It first made anchor near the deserted James Island, opposite the Ñomi town of Jufure and the French post at Albreda. The English at that period left the Ñomi trade to the French; but they needed Ñomi help for the trip up the river, and the first step toward getting that help was a series of payments the English considered to be an anchorage fee, though the people of Ñomi recognized them as the etiquette of gifts to establish a social relationship between strangers. In this first stage, the Mansa of Ñomi received ten gallons of rum. The Alkaati of Jufure got two iron bars, and other miscellaneous gifts of wine, cider, or other beverages were paid over to those who performed small favors; but the total cost at this stage was only about £1.85.[1]

The advance beyond Ñomi had been the subject of a long controversy. The Mansa of Ñomi demanded a toll from ships that sailed further, just as he charged tolls for the juula caravans that came overland to trade with the French at Albreda. English merchants resented these charges, and their resentment led to recurrent violence through the 1750's and to the Anglo-Ñomi war of 1765–68; but Ñomi continued to collect a toll amounting to a prime cost value of £16 to £20 per ship until 1823. The key to Ñomi's ability

1. This hypothetical account of a "normal" trade experience is based mainly on Captain Heatley in *Board of Trade Report*, part 1, and A. R. Onslow, 13 November 1788, *Board of Trade Report*, part 2.

to collect, however, was not British military weakness. It was the fact that the English needed broker-interpreters from Ñomi, and these specialists could only be recruited with the Mansa's permission. Mansas of Ñomi had long been using this leverage against the English. As early as 1733, one Mansa had made it a crime punishable by enslavement to serve as a broker-interpreter on a European ship that had not paid tolls.[2]

By the 1780's, most ships hired extra crew in Ñomi as well. These temporary sailors, called butlers, took over work like rowing boats, taking on wood and water, and generally relieving the overseas crew of heavy work in an unaccustomed climate. Butlers were also cheaper labor than English sailors, since they were paid £.30 a month, against the English sailor's wage of £1.50 (see *Supplement,* appendix 14), and the availability of temporary labor made it possible to sail with a lower manning scale for the rest of the voyage.

The skilled staff taken aboard in Ñomi were called linguists and messengers, usually two of each, but they did more than interpret and carry messages. The first linguist stayed on board the ship to act as interpreter and broker in dealing with the shore-based broker hired by the caravan leader or other seller. He earned a salary of £1.50 per month plus a commission of £.10 for each slave purchased, which meant that his actual monthly earnings could be as high as those of a Senegalese riverboat captain. The second linguist earned only £1.20 and keep, and his job was to work on shore trying to attract trade, sometimes buying slaves or provisions. Messengers worked still further out to let people know a ship was coming or to direct caravans to the point of trade.

In the 1780's, English sailed directly upriver to Ñaanimaru to begin their trade in the kingdom of Ñaani, though they might later go higher still if supply turned slack. On arrival, the captain presented the usual gifts to the small value of about £.60, which the Europeans again took to be an anchorage fee. The ship could then begin advertising its wares by sending the messengers ashore to drum up business, perhaps outfitting a pulling boat to go further upriver with one of the linguists in charge. Gradually, the brokers from Ñomi made contact with local brokers and brought them on board one at a time. All the brokers distinguished between the "single trade" of small lots and the "coffle trade," in which an entire caravan could be sold at a single transaction, but the procedure was the same in both. The land-based broker on his first visit asked only about the number of bars being offered for each kind of merchandise, and about the general quality and assortment of the cargo from Europe. He made this kind of survey of all ships in the river and of land-based Afro-European slave traders before returning to the ship or trader that seemed to offer the best prospect. This time he brought the owner of the slaves or other merchandise, so he and his client could bargain against

2. Debat to African Committee, Gambia, 1 August 1759, T 70/30; Charles O'Hara, despatch of 15 September 1768 and associated despatches in CO 267/14; Mbaeyi, "British Barra War," *JHSN,* 3:623–31; Moore, *Travels,* p. 67.

the shipboard broker and the supercargo. They first sought agreement on price of the African merchandise in bars, then on the assortment of the European goods to be paid in return. With these two points settled, they sent ashore for the produce or slaves. Slaves were inspected by the ship's surgeon, who could still reject or demand variance in price on grounds of physical condition. Once that test was passed, the captain paid over the goods, holding out one bar per slave for the king of Ñani and a further half-bar for the Tubabmansa of Ñaanimaru, a toll equal to about 1 per cent of the purchase price. Finally, the captain made the final ceremonial payment, the "cut cord," theoretically for loosening the slaves from the rope that had tied them during the trip but actually, by now, the final seal of solidarity between buyer and seller. With minor variations, this etiquette in the slave trade was remarkably persistent and much the same in all parts of Senegambia.[3]

In addition to the fees and tolls collected from the Europeans, local brokers and government officials collected equivalent payments from the African strangers who came to trade. In these transactions, the saatigi of the caravan often acted for the whole body of slave owners, serving as a broker who took a commission before passing the balance to the owners themselves, but he also worked with a local landlord-broker who provided a variety of services and guarantees. The landlord-broker was a nearly universal institution of West Africa, though the local variations were many. Here, for example, the jaatigi, as he was called in Malinke, acted as a broker alongside the saatigi. In the central Manding region, however, in places like Bamako or Jene, or at Madina in Xaaso, the landlord was an agent and a paid confederate helping strangers deal with the local people, but the individual who actually organized the exchange was another kind of market specialist called a *tefe.*[4]

Other variants of landlord-brokership were found in other parts of Senegambia and at earlier periods. Many of the Alkaati in Senegambian ports of the late seventeenth or early eighteenth centuries were government officials, landlords, and brokers all in one. In Portudal, in Bawol, for example, the Alkaati had a variety of houses available for assignment to visiting merchants. Some of the Tubabmansa on the upper Gambia did the same, supplying accommodation, acting as agents to buy provisions in the town, arranging interviews with the ruler or other higher officials, if such were necessary. Even the permanently established posts of the Afro-Europeans or independent European traders on the Gambia toward the end of the eighteenth century had a man to perform similar intermediary functions It was usually a local village head who accepted gifts and other payments on terms the

3. For variants on this pattern see La Courbe, *Premier voyage,* p. 195; "Mémoire concernant le commerce," enclosed with Commandant Gorée to CI, 4 July 1741, ANF, C6 12.

4. Meillassoux, "Kafo de Bamako," pp. 209–10; Monteil, *Djenné* (Paris, 1932), pp. 259–60; Monteil, *Khassonké,* pp. 125–27.

Europeans thought were ground rent. He then served as their protector and agent in dealing with local authorities. By the nineteenth century, even Europeans were acting as landlord-brokers. In Bakel, the visiting juula, who would once have gone automatically to one of the Soninke clerics as landlord, chose instead to stay with one of the *tubankooɓe* (Senegalese or European traders), who could offer the same range of services and were more effective intermediaries with the Senegalese government that now ran the town.[5]

Senegalese practice in general was close to that of the Gambia. The *maître de langue* was like the Gambian linguist in being broker as well as translator. Even the pay was on the same basis, a flat salary plus a commission on purchases. For that matter, interpreters were needed on either river only by traders fresh from Europe. Wolof was the principal trade language on the lower Senegal, and all French who lived long in Saint Louis learned enough to carry on their business. It was much the same on the Gambia, where Portuguese creole, the trade language of the seventeenth century, gradually gave way to Malinke, which became dominant by the end of the eighteenth. The maître de langue as a supplementary broker was therefore an important feature only of the ship trade along the Gambia, the Gajaaga trade, and the gum trade along the Senegal—in all of which Europeans had not yet accommodated to local custom and therefore needed an extra layer of brokerage, much as the early English and French traders had needed the Afro-Portuguese.[6]

Market Imperfections and Administered Prices

While the Senegambian economy was fundamentally competitive, competition was imperfect, as it is in most economies simply because the model of perfect competition is an analytic device, not a description of reality. Many factors reduced competition—imperfect economic contact between markets, difficulties in transportation, political interference, even geography. The Senegal was more naturally suited than the Gambia to restricted competition because oceangoing ships could not slip past Saint Louis as they

5. Moore, *Travels*, p. 127; Hull, "Voyage to Bundo," p. 1; Bruë to Collé, 9 December 1716, ANF, C6 5; Brüe to Violaine, 23 October 1719, ANF, C6 5; Saint-Adon to CI, 20 April 1729, ANF, C6 11; Adanson, *Voyage,* p. 108; Governor to Commandant Bakel, 31 December 1834, 13 G 204; Hammady Madi Sy, Medina Kojalaani, CC, T 7 (2).

6. Saugnier, *Voyages,* p. 276; Thomas Thurloe to RAC, 28 May 1678, T 70/10; unsigned, undated annotation of Labat, c. late 1740's, ANF, C6 29; Moore, *Travels,* p. 39; Saugnier, *Voyages,* p. 276. Even the salary of the maîtres de langue on the Senegal was similar to that of a linguist on the Gambia. The Senegalese got 8 bars a month, while the Gambian got 10. On the other hand, the commission per slave was 2 bars per slave in Saint Louis and only 1 bar per slave on the Gambia. But this may not have affected total income very much, since more slaves in larger lots were traded on the Gambia. (Sénégal, Dépenses Général, 1784, ANF, C6 16.)

could past James Island. This meant, among other things, that the government in Saint Louis could successfully support price controls through monopolies like the Galam Companies. In addition, gum, in the short run, was peculiarly insensitive to economic demand. Most Senegalese commentators in the early nineteenth century were convinced that it had a very low price-elasticity. Productivity was determined by weather and political stability at the gum forests and along the routes from there to the market, and gum was mainly a Senegalese, not a Gambian export.

In the background is the undeniable fact that the Compagnie des Indes and the Royal African Company were created and run in the frank hope of extracting a monopoly profit. Both had a legal monopoly over their respective national sectors of Senegambian trade. Both failed to make their legal right a practical reality. Though they were in continuous competition with one another, they hankered after controlled prices that would have staved off the financial failure that finally overtook them both. The natural solution might seem to be combination to fix prices. The two companies tried that briefly in 1700, setting prices for the imports and exports of the Gambia to force out the English private traders who threatened them both,[1] but the scheme failed, and efforts to do the same at later dates failed as well, probably because of the intensity of national competition for overseas trade.

The attempt to fix prices by the exercise of force was possible from the African side as well. In 1722, for example, the Brak of Waalo, Yeerim Mbañik, visited Saint Louis with a considerable army in order to press for a 20-per-cent increase in the bar price paid for slaves and a 33-per-cent decrease in the price asked for rum.[2] Pressure of this kind could sometimes be effective, especially in the short run, or in times when the balance of locally available power lay on the African side; but it was hard to sustain over a period of time, and African political authorities were more concerned with their own revenue than they were with the economy at large.

The more common and more successful device was to make a special deal with a trading company in favor of the royal exchequer, and these deals could sometimes amount to a genuine administered price. During the early eighteenth century, the French at Saint Louis and Gorée had special arrangements with the Damel of Kajor. The two parties agreed on a three-tiered price structure—one tariff for the Damel's personal trade, a second for his royal officials, and a third for the common people. Even the form of these prices was different from the usual bar prices of the period. The tariffs were not expressed in bars, but as separate schedules for each major export, listing its value in each common import.[3]

---

1. Bruë to Corker, Albreda, 20 April 1700, ANF, C6 29.
2. Julien du Bellay to CI, 28 December 1722, ANF, C6 7.
3. "Mémoire général sur le commerce du Sénégal," 1718, ANF, C6 14; Labat, *Nouvelle relation,* 4:235–37.

These arrangements are interesting evidence that the bar-price system was not universal and that barter-like trade survived into the eighteenth century, but they were not very important to the whole picture of Senegambian trade. The essence of that situation was an African would-be monopolist confronting a European would-be monopolist in circumstances where neither one had the slightest chance of commanding enough of the market to make his monopoly economically effective. The attempt was little more in the end than part of the complicated payoff that passed between major European firms and the local rulers.

It resembled the usual European effort to pay different prices to different categories of customer. Both the English and the French at some period paid more to the Afro-Portuguese than they did to other suppliers. They also tried to make their posts attractive to the big juula caravans from the interior by paying higher prices than they paid to the small-scale local trader, who brought little more than his own surplus production from the near vicinity. Though these arrangements were undoubtedly important weapons in trying to control the Senegambian trade, they were probably no more important as a source of imperfect competition than the present-day quantity discount or favorable deal for favorite customers.[4]

A more continuous influence toward imperfect competition was the price agreement between an African authority and the Europeans trading in his area. Like the prices on the Damel's list, these prices were administered and influenced by the play of supply and demand in the market place only in the long run. But the absence of market forces may be more apparent than real. The African institution underlying such agreements was often a form of collective bargaining, in which a single agent bargained for a group—possibly a town head, for all the people in his town. Collective bargaining of this kind could be invoked whenever the arrival of a caravan or a group of strange produce buyers created a situation of few buyers and many sellers. The practice was invoked from an early date for transactions with the Europeans. La Courbe, in 1685, described a millet-purchasing expedition to the lower Senegal, where the many potential sellers bargained on a price through the village head. Once that was settled, La Courbe was able to fill his twenty-ton ship in a day and a half—incidental evidence that surplus grain was marketed in considerable quantities.[5]

The Gajaaga trade practice at that time was similar. Three or four of the principal caravan leaders bargained collectively with the Europeans, for the whole group of African sellers, until a price was set for the season. Europeans preferred this system to a more open competition. One French official in 1734 argued that an agreed and steady price, even though it might be higher

4. "Mémoire concernant le commerce," enclosed with Commandant Gorée to CI, 4 June 1741, ANF, C6 12.
5. La Courbe, *Premier voyage,* pp. 98–99.

than was absolutely necessary, gave African merchants something they could count on and therefore encouraged a larger and more stable turnover than was otherwise possible. Lamiral, the Saintlouisien advocate of free competition at the time of the French Revolution, argued for collective bargaining between a representative of the Senegalese traders and the African merchants in Gajaaga. His fear was that Africans would hold their goods until the end of the high-water season, when they knew the Senegalese had to leave. Then they could drive a hard bargain.[6]

The preferred practice in the Gajaaga trade throughout the eighteenth century and on into the early nineteenth-century era of the gum trade was a bargained price. The evidence is not clear, however, that the preferred practice was the actual practice. A recurrent problem of the gum trade was that people on both sides had an interest in breaking the collectively agreed price, which made the agreement hard to enforce. At least in the Bundu provision trade of the 1730's, local conventions governed the practice to be followed if the initial price agreement broke down. There, the bargained price governed both the number of bars and the assortment for payment. If the buyer was forced to break the agreed assortment for lack of goods, the seller was entitled to change the bar price as well.[7] This and other evidence of chronic quarrels and rearrangements of initial price agreements suggests that the prices were bargained collectively at the beginning of the season and then changed by further collective bargaining as conditions changed, all of this accompanied by an unknown amount of trade outside the agreement. Even when the Senegalese end of the trade was in the hands of a legal monopoly like the Galam Companies or the Compagnie des Indes, the multitude of laptots had their own small cargoes to trade and their own trade contacts in the Gajaaga towns. It was also a recurrent complaint that the Moors and the juula alike were so price conscious they would travel many extra miles, regardless of cost, in order to sell high and buy low.[8]

Credit and Commercial Paper

Both Europeans and Africans were opposed in principle to the use of credit in circumstances like those of Senegambian trade. The Europeans were suspicious of loans across cultural boundaries, beyond the jurisdiction of "civilized' governments whose courts could help guarantee repay-

6. "Nouvel arrangement touchant la concession du Sénégal," BN, FF, NA, 9341, ff. 33–98; Lamiral, "Plan d'administration," 1791, ANF, C6 20.
7. Saint-Adon to CI, 2 December 1736, ANF, C6 11.
8. See, for example, Brossard to Governor, Bakel, 29 October 1853, ANF-OM, Sénégal IV 18.

ment. The Senegambian juula were Muslims as well as merchants, and Islam prohibits loans at interest.

But Muslims and Christians alike found a way around their early reluctance. For Muslims, the most convenient device was to make a contract in kind—so much millet today will be repayed with so many kola nuts in six months' time. The form is therefore a speculation in "futures," but the expectation on both sides would allow for a profit equivalent to interest. Many Muslims hold and have held that this practice is proscribed by Islam and *bida,* but it was and is extremely common in Senegambia.[1]

For Christians the advantage of lending to Africans in spite of the risk was not only the interest payments but the fact that loans gave the lender a competitive advantage over other buyers. The practice of lending in order to secure a quasi monopoly over the business of the debtors was suggested by the Gambia staff of the Royal African Company as early as 1677.[2] It began in the late seventeenth century and continued through the eighteenth and nineteenth centuries in a pattern of growing involvement by European capital in African trade.

Senegambian credit relations, however, were far less one-sided and far more complex than the usual oversimplified picture of the rich European lender and the poor African creditor. The books of the Royal African Company of the 1730's are a useful illustration of the possibilities. By that time, the Company had outstanding loans up to the value of £3,000 sterling or more on the Gambia alone, a sum nearly one-third the amount of its total annual subsidy from the British Parliament. The sum is large, but hardly surprising. The surprise comes from the fact that the Company was a net debtor. Taking the January 1 financial position on alternate years from 1735 to 1741, the Company's Gambia debts exceeded its Gambia credits by about 25 per cent. (See table 7.4.) A large number of the important creditors, however, were Europeans and often the Company's own servants to whom it owed back salary or other claims, while most of the debtors were people with African or Portuguese names having an average indebtedness of about £20 each. Taking only creditors or debtors with obviously African and Portuguese names, the Company's outstanding credits were about twice its debts at the beginning of 1737, 1739, and 1741.

The Company's books for the 1730's also show how it financed its suppliers. The typical operation was for the Company to loan an assortment of goods with a total value of 35 bars in return for the future delivery of "one good slave" at a time not specified but presumably within the year. Since the Company paid 40 bars for the cash delivery of "one good slave" in these

1. Hammady Mady Sy, Medina Kojalaani, CC, T 7 (2); Bakou Kaba, Tumbura, CC, T 13 (1).
2. Thomas Thurloe to RAC, 15 March 1677/78, T 70/10.

Table 7.4
Credit Position of the Royal African Company at James Fort, the Gambia
1735–41

Year	Total owed to RAC (£)	Number of debtors	Percentage of Portuguese or African names among debtors	Total owed by RAC (£)	Number of creditors	Percentage of Portuguese or African names among creditors
1735	2,192.30	79		3,799.60	52	
1737	2,662.69	136	73	4,267,37	58	39
1739	3,347.43	163	86	1,738.47	35	46
1741	3,107.68	148	85	4,345.26	50	28

Source: Statements of the position as of 1 January of each year, Gambia Accounts, T 70/563, 567, 571, and 575.

years, the discount of 12.5 per cent under current market represented the interest on a loan. The opposite operation was also common. A slave dealer with slaves to sell but no wish to take payment in the goods the Company had on hand could deliver the slaves against the promised future delivery of an itemized list of goods, usually to the total value of 45 bars or about 12.5 per cent premium over current market.[3]

Loans of both kinds were especially common at posts like those of Gajaaga, with their periodic isolation from the coast, and the practice was closely linked to the economics of holding slaves for sale. The Soninke clerics could hold their trade slaves more cheaply than the French could do at the fort. The Baacili secular rulers, on the other hand, captured slaves but rarely dealt in slaves, and they were anxious to get rid of their captives regardless of the season. They would therefore sell at the low, dry-season prices in return for a promised list of goods to be delivered when the river rose and the boats came up from Saint Louis. In this instance they might have to forego interest in order to avoid the difficulty and danger of holding captives they had taken themselves.[4] The amount of credit received in this form, however, was limited by the facilities for holding slaves at Fort Saint Joseph, and by the fact that the cost of holding slaves was greater than the interest for an equal period of time. Interest was about 50 per cent per year in Gajaaga in the 1740's. It was not worthwhile buying slaves on credit, therefore, unless the slaves could be shipped immediately. The French Company's tendency in Gajaaga of the 1720's and 1730's, however, was to receive interest-free credit from the Baacili, while at the same time extending credit with interest to the

3. These transactions occur frequently in the Gambia Accounts from 1727 through 1741 in the T 70 series, PRO.
4. Levens, Report of 10 July 1725, BN, FF, NA, 9339, f. 145.

Draame and other clerical families who traded further into the interior, often taking substantial loans of £200 to £300 sterling.[5]

African loans to European traders were largest in emergencies. During the Seven Years' War, when the English blockaded Saint Louis, the French Compay went on taking delivery of gum from the Moors on credit that amounted to a prime-cost value of nearly £1,000. The Company also went on buying millet and oxen on credit from Fuuta in order to feed Saint Louis. Some of the Moors extended credit to English traders as well during the English occupation of Fort Lewis in 1758–79, but the practice of selling to Europeans on credit was less and less common after the end of the eighteenth century. In the nineteenth, the flow of credit was very heavily in the other direction, though the Senegalese traders in Gajaaga ran short of goods in 1822 and again in 1827–28 and both times were forced to buy on credit.[6]

Credit relations between the Europeans and African states had obvious political overtones, but political loans were less common and less profitable than might be expected. The men-on-the-spot were often tempted to make loans to particular African political leaders for the purchase of war materials, but this was always discouraged in Europe for the obvious reason that a loan of this kind was hardly more than a wager on the uncertain outcome of a political contest. It was done, however, from time to time. In 1722, for example, rulers of Kajor and Bawol each planned to conquer the other kingdom. The Teeñ of Bawol borrowed the value of 18 to 20 slaves from the Royal African Company at Portudal. The Damel then borrowed the value of 5 slaves from the Compagnie des Indes at Saint Louis. The home office complained, but the French Company, at least, kept throwing good money after bad to protect the original investment. By 1726, the Damel's debt to the French had risen to 107 slaves, while the Teeñ himself owed them 41.[7]

Commercial loans in a productive enterprise were far more likely to be repaid, but collecting was not always easy if the borrower lived some distance away from the posts. In the early eighteenth century the British preferred to lend to Afro-Portuguese from the Gambia rather than to juula from the hinterland, just as the Compagnie des Indes preferred the Soninke of Gajaaga to other debtors. But both companies and their successors did, in

5. Saint-Robert to CI, 18 July 1725, ANF, C6 9.

6. Conseil du Sénégal to CI, 3 October 1757, CO 267/12; Le Bart to CI, Málaga, 30 November 1757, ANF, C6 14; John Barnes to African Committee, Fort Lewis, 27 August 1764, T 70/37; Lelieur de Ville-sur-Acre, report on Galam Voyage of 1822, ANF-OM, Sénégal IV 15, and report of 18 March 1828, ANS, 1 G 11.

7. Saint-Robert to CI, 28 December 1722, and Julien du Bellay to CI, 3 May 1722, ANF, C6 7; RAC to Glynn, 27 June 1732, T 70/55; Levens, Report of 10 July 1725, BN, FF, NA, 9339, f. 145 (copy also in ANF, C6 9); Saint-Robert to CI, 18 July 1725, ANF, C6 9; Director Saint Louis to CI, 7 July 1726, ANF, C6 10.

fact, lend to Africans who came from a distance. Yuuba Jaalo of Bundu was a regular and significant debtor of the Royal African Company after his return to Africa. Somewhat later, Dr. Laidley, the Gambia trader who helped Mungo Park, had money lent to juula in Xaaso and in Jara on the Malian sahal, beyond the range of any European traveler up to that time.[8]

No government sanction was available to force repayment, but loans were repaid even at this distance; and the main sanction (beyond the debtor's interest in borrowing again from the same source) was the solidarity of the juula as a social group, combined with the Senegambian notion of community liability. If a European ship committed acts of aggression on the coast or riverbank, the next European ship to appear was attacked in reprisal. If an individual defaulted on a loan, the creditor could seize another juula from the same ethnic group, preferably from the same village, if at all possible from the same lineage. The luckless scapegoat could then be held until the real debtor paid up, and the social pressure of the merchant community could force him to do so. In the case of government indebtedness, the annual gifts were one source of pressure, since they could be suspended or reduced as a form of punishment.[9]

Special variations of commercial practice grew up within the individual trade diasporas. Among the Afro-French of Saint Louis and Gorée, they were often based on French law, adjusted to a society that was only partly literate. Most of the active traders who actually went upriver were financed by capitalists from Saint Louis, sometimes the European firms, sometimes Africans who had already accumulated capital through trade. In the Gajaaga trade of the late eighteenth century, the usual contract was a "future" in slaves. Toward the end of the dry season, a lender paid 120 to 130 bars per slave to be delivered after the high season, thus giving six-months credit. Most of these bars were "heavy" bars, so the total paid would have been the value of £15 to £20. Once in Gajaaga, the trader could buy slaves for only 70 bars, and fewer heavy bars than he had collected—say, a value of £6 or £7. His markup of more than 100 per cent should have allowed for his profit, while the lender ended with a slave worth £25 to £30, for which he had paid £20 less than six months earlier, and his only risk was a drop in the price of slaves or an inability to collect the debt.[10]

8. Saint-Robert to CI, 18 July 1725, ANF, C6 9; Park, *Travels,* 1:126–30, 170; T 70/563–75.

9. Moore, *Travels,* pp. 80–81, 111–13; Memorial from Masters of Vessels Trading at Ñanimaru, 4 July 1764, CO 267/13; Mémoire générale sur le commerce du Sénégal, ANF, C6 14 (1718); Park, *Travels,* 1:450.

10. This account of the Gajaaga trade c. 1785 is based principally on Saugnier, *Voyages,* esp. pp. 270–83. The example comes from a period when slave prices in Senegambia were near their all-time peak, which may have brought windfall profits

Alternate arrangements made it possible to spread the risk more widely. Slaves could be considered the lender's property from the moment of acquisition in Gajaaga, and at that moment the borrowing trader would switch from his first role as entrepreneur to become a mere agent. In this way, the borrower took the risk for the trip upstream and the purchase, while the lender assumed any losses during the trip back down—but to compensate for the greater risk, the capitalist paid only the value of £11 for the "future." Or, if he wanted to assume the whole risk himself, he could outfit a boat and hire a captain to make the whole voyage on his account.

Commercial contracts in Saint Louis were confirmed by an oral ceremony in the presence of the mayor. The two parties appeared with at least three witnesses and a number of guarantors, usually relatives of the debtor. The terms of the agreement were stated and then written down, not as so many bars, but as an itemized list of trade goods turned over to the borrower and of the commodities he would repay at the end of the period. The lender then made a small gift to the mayor and each of the witnesses, and the agreement was closed. If the debtor failed to repay at the stated time, the guarantors became responsible. On complaint to the mayor, their property could be seized along with that of the debtor. Slaves who were seized, however, could not be sold unless they were trade slaves; domestic slaves simply worked for the lender rather than the debtor. The mayor's function in all this was not simply to enforce the contract but also to arbitrate between the parties. If it could be established that the debtor's failure was simply bad luck, the loan could be extended for a second season as a chance to recover the loss; but this time the contract would call for a higher rate of interest and stiffer guarantees of repayment.

The historical record tells much less of credit relations within the purely African trade diasporas. They must have had institutional patterns for commercial loans, since they borrowed from and lent to the Europeans on the coast, but the network of credit that must have existed left no substantial evidence.

The record is equally vague about transactions later associated with banking. Bills drawn on London or Paris, for example, were a common means of payment in the coastal entrepôts. African traders were also willing to accept commercial paper toward the end of the eighteenth century and later, though when it was introduced and how much it was used remain a mystery. The clearest evidence comes from Mungo Park's account of his first journey into the interior in 1795–97. Dr. Laidley, the private trader based at Pisania on

higher than usual to the Saint Louis capitalists; but Saugnier regarded this arrangement as unusually favorable to the traders who made the trip, and pointed out that the capitalists expected a rate of interest in the neighborhood of 50 per cent.

the Gambia, gave Park bills drawn on various of his debtors in the interior, mainly caravan leaders to whom Laidley had given advances. In two cases, Park was able to collect from these men by presenting Laidley's bill, picking up goods to the value of two slaves at Konaikari in Xaaso and the value of three at Jaara in Kaarta. On the return journey, Park arranged for Karfa Ture, a saatigi at Kamalia near Bamako, to bring him through to the Gambia. In order to make sure that Karfa would be paid if he himself should die along the way, he gave Karfa a bill drawn on Dr. Laidley for the value of one good slave, and this was apparently perfectly acceptable. Two decades later, when Major Gray followed Park's first march eastward from Wuuli, Gray found himself short of goods to pay the Almaami for transit across Bundu, but the Almaami was willing to accept an order on the Gambia for 120 bottles of gunpowder, 20 trade guns, and a blunderbus.[11] We are left with this tantalizing and specific evidence but nothing more than guess as to the origin or full extent of these practices.

11. Park, *Travels*, 1:126–30, 170; Gray, *Western Africa*, p. 116.

8 | EXTERNAL TRADE

External trade usually comes first in writing about African economic history, mainly because the historiographic tradition was laid down by Europeans who first saw Africa through the commerce that linked the two societies. This time it has been left till last, partly to help maintain a Senegambian perspective, partly because the aggregates of imports and exports bring together and summarize topics like the slave trade or production for export that have already been discussed in a narrower context. When the aggregates are assembled and the quantitative records, projections, and estimates are laid on the line for interpretation, they raise some serious questions about the older interpretations, not only of Senegambian economic history but of precolonial African economic history in general. In suggesting a reinterpretation of Senegambian economic history, they suggest that similar reinterpretations may well be required for other regions too.

The received wisdom about the precolonial trade of West Africa is that Africans exported mainly slaves and received in return worthless goods such as cheap gewgaws, beads, rum, and firearms. As an overtone, it carries the judgment that the Europeans hoodwinked a group of ignorant savages into parting with something of considerable value in return for nothing, or even for goods that were positively harmful—called in the period of enforced suppression the "arms traffic" and the "liquor traffic." For all of this time, from the first Portuguese voyages down the African coast in the fifteenth century to the early nineteenth century, African economies were taken to have been stagnant, static, or perhaps even retrograde as production and living standards were reduced by the slave trade.

Then, the thesis continues, in the first decades of the nineteenth century, humanitarians in Europe and America finally recognized the basic immorality of this system and forced their respective nations to bring the slave trade to

309

an end. At first, the African economies continued in their accustomed stagnation, till they were gradually revived by the activities of a new group of European merchants offering "legitimate trade," exchanging European manufactures for such products as palm oil and peanuts. As a result, Africa was linked to the world markets in an "economic revolution" of rising exports, rising production, and rising gross national product—though "national" product was something of a misnomer, since most of Africa was on its way into the colonial period before the economic revolution was well under way.

This economic revolution was first identified by McPhee, who placed it, for British West Africa at least, in the period between 1895 and the First World War. Since McPhee's time, others have revised the outline in various ways. An influential interpretation by Eric Williams tended to change the European motives from humanitarian to economic self interest. Still others have tended to push the early phases of the economic revolution back in time to have it begin about 1880, as early as 1850, or occasionally in the 1830's, but not earlier.[1] Robert Szereszewski, writing about Ghana in 1965, still located the core of the revolution in 1891–1911, as McPhee had done, and for him the economic order that had gone before was dominated by "traditional agriculture and collection of forest produce, traditional crafts—and by trade flows whose nature in terms of organization, conveyance, spatial incidence and type of commodities had not changed significantly over centuries."[2]

The standard view is not completely wrong in all respects, and much of it was based on solid and well-conducted research dealing with the period of the "economic revolution" itself. The problem is that some historians have been too willing to accept, and to interweave into their own specific research, some of the assumptions earlier Europeans had made about Africa—usually without research. Among these was the belief that African economies must have been static. It follows from the myth of a savage Africa, and it led to the assumption that any deep-seated change must have come about on European, not African, initiative. That, in turn, goes back to the assumption of African weakness and perhaps inherent inferiority. This belief that Africans were and had always been economically, politically, and militarily weaker than the West drew something from the actual power relations that existed from the middle of the nineteenth century, coupled with the easy assumption (for Europeans) that things had always been that way. And, from about that time

1. Alan McPhee, *The Economic Revolution in British West Africa* (London, 1926). For a recent synthesis see C. W. Newbury, "Trade and Authority in West Africa from 1850 to 1880," in L. H. Gann and Peter Duignan, eds., *Colonialism in Africa*, 3 vols. to date (Cambridge, 1967–),1:66–99.

2. R. Szereszewski, *Structural Changes in the Economy of Ghana 1891–1911* (London, 1965), p. 1.

onward, the sentiment could draw endlessly from the well of European pseudoscientific racism.

One approach to a sounder understanding is to move consciously beyond the old assumptions and look for a more measured view of Afro-European commercial relations in the precolonial period. We now know enough about the enormous changes that industrialism brought to Europe to recognize that most of the difference in relative power, as it was seen in the nineteenth century, was comparatively recent in origin. That is, Europe jumped ahead in a long wave of technological advance beginning a little after the year 1000, and the speed of scientific progress was especially striking after the seventeenth century. Africa, along with the rest of the world, was left behind. It looked comparatively static to nineteenth-century Europeans overwhelmed by their own rails and steam, but Africa was no more static than other societies outside the West. One of the big problems, for which the study of Senegambia is only a part of a clue, is to understand how societies whose pace of technological change was very different interacted economically. The mythic character of the old stereotype of gewgaws for slaves has already been exposed by the scholarship of the past ten or fifteen years. The next step is to move forward with the considerable body of quantitative data available and to see how far trade data can serve as a set of socioeconomic indicators of other changes in African societies.

So far, historians have not pushed very far toward a quantified economic history of precolonial Africa. The Senegambian data assembled here and in the *Supplement,* appendix 15, are therefore sometimes more puzzling than helpful. When they contradict older, nonquantified historiography, three possibilities are open. Either the data are wrong, Senegambia is an exception to the general West African pattern of change, or the older historiography is wrong about the whole region. Comparable data from other regions will no doubt clarify many points that for the moment must be tentative, while other points will be corrected or contradicted. Appendices in the *Supplement,* appendix 15 in particular, are intentionally fuller than they need be so that other scholars can replicate the method to arrive at comparable data, while the text of this chapter will seek to explain what seems to be explicable at present, and mainly for Senegambia alone.

Imports

With its unique position of facing at once on both the Atlantic and the desert, Senegambia could hardly be a type-case for all West Africa, though it might exemplify certain common patterns. Senegambian differences are obvious as early as the seventeenth century, when iron imports were far heavier than they were elsewhere, coming to about half the total of Senegambian imports in mid-century.[1] The explanation in this case is easy; coastal Senegambia had no significant iron industry of its own, while most of the rest of West Africa did. The result is also obvious in the development of iron-bar currency, while other coastal regions went to gold dust, cowries, brass manilas, or various textiles.

But iron bars are a semimanufactured product; the iron had to be processed before it could be used. This fact strikes at the deeper implications of the gewgaw myth. The myth implies that Africans foolishly bought articles of adornment or luxuries that served no basic human need, and in return for a basic resource—human beings. In fact, the iron was not only a raw material for the Senegambian smiths; much of it became capital goods. Though some went into lance and javelin heads, most took the form of hoes and other tools for the further increase of Senegambian agricultural productivity.

The place of iron among Senegambian imports declined after the mid-seventeenth century, but it still came to a third of all imports in the 1680's. The high proportion of iron was a principal mark distinguishing Senegambia from other parts of West Africa. The Royal African Company's account books from the London office and from the Gambia are compared in table 8.1. The dates are slightly different, and some differences would be expected on other grounds. As a cloth-manufacturing and cloth-exporting region, Senegambian cloth imports should be low, and they were.[2] Arms and ammunition held about the same place they did elsewhere, again as expected. The striking and unexpected difference is in the important place of beads and semiprecious stones, and of silver, which was mainly used at this period as raw material for the jewelry industry. This was no short-term fluke but a continuing feature of the Senegambian market, as is illustrated by column 2, which gives the distribution of imports by commodity in the 1730's. In fact, columns 1 and 2 for the Gambia have a clear family resemblance to one another, even though they were samples a half-century apart, while both are different from the general African pattern of column 3. Changes between the two periods are nevertheless significant—a continued fall in raw iron, a rise in silver and firearms, and a shift of luxury imports from beads to textiles. The difference between the columns also underlines a point often made by contemporaneous

1. Dapper in *BIFAN*, 32:538.
2. The 1680's figure for textiles, however, may be too low, since it is considerably lower than is usual for Senegambia at other times or for other parts of West Africa at that time. The fault may be in the difficulty of making a significant aggregation of different *kinds* of textiles, none of which was important enough by itself to be taken into account. Common sense would indicate a guess that the figure was really closer to that shown for the 1730's.

Table 8.1

Gambian Imports 1683–88 and 1731–41 Compared to Royal African Company's
Exports to Africa 1680–82

Commodities	(1) Gambian imports 1684–88		(2) Gambian imports 1731–41		Royal African Company exports, 1680–82	
Metals and metalware		33.7		34.6		22.4
Iron bars	24.9		8.2		11.1	
Silver coins	4.2		16.3		–	
Copper rods	1.0		.8		4.5	
Brassware	1.7		7.6		4.9	
Pewterware	1.9		1.7		1.9	
Woolen cloth		1.4		3.1		28.1
Perpetuanas	–		–		13.9	
Red cloth	1.4		3.1		–	
Says	–		–		13.3	
Welsh plains	–		–		0.9	
Indian textiles		1.6		7.5		18.3
Allejaes	–		–		1.0	
Bafts	–		2.3		1.4	
Brawles	–		–		2.5	
Guinea stuffs	–		–		1.9	
Long cloths	–		5.2		2.8	
Longees	–		–		1.2	
Nicconees	–		–		2.3	
Pautkes	–		–		1.6	
Tapseels	1.6		–		3.6	
Other textiles		1.0		11.2		14.4
Annabasses	–		–		3.5	
Carpets	–		–		0.1	
Silesias (linen)	1.0		4.4		4.7	
Sheets	–		–		5.4	
Boysados	–		–		0.7	
Fringe	–		5.4		–	
Manchester cloth	–		1.4		–	
Cutlery and weapons		8.1		13.8		6.4
Firearms	1.5		8.9		2.7	
Gunpowder	1.2		4.9		3.1	
Knives	–		–		0.6	
Swords	5.4		–		–	
Cowrie Shells	–	–	–	–	7.2	7.2
Brandy	14.1	14.1	4.2	4.2	–	–
Beads and semi-precious stones		39.9		25.7		3.1
Glass beads	13.9		11.3		1.8	
Coral	7.0		1.9		1.3	
Amber	11.4		–		–	
Crystal	7.6		8.5		–	
Carnelians	–		4.0		–	
Total	100.0	100.0	100.0	100.0	100.0	100.0

Sources: K. G. Davies, *Royal African Company*, pp. 350–57; T 70/546. See *Supplement*, appendix 15.

observers on the coast: the African demand rather than the preference of the English supplier determined what was and was not imported.

The English imports to the Gambia, however, were only a part of the picture. Although French archives contain nothing as detailed as the Gambian accounts of the mid-1680's, an official of the Compagnie des Indes made a survey of Senegalese demand in about 1718. The pattern of imports again bore a family resemblance to that of the Gambia. (Compare columns 7 and 8, table 8.2.) But the survey of the Compagnie des Indes went further still and separated the estimated imports into local market areas, showing that the pattern as a whole was in fact the sum of quite disparate subregional demands for European goods. The Gambian pattern must also have been the sum of similar and diverse demands.

The patterns in the 1718 survey tend to confirm what was already known about the economic characteristics of each sub-region. Waalo and northern Kajor, for example, produced no iron of their own; their heavy demand for European iron would be expected. Gajaaga, with its own iron industry and close ties to that of Bundu, would be expected to buy less from overseas. In fact, the survey shows that it bought none at all. The middling demand from the hinterland of the petite côte and the lower Gambia also follows expectations, since that region bought iron from the interior as well as from the Europeans. And textile imports follow expectations in much the same way. High imports went to places like southern Mauritania, with negligible production of its own, while places that were themselves net exporters of cloth bought much less of the European varieties.

Other aspects of the distribution are harder to explain, or at least the explanations have to be more speculative. Beads and semiprecious stones, for example, show a skewed distribution, with the greatest demand in the south and east, least in the west and north. In part, this preference is reflected in the high value placed on amber in eastern Senegal and the Niger valley, down to the recent past. But amber, coral, and carnelians were also well suited to the overland trade on account of their high value and low bulk. Cowries were sent east where they had monetary value, and the distribution of firearms follows from the fact that they were not yet in common military use beyond the coastal region.

Other imports (too low in value to appear on table 8.2) also show a distribution pattern that fits what is known about Senegalese society at that time. Paper consumption is an index of literacy and hence of Islamic learning. It accounted for some 3.5 per cent of expected sales to Gajaaga, 1.5 per cent to the region of Saint Louis, 1.6 per cent on the Gambia, and little or nothing elsewhere. Since Fuuta Tooro was joined to Saint Louis in this survey, the Saint Louis figure would reflect the strength of Islam there and in northern Wolof country; and brandy consumption is an inverse fit, since serious

Muslims drank little. Thus the high consumption by the Sereer of Siin, which continued into the twentieth century as the least Muslim region in Senegambia.

Table 8.3 carries the pattern of Senegambian imports on into the early nineteenth century by half-century intervals, though with a gap for lack of data on the 1780's. What information is available, however, suggests that the new pattern of the nineteenth century emerged after the 1780's rather than before, leaving the distribution of imports remarkably stable over the century 1690–1790. The slightly different mix of goods imported to the Gambia as distinct from the Senegal also persisted, as the English imported more beads, semiprecious stones, and weapons, while the French continued to meet the high demand for textiles in their trade region. Some quality differences may also have reinforced local preferences, if we can believe the French traders who thought they sold more textiles because their customers preferred French goods to English, just as they complained chronically of the quality of firearms and gunpowder sent out from France.

Within any category of imports, such as textiles or brassware, the Senegambian taste was remarkably constant in regard to a few items, but otherwise extremely fickle about style and design. Several of the constant market preferences persisted from the early days of trade with Europe, simply because people were used to certain products the Dutch or Portuguese had first supplied. This meant that English and French traders of the eighteenth century had to draw from the old source of supply or else copy the designs. "Flemish" knives, for example, were a staple of the trade. In fact, the original ones came from Solingen, not Flanders, though a few were made in the region of Liège and Namur. But the English began to produce their own Flemish knives even before the end of the seventeenth century.

Brass pans of the type known as Guinea pans, on the other hand, originated as a straight-sided Spanish pan about 21 cm high. With time, the pans became shorter and came in a variety of different sizes. The French made three, one at 1 kg, one at .75 kg, and one at .50 kg (varying in size from 31 cm diameter by 8 cm depth for the largest to 22 cm diameter by 5.5 cm depth for the smallest). But even a steady seller like the Guinea pan could come and go in fashion. In the late 1740's, they were a drug on the market in Gajaaga, only to come back in 1754 and 1755, when nearly 20,000 were sold.[3]

The gewgaw image of the African trade originated with glass beads, which were extremely cheap and sold in large quantities. The price of ordinary beads manufactured in Venice or Holland varied between £80 and £120 a metric ton, and they were usually sold in Europe by weight. In Africa, on the

3. Dapper, *Description de l'Afrique,* p. 236; Conseil du Sénégal "Nouvelles observations sur la qualité des marchandises," 10 June 1736, ANF, C6 11. Conseil du Sénégal, 31 July 1755, ANF, C6 16.

Table 8.2

Regional Internal Distribution of Senegambian Imports, 1718, Expressed in Percentages of the Total
Value of Imports

(Estimated imports by Compagnie des Indes, 1718, by regions)

Commodity	(1) Waalo and northern Kajor	(2) Trarza	(3) Gajaaga	(4) Bawol and south Kajor	(5) Siin	(6) Lower Gambia	(7) Total CI	(8) Gambian RAC imports of 1731–41
Metals and metalware	31.7	11.7	33.1	28.6	27.1	29.6	29.2	34.6
Iron bars	18.3	–	–	10.4	10.2	8.2	8.5	8.2
Silver coin	9.0	11.7	20.1	15.6	16.9	8.2	12.8	16.3
Worked silver	.7	–	–	1.5	–	–	.4	–
Copper	3.7	–	–	.2	–	.8	1.0	.8
Brassware	–	–	–	.9	–	12.2	3.8	7.6
Pewterware	–	–	13.0	–	–	.2	2.7	1.7
Textiles	33.8	83.1	6.7	25.1	11.0	11.3	23.0	21.8
Clothing	1.6	–	–	1.1	–	1.6	1.0	–
Cutlery and weapons	7.9	1.9	0.6	12.3	2.5	3.0	5.3	13.8
Firearms	4.1	–	–	7.4	–	–	2.3	8.9
Ammunition	3.8	–	–	3.7	2.5	2.1	2.2	4.9
Swords	–	–	0.6	1.2	–	0.8	0.6	–
Flemish knives	–	1.9	–	–	–	0.1	0.2	–
Beads and semi-precious stones	22.4	–	49.5	20.9	30.5	49.2	34.0	25.7

Food and spices (cloves and salt)	0.3	—	5.3	0.4	—	—	1.2
Misc. manufactures (paper, mirrors, combs, padlocks, etc.)	2.1	3.2	3.5	—	—	1.6	1.8
Brandy or spirits	—	—	—	11.0	25.4	2.0	3.6
Cowries	0.2	—	1.2	0.6	3.4	1.6	1.0
Total	100.0	100.0	100.0	100.0	100.0	100.0	100.0

Sources: Cols. 1–7, "Mémoire général sur le commerce du Sénégal," [1718 or 1719] ANF, C6 14, a projection of the future needs of each department of the Senegal trade of the Compagnie des Indes. Col. 8 from table 8.1, col. 2.

Table 8.3

Estimated Proportions of Certain Major Imports
in Senegambian Total Imports
1680's, 1730's, and 1830's

Commodities	1680's (per cent)	1730's (per cent)	1830's (per cent)
Metals			
Iron	24.9	21.2	1.5
Silver	4.2	10.2	3.9
Copper	1.0	0.5	–
Brass	1.7	4.8	–
Pewter	1.9	1.1	–
European textiles	2.4	9.7	25.0
Indian textiles	1.6	18.5	33.9
Cutlery and weapons			
Firearms	1.5	5.6	6.0
Gunpowder	1.2	4.0	3.8
Cutlery	5.4	1.0	–
Beads and semi-precious stones	39.9	18.0	8.8
Spirits	14.1	4.8	7.1
Paper	–	0.5	–
Tobacco	–	–	10.0

Sources: Sample of 1680's based on Gambia only, from table 8.1. Data for 1730's from table 8.1 (for Gambia) and *Supplement* table A15.1 (for Senegal), weighted in proportion to export values, 37.2 per cent for Senegal, 62.8 per cent for Gambia. Data for 1830's from *Supplement* tables A15.1 (for Senegal) and A15.2 (for Gambia), weighted in proportion to export values of 1832–34, at 25.8 per cent for Gambia and 74.2 per cent for Senegal, the weighted total then adjusted for estimated silver imports. See *Supplement*, appendix 15.

other hand, they were often sold by a conventional measure called a mass, made up of 12 "branches," in turn divided into 10 "strings." Since the weight of the individual beads varied a good deal, the weight of a mass could differ from one type to another by a factor of two to three. This implied a real difference between cost and selling price, depending on type—and anywhere from a dozen to forty different styles and types were normally stocked in the

Senegal trade. The result is a large area of uncertainty and a wide spread of £/bar ratios between different beads, even though none of them had an especially low £/bar ratio.

Nor were all beads in the category of the cheap glass beads. Large and medium stones of amber cost at least £3 per kilogram in eighteenth-century Europe, rising to the range of £10 to £14 in the early nineteenth. Carnelians from Bombay (*cornalines* in Senegalese French, *arrangoes* in Gambian English) cost as much as £.43 each at the beginning of the eighteenth century, and coral at £5 to £10 a kilogram was clearly in the luxury class and was also near the top of the range of £/bar ratios. Even crystal was far from cheap. A thousand stones of no. 22 (one of the better grades, though not the best) sold in the range of £1.50 to £2 in the last decades of the seventeenth century.[4]

Textiles were like beads in variety and changing fashion. At one time or another, Senegambians bought virtually every type of cloth available in Europe or India, though only a few remained on the import lists decade after decade. Among European textiles, the most popular of all over the long run was the linen called Silesias or Slesias by the English, platilles by the French. As the English name suggests, it originally came from Silesia by way of Hamburg and Dutch trade links. By the middle of the eighteenth century, however, the English made their own Silesias, and Bretons too were experimenting with imitations.[5]

European textiles, however, were less popular than Indian cotton goods. The most consistently popular were the types known in English as niconees and tapseals, though neither became dominant in the way that the pièce de Guinée finally conquered the Senegalese market in the early nineteenth century. Both were woven mainly in western India, tapseals in Cambay and Ahmadabad in Sind, niconees in Broach and Baroda. Both were light cloths patterned on the loom, about 8 to 9 meters long by 1 meter wide. Tapseals, however, were of mixed silk and cotton, while niconees were a striped calico.[6]

Information on other types is apt to be more elusive, because of the

4. Price information about Senegambian imports is most readily available in the Invoice Books, Outward, of the RAC, T 70/921 and succeeding volumes, in the Gambia account books, T 70/836 and succeeding volumes, in the annual customs statistics from 1832 onward in Statistiques coloniales and Gambia Blue Books in the PRO, both annual series. Occasional inventories and lists fill in periods not covered in the longer series, such as the returns for Sénégal et dépendances, 1 January 1818, ANF-OM, Sénégal XIII 72, or the inventory by N. M. Michel of Nantes, April 1704, quoted in Gaston Martin, *Nantes au xviiie siècle: L'ère des négriers (1714–1774)* (Paris, 1931), pp. 48–52.

5. Chambon, *Le commerce de l'Amérique par Marseille, ou explication des lettres-patentes du roi,* 2 vols. (Avignon, 1764), 2:395–96.

6. Irwin and Schwartz, *Indo-European Textile History;* Chambon, *Commerce par Marseilles,* 2:385 ff.; R. Wissett, *A Compendium of East Indian Affairs,* 2 vols. (London, 1802), vol. 2, no pagination.

different names used for similar cloths and the similar names for different cloths. The contrast between the light "Guinea stuffs" of English usage and the heavy, indigo-dyed pièce de Guinée is an obvious example. One textile that went by the name "long cloth" was equally confusing. Toward the end of the seventeenth century, it was an Indian cotton, and it was long—about 34 meters in each piece. It was available in blue, white, or brown, originally from Golconda but later from Madras as well. By the nineteenth century, however, the term "long cloth" had been transferred to a Lancashire calico. Meanwhile, still another Indian textile was called longee, but this time the name was derived from the Hindi *lungī*, meaning a body wrapper.[7]

Several terms for Indian textiles began, like long cloth, as simple descriptions which became more and more specified until they meant definite types with set standards. This was the history of the bafatas, which became the English bafts. In much the same way, *alacha*, meaning striped, became Anglicized and specified until it ended as the allejae or allejar, a light striped cotton from Coromandel in either blue and white or red and white. The size of the piece was also fairly standard over long periods, but it *could* change without the change showing on the record. Most, however, were about 14 or 15 meters long and 1 meter wide—a size that was standard for bejutapauts of heavy blue or blue and white cotton, or for the lighter chelloes or chelas, patterned on the loom. Aside from the familiar tapseals and niconees, however, other cloths tended to come and go on Senegambian shipping lists, with the pauktas, brawles, and long cloths of the late seventeenth century giving way to new types like chelloes and bejutapauts in the middle of the eighteenth.[8]

Changing tastes, types, weights, and sizes make it hard to trace changing patterns of manufactured imports, but a few of the most important were uniform enough over time to leave a usable record. Two estimates or orders for goods needed by the Compagnie des Indes, centering on 1718 and 1753 respectively, make it possible to construct index numbers measuring the changing prices and quantities of six selected imports over a period of 120 years.[9] The results in table 8.4 and figure 8.1 cannot be accurate to the last

7. H. Yule and A. C. Burnell, *Hobson-Jobson* (London, 1903), p. 519; Irwin and Schwartz, *Indo-European Textile History*, p. 67.

8. Irwin and Schwartz, *Indo-European Textile History*, pp. 57–58, 62; Wissett, *East Indian Affairs*, vol. 2; O. Rinchon, *Le trafic négrier d'après les livres de commerce du capitaine gantois Pierre-Ignace-Liévin Van Alstein*, vol. 1 (Paris, 1938), pp. 100–101.

9. These index numbers follow the indications of R. G. D. Allen, "Index Numbers of Volume and Price," in R. G. D. Allen and J. E. Ely, eds., *International Trade Statistics* (New York, 1953), pp. 186–211. The value in each case is the quantity imported times the price in Europe, f.o.b. The index of volume or quantity traded is established by reference to the prices in the base year. That is, volume equals current year's imports at 1718 prices divided by 1718 exports at 1718 prices x 100, to translate into a base-100 index number.

Table 8.4
Index Numbers for the Value, Volume, and Price
of Selected Commodities Imported into Senegambia,
1718, 1753, and 1838
(1718 = 100)

	1718	1753	1838
Silver			
Annual average value	100	76	294
Quantity	100	76	294
Price	100	100	100
Firearms			
Annual average value	100	462	1,397
Quantity	100	798	1,292
Price	100	58	108
Gunpowder			
Annual average value	100	60	985
Quantity	100	238	33,149
Price	100	25	30
Iron			
Annual average value	100	115	59
Quantity	100	187	94
Price	100	62	62
Brandy			
Annual average value	100	51	201
Quantity	100	403	1,317
Price	100	13	15
Pièces de Guinée			
Annual average value	100	222	74,947
Quantity	100	339	110,373
Price	100	66	68

Sources: Data for 1718 and 1752–54 from *Supplement* table A15.3, with price of guns adjusted to that of trade guns for all dates. Data for 1838 is the annual average of 1836–40 as reported in *Statistiques coloniales* for those years.

digit, but they measure such enormous changes that absolute precision is not needed to show an underlying pattern. Virtually all quantities increased sharply over the period, while all prices dropped. Prices tended to level out in the second interval (from the 1750's to the 1830's), but quantities continued to increase overall as rapidly as they had done up to the 1750's.

The performance of these major imports over an extended period separates them into three pairs. Iron and silver, the long-important raw materials for the Senegambian smiths, remained comparatively steady in volume and price, though a progressively smaller part of all imports. A second group, consisting of firearms and brandy, had steeply falling prices over the first interval, matched by rising volume. After 1753, however, prices stabilized, but volume continued to rise as rapidly as ever. (See figure 8.1, where the rate of change on the semilogarithmic graph is represented by the angle of the line.) The third group, guinées and gunpowder, began with slightly lower rates of increase in volume, which turned to spectacular increases after the 1750's.

Several aspects of this pattern are significant. Import prices, at least, seem to have had little or nothing to do with demand—Senegambians bought more from Europe because their earnings from exports made it possible, and their

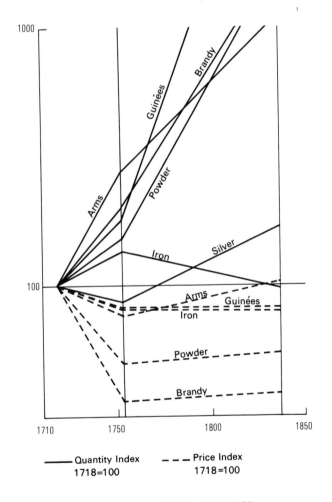

8.1 Senegambian Imports by Quantity and Value, 1718–1838

UWCL

choice of what to buy was made for other reasons than price. The enormous increase in the purchase of guinées, for example, is simply a reflex of the increase in the gum trade. The Moors who supplied the gum had the purchasing power, and textiles were what they wanted. But the brandy purchases raise another kind of question. If the spatial distribution of brandy imports in 1718 followed the spatial distribution of non-Muslim populations, the rise in brandy imports suggests that Islam may have been declining; but other kinds of evidence point to a rise of Islam in this period before the outbreak of the religious wars. The better explanation, though still speculative, is that rising brandy imports indicate a shift in power within Senegambian societies, as the ceddo and the military generally increased in wealth and power at the expense of the clerics and the Muslim peasantry.

The rise of firearms and gunpowder is also a quantitative indicator of trends that were already clear from qualitative evidence. Firearms had not been an important aspect of Senegambian trade in the sixteenth or early seventeenth centuries. Senegambian military power at that time depended more on horses, which the Portuguese furnished; and the Portuguese for their part frequently embargoed the export of iron or firearms to Africa, though some certainly came through.[10] Mid-seventeenth-century travelers were unanimous in their descriptions of Wolof warfare as dominated by spear and javelin for the cavalry and poisoned arrows for infantry. As late as 1677, the Wolof were still making little use of firearms for warfare, though arms were beginning to be imported in small quantities. The real switch, for the coastal zone, was in the 1680's and 1690's.[11]

Up to a decade or so ago, the lateness of that date would have been surprising, since the stereotype of arms and gewgaws in exchange for slaves was the accepted view for the whole four centuries of the slave trade. Recent new research has revised the old view, so that firearms are now seen as a significant factor in Afro-European relations only in the eighteenth century and later. The problem for musketeers was that reloading was slow, taking a minute or more, which put them at the mercy of a cavalry charge, in open country, or of rapid fire by archers using poisoned arrows, in thick brush. In Europe the significant change in the seventeenth century had been the development of rapid-fire field artillery,[12] but the Europeans did not use that

10. Rodney, *Upper Guinea Coast*, pp. 173–77.

11. Alexis de Saint-Lo, *Relation du voyage au Cap Verde* (Paris and Rouen, 1637), p. 118; C. Jannequin, *Voyage de Lybie au royaume de Sénégal* . . . (Paris, 1643), pp. 152–53; Chambonneau in Ritchie, "Deux Textes," *BIFAN*, 30:324–25; Comte d'Estrées, "Mémoire tant sur l'arrivée des vaisseaux du Roy au Cap Vert et leur ses jour en ces rades que sur le Commerce qu'on peu faire à ces costes jusques à la rivière de Gambie," BN, Mélanges Colbert, 176:ff. 225–32.

12. See G. White, "Firearms in Africa: An Introduction," *JAH*, 12:173–85 (1971); R. A. Kea, "Firearms and Warfare on the Gold and Slave Coasts from the Sixteenth to the Nineteenth Centuries, *JAH*, 12:185–213 (1871); Cippola, *Guns and Sails*, passim.

weapon overseas until well into the eighteenth. For Senegambia, the key change in Europe was the development of cheap and ordinarily reliable flintlocks in the 1690's. Very few changes in the basic form of muzzle-loader took place for more than a century and a half after that, and guns of the same type were still manufactured for sale in West Africa into the twentieth century.

The result was the ordinary musket or "trade gun." Its cost was remarkably uniform between French and British suppliers and between one decade and another. The higher cost shown for 1718 in table 8.4 came about only because the official estimates of that date were based on the more expensive buccaneer gun. The common trade gun sold for £.40 to £.80 in the late seventeenth century, £.40 to £.50 in the eighteenth, and £.40 to £.60 in the early nineteenth. But the trade gun was not alone; other guns sold for several times the price, though in much smaller quantities. In 1777, for example, the Compagnie des Indes offered a range from trade guns that cost £.336 in France, through to the top of the line, a double-barreled gun costing £1.25. By the 1820's, the variety was even greater, from the ordinary trade gun costing the equivalent of £.48, through seven other types, to a double-barreled gun costing £3.68. Even the cheaper guns had to be selected with an eye to local taste: in the 1780's, the Moors and the Soninke from Gajaaga eastward preferred their guns bronzed or gilded, with silver trim, while copper trim sold better in the Gorée markets, and steel trim was preferred on the lower Senegal.[13]

Once the coast was armed, the interior followed. The Moroccan forces using guns along the desert fringe after 1719 (and occasionally earlier) were one incentive, though not so powerful as might be anticipated, since the Moroccans were sometimes beaten by armies without guns. In spite of the fact that the Compagnie des Indes tried sporadically until 1736–37 to prevent the sale of guns in the interior, the English on the Gambia were willing to supply all comers. Fuuta Tooro began to convert to firearms for warfare in the 1730's, and guns were sold freely in Gajaaga from 1737 onward. Some African rulers even managed to get artillery. Saatigi Konko Bubu Muusa of Fuuta Tooro captured a French ship on the Senegal and took the cannon for the defense of his own tata. As head of artillery, he appointed an Afro-Frenchman named Violette, who had learned to handle cannon in the Senegal river trade.[14]

Experiences of this kind occasionally convinced some Europeans of the danger of selling guns to potential enemies, but embargoes for security reasons were comparatively rare and ineffectual, though Saint Louis refused

13. "Réponses aux plaintes de M. de Paradis," 1777, ANF, C6 17; "Tableau détaillé des coutumes, 1829," ANS, 13 G 16; Saugnier, *Voyages,* pp. 287–89.

14. Saint-Adon to CI, Gajaaga, 2 December 1736, Conseil du Sénégal to CI, 15 June 1736, and Saint-Adon to CI, 20 April 1737, ANF, C6 11.

to sell powder to the Moors for a time in 1716, and as late as 1847 it briefly prohibited the sale of arms and munitions, for fear they would fall into the hands of Eliman Bubakar of Dimar, in Fuuta.[15] But the main drive was for profit, not security. After 1737, guns were restricted in Gajaaga, but only to exact a monopoly price by insisting that muskets count as "heavy bars" and refusing to give more than one gun per slave in the assortment of goods. The period of quasi monopoly ended in the 1750's, however, as competition from the Gambia forced the French company to drop its restriction.[16]

Firearms were nevertheless slow to move beyond Gajaaga. When Mungo Park passed through Kaarta in 1795, neither Kaarta nor Segu used guns extensively, even though they fought (and often won) against states that did. By the middle of the nineteenth century, Kaarta had finally taken up guns, but they were still rare in out-of-the-way places like eastern Bambuhu and the region further south and east.[17]

This gradual spread inland over a period of nearly two centuries is consonant with the import data that show a steady increase in the sale of guns, combined with a still more rapid increase in the sale of gunpowder. (Other things being equal, the fact that the sale of gunpowder rose more rapidly than that of guns implies that many of the guns were not replacements but were sold to new users.)

Changes in the volume of the gun traffic correlates badly with the changes in the volume of the slave trade. The slave trade reached its maximum volume in the 1730's and then declined. The gun traffic of that decade was barely getting started, and it reached its peak volume a century later when the slave trade was legally finished and actually insignificant. In addition, the Bambara wars of the far interior that actually supplied the bulk of the slaves throughout the eighteenth century were mainly fought with other weapons. For Senegambia, at least, the "arms for slaves" portion of the stereotype simply does not hold. Indeed, the fact that the damaging impact of the arms trade and the slave trade were somewhat separated in time for Senegambia suggests that they represent two different evils from the broader world of Atlantic commerce, and a greater effort to separate their consequences for other parts of Africa might yield more accurate analysis than we have had so far.

Another way to examine the implications of changing imports is to regroup them in broad categories related to economic development. Table 8.5 distinguishes raw materials, consumer goods, and nonproductive goods whose value to the health and well-being of Senegambian society was either neutral or

15. Bruë to Collé, 9 December 1716, ANF, C6 5; Arrêté of 25 October 1857, ANF-OM, Sénégal IV, 19.

16. Conseil du Sénégal to CI, 24 February 1752, ANF C6 13; statement of the Conseil, 31 July 1755, ANF, C6 14.

17. Raffenel, *Nouveau voyage,* 1:436.

Table 8.5
Senegambian Imports Grouped according
to Development Potential, 1730's and 1830's
(Major imports only, in percentages of total
major imports)

	1730's		1830's	
Raw materials				
Iron	21.2		1.5	
Silver	10.2		3.9	
Total		31.4		5.4
Consumer goods				
Brass and copperware	5.3		—	
Pewter	1.1		—	
Textiles	28.2		58.9	
Beads and semiprecious stones	18.0		8.8	
Paper	.5		—	
Total		53.1		67.6
Nonproductive goods				
Arms	6.6		6.0	
Powder	4.0		3.8	
Spirits	4.8		7.1	
Tobacco	—		10.0	
Total		15.4		26.9

Source: Table 8.3

negative. Over the century between 1740 and 1840, Senegambia's foreign trade increased enormously because Senegambia sold more to Europe at higher prices. But the returns in the form of imports may not have been those best calculated to increase Senegambia's own productive capacity. A greater capability of further growth might have come with a trend toward more raw materials, fewer consumer goods, and fewer nonproductive goods. The actual direction was the reverse, in all three categories. The change in the first two categories was clearly a reflex of European industrialization, but not in the sense that European industrial products had begun seriously to penetrate the Senegambian market in competition with Senegambian producers. The most important single change was the enormous increase in textile imports, but this was Indian cottons two-to-one against the European machine-made European product, and the guinées went mainly to the gum region. Senegambian iron production apparently held its own, and Senegambian textiles must have held their own outside the south-Mauritanian market.

Until the 1830's, in short, Senegambia had been pulled into the fringe of the industrial world as a supplier of raw materials, but not yet as a market for manufactured goods. The main new imports were Indian cloth, American tobacco, and some American rum alongside the French brandy. It could be argued that this was an "economic" allocation of Senegambian resources, because the market will naturally reflect the consumers' preferences. The problem is whether the consumers wanted what was conducive to economic growth. The rising percentage assigned to nonproductive goods is one aspect of the problem. Another is the fact that nothing in the table of imports, at least, shows any indication of capital investment. This is no sign that capital investment was stagnant or declining, since the increased commerce was based in part on Senegambian capital, but it does suggest that Senegambia was not falling into step behind the economic advance of industrial Europe.

Another way of seeing the pattern is to return to the stereotypes about the slave trade. The arms and gewgaws myth was just that, but now in the 1830's it begins to fit far better than it fitted during the era of the slave trade. This is no justification of the slave trade, but it does suggest that the transition from the slave trade to "legitimate trade" was not all that it might have been for the economic future of the region.

Another kind of index based on the same data is provided by distinguishing goods used mainly by women—silver for jewelry, beads, and semiprecious stones—as opposed to those consumed mainly by men—brandy and tobacco. Over the century 1740 to 1840, the first category dropped by 55 per cent, while the second more than tripled. Any argument based on these data has to be completely speculative; it could be evidence that men chose to spend more on drink and less on the adornment of their women—by extension a shift in preference from sex to alcohol. Or it could indicate a shift in authority over consumption decisions from women to men—and in this context it is all too

Table 8.6
Changing Proportions of Major Senegambian
Exports in Total Exports,
Half-Century Intervals, 1680's to 1830's

Commodity	Per cent of major exports			
	1680's	1730's	1780's	1830's
Gold	5.0	7.8	0.2	3.0
Gum	8.1	9.4	12.0	71.8
Hides	8.5	–	–	8.1
Ivory	12.4	4.0	0.2	2.8
Slaves	55.3	64.3	86.5	1.9
Wax	10.8	14.5	1.1	9.9
Peanuts	–	–	–	2.6
Total	100.0	100.0	100.0	100.0

Source: *Supplement* tables A15.6 and A15.9

easy to conjure up the stock characters of Senegambian history, the eigh-teenth-century signare and the nineteenth-century ceddo. The serious point here is that this quantitative study of foreign trade shows many things that fit well with other kinds of evidence, while raising new questions that can only be answered, if at all, by new qualitative research.

Exports

The production, extraction, and shipment of individual Sene-gambian exports has already been discussed, but the changing value of total exports is also significant. The most obvious point to the data assembled in table 8.6 is that Senegambia was consistently a one-export region. One product made up more than half the value of its exports from the early seventeenth century to the present. In the early seventeenth, it was hides. The sample for the 1680's marks a period when slaves topped the 50 per cent mark, the slaves continued dominant until at least the 1790's. By the 1830's, however, gum had become what slaves had been, and a further sample in the 1880's or the 1930's would show peanuts in the place of gum. Senegambia, in short, adjusted again and again over a span of three centuries to a combination of changing demand from overseas and changing supply conditions at home. The "peanut revolution" of the nineteenth century was only the last of a series of "commercial revolutions." Nor were the shifts merely the emergence of a principal export from among a group of leaders. It was all or nothing for hides, slaves, and peanuts—leaders for a time, but less than 1 per cent of all exports before or after. Even gum, the most consistent of all, dropped below 10 per cent at one stage.

Running counter to the rapid shift from one export commodity to the next, the money value of all Senegambian exports rose consistently from one half-century to the next, the percentage increase at each interval being slightly higher than the one before. (See table 8.7.) The total value of exports, however, was the volume of goods exported times the prices at which they were sold. It is possible to assess separate roles for volume and for price of each major export, as in table 8.8, though not for all exports together, because the commodity makeup of total exports shifted constantly through time.[1]

The index numbers of volume and price shown in table 8.7 are therefore approximations of reality. They are not measures of what actually happened

1. For the mathematical explanation of this point see Allen, "Index Numbers," pp. 195–96.

Table 8.7
Index Numbers of Price, Volume, and Value
of Total Senegambian Exports at Half-Century Intervals
1680's–1830's

Change between 1680's and 1730's, export proportions held as of 1680's; 1680's = 100	

Annual value	242
Annual volume	184
Price level	134

Change between 1730's and 1780's, export proportions held as of 1730's; price and quantity levels of 1730's = 100

Annual value	299
Annual volume	84
Price level	467

Change between 1780's and 1830's; price and volume indices based on 1780's = 100

Annual value	322

Volume with export proportions held at level of the 1780's	162
Volume with export proportions held at the level of the 1830's	3,412
Volume at geometrical mean of the above	743
Price level with export proportions as of the 1780's	92
Price level with export proportions of the 1830's	383
Price level at the geometrical mean of the above	188

Source: *Supplement*, tables A15.6 and A15.9. See text for mode of calculation.

but of what would have happened if the balance of commodities among Senegambian exports had remained frozen at the base percentages throughout each fifty-year period. To prevent even more distortion, it is necessary to begin again with a new base for each interval, rather than carrying index numbers through the whole period, as is done with individual commodities in table 8.8.

Where the proportions of export commodities did not change greatly, as in the interval 1680's to 1730's, the distortion may be quite small. In that instance, the might-have-been figures help to explain that the actual 140 per cent in export values was caused by a relatively balanced increase in both price and volume.[2]

2. The degree of probable inaccuracy is indicated by the fact that a true index number for volume times the true index number for price should equal the total value of the year's exports. This is much more nearly true in table 8.7 for the interval 1680's–1730's than for any other.

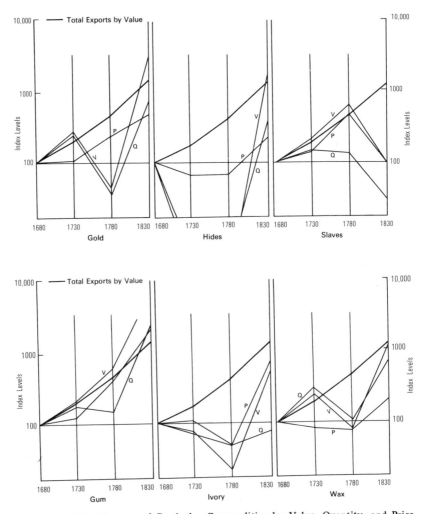

8.2 Senegambian Exports of Particular Commodities by Value, Quantity, and Price, 1680–1830   UWCL

The next period from the 1730's to the 1780's shows a very different set of circumstances. The total value of the exports increased threefold, or slightly more than the increase up to the 1730's; but the volume of every single major commodity declined, and the increase in value was entirely a matter of rising prices, especially a very steeply rising price for slaves. This pattern is not well explained by any of the direct evidence. It could result in part from the fact that the great companies were no longer operating in the 1780's, and

European shore establishments were much reduced in size. It must have been influenced to some degree by the disastrous drought of the 1750's, and it was apparently influenced by political conditions in the Bambara country to the east, the chief supplier of slaves. In this situation, which might have meant lessening income from exports and hence less money to pay for imports, the Senegambians were pulled through by the windfall of rising slave prices. This was simply coincidence. The 1780's were the peak decade of the Atlantic slave trade, and the prosperity of the tropical plantations in the Americas led planters to bid up the price paid for slaves in Africa, even though Senegambia did not respond with increasing numbers sent into the trade.

Table 8.8
Index Numbers for Value, Volume, and Price of Major
Senegambian Exports at Half-Century Intervals
1680's to 1830's
(1680's = 100)

Commodity	1680's	1730's	1780's	1830's
Gold, annual average:				
Value	100	379	34	1,831
Volume	100	348	25	1,035
Price	100	109	134	177
Gum, annual average:				
Value	100	279	1,066	26,886
Volume	100	211	161	1,695
Price	100	133	664	1,586
Hides, annual average:				
Value	100	1	1	2,897
Volume	100	2	2	442
Price	100	60	60	656
Ivory, annual average:				
Value	100	79	14	692
Volume	100	66	37	68
Price	100	119	38	1,010
Slaves, annual average:				
Value	100	281	1,130	105
Volume	100	170	146	22
Price	100	165	776	478
Beeswax, annual average:				
Value	100	325	72	2,794
Volume	100	432	105	1,039
Price	100	75	68	269
Total value, major exports	100	242	723	2,325

The final interval has a serious problem of measurement, involving a shift from exports dominated by the slave trade to the new leadership of gum. The index numbers constructed as though the basket of exports were constant as they had been in the 1780's bear no resemblance to reality, nor do current-weighted index numbers based on the new conditions of the 1830's. Both kinds of index numbers are shown on table 8.7, as is another possibility, the geometrical mean of the two.[3] Even that is not a fair reflection of reality, though it is an improvement over the others. For a reasonable approximation of reality, it is necessary to follow the movement of individual commodities shown in table 8.8. But the three different kinds of index all agree on one point—the volume of exports over this interval rose much faster than prices, returning to the pattern of the first interval and reversing that of the second.

The fall of the slave trade and the rise of gum also had special implications within Senegambia. The income from the slave trade went to the suppliers and to the traders along the main east-west routes, while the income from the gum trade went to the masters of the gum forests and to a different group of traders. With a ten-fold increase in the volume of gum exports, coupled with a 240-per-cent rise in price, a massive shift of income took place. But the rate of growth in exports generally was such that the gains of the Senegal valley were not necessarily balanced by losses elsewhere. This fact becomes clear by reference to the base-weighted volume index, which minimizes the importance of gum. Even on this basis, the increase in volume was 162 per cent, or nearly as great as it had been over the first interval, and the prices of hides and ivory went up even faster than gum prices did. Although slave prices lost 38 percent and slave volume declined, the loss was more than compensated by the boom in hides, wax, and ivory.

These data in tables 8.7 and 8.8 also reflect on some of the standard interpretations of the slave trade, especially on its decline and fall. The "humanitatian" interpretation often stresses the profitability of the slave trade in the nineteenth century, showing that it was abolished by men of good will against the financial interests of those who continued in the trade, and at great cost to the British taxpayers. The undertone, sometimes explicit, is to praise the generosity of the "legitimate traders" and to condemn the greed of those who continued the evil but profitable trade in slaves. This view has some things to recommend it, since some humanitarians did act from principle and some slave traders did continue in the trade because they still made a profit; but it will have to be modified by the knowledge that (at least for Senegambia) the rising demand was in the sector of legitimate trade.

3. The geometric rather than the arithmetic mean is called for here, since the index numbers are actually proportions. In this case, the geometric mean of volume index numbers is the square root of the product of the volume index 1830's times the volume index 1780's—and the equivalent calculation for price indices.

Still another assumption often found in older works on the slave trade is that Africa had virtually nothing but slaves to sell, leaving a choice of slave trade or no trade at all. This may have been nearly true for other regions, but it was not true of Senegambia, where the average slave exports from the 1680's through the 1830's came to only about 52 percent of the total value of export trade. If only the century at the height of the trade, between the 1680's and the 1780's, is taken into account, the slave trade was still less than 70 percent of all exports by value. (Table 8.6.)

Some other measurements help to lend perspective to the growth pattern of Senegambian foreign trade. The value of Senegambian exports, for example, rose even more rapidly than equivalent index numbers for the foreign trade of the most developed countries in Western Europe. (Table 8.9.) It is important to remember that Senegambia began with a much lower base, so the full impact of this growth would not be equivalent to the changes taking place in eighteenth-century Europe. On the other hand, the per capita value of foreign trade was not far different in order of magnitude from those of the less-developed Western countries in this period. Even without adequate population data, it is possible to make rough estimates based on alternative guesses of the probable population. As of about 1960, Senegal and the Gambia together were thought to have about 2,500,000 inhabitants, and another 500,000 should also be counted, those who were part of the commercial region in southern Mauritania or east of the Faleme. The eighteenth-century population was probably lower than that, but 3,000,000 can be taken as a maximum estimate. At that figure, the annual value of Senegambian foreign

Table 8.9
Increase in Value of Senegambian Foreign
Trade Compared to the Trade of England
and France, 1680's to 1830's
(1730's = 100)

Territory	1730's	1780's	1830's
Senegambia	100	299	962
England	100	144	550
France	100	244	456

Sources: Senegambian export values are the annual averages from tables A15.6 and A15.7 of the *Supplement*. European values are from Michael G. Mulhall, *Dictionary of Statistics*, 4th ed. (London, 1899), p. 128, taking the one-year figure for 1730, 1780, and 1830 as indicative of changing values over the interval.

trade in the 1830's would have been about £.14 per capita. Guessing at a population of 1,500,000, foreign trade would have come to about £.28 per capita. This is less than similar estimates for any European country around the year 1800, when Italy was lowest among major countries, with an estimated per capita foreign trade of £.60, and Britain was highest, with about £6.20.[4] Taking the earlier date of 1720, before Europe began to make significant steps toward industrialization, per capita foreign trade for both Italy and France was as low as £.30. The comparison suggests that Senegambian foreign trade was probably less than the range of per capita international trade among European nations, but the difference between highest and lowest European rates was greater than the difference between Senegambia and the lowest European rate.

The Terms of Trade

It is also useful to pass beyond export and import data as separate entities and examine the combination of the two in the form of changing terms of trade. That concept is often misunderstood, and it can mean several different things, even in its technical sense. Nontechnical usage, however, sometimes suggests that the terms of trade can be favorable or unfavorable, in the sense of a good bargain or a bad bargain. Technically speaking, terms of trade are always relative to a specific time. They are simply index numbers, measuring the difference from some other situation defined as equal to 100.[1]

In fact, the terms of trade are not a single measure but a series of measures, each concentrating on different aspects of exchange. The most common of these measures is the net barter terms of trade—which compares the changing price of the basket of goods usually purchased against the prices of the basket of goods sold in exchange, ordinarily imports against exports, with the price of each commodity weighted according to its relative importance. The net barter terms of trade, in short, are simply the export price index divided by the import price index, the quotient multiplied by 100. If prices shifted in favor of the country under consideration, the terms of trade index would rise above 100, so that 120 indicates a 20-per-cent improvement in the overall price situation, while 80 indicates a 20-per-cent shift in the opposite direction.

The gross barter terms of trade are exactly the same kind of measure, but

---

4. These European estimates are from W. W. Rostow, "The Beginnings of Modern Growth in Europe: An Essay in Synthesis," *Journal of Economic History,* 33:547–79 (1973), p. 558.

1. See Allen, "Index Numbers," passim.

using the changing volume of trade rather than the changing prices. That is, they would use volume indices like those in table 8.8 in place of the price indices. For Senegambia, unfortunately, accurate indices of import volumes are not available for most periods. Neither gross barter terms of trade nor "income terms of trade" combining volume and price are therefore possible before the nineteenth century, but table 8.10 summarizes the net barter terms of trade over each of the three half-century intervals.

When import and export prices were considered separately, it was important to have uniform conditions for each series. That is why import prices were recorded as they appeared most frequently in the historical record—the prime cost, f.o.b. a European port. Export prices were taken as *they* were most frequently recorded—the price paid to the African supplier in the Senegambian port. The fact that conditions were not identical for imports and exports makes no difference so long as each is treated as a separate series of index numbers. An accurate terms of trade index, however, can only be made from these indices if they are reduced to the actual value of the commodities at the point of entry or departure from Senegambia. In fact, the handling costs from the purchase of goods in Senegambia to their shipment tended to decline as time went on. Since the handling costs were especially high for slaves, the average handling cost dropped steeply as slaves began to be a smaller and smaller part of total exports. On the import side, freight rates also dropped steadily throughout the eighteenth century.[2] Neither of these changes can be measured as precisely as one might wish, but it is more accurate to adjust with the roughest kind of estimate than to leave them out of account altogether.

On the side of handling costs, the cost of bulking and preparing slaves purchased nearby for shipment from a coastal point apparently dropped from about 60 per cent of the purchase price in the 1730's to about 33 per cent in the 1750's.[3] This drop in costs accompanied institutional changes that shifted bulking and handling from Europeans to Africans and Afro-Europeans. This change was centered in the second interval, between the 1730's and 1780's. It therefore seems appropriate to assume a general 50-per-cent drop in bulking and handling costs in that interval. The decrease in the slave trade, with its high handling costs, justifies an estimate of a similar drop of 50 per cent between the 1780's and the 1830's. The crude data of table 8.10, column 1, can therefore be adjusted as indicated in column 2.[4]

2. D. North, "Sources of Productivity Change in Ocean Shipping, 1600-1850," *Journal of Political Economy*, 76:953–70 (1968).

3. See *Supplement*, appendix 8.

4. If the cost of bulking and handling is taken at 50 per cent of the price paid the African seller at a coastal point in either the 1680's or the 1730's, the suggested rate of reduction would cut it to 25 per cent of that price in the 1780's, and 12.5 per cent by

Table 8.10
Senegambian Net Barter Terms of Trade
Half-Century Intervals, 1680's to 1830's

Decade	Export price index		Import price index		Terms of trade index		Continuous adjusted indices 1680's = 100		
	(1)	(2)	(3)	(4)	(5)	(6)	Export	Import	Terms of trade
	Crude	Adjusted for handling costs	Crude	Adjusted for freight rates	Crude	Adjusted			
1680's	100	100	100	100	100	100			
1730's	134	134	98	90	137	149	134	90	149
1730's	100	100	100	100	100	100			
1780's	467	389	134	122	349	319	521	110	475
1780's	100	100	100	100	100	100			
1830's	188	169	83	78	227	217	880	86	1,031

Source: Tables 8.7 and *Supplement* tables A15.10, A15.11, and A15.12.

336

Import prices also have to be adjusted from the f.o.b. values at a European port to the c.i.f. values (landed before payment of duties) in Senegambia—in effect, an adjustment for the cost of ocean freight. Freight rates are estimated to have declined at a rate between 0.5 per cent and 1.0 per cent per year in the eighteenth century. This suggests a mean drop of 37.5 per cent over each half-century interval. The crude data of table 8.9, column 3, are therefore modified by appropriate reductions in freight rates as indicated in column 4.[5]

As a result of the changes in columns 2 and 4, a set of modified terms of trade indices can be set alongside the crude rates given in column 5. In fact, the two adjustments counterbalance each other, and the terms of trade are not very much affected. (Column 6.)

One problem with the interpretation of these shifting terms of trade over fifty-year intervals is the necessary imprecision about the shifts and turns that may have taken place in the shorter run. Even though annual time series are not possible for the whole period, partial annual series are available, and they help to illustrate some of the briefer fluctuations that must have gone on. One source of fluctuation, for example, was the alternation of war and peace in Europe. An annual import price index can be worked out for the years 1671–1704 and 1727–41. (See *Supplement*, table A15.10.) Figure 8.3 illustrates the rise of European prices in response to the war between France and England that began late in 1688. The price rise from beginning to end was on the order of 54 per cent, and that was simply the rising European cost of Senegambian imports. On top of that would be much higher ocean freights from scarcity of shipping, high insurance rates, and so on. An index adjusted to c.i.f. prices must have risen to at least 200, while the prices paid for Senegambian exports may well have dropped for lack of ships to carry them away. A conservative estimate for the period 1693–97 would put the import price index at 200 or more and the export price index at 90 or less, implying a net barter terms of trade index of 45 or less. This must have been the condition again during the War of the Spanish Succession from 1702 to 1713 so that, rather than having a gradual shift toward improving terms of trade over the first interval, about 20 of the 50 years were war years with much worse terms of trade. The use of the four test decades as a touchstone for the long-term trends is legitimate because they were all mainly decades of peace, but

---

the 1830's. To convert from the prices paid the supplier to an estimated f.o.b. price, the export price index number for each period can be increased by the suggested percentage. It is then necessary, however, to adjust once more to return the whole index series to 100 for the base date in each case. The results of these modifications appear in table 8.10.

5. If the cost of the freight from Europe to Senegambia is 50 per cent of the prime cost in the 1680's, then progressively 31.3 per cent in the 1730's, 19.5 per cent in the 1780's, and 12.2 per cent in the 1830's, the crude import price index can be reduced by the appropriate percentage and then readjusted so that the new base will still be 100.

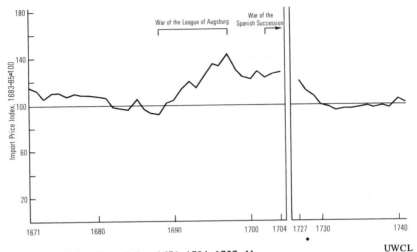

8.3 Gambia Import Price Index, 1671–1704, 1727–41   UWCL

it has to be kept in mind that the periods of warfare at sea were periods when the terms of trade probably turned against Senegambia in the short run, and such periods were about half of the elapsed time between 1688 and 1816.

One other kink in interpreting Senegambian terms of trade is a fact we have seen at several points—that the Senegambian totals are aggregates of individual subregions that might have been differently affected. This becomes clear in the early nineteenth century, as data become available for Senegal and the Gambia separately. Senegambia of 1823–50 (see tables 8.10, 8.11, and figure 8.4) no longer responded to the pulse of European war, and, in this period of the long peace, it responded very rapidly to fluctuations in the European commodity markets. Contrary to the experience of the late seventeenth century, where the most important fluctuation occurred with the import prices, the crucial short-term shifts were now in the export prices—though the long trend over the quarter-century came from cheaper imports. Export-price fluctuations were sharpest for Senegal, if for no other reason because of its overwhelming dependence on gum. The Gambia, with nearly equal dependence on wax, hides, and gum, had some protection against a sharp price deviation in any one of them, but even so, the Gambia could have a 20-per-cent shift in its favor in a single year (as in 1830) or could take a windfall loss of nearly a third (as in 1831 to 1833).

For Senegal, the years of high gum prices were often years of high production as well (as in 1836–37 and 1844–45), but years of low volume could also be years of low price, so the multiplier worked in either direction to produce a pattern of boom and bust. Between 1845 and 1846, for example, the overall terms of trade turned against Senegal by 60 per cent, on top of a 27-per-cent decrease in gum exports. At the time, the full impact of these shifts would be felt only by the commercial community and the gum suppliers, since these decades were still transitional between the era of the enclaved trade centers and the colonial economy to come. With the development of large-scale peanut cultivation, the fragility of monoculture and dependence on the European market would join the older fragility of life on the desert's edge.

It would be a mistake to overemphasize the terms of trade as a general economic indicator, especially for early periods. Until well into the nineteenth century, imported goods would have counted only as a small fraction of any cost of living survey. Economists are also rightly suspicious of terms of trade studies that extend beyond a decade or so. The incommensurates in trying to allow for the changing price of "one automobile" from 1914 to 1934 to 1954 are simply too great to make the calculation very useful. On the other hand, a primary producer like Senegambia in the preindustrial era bought and sold many things that did not change very much over a period as long as two centuries. In this sense, a half-century of preindustrial change might not equal a decade's technical change in the industrial era. But the preindustrial era was also the prestatistical era, and data for that period are neither so plentiful nor so accurate as they would be for later times.

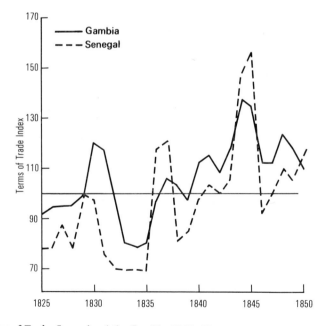

8.4 Terms of Trade, Senegal and the Gambia, 1825–50

UWCL

In spite of these problems, the main question is not the absolute accuracy of the measure but whether it is accurate enough to carry the interpretive load placed on it. A present-day economist trying to predict economic performance as a basis for monetary or commercial policy would need far more accuracy than the historian looking for long-term patterns of economic change.

The data are easily accurate enough to support the generalization that, in spite of the probability of strong contrary swings in wartime, the net barter terms of trade shifted consistently in favor of Senegambia over a period of nearly two centuries. Even if the accuracy of the estimates is no closer to reality than half or double, the overall shift to Senegambia's advantage from the 1680's to the 1830's would have been within the range of fivefold to twentyfold. Or, as a median estimate, the Senegambians at the end of the period received about ten times as much as they had received 150 years earlier for the same quantity of goods exported.

Furthermore, except for the half-century 1740–90, the shift in net barter terms of trade was simultaneous with a remarkably steady increase in the volume of exports. Thus, though income terms of trade are not measurable, the Senegambian gain in income terms would have been still greater than the gain in net barter terms.

The fundamental cause of the shift in Senegambia's favor is apparent in the broader Atlantic economy. The change in the net barter terms over both the first and second intervals—for the whole century from the 1680's to the 1780's—was carried by the rising price of slaves. That rise originated in turn with the rising production on tropical American slave plantations, and beyond that with a demand for tropical staples on the European market.

The continued shift in net barter terms over the next interval to the 1830's, however, depended on direct rather than indirect European demand for exotic products, this time gum, hides, ivory, and beeswax. The new phase was related to the rise of the industrial economy in Europe, while the earlier phase was not; but industrialization had not yet progressed to the point that Senegambia profited greatly from lower prices for European products. Industrial Europe could afford to pay well for raw materials, and the payoff of industrialization also appeared on the Senegambian import side in the form of diminishing prices for European goods—especially from the 1780's to the 1830's in a falling price of machine-made cotton cloth. It is worth noting that this general drop in import prices from an index number of 211 in the 1780's to the base of 100 in the 1830's is almost exactly parallel to a similar drop in the import price index of the United States over the period from 1815 to the 1830's, and it may have been a common pattern for most of the less-developed world in those decades.[6]

---

6. Douglas North, *The Economic Growth of the United States from 1790 to 1860* (Englewood Cliffs, N.J., 1961), pp. 89–90, 242.

A third phase, with a somewhat different basis, began in the 1830's, again with import prices moving in parallel to those of the United States. Unlike the previous period, Senegambian exports no longer rose in value, and the continued shift of the terms of trade in Senegambia's favor was carried entirely by a continued drop in the prices paid for imports, though that decrease was now much less steep than it had been in the early decades of the century. In effect, overseas producers had, by this time, responded to the new level of European demand, represented by the fantastic rise in the prices of gum, ivory, and hides over the early decades of the century. The initial price increases had done their work, and prices could be allowed to work their way gradually downward. The same phenomenon was to occur with the prices offered for palm products at about this same time and with peanuts just a little later. In each case it began a sharp turn of net barter terms in favor of the extra-European supplier, followed by reversal as the competition of many primary producers shifted the terms back in favor of the industrialized society.

It would be interesting to know whether this was a common worldwide phenomenon—whether shifting terms of trade resembled the Senegambian experience in other non-European countries from the seventeenth century onward. Unfortunately, quantitative studies are still lacking. Gisela Eisner's work on Jamaica, 1830–1930, overlaps by only twenty years, and Jamaica's special circumstances during the first decades after slave emancipation are too different to make the comparison very useful for the period before 1850. The shifting terms of trade from 1832 to 1930, however, were not far from the pattern that had begun for Senegambia in the second quarter of the nineteenth century.[7] They moved over the long run mainly in response to changes in import prices, but only through a range of 53 index points—compared to a range of 60 index points in the Senegambian fluctuations of 1826–50. Both the Jamaican or the Senegambian nineteenth-century pattern is therefore very different from the really wild fluctuations that marked Senegambian terms of trade before the 1830's.

For Senegambia, it is clear that the world markets offered economic terms that were increasingly attractive from the 1680's onward, at least on the surface. It is equally clear that the abrupt shifts in price moved the Senegambian economy through a series of monocultures (at least for the export sector) in response to changing external demand.[8] More advantageous exchange, therefore, exacted one kind of price in the form of continuous adjustment, which inevitably brought windfall gains to some and losses to others.

7. G. Eisner, *Jamaica, 1830–1930* (Manchester, 1961), esp. pp. 257–60.
8. Something similar happened in Jamaica over the century of Dr. Eisner's survey, as sugar gave way to bananas, with sugar 60 per cent of the whole export value in 1830 and bananas 57 per cent by 1930. (Eisner, *Jamaica*, p. 238.)

It is important not to interpret the net barter terms of trade as an index of the social costs or social benefits that flowed from a commercial relationship. Some people assuredly received an increased return over a period of time for the goods that were sold, but this was hardly a social benefit in the period when most of those goods sold were slaves. It was less a social benefit than it might have been in the early nineteenth century, when the trend ran toward unproductive imports rather than those that might have strengthened the economy as a whole.

It is also important not to overemphasize the role of external trade in the Senegambian economy. Only a small part of the gross territorial product entered interregional trade, and only part of that moved by sea. Information about external trade is not important because external trade was important. It is important because it provides measurable evidence about the early and tenuous links between a part of the non-Western world and the preindustrial West—links that were still comparatively weak but were in time to become overwhelming.

INDEX

JACKET DESIGNED BY SYLVIA SOLOCHEK WALTERS
COMPOSED BY THE COMPOSING ROOM, GRAND RAPIDS, MICHIGAN
MANUFACTURED BY MALLOY LITHOGRAPHING, INC., ANN ARBOR, MICHIGAN
TEXT LINES IN PRESS ROMAN, DISPLAY LINES IN BASKERVILLE

ᗐᗏ

Library of Congress Cataloging in Publication Data

Curtin, Philip D
Economic change in precolonial Africa.

Includes bibliographical references.
1. Africa, West—Economic conditions. 2. Slave-
trade—Africa, West—History. 3. Africa, West—
Commerce—History. I. Title.
HC503.W4C87   330.9′66′301   74-5899
ISBN 0-299-06640-1 (v. 1)